OAK

Oak

A British History

Esmond Harris, Jeanette Harris and N. D. G. James

WIND*gather*
PRESS

Oak

A British History

Published by: Windgather Press Ltd, 29 Bishop Road, Bollington,
Macclesfield, Cheshire SK10 5NX, UK

Distributed by: Central Books, 99 Wallis Road, London E9 5LN

British Library Cataloguing-in-Publication Data
A catalogue record for this book is available from the British Library

ISBN 0 9538630 8 5

Typeset by Carnegie Publishing Ltd,
Chatsworth Road, Lancaster
Printed and bound by The Alden Press, Oxford

Contents

The early climate of Britain. Tree species in the distant past. The arrival of oak in Britain after the ice age; dating oak timbers and artefacts by radiocarbon dating and dendrochronology, pollen analysis and climate changes. The gradual influence of man on the natural woodland. Use of oak in timber circles and trackways. Early use of oak for housing and its importance to man for fuel, tanning, charcoal and artefacts. The Celts, the Roman invasion and their influence on the woodland cover.

Tree clearance, particularly of oak, coppicing, woodland regeneration, clearing for pasture. The Sweet and Meare Heath tracks. Early protection of woodlands by enclosure. Destruction of oak woods for iron smelting and glass manufacture. Woodland regeneration. Evelyn's recommendations for woodland management and subsequent texts with regard to oak. Methods used to establish oak in the past by natural regeneration, transplanting and direct sowing. Protection of young oak woods and first use of conifers as 'nurses'. Old nursery practices compared with modern techniques. Suitable soils and silvicultural systems for oak. The relevance of the past to today's practice; modern methods. Tree shelters and their particular value for oak.

Management of oak woodlands in the past by the Romans and Anglo-Saxons. Forest laws. The Domesday Survey, Royal Forests, management by the monasteries and tenants' rights. Management systems: high forest, coppice with standards, simple coppice. The importance of coppicing, medieval hunting forests and timber production, coppice with standards, wood pasture. Henry VIII's statute. Over-cutting of oak woods, shortage of fuel wood, rising demand for charcoal for iron smelting, open-grown oak trees for ship building and laws to ensure its provision. Concern about supplies of oak. Proclamation by James I to restrict felling for glass manufacture. Evelyn and other writers' recommendations for growing oak in mixture, nursing of oak and pruning. Eighteenth-century forest practices. The introduction and general use of conifers as nurses. Production of oak plants in nurseries. The problem of epicormics on oak. Recognition of sessile oak as a separate species. High prices obtainable for tan bark during the Napoleonic wars. Reduction in need for ship timber. Influence of continental practice on yield control. Shake in oak timber and the influence of soils. References to successful growing of oak in the historical literature. Nursing and pruning. Lessons for the successful growing of oak today.

The paramount place of oak timber and its secondary products over many centuries. Historical uses of oak for tan bark and charcoal. The special characteristics of oak: durability, cleavability, strength and good working qualities suitable for a wide range of uses, such as in cooperage, houses, ecclesiastical buildings, furniture and carving. Oak for barrels, casks, spelk baskets, shingles and in church carving. Oak as the principal timber of the village carpenter. Present day restorations and craft uses of oak. Decorative features of oak timber – 'brown oak', 'bog oak', 'pippy oak' – in the past and today.

The importance of oak in the earliest boats and ships, archaeological evidence of oak in boats and ships, use of 'clinker' construction by the Saxons and Vikings. The Ferriby, Nydam and Dover boats. King Alfred's navy. The adoption of 'carvel' construction for stronger ships, merchant vessels and fishing boats. King Henry VIII's navy and increasing world trade requiring merchant ships. Oak for 'treenails' and 'compass wood', the latter requiring large trees. Increasing shortages of ship-building oak, particularly 'grown' timbers. Elizabeth's concern about the destruction of oak forests, particularly near navigable rivers. Different methods of growing oak for compass timber and for planks; steamed timber when grown oak not available. Replacement of oak 'knees' by iron and eventually of wooden ships too. Bristol pilot cutters and Scott's *Discovery* at the turn of the twentieth century, the last ships to be constructed of oak. Revival of building in oak for the mine sweepers of the Second World War. The use of oak bark for tanning sails. Use of oak in present day boat restoration projects and replicas.

Myths, legends, 'mistletoe oaks', poems and people associated with oak. Oak trees and mistletoe sacred to the Druids. 'Mistletoe oaks'.

Illustrations

Figures

(Copyright is held by the authors unless otherwise indicated)

Colour plates (between pages 146 and 147)

Foreword

The Lord Clinton DL,
President of the Royal Forestry Society
of England, Wales and Northern Ireland

As President of the Royal Forestry Society, it is a privilege to write a foreword to this unusual book. Esmond and Jeanette Harris have produced what I believe is a masterpiece, making use of N. D. G. James' original concept and their own up to date knowledge of the oak tree, its history and its cultivation. The book therefore encompasses the work of three authors, on a subject which in itself needs many hours of research, wide knowledge and an eye to the future.

As someone who has known the present writers as well as the late N. D. G. James, the subject becomes even more valuable in a book that will be a pleasure to read. Its strength lies, like oak, in the time it has taken to mature. It should be on everybody's bookshelf who has an interest in the subject of our National Tree.

Preface and Acknowledgements

For a long time as a practising forester it had seemed to me that twentieth-century foresters in Britain had forgotten much of the earlier knowledge about growing oak and this was reinforced by my occasionally dipping into old forestry textbooks. These give detailed prescriptions for growing oak and emphasise the importance of growing it with other species rather than as pure stands. They describe methods of early shaping and pruning as well as the sites upon which oak will succeed but today we are largely ignorant of them.

When I was invited to complete a book on the history of oak in Britain, originally conceived by the late N. D. G. James, the opportunity was there to explore the lessons of the past more fully and to glean from them what is still relevant today. This is timely in view of the recent resurgence and interest in growing broadleaves in Britain. Oak must be the paramount broadleaf species, albeit one of the most difficult to grow well. The Forestry Commission Broadleaved Policy of 1985 (Forestry Commission 1989), which arose from the Institute of Chartered Foresters/Forestry Commission Symposium 'Broadleaves in Britain' of 1982 (Malcolm *et al.* 1982), has undoubtedly resulted in some unsightly and poor scrubby woodlands, particularly of oak. Perhaps some of the lessons from the past highlighted in this book will lead to an improvement in our oak woods in the future. Oakwoods can provide a wonderfully versatile and attractive timber as well as resourceful habitats for a wide range of wildlife species.

This book would not have been possible without the use of N. D. G. James's extensive private collection of old forestry text books. They have been drawn upon heavily to provide the historical picture encapsulated in chapters two, three, four and five and for the account of silvicultural techniques used in the past which features in chapters two and three. Many of these are still relevant today.

The book though is not just about how to grow oak. It places oak in its ecological setting in Britain, traces its economic importance and gives a perspective for growing and managing oak woods for the future.

To be asked by N. D. G. James' two sons to complete the work started by their father was a privilege which became a challenge as the breadth and potential for the book grew. Throughout, my wife J. A. Harris undertook the hard work of extensive background reading in the old books and much of the initial drafting. We hope some of our pleasure in putting oak in its historical

Preface and Acknowledgements

context will be passed on through the pages of this book to those who today enjoy oak woods and the beautiful objects still being made from oak timber.

We are grateful to Professor David Harris of University College, London, for his guidance and helpful comments on chapter one, to John Woolls B.Sc. (forestry) for reading the whole manuscript and to Veronica Wallace B.Sc. for improving its presentation and use of English.

Esmond Harris
Calstock, Cornwall, December 2002

To the memory of N.D.G. 'Jimmy' James, a great forester, a courageous soldier and an eminent author. Above all, a man of humour and sensitivity. A true friend to all those who shared his many interests.

CHAPTER ONE

The Early History of Oak in Britain

Loo the ook, that hath so long a norisshynge
From tyme that it first begynneth sprynge,
And hath so long a lif as we may see.
Chaucer – The Knight's Tale

Investigating the history of oak

We know much about oak in Britain before recorded history. Oak occurs throughout the temperate world and the two native oaks, pedunculate oak (*Quercus robur*) and sessile oak (*Q. petraea*), are not confined to Britain. Pedunculate oak is found in Europe, South West Asia and North Africa; sessile oak, with a more northerly distribution, is found in Europe and West Asia. Recent work on the genetics of oak has shown that all species of oak have a large number of genes in common world-wide but they hybridise freely and there are strains of oak which only differ slightly in their genetic make up (Ferris 1996).

Oak belongs to the flowering plants, or Angiosperms, which begin to appear in the fossil record in the warm period known as the Cretaceous (about 144 million to 66 million years ago). Towards the end of this period, world climate was cooling and this seemed to have helped the evolution of the flowering plants. The following period, the Tertiary (66 to 1.6 million years ago) was still warm at the beginning and fossil remains found in Britain in the rocks of this period include redwood (*Sequoia*), swamp cypress (*Taxodium*), both now North American species, Southern beech (*Nothofagus*), which is now a southern hemisphere species, and a range of tree species now found in East Asia. As the climate went on cooling towards the end of the Tertiary and became more temperate in nature, species more familiar to us today appeared. These included oak (*Quercus*), beech (*Fagus*), hornbeam (*Carpinus*), hazel (*Corylus*), alder (*Alnus*), elm (*Ulmus*), birch (*Betula*), maple (*Acer*), spruce (*Picea*) and pine (*Pinus*).

The next period, the Quaternary (1.6 million years ago) saw further cooling of the earth and the onset of the Ice Ages. Until recently, it was assumed that there had been four ice ages and the last one was taken as a base line for the natural plant and animal life of the British Isles. It was conveniently postulated that the ice swept everything away and that the land of Britain emerged from the ice devoid of vegetation. This simple explanation is not now borne out by the known facts. How has this fuller understanding come about?

FIGURE I
Wistman's Wood,
Dartmoor.
MICK SHARP

1

The last few decades have seen major advances in the methods used to interpret prehistory. Natural radioactivity within materials has provided a number of methods which can be applied in different ways to date them. Radioactive elements change over time into more stable elements and the time taken for this to occur can be measured. The rate of decay, or change, from the radioactive isotope (the form of the element with a particular atomic weight) to the more stable form (with a different atomic weight) is expressed in terms of their half-life (the time taken for half the radioactive form to decay into a stable form). By measuring the proportions of these isotopes in samples, dates can be calculated. For instance, the dating of the oldest rocks has become more accurate by measurement of the decay of rubidium–87 into strontium–87 as the half-life is very long; potassium–40 decays into argon–40, with a half life of 1,310,000,000 years and is suitable for younger rocks; whilst the decay of uranium–234 into thorium–230, with a shorter half-life, is suitable for dating the youngest rocks.

In a similar way, radio-carbon dating depends on the rate at which carbon–14 (C–14) decays to nitrogen. C–14 is produced in the atmosphere by cosmic rays. These have a high neutron content and the neutrons react with N–14 (nitrogen) and form C–14 (carbon), which is then taken up by plant material together with other forms of carbon (Switsur 1986). After the plant dies, no more C–14 can be absorbed and the C–14 then changes back to N–14, half the C–14 being lost in 5,730 years. The amount of decay, measuring the proportion of C–14 to C–12, can be calculated, giving a date at which a plant died. Early methods of carbon dating required large samples but the technique of *accelerator mass spectrometry*, which is more efficient in separating out and evaluating the proportion of C–14, enables the use of very small samples to give results. Radio-carbon dating has limitations, however. The amount of C–14 in the atmosphere has not been constant in the past, it was high about 9600 BP (before present, i.e. dating backwards from 1950) and is artificially high again now due to the burning of fossil fuels and nuclear explosions (Hedges and Gowlett 1984). Thus carbon dates differ increasingly from calendar dates the further back they go, so that adjustment, or calibration, has to be made. Calibrated dates are usually expressed as years BP, uncalibrated dates as years bp; this is the convention followed in this book. The radio-carbon method can be used on a variety of materials and has been used to date oak artefacts, such as wood and charcoal. Another technique known as 'thermoluminescence', which determines past radiation dosages, is used on burnt materials, especially flint.

The use of oxygen isotopes has thrown new light on climatic change during the ice ages. Oxygen occurs as oxygen–16 and oxygen–18. Once fixed in ice layers, or in small animal shells in ocean sediments, the proportions remain stable and indicate the climatic conditions at the time. In glacial periods, oxygen–16 evaporates from the sea leaving it with more oxygen–18. Water is locked up as ice, the sea level falls and the atmosphere becomes drier. Conversely, in warmer periods the situation is reversed; water is released as ice melts, rainfall increases and sea levels rise. From numerous cores taken from ice and the oceans containing layers of sediments, a picture has been built up of the climatic changes in the last 2 million years. Instead of four major ice ages the cores show a series of fluctuations with three overlapping cycles of cold and warmth of about 20,000 years, 40,000 years and 100,000 years. Some of these fluctuations are much warmer or much colder than others and the coldest period of the last fluctuation is now dated at 18,000 years ago in the northern hemisphere. Cooling in the southern hemisphere in the last glacial period is now known to have preceded that in the northern hemisphere by about 3,000 years. Maximum warming following the glacial period also occurred earlier by 3,000 years in the southern hemisphere, i.e. 9000 BP compared with 6000 BP in Europe (Salinger 1981).

The trees found in Britain during the warmer phases preceding this last glacial advance included oak, ash, Montpellier maple (*Acer monspessulanum*), wingnut (*Pterocarya*) and yew (*Taxus*) in the warm, wet periods, with spruce, fir (*Abies*) and hemlock (*Tsuga*) being found in the colder, drier phases (Sutcliffe 1985). In the last warm phase, initial colonisation by birch and pine followed by oak, hazel and elm was shown by one study (Pitts and Roberts 1997). In the context of this development it is significant to note that oak requires a minimum period of 140 days a year when the temperature exceeds 10°C for satisfactory growth and much warmer conditions for good growth.

Glacial and non-glacial periods are also reflected by changes in sea level; the level falls in cold periods and rises in warmer times. Research is now giving us a global picture of these changes. At the same time, it is becoming evident how varied the extent of glaciation was and how the warm, wet periods varied on different continents and hemispheres (Salinger 1981).

Determination of the presence of particular trees, shrubs and herbaceous plants in the past relies mainly on a technique known as pollen analysis. The pollen of a species is identifiable from that of other species by the patterns on its outer coat unless the species are very closely related, such as the two oaks found in Britain which cannot be separated. By examining pollen from certain sites (it is preserved in some soils such as peat, river and lake muds, better than in others), a picture can be drawn of the vegetation existing at the time that a particular peat or mud layer was formed. The identification and interpretation of the amounts of pollens is a specialised subject and adjustments have to be made for various factors. These include the amount and type of pollen produced. For example, hazel produces large quantities of wind-blown pollen that preserves well, so is often over-represented in a soil layer. Hazel flowers early in its life and will also flower heavily within two to three years of coppicing. Oak is also wind-blown but does not produce such abundant pollen as hazel so that it is often under-represented in samples (Godwin 1975). Wind-blown pollen can be carried for long distances, up to 5 degrees latitude (about 250 miles) (Woillard 1979); hence the presence of pollen does not necessarily mean that the trees grew nearby. Also, streams may carry pollen into ponds and lakes from elsewhere. In contrast, trees relying on insects for pollination do not produce such large quantities of pollen and so are not so well represented in samples. Some pollens preserve less well than others, e.g. those of maples. The type of pollen found in samples shows whether the vegetation at the time was woodland, grassland or arable.

In addition to pollen, artefacts made from natural materials such as seeds, spores, wood and charcoal can be studied in deposits to show the presence or absence of certain species. All can be dated by the radio-carbon method. The type and species of animals in deposits, which can include woodland beetles, molluscs, marine organisms and other animal remains, all help to build up a picture of climatic and vegetation change.

Oak in prehistoric Britain

What do all these investigations tell us about oak in Britain in prehistoric times? First of all, that oak has been here for over one million years, appearing in the warmer periods of climatic change, being found in Tertiary remains and in the many following inter-glacials. Some of the glacial episodes were far more severe than the latest one, which has always been regarded as providing the 'clean sheet' for Britain's vegetation. Where did oak and the other species go then and where did they come back from?

It is generally accepted that as the ice expanded its range, trees and plants were pushed south. The land masses were not as they are now because a huge quantity of water was locked up as ice. When the polar ice extended, water was taken up from the oceans, thus lowering the sea level. The weight of the ice on the land caused sinking and in some cases earth movements also occurred. It has been suggested therefore that vegetation may have migrated west as well as south on land exposed by the lowering sea levels. As a result of recent research this theory has become more plausible. It is now established that sea levels in the last glaciation were up to 150 metres below present levels. This meant that land was exposed in what is now the North Sea, to the west and south of the British Isles, and to the west of France and Spain. Changes in ocean circulation also took place but little is known yet about the effect this had on the temperature of these exposed land surfaces. It is known, however, that changes in the direction and increased warmth of ocean currents cause land temperatures to rise, allowing vegetation to colonise rapidly (Salinger 1981). One study showed that in the last inter-glacial, although the ocean temperature at minimum glaciation was similar to today, Europe was warmer than it is now (Sutcliffe 1985). As the ice melted, sea levels rose but at the same time, land that had been under the weight of the ice rose, in some cases forming raised beaches such as those to be seen in Scotland.

The latest glaciation is now believed to have reached its maximum extent 18,000 years ago in Europe. In Britain, this last advance of the ice was not as extensive as some of the previous glaciations. The land surface affected by the ice sheet covered most of Wales except the south, the Cheshire plain to Lincolnshire and the rest of Britain to the north of this line. To the south the vegetation was tundra giving way southwards to open forest and grassland. From 17000 BP warming took place, being relatively rapid between 15000 and 12000 BP, then slowing and finally reaching the period of maximum warmth about 6000 BP (Salinger 1981). A rapid rise in temperature about 13000 BP enabled vegetation to move in from ice age refuges and colonise the land surface quickly.

Radio-carbon dating, thermoluminescence techniques, pollen studies and other research establishing changes in flora and fauna have all increased knowledge of the events which followed the retreat of the ice. Using the results from pollen studies, maps of the advance of tree species have been compiled (Figure 2). Pollen of a particular tree or plant species is sampled for abundance in sediment layers, radio-carbon dated and the results plotted on a map. Pollens of the same age and frequency are joined together by a line showing how far and from which direction the tree or other plant species had colonised by a

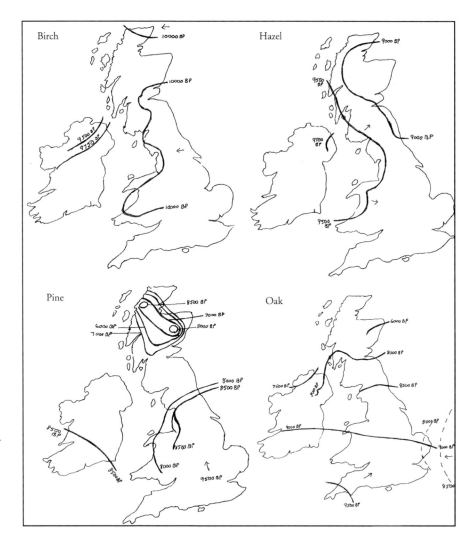

FIGURE 2
Isochrone contour maps showing the arrival and spread of some tree species in Britain. Sources: Godwin (1975), Bennett (1983) and Birks (1989).

AD / BP:BC	Period	Climate	Temp. warm:cold	Vegetation	Animals	Man and Oak
1901–1950		Warm				Shortage of 'grown' timber for ships.
1721–1900		Cool			Roe deer extinct, England	Forest decimation for iron smelting.
1540–1720		Cold			Wolf, wild boar extinct	Black Death, forest rejuvenation.
1301–1539		Cool				Forest exploitation.
951–1300	Little Ice Age — Warm	Warm		Natural vegetation increasingly replaced by managed landscape		Anglo-Saxon period. Famine, wars, plague, forest rejuvenation.
801–950		Cold			Bear extinct	Ditto.
651–800		Warm			Beaver extinct	Ditto.
350–650		Cold		Ditto		
1–350		Warm		Ditto		Roman period. Oak for smelting, building, roads, bridges. Forest decimated.
BP:BC						
2001:1	Sub-Atlantic	Cold Wet Summers		Oak preserved in peat		Iron Age. 'Dover boat'. Hill forts. Heavy plough.
2500:500	Sub-Atlantic	Severe Winters		Blanket bog forms		Oak forest clearance on heavy soils.
3000:1000	Sub-Boreal					Bronze Age. Itinerant smiths. Stonehenge and Woodhenge built. Oak used to smelt copper.
3500:1500	Sub-Boreal			Beech, hornbeam		
4000:2000	Sub-Boreal			Ash & lime decline in south		Ploughing. Lime forests felled on easily worked soils.
4500:2500	Sub-Boreal	Cooling		Elm declines		
5000:3000	Atlantic	Climatic		Oak grows to large sizes		Flint mines active producing axes for forest clearance.
5500:3500	Atlantic	Optimum		Lime reaches max. (Midlands)		
6000:4000	Atlantic	Wet		Oak reaches max. spread (Scot.)		Sweet Track built. Timber circles. Plough marks.
6500:4500	Atlantic	Warm				Neolithic period begins.
7000:5000	Atlantic			Large oaks	Aurochs extinct	Acorns as food.
7500:5500	Atlantic	North Sea & Channel Flood		Lime (S. East)		
8000:6000	Boreal	Warm and Dry		Oak all Britain except N. Scot.		Fire used for clearing forest (pine) in uplands.
8500:6500	Boreal	Warm and Dry		Alder, ash		
9000:7000	Boreal	Warm and Dry		Oak (East Anglia)		
9500:7500	Boreal	Warm		Hazel, pine, oak (S. West), elm		Hazel nuts as food, axes used to fell trees.
10000:8000	Pre-Boreal	Warmer		Birch, willow, juniper, aspen	Elk, red and roe deer, boar, marten, beaver, wolf, aurochs	Forest cleared by fire.
10500:8500	Young Dryas			Cold steppe grassland		
11000:9000	Young Dryas	Cold				Mesolithic Period begins.
11500:9500	Allerod			Birch, willow		
12000:10000	Allerod			Grassland, open forest S. Britain	Saija, musk ox, horse, bear Norway Lemming	
12500:10500	Allerod	Warm		Tundra S. Britain		
13000:11000	Older Dryas	Cold		Cold steppe grassland S. Britain		
14000:12000						
15000:13000		Warming				
16000:14000						
17000:15000				Tundra in Southern Britain	Lemming, reindeer	Palaeolithic Period.
18000:16000		Maximum Glaciation				

TABLE 1. The development of tree cover and exploitation of oak in Britain.

certain date. This produces an *isochrone contour* or *map*. An atlas of pollen maps has been published by Huntley and Birks (1983).

The time between the post-glacial period and the present day is divided into a number of periods which are named and dated (see Table 1), providing a framework for post-glacial studies. The periods of the Older and Younger Dryas, separated by a warm period, saw birch, dwarf willow (*Salix*), grasses and an arctic vegetation developing by 12000 BP. The Boreal period found rapid colonisation by willow, birch, juniper (*Juniperus*), hazel and pine. The isochrone maps show birch to have invaded mainly from the land-locked North Sea and that its spread to the west was well established by 10,000 BP. Pine came in from the south of Britain and was widely distributed by 9000 BP. There is evidence that Scots pine (*P. silvestris*) invaded Scotland from two separate directions, unrelated to the main colonisation in England. Work on substances (called iso-enzymes and mono-terpenes) found in Scots pine has shown that the eastern and western populations are different (Kinloch *et al.* 1987). These results indicate invasion from land west of present-day Scotland as well as from the North Sea.

Hazel came from the south into the area around the Irish Sea, spreading west into Ireland and east into England 9,500 years ago. Oak first invaded from the same direction and was relatively abundant in Cornwall 9,500 years ago. The invasion by oak and hazel from the south-west indicates a land refuge in this direction, perhaps warmed by the Gulf Stream. By the time of maximum warmth about 6,000 years ago, oak had colonised most of Scotland south of Loch Ness.

It is interesting to see from Figure 2 that oak and pine spread north at roughly the same speed although it might be expected that trees such as pine, with lighter seeds, would spread more quickly. Work in America has shown that trees with wind-blown seed or animal-carried seed in fact colonise at about the same rate. In this American study migration rates were found to be rapid; the migration rate of white pine (*P. strobus*) was equalled by the oak, at 350 metres per year. It was calculated that the forest could advance by 1 to 8 kilometres a generation depending on the age of fruiting and longevity of the species (Moore 1987). In Britain, birch preceded oak and probably provided the protection which oak prefers in its early years as it is not a full ligh-demanding pioneer like birch and pine.

As it is not possible to distinguish between the pollen of English, common or pedunculate oak and sessile or durmast oak, some of the pollen data may represent one species and some the other. A study in East Anglia showed two pollen peaks, one about 9,000 years ago and another 1,000 years later (Bennett 1983). From the known ecological requirements of the two species it could be postulated that the first peak represents common oak. This species withstands severe winters and late frosts better than sessile oak (Ellenberg 1988) and might be thought more suited to the continental conditions which prevailed in that area at that time when the North Sea area was still land. Indeed, some colonisation must have come from the east: oak has been dredged up in the

North Sea and dated at about 8500 BP (Godwin 1975). By the time of the second peak, 1,000 years later, the climate was both warmer and wetter and thus more suitable for sessile oak. Work is now being carried out on the DNA of oaks and this should produce interesting results. Already groups with different DNA profiles are emerging. Common oak in East Anglia has a different genetic profile to other common oaks, which may reflect colonisation and isolation in this area (Ferris 1996).

It can therefore be speculated that the initial invasion of oak at about 9500 BP in the South West was sessile oak, the conditions being warmer and wetter on the west coast. Most of the present oak woods in the South West are indeed sessile oak, the high elevation dwarf oakwoods of Dartmoor being an exception. There, Wistman's Wood (Figure 1; Plate 1), Black Tor Beare and Piles Wood are predominantly pedunculate oak. Although old woodland sites, the present trees may not be natural (Simmons 1965). These three unusual, small oak woods have been studied by many people and their conclusions have been summarised by Harvey (1977). The anomaly of common rather than sessile oak could indeed be explained by re-planting, probably for pannage, with the species which was used in preference in the sixteenth and seventeenth centuries because a better and more profitable acorn crop is produced by it. All three woods have been exploited in the past: first by early settlements and later by tin miners as there is evidence of tin streaming nearby; the sale of Black Tor Wood for felling is recorded in 1620 (Christy and Worth 1922). The whole question of the natural distribution of the two oaks is masked by man's interference and his extensive planting of common oak. (Common oak was grown for crooked beams for buildings and ships and it was important as a supply of mast for livestock, especially pigs, because the acorns are larger, fall more readily from the tree and a heavier crop is produced). The common oak also flowers at a younger age than sessile oak and so produces mast (seed) sooner in its lifetime. However, the ranges of the two oaks overlap and where both species are growing together hybrids can be found showing characteristics of both.

Between 7000 BP and 5000 BP (5000 BC to 3000 BC) the warming of the land reached what is known as the 'climatic optimum', when mean temperatures were 2.5°C higher than they are today. At this time the warmth-loving oak reached its furthest extent north and its highest altitudes. Although present earlier, ash (*Fraxinus*) and lime (*Tilia*) also expanded rapidly at this time. Alder, too, benefited from the warmer, wetter conditions of this Atlantic phase although it had been present many years earlier. The period represented the maximum extent of forest cover in Britain, which included rowan (*Sorbus*), bird cherry (*Prunus padus*), elm, probably wych elm, yew and holly (*Ilex*). As the climate warmed, the sea level rose until Britain was finally separated from Europe 7,000 to 8,000 years ago and new tree species were unable to invade unassisted. Woodlands that had colonised land exposed between the glaciations in the North Sea area and to the west of Britain were submerged. Oak is still dredged up in the shallow North Sea and the remains of these forests can be seen on the coast, whilst folk memory of these events may have given rise to the land of Lyonesse in Arthurian legend.

Oak trees growing in the climatic optimum reached great sizes, due to the warm temperatures, the rapid rise in carbon dioxide levels, abundant moisture and virgin soils as yet not degraded by leaching and agriculture. That this was so can be seen in some of the large trees preserved in bogs and fens which are still dug up today. In the sub-Atlantic period which followed, the mean temperature fell and these trees suffered from a rising water table which restricted root growth to the surface, rendering them unstable and wind blew them over. The climate deteriorated and peat formed over them so that the timber was preserved.

Such trees have had an important role in improving dating techniques by dendrochronology, the science of dating tree rings, and have been used to make radio-carbon dating more reliable. Oak is proving particularly valuable in this respect because tree rings are 'able to provide accurate dating frameworks for other, less precise, dating methods that have previously relied largely on topographical differences, such as pottery dating and the evolution of carpentry techniques' (Bridges 2001). Trees in the temperate latitudes show annual growth patterns in the form of rings, where the spring and summer wood of each year's growth is laid down in contrasting less dense and more dense layers. The first tree ring chronology was developed by Douglass in America in 1929 on pine and later extended by the discovery of the long-lived bristle-cone pine (*Pinus aristata*), which enabled a chronology of known dates of over 8,500 years to be established (Pilcher *et al.* 1984). These known dates provided a check for radio-carbon dates to be calibrated against.

In Europe, no such long-lived trees existed and the climate does not show such extreme variations. Different trees and methods were employed. Oak was used as it is a long-lived tree, 'compared with other species, is durable and also well represented in the historical record' (Bridges 2001), and large old trees remain preserved in bogs. A chronology was developed in Ireland mainly from bog oak. This was cross-matched with other chronologies obtained from oak from English and German sites using archaeological timbers, bog oak and river valley oak. Unlike the bristle-cone pine, these trees grew at low altitudes. Sequences of tree ring widths with patterns of wide and narrow rings from various sources were examined. These reflected the environmental conditions at the time and sequences were thus produced that could be recognised over a wide area. One example is a volcanic eruption in China in 208 BC which had world-wide effects, showing up in narrow tree rings in Ireland, Germany and America (Milner 1992). Another was the eruption of Thera in the Mediterranean in 1628 BC.

Chronologies for oak were thus cross-matched so that eventually a full, master chronology for oak was obtained extending back over 7,000 years (Pilcher *et al.* 1984). This could be linked to the chronology for bristle-cone pine. A chronology for post-glacial pine in Europe has now been linked to the oak chronology and takes European dates back to 10000 BP (Day and

Mellars 1994). As a result, radio-carbon dates can now be calibrated and produce accurate results of great importance to archaeology. A recent example of oak timber being used for dating and thereby correcting previous understanding of traditional building techniques, was at the Priory Barn in Hertfordshire which modified a previous carbon date and thus its history. It was established that external weather boarding started to replace wattle and daub much earlier than had previously been thought.

It has often been suggested that Britain's forests at the climatic optimum were mainly oak. This is a simplistic view. The natural forest, before man's intervention, was a mixture of species similar to but with fewer species than untouched forest in China today (Harris and Harris 1987). Besides oak, elm, birch, rowan and lime must have been major components in the south west of Britain, with alder, poplar (*Populus*) and willow in the wetter areas. However, it is now thought that by the climatic optimum man was almost certainly having an impact on the forest.

After the ice had begun to retreat, animals moved north into Britain and were followed by Mesolithic hunter-gatherers. At this period animals of the open grasslands were hunted. Birch, followed by pine and oak, then invaded and by 9500 BP animals typical of woodland conditions make their appearance in the archaeological record and were being exploited by man. People lived in small groups and in addition to hunting, exploited other natural resources and to begin with their impact on the trees was probably not significant. Small trees were felled to build both temporary and more permanent, larger dwellings, and some tree selection must have taken place. Pine in particular would have provided straight poles and was not difficult to fell. It has been shown that flint axes are very efficient in felling and splitting oak. Willow, aspen, birch and hazel too were available: poplar rafters in the form of whole young trees are still used in north China today (Harris and Harris 1987).

As settlements became more permanent, it was not long before larger timbers were being cut for housing and numerous sites have now been excavated with the remains of the post holes still evident. Archaeological remains dated at 7500 BP have been found with round posts, including oak, used in the construction of huts, the floors of which were made of small timbers of split birch and pine, overlaid with birch bark. To fell and split trees, flint axes were used and evidence of trees felled in this way has been dated to 9000 BP, though axes must have been in use for this purpose much earlier elsewhere in Europe. Hazel nuts have been found on many Mesolithic sites and were an important part of the diet. Hazel was an early coloniser (with pine) and to provide a food source, deliberate clearing (by fire) of the forest may have been undertaken to encourage the bushes to flower and fruit, which they would not do in the shade. There is also some evidence that other plant foods may have been positively encouraged (Zvelebil 1994). Acorns are not often found on early sites as they do not preserve well, though they became a food source later for both man and animals (Mason 1992). Before they can be eaten, the tannin needs to be leached out of the acorns to render them palatable

(Dimbleby 1978). Felling or burning pine would in itself encourage the broadleaved element to coppice. Hazel would therefore be encouraged by the removal of pine as cutting or low intensity surface fires enable oak and hazel to sprout again quickly and to dominate the vegetation (Wang 1961; Rowe and Scotter 1973). Today, in north China, the felling of pine has resulted in oak coppicing freely and preventing pine regeneration (Harris and Harris 1987). In contrast, hot fires, more typical of sporadic natural fires where the litter has built up on the forest floor, destroy plant cover, especially on dry sites and thereby favour pine regeneration (Larsen 1980). Evidence of man clearing forest 8,000 years ago and pine disappearing as a result has been found in upland Yorkshire (Simmons and Innes 1981), whilst many instances of clearance are recorded by Zvelebil (1994). Once the deciduous forest became dominant it would be much more difficult to burn and was probably felled or ring-barked to provide clearings. Unlike most conifers, hardwoods coppice when felled and so would regenerate the forest, eliminating pine. Oak may therefore have been helped to become a major part of Britain's vegetation by the human activities of felling and burning pine, thus preventing its regeneration.

The transition to the Neolithic is today considered to have been gradual and scattered, spreading to Britain from eastern Europe about 5,500 years ago. Recent work now indicates that agriculture arose in one or two centres in south west Asia, possibly due to climatic changes at the end of the last ice age. It then spread with the migrations of the rising population of Neolithic farming people; this has been confirmed by research work into population genetics (Cavalli-Sforza 2000). It is now thought that the spread of ideas was important. Recent work on European genetics has shown that two thirds of the population have a Paleolithic ancestry compared with about one third derived from Neolithic farmers (Sykes 2001). Alluvial areas were first exploited as the soils were most suitable for agriculture. In areas marginal for agriculture, farming and hunter-gathering lifestyles may have complemented each other (Harris and Hillman 1989). Farming gradually became more and more important and as populations increased man began to have an impact on the once extensive forest. By this time, oak had spread widely and during the climatic optimum grew to large sizes. As people settled, buildings became more elaborate and permanent, use being made of durable oak timber. The long houses of the early farmers were substantial structures in which big timbers, especially oak, were used, after felling and splitting with flint axes. As well as being used in domestic housing, large oak timbers were employed in the construction of sacred sites, timbered graves, temples and timber circles. Some of the oak posts were massive when one considers the technology available for felling, transport and handling; many were a metre or more in diameter.

In Britain, many timber circles existed and some pre-date stone circles such as Stonehenge. The tenons on the stones to hold the lintels at Stonehenge were unnecessary; they reflect the use of wooden tenons which would have fixed the lintels of timber circles (Gibson 1994). The shaping of these wooden joints also shows sophistication in the use of tools. Timber circles have been dated back to 5,500 years ago so man by this time must have been affecting the composition of the natural forest through his use of timber. The function of these circles is not fully known but they are thought to represent a calendar or to predict the equinoxes and other astronomical events, which would have been important to farming people.

Other uses were by then being found for oak. Dugout canoes of oak logs have been found, probably fashioned with a flint adze, a tool which has retained its shape and function until the present day, flint being replaced by iron or steel. A Bronze Age canoe from about 4,000 years ago, found in Yorkshire, was constructed of split oak planks, sewn together with yew withies, made waterproof by filling the gaps with moss (Dimbleby 1978). By the Bronze Age, oak was being used for coffins and in some cases the enclosed bodies have been well preserved by the tannin in the timber.

The wheel became important for transport about 5,000 years ago in Europe. Early solid wheels were made of oak or elm, both being tough timbers. Elm was an important tree providing not only timber, fibre and animal fodder but also a food source as the protein-rich cambium was eaten in the spring (Dimbleby 1978). Animals today also strip the bark of elm for the same food source. Since both these activities result in ring-barking of the tree, this may be one of the causes for the decline of elm in the forest record. Dutch elm disease has also been suggested as causing the elm decline (Moore 1984). Another reason for the decline in elm pollen at this time could be the coppicing of elm as animal fodder, which is still occurring today in Romania (Lines personal communication). Repeated coppicing would have prevented the elm from flowering but would have produced large, young palatable leaves for fodder. Any of these causes would increase the proportion of oak to the other species existing in the remaining low-lying forest. At about the same time as elm declined, so too did ash and lime. Lime was also an important tree for bark fibre (for making rope) but stripping the bark would have killed the tree. Lime timber is easily worked and beehives were made from hollowed trunks. Removal of lime for these uses would again have favoured oak. Ash was a useful timber and a good fuel wood as it can be burnt green. However it relies on open ground for regeneration and the impact of domestic grazing animals on young seedlings cannot be ignored. Oak survived over other species, both because it coppiced so freely and because it was valued for many uses.

It was about this time that man began clearing the forest more systematically for farming rather than using the less intensive slash and burn technique. Lime forest was felled in southern Britain as it grew on fertile soils suitable for agriculture. The cultivation of open ground would also have prevented ash regeneration. Because the plough by then allowed better cultivation, there was a rapid rise in the demand for flint axes for clearing forest and flint mines, or 'factories', were opened in Poland, Belgium and at Grimes Graves in Norfolk, the axes being exported over long distances.

That wood had been in use for a long time is illustrated by the discovery of a yew spear at Clacton, dated at about 400,000 years ago. The discovery of the 5,200-year-old corpse in the Alps in 1991 (Spindler 1994) provided an insight into how man then used different woods. A sophisticated knowledge of the properties of various woods for different purposes is evident, such as yew for his bow, ash for a dagger handle, lime fibre for rope, hazel frames and birch bark for containers. Birch sap was boiled to a tar and used as a glue. Collecting sap and stripping the bark of birch would again kill the tree and would have had an influence on forest composition.

The tannin-rich property of oak was early recognised and exploited. Tanning prevents skins from decomposing and renders them soft and pliable for clothing and other uses. Tanning was first undertaken by smoking, using plants other than oak but the resulting product was not very soft. Oak bark and galls are rich in tannin and produce a better leather. They have been recorded as being used for tanning in the Neolithic period; the same process is still used today. Oak trees were felled when the sap was rising in the spring and the bark was then easily stripped away. The bark was stacked for about a year and then steeped in water. It was then placed in alternate layers with the leather until the required texture was achieved.

Timber was also used to make trackways on soft ground in locations such as the Fens and the Somerset Levels. To make the tracks, birch brushwood was first laid down, then poles were placed longitudinally. Finally, these were overlaid transversely with split and round logs of alder, birch and oak. The range of timbers used is evidence of early coppicing. This is discussed further in Chapter 2.

Oak timber was also used for smaller items requiring strength. Eel spears have been found with oak hafts. Oak was used to make fish and animal traps. Tread traps made of oak with a horizontal flap to catch animals are known from the Bronze Age. When an animal trod on this, a wooden spring was activated and the animal was caught by its foot (Dimbleby 1978).

Oak was important as a fuel, perhaps not so much as firewood as it is slow to dry but rather in the form of charcoal, which is more easily transported and hotter burning. Oak charcoal is found on many sites and can be identified by typical characteristics. Charcoals on archaeological sites provide evidence of the tree species being used which were probably growing not too far away. On early Bronze Age sites, charcoal for copper extraction was derived from oak, alder and hazel (Dutton and Fasham 1994). The technique of smelting copper and the later production of bronze developed first in eastern Europe. In the heyday of Mycenae, about 1500 BC, minerals were in great demand and traders travelled west in search of copper, gold and tin (Barber 1983). At this time, metal smiths travelled widely practising their trade, producing bronze objects which became status symbols and are found in burials of important people of this period. Until recently, the evidence for early copper mining in Britain was lacking but over twenty sites have now been identified in use 3,800 years ago (Dutton and Fasham 1994). The mineral resources of Britain were therefore being exploited quite early, probably at the end of the Neolithic in the uplands (Mellars 1986). Large amounts of charcoal, probably mainly of oak, must have been used to extract them from their ores.

The climate now began to cool. It has been estimated that there was a fall of nearly 2°C in average temperatures between 1000 and 750 BC (Cunliffe 1986), which resulted in the extensive formation of blanket bog. It was at this time that substantial remnants of oak forests were preserved in peat, the climatic conditions for the growth of oak having become marginal. At this time iron became important as metal for tools; the ore was mined and smelted here. The strong, mould-board plough enabled the cultivation of heavy soil, allowing more forest to be cleared in lowland areas. Written accounts began to appear such as the writings of Pytheas the Greek (320 BC) and the Romans, recording the way people lived in western Europe; the Druids of the Celtic religion are chronicled. Groves of old oak trees assumed great sacred importance and may have been remnants of the old forest. Sacred groves of old trees became important in Greece when forest cover declined (Perlin 1989); in China many of the old trees are only preserved round temple sites.

Trade with Britain for minerals increased. Depletion of the forest continued for both agriculture and the production of charcoal for smelting, oak being particularly good for this purpose. By about 1000 BC forest cover on Dartmoor, for instance, had almost gone (Barber 1983) leaving only a few remnants. The same was true on other upland sites. Iron Age forts also made use of timber as did domestic dwellings; thus substantial quantities were used, with oak being preferred for its durability and ease of cleaving (see Chapter 4).

The Romans and after

The mineral wealth of Britain was one of the reasons for the Roman invasion. The Romans mined copper, lead, silver, gold, tin and iron. Vast amounts of timber were felled for smelting the various ores, especially for iron in Kent, the Sussex Weald and Forest of Dean, decimating the oak forests (Meiggs 1982). Charcoal was used in glass making and salt production, whilst the Romans also used timber for fuel to heat houses and baths. The properties of various timbers were well known and oak was specified for lintels and beams in temples and houses. Ships in the Mediterranean were built of various timbers but the keel was often of oak, to withstand the stresses placed on it. Boats on the Western seaboard were almost always of oak planks which could withstand the Atlantic seas. Oak timbers were used for houses, forts, roads, bridges and quays and the Romans must have felled large areas to meet these demands. The shortage of big oak timber becomes evident when it is recorded that large timbers were removed from abandoned forts for use elsewhere (Meiggs 1982). Land was also cleared for agriculture as the population grew under Roman rule. In the period 100 to 300 AD it is estimated that the production of iron alone destroyed 180–500 square miles of forest (Perlin 1989).

As resources of wood were exhausted in the south of Britain, mining took place to the north and west, so that by the time the Romans left the tree cover of Britain had been drastically altered, except in Scotland. The ensuing times of unrest allowed woodland to regenerate. The climate fluctuated at this time; Bede records famine about 400, saying 'famine left a lasting memory of its horrors' (Sherley-Price 1955). Cores from Greenland (Herron *et al.* 1981) showed little summer ice melt and the cold summers meant crops failed. In addition plague decimated the population. All these factors gave the forest a chance to regenerate and recover whilst at the same time management of the remaining forest became increasingly important (see Chapter 3).

By this time, old oak trees must have been significant landmarks and important as boundary markers. Bede records that Augustine in 603 'summoned the bishops and doctors of the nearest British Province to a conference at a place still known to the English as Augustine's oak which lies on the border between Hwiccas and the West Saxons' (Sherley-Price 1955). A later gathering was attended by seven British bishops: 'We are not told where they met Augustine ... a good case has been made out for Abberley in Worcestershire, near the Herefordshire border. There was an ancient tree here called Apostle's Oak, famous enough to give its name to the parish of Rock, originally R(oak), in which Abberley was included until 1289' (Finberg 1974). The tradition of named oaks thus goes back a long way; probably St Augustine's Oak is the first recorded named oak.

CHAPTER TWO

Propagation and Raising

The thorn is mother of the oak.

Anon.

As oak became of increasing economic importance its propagation became increasingly sophisticated. More has been written about how to grow oak woods than woods of any other species of tree. Here we will see how these ideas and practices evolved over the centuries with regard to oak in particular and consider what is still relevant today.

Tree clearance was undertaken in Britain early in the colonisation of the land by hunter-gatherers; this involved clearing a great deal of oak. At first trees were destroyed using fire and there is now evidence that this led to the formation of heaths and moorland, which provided grazing areas for game, making it easier to locate and hunt the animals. Trees were also felled for dwellings and post-hole remains have been found as early as 9000 BP (Mithen 1994). By the Neolithic (5000 BP) larger trees in the primary forest were felled for dwellings and for constructing the timber circles which preceded stone circles.

To begin with, woodland was left to regenerate itself by natural seeding or by coppice sprouts from cut stumps. At some stage it must have been realised that coppicing and pollarding were two ways of providing a constant supply of wood of usable sizes. Coles and Coles (1990) tell us that: 'The Somerset Levels have revealed evidence of coppicing and pollarding from *circa* 4000 BC onwards and this is the earliest sign of woodland management so far recorded anywhere in the world'.

A trackway built across swampy ground in the Levels was discovered by a Mr Sweet whilst peat cutting. This track is now known as the 'Sweet Track', from which in 1990 oak timbers were dated by tree ring chronology to 3806 BC (5806 BP). This track was made from cleft oak planks split with axes and wedges, about 3.4 m long and 60 cm wide, held together mainly with hazel and alder pegs but also with some elm, ash and holly (Coles and Coles 1990).

The Sweet Track had been preceded by an earlier track in the same area made of hazel posts and split ash and lime trees. Flint and stone axes were found in the area as well as a yew mallet dating to 3000 BC. Other tracks in the Levels were made of hazel hurdles constructed of coppice material and have been dated to 3500 BC. The Meare Heath Track, also in the Levels, dates

FIGURE 3
Pedunculate oak
acorns, Wistman's
Wood, Dartmoor.

JEAN WILLIAMSON

17

from 1400 BC and is made almost entirely of oak. These trees 'were smaller, younger and less suitable for producing quantities of good planking and were probably felled from secondary woodland' (Coles and Coles 1990).

The oak timbers of a track found at Flag Fen in Cambridgeshire have been dated at 3500 BP and these showed 'the distinctive tree bases that result when oaks and willows are trimmed to ground level to foster the growth of standard sized poles' (Fagan 1995). Many trackways have also been found in Ireland on wet ground. One of these was made of oak and ash, incorporating both roundwood and split stems. Tree ring analysis of the oak gave a felling date of 2259 BC (Raftery 1992).

As it became more important to have a supply of wood near settlements for building, fuel and animal fodder (leaf hay, especially from ash and elm foliage, and oak twigs) it must have been realised that supplies of wood needed to be maintained and deliberate management then probably resulted. Grazing animals and pigs needed to be kept out of coppice woods if the woods were to re-grow successfully after felling. Thus the cultivation of parts of the forest, which included oak and other trees, produced coppice woods in Britain for the first time. This probably dates back at least 6,000 years; we might today consider this as early forest management.

The cultivation of trees by seed for both ornament and utilitarian purposes was carried out by the Persians in ancient times who planted trees in lines with those in one row between those of the next in order to give trees adequate space. This was known as the 'quincunx' and was much later advocated by many eighteenth- and nineteenth-century silvicultural authors. Tree cultivation was also well understood by the Egyptians, while in Greece in the eighth century BC Homer's epic poem, *The Odyssey*, includes a passage describing Ulysses' father planting trees in the hope of his son's return. It was developed further by the Romans. By then in Italy the different ways in which wood was grown and the use to which it was put were clearly defined. Cato in 200 BC advocated self-sufficient estates growing various crops. These included vines, willows, fruit orchards, coppice woods (*silvae caedua*), the latter for poles and firewood, also 'mast woods' (*silvae glandiferae*) for fattening pigs; usually of oak or beech. Varro in 47 BC planted pines and cypresses on farm boundaries and recommended oak for use as vine stakes; whilst Columella (first century AD) advocated coppicing oak to supply stakes for vine supports on a seven-year cycle (Meiggs 1982). In Gaul, *silvae materiariae*, or high forest, was also distinguished (Linnard 1982). Roman rule in Britain must surely have promoted these practices, with coppice woods near settlements providing stakes, poles and fuel-wood, with building timber from high forest. Oak coppices were probably established near Roman villas to provide vine poles, just as they were in Italy. Any standards in coppice and larger old oak trees in high forest, including mast woods, provided the larger building timbers, tan bark and acorns for animal fodder.

Regeneration in coppice would have been from sprouts growing on the felled stumps and in high forest and mast woods by natural seeding (probably helped by the rooting of both domestic pigs and wild boar) and planted acorns; by the eleventh century deliberate planting, probably with acorns rather than young trees, was being recorded. [The] 'King of Gwynedd is said to have improved the husbandry in his kingdom by "planting old woods" and making orchards and gardens' (Linnard 1982). Linnard also suggests that the early Cistercian monasteries in Britain practised a high level of forest management, such as that recorded for their counterparts in Bavaria, where 'the forest ordinance ... dating from the second half of the thirteenth century gives details of the forester ... it also indicates an appreciation of the importance of suitable forest floor conditions for natural regeneration' (Linnard 1982).

In 1359 the Black Prince is recorded as requiring one of his Stewards to see that his underwood was fenced after cutting when he instructed him 'to enclose the woods so cut down with a hedge so that beasts may not enter and do damage to the young growth'. There is record of tree planting in Scotland in the 1300s near houses of importance and by monasteries (Anderson 1967). In 1457, King James II of Scotland commanded that 'all tenants ... [should] plant woods and trees' (Hunter 1883). In the fifteenth century 'cultivation of trees and woods of the New Forest was undertaken' (Brown and Nisbet 1894).

From the Romans onwards woodland regeneration was active, primarily sustained by coppice regrowth, encouraged and enclosed until established. In other woods regeneration was by natural seeding, if necessary supplemented by 'dibbling' acorns into holes made with a stick. Until 1500 there was little need to create new woods as the land was still sufficiently wooded for the size of the population and the demands upon woodland.

The Tudor era saw less unrest than had prevailed in the past and Britain was not disrupted by civil wars. Trade and manufacturing increased and woods were felled to create more pasture and arable land. When the monasteries were dissolved new landowners took the opportunity to exploit the woods for profit. This increased felling caused Tusser in 1577 to state 'that men were more studious to cut than to plant trees'. Planting must also have been undertaken, though, as Holinshed (1577) states 'plantations of trees began to be made for the purposes of utility'. In Scotland, Anderson (1967) records leases which referred to plantations as early as 1510. In the more settled conditions landowners and those who had profited by trade built residences in which internal decoration, particularly oak panelling and oak furniture, became prominent features. Shipbuilding increased with trade and the iron-smelting industry began to decimate woods for their charcoal. The result was a great demand for wood, particularly oak, and fears were expressed about future supplies. This led to the Statute of Woods of 1543, which is discussed more fully in the next chapter.

By the mid-sixteenth century leases began to stipulate that a tenant should plant a specified number of timber trees during his tenure. In Wales: 'For example, a lease of 1564 required the tenant to plant 180 trees, either oak, ash, elm, poplar or walnut' (Linnard 1982). In Scotland too, the shortage of wood was being felt and an Act in 1503 required 'every Lord and Laird ... [to] plant at least one acre of wood where there is no great woods nor forests' (Hunter 1883). By the end of the sixteenth century a number of landowners were actively seeking to regenerate their woodlands. In 1580, Lord Burleigh (1520–98) is credited with establishing the first pure oak plantation in Windsor Park when an enclosure of 13 acres was sown with acorns (Albion 1926), though Brown and Nisbet (1894) give the date as between 1550 and 1560.

Such woodland regeneration by enlightened landowners did not diminish the rate of destruction of existing woods for iron-smelting and glass manufacture. Thus the management of woods and their regeneration became increasingly important as virgin supplies dwindled and the shortage of wood for shipbuilding became of concern. At the same time the cultivation of trees for both ornamental and practical purposes increased. Norden in 1618 argued that: 'Lords [as well] as tenants [should] plant for every sum of acres a number of trees or to sow or set a quantity of ground with acorns' (Perlin 1989). Standish (1611) also advocated that new woods should be planted. There was a significant development at about this time when it was realised that it was an advantage to raise oak seedlings in nurseries for planting out in woods. One of the earliest nurseries raising oak seedlings was described by Church in 1612 thus: 'And in this garden or nursery thus made you may, when they are grown to 3 foot high, remove of them how many you please' (James 1981).

Evelyn and his successors

It was not however until the publication of John Evelyn's *Sylva* in 1664, after much woodland had been destroyed during the Civil War, that the planting of woods for timber began to be taken seriously. Evelyn's book drew on many sources, including classical authors and those of the sixteenth and seventeenth centuries, such as Fitzherbert, Miller, Plot, Church and Tusser. Its purpose was to inform landowners how to raise oak and other trees. He set down in detail the practical knowledge of that time. Some of his ideas must have come from his father who managed the woodlands on the family estate at Wootton House in Surrey. Much of what he wrote is quoted in many subsequent books on the raising and cultivation of oak. His literary style makes difficult reading, so the following gives a brief account of his ideas.

Evelyn was convinced that planting young trees from a nursery was the best practice and 'that an acorn … shall in two or three years outstrip a plant of twice that age which has been either self sown in the woods, or removed' [lifted and replanted elsewhere]. He thought that the nursery-raised plants grew straighter, made better roots and grew well as they were not either shaded or 'dripped' on by overhead trees. He quotes Virgil:

> Trees, which from scattered seeds to spring are made
> come slowly on for our grandchildren shade.

Although we have little doubt about this today, not all subsequent authors agreed with him and over the succeeding 150 years or so two schools of thought existed, those who advocated planting the acorns where they were to remain (known today as direct seeding) and those who maintained that oak seedlings grown in a nursery and then planted out in the woods did better. For direct seeding, in fields that could be ploughed, a clean seed bed was essential. After ploughing, two crops of turnips were taken to control the weeds and then the acorns were planted. Evelyn was aware that young oak needs shelter and to give the young plants shade and protection he recommends sowing the acorns with furze and broom or growing them under a crop of oats. Today Evans (1984) tells us that direct sowing, though often tried, has seldom been a success. Very large quantities of seed are needed, up to 100,000 per hectare to be successful, and there are high seedling losses from mice, bird and squirrel predation. The resultant stocking tends to be patchy, with seedlings crowded in places and many gaps. 'One benefit claimed for direct sowing is that because root growth of the seedlings is continuous and not broken by transplanting, both early growth and final tree stability are improved. No experiment has ever shown support for either of these claims for direct sowing, though there is some evidence that initial root development and symmetry are better, or that planted trees are in any way unsatisfactory' (Evans 1984).

For a 'seminary' or nursery, Evelyn says that the ground should face south-east and be protected from the north and west (whereas today we would avoid an easterly aspect because damage by late spring frost is greatest where plants are thawed rapidly by the early morning sun). The area should be well fenced to keep grazing animals (cattle, deer, hare and rabbits) out. It needs to be ploughed or trenched (double dug) with a spade, especially on a clay soil and well weeded before the acorns are sown. He quotes the Roman philosopher Boethius:

> He that for wood his field would sow,
> Must clear it of the shrubs that grow,
> Cut brambles up and the fern mow.

Evelyn stipulates that acorns should be collected from 'fair thriving trees'; another point we would emphatically agree with today. If they are not to be sown in October they should be put in sand, layer upon layer (known now as 'stratification') and sown in early spring, thus reducing the damage from vermin – mice, voles, pigeons, rooks and pheasants – which eat winter sowings. Clearly he was aware that acorns do not store well and are best sown immediately after collection in the autumn.

Evelyn goes on to describe how acorns in the nursery should be sown like beans one foot apart in drills, the drills to be two feet apart and covered by rake, as he was of the opinion that broadcast seed left gaps. The acorns are best sown in the autumn but as mentioned above vermin need control to avoid too much loss. He considers it unnecessary to add fertiliser to the young plants, especially if the land has been prepared by growing a crop of turnips beforehand which have been eaten off by sheep. As well as the soil being

enriched, the weeds are also controlled by this practice. The importance of
weeding and watering the young trees until they are ready to be planted out
in the wood is emphasised:

> Hough (hoe) in the spring, nor frequent culture fail,
> Less noxious weeds over the young wood prevail.

When the tops of the seedlings touch each other they are to be singled to
two to three feet apart and the seedlings planted elsewhere to be grown on
at 18 inches apart (as they were too valuable to be discarded). A mulch is to
be put between the rows to protect and help to retain moisture for the roots
(it no doubt also kept down weeds) and the trees should be kept well watered.
The mulch is provided by 'scattering a little mungy half rotten litter, fern,
bean haume, or old leaves among them, to preserve the roots from scorching,
and to entertain the moisture'. When the seedlings were two to three years
old they were lifted and planted out in their future situation at final spacing
of about 40 feet, surrounded by ash, chestnut and other trees for shelter and
protection.

He directs that the roots should be handled carefully when the seedlings
are lifted from the nursery beds. Evelyn acknowledges that some foresters
transplant the seedlings in the nursery before planting them out in the woods.
'Transplanting of young oaks gains them ten years advance, some happy
persons have affirmed.' If this is to be done, he recommends cutting back the
tap root, reducing the head and planting in loose soil to encourage the fibrous
roots. (Subsequent authors have varied in their advice whether to transplant
or not.) When moving the plants from the nursery care should be taken to
leave soil on the fibrous roots; this was indeed suggested by Theophrastus as
long ago as 300 BC and Cato, writing in 200 BC, advised binding mould
round the roots and transporting in baskets to preserve the soil. Evelyn goes
on to say that the hole in which the tree is to be planted should be friable
and not compacted, 'never to enter your stem deeper than you found it
standing, for profound burying very frequently destroys a tree'.

After being planted out in their 'final situation', 40 feet apart for pedunculate
oak and 25 for sessile, he advocates cutting the plant back to one inch above
the ground after two years (when there has been root growth) and then
later selecting a single strong shoot and pruning the side branches. 'By this
means the Oak will become excellent timber, shooting into straight and single
stems.' When planting out in the woods he says, 'some advise that, in planting
of oaks etc., four or five be suffered to stand very near to one another, and
then to leave the most prosperous when they find the rest to disturb its
growth; but I conceive it were better to plant them such distances as they
may least incommode one another.' He also states that it was better not to
plant out oaks that were too large, saying, 'but as for those who advise us to
plant oaks of too great a stature, they hardly make any considerable progress
in an age and therefore I cannot encourage it'. This is a lesson we still need
to learn today.

The final area in which the seedlings are planted also needs to be fenced in some way as:

> Sow acorns, ye owners that timber do love,
> Sow haw and rye with them the better to prove,
> If cattle or coney may enter to crop,
> Young oak is in danger of losing his top. (Tusser 1557)

Evelyn emphasises that oak can be grown on a variety of soils: rich deep loams are best for good oak timber but as these soils were also the best for agriculture they were not so readily available for planting with trees.

Almost all that Evelyn recommends above remains pertinent today: the importance of seed collection from good trees, sowing in autumn rather than storage over winter, the greater success of seedlings grown in a nursery when planted out compared with those from direct sowing, the importance of weed control in the nursery, the care of roots whilst transplanting, the value of cutting back tap roots, the greater success of small transplants over large plants and the need of shelter for oak and thus for planting in a matrix of other species; also the success with which oak can be cut back in order to encourage a single leader or indeed if fire has passed through a young crop.

The latter half of the seventeenth century saw the publication of a number of books on forest trees as more and more landowners turned to establishing plantations; at the same time enclosures were being planted in the Royal forests. A list of such books can be found in James (1981). For example, an enclosure of 10,000 acres was commenced in the Forest of Dean in 1668 under the Dean Forest Reafforestation Act of 1668. By 1671 Pepys recorded that 8,000 acres were planted: 'in divers places (especially where there are bushes) the oaks come up very well but not so in the bare places' (Hart 1966). For the New Forest, an act was passed in 1698 allowing the enclosure of 6,000 acres and a further 6,000 acres twenty years later.

By the end of the eighteenth century the number of books describing how to grow trees increased, many repeating much of Evelyn's *Sylva*. All stressed the importance of growing oak on good soils and many plantations were established on ploughed fields, the acorns being sown with cereals or pulses which were then harvested over the oak seedlings, or fields were ploughed and transplants from the nursery set out at final spacing with underwood planted between. Many authors preferred the establishment of woodlands by means of direct sowing. Bradley, in 1718, stated: 'I would advise that every plantation of oaks be set from acorns on the very spot where they are to remain.' In 1717 Moses Cook produced *The Manner of Raising, Ordering and Improving Forest Trees*. Many of his recommendations are similar to Evelyn's but in contrast, he is very much in favour of transplanting oak trees in the nursery whilst they are small, observing that when they are moved late to the planting ground from the nursery without transplanting, the tap root is easily damaged. He would lift seedlings when two to three years old and cut the tap root, and then plant on land ridged with a plough so that the growth of fibrous roots was then encouraged, an effect achieved today by undercutting. He emphasises the importance of planting the right tree on the right soil for good growth, confining oak to be grown as timber to good loams. Although oak will grow on other soils, for light soils he recommends beech, holly and hazel; ash and elm on clays; ash, hornbeam and sycamore, with alder, willow and poplar, on moist soils.

Buffon, writing in 1739, observed that acorns sprouted in 'thin' places (where there is a light canopy) within a wood and that oak seedlings appeared naturally in uncultivated fields. Ellis (1745) also commented on oak seedlings colonising meadows near woods, a situation commonly seen today, as an indication that oak seedlings need light. Buffon carried out extensive experiments on how to establish oak in an area which he divided into trial sections. One section was ploughed three times, another twice and another once. In other sections the acorns were dibbled in without ploughing or were scattered on the grass; some were planted with seedlings lifted from the wood or planted with seedlings raised in nurseries, some of these were planted in spring and some in autum. In others acorns were sown an inch deep and some six inches deep; acorns were sown with oats; some soaked before sowing and some sprouted in earth over winter. The trees taken from the nurseries 'almost all succeeded' whereas 'the trees, big and small, which I had taken out of my coppices, perished the first or second year'. The acorns which had been sprouted in earth over the winter and then dibbled in were also successful. In another experiment he divided an area into two parts and dibbled in acorns on bare ground on one and in amongst bushes of thorn and juniper on the other. Although both areas had seedlings in the first year, by the fifth there were few left on the bare ground but on the second area a young wood became established amongst the bushes (an effect achieved today by the use of tree shelters). He therefore concluded that in the early years the seedlings needed shade and shelter from frost and wind. He also observed in one dry summer that the oaks which had not been weeded after July survived better than those where the weeding had been carried out all summer, as the latter plants had not had enough moisture and he concludes that it would have been better to have left the weeds (which would have reduced evaporation from the soil and provided shelter).

Buffon's ideas probably came from Germany, as did much forestry practice in the eighteenth and nineteenth centuries. Matthews (1989) tells us that at this time 'many fine oak stands were raised by dibbling acorns, often in conjunction with field crops'. This practice eventually fell out of favour and is not used today, other than by occasional woodland owners who push a few acorns in the ground as they walk round their woods; its failure in Britain almost certainly being due to heavy predation of the acorns.

Batty Langley, writing in 1740, was another author who preferred setting acorns out in their final situation on open ground, not overshadowed by trees, as the resulting seedlings need less watering and staking. On rich soils he advised sowing an underwood six to seven years later, especially if ash was also planted, so that the ash did not outstrip the oak and remove too many nutrients. By this time, seedlings could easily be purchased from commercial nurseries rather than raised in the landowner's own nursery; he warns that 'we should be careful, how we buy trees from Nurseries, where they have been grown without being transplanted'.

Haddington (1761), who is credited with the first use of conifers to nurse oak, had read books on raising oak and other trees, including Cook and Evelyn. He says of Evelyn: 'his language is affectedly cramp; he shows, in my mind too much regard to the age of the moon, and other niceties, ... He is tedious, and makes too many digressions; but in the main is a good author.' The reference to the moon was to Evelyn's rule that tree felling should take place when the moon was on the wane and planting when the moon was waxing. There are also other statements in Evelyn which we now find rather naive, such as the rule that when trees are transplanted they should be replanted in exactly the same aspect as they were before. Haddington was a practical author who is credited with the first use of pine to nurse oak. He began, however, by preferring direct sowing and planted acorns in areas intended to become woodland, stating: 'I think it is by far the best way, if the field-mice could be kept from destroying them: ... Where the ground was bare ... the acorns did very well' but he failed to control grass in the fields planted and lost many seedlings, so resorted to growing the seedlings in a nursery first.

In 1754 the Royal Society of Arts, in order to improve standards and encourage planting, offered medals for good plantations of oak and newly introduced species, especially conifers. This led to landowners trying out new species in their woods and looking for profit as well as pleasure from trees. The Edinburgh Society of Arts, which came into being in 1755, included similar objectives in its aims (Anderson 1967).

By the time of the publication of Evelyn's sixth edition in 1766, which contained extensive notes by Dr Hunter, many landowners were using *Silva* as a basis for tree culture and regeneration but were also developing their own techniques for raising oak and establishing plantations. Hunter quotes at length how trees were raised at Welbeck in Nottinghamshire. Although in many respects Evelyn's principles and practices were followed, other techniques were also employed. For instance, Hunter says that at Welbeck when oak was planted out in the wood, small birch seedlings were also planted thickly between the oak, whilst evergreens (holly, laurel, yew and juniper) were planted around the edge of the wood to provide shelter, either mixed or in pure groups for variety 'but so as to make a regular screen or edging. Our design ... is to make the outsides of the wood as if scalloped with evergreens.' Hunter goes on to say that at Welbeck when oak plants were lifted in the nursery, they were first placed in trenches and covered with soil to keep the roots moist and frost free. Only as many as could be planted in a day were then taken to the planting site. This is an early reference to what we now know to be so important, proper handling and care of transplants. The plants were pruned if the root or head was excessive. Planting holes were dug, the subsoil from the bottom being placed down the slope if on a hillside, to retain moisture.

After planting the tree was trodden in firmly. Finally, extra acorns were also set amongst the planted oak and birch. At the end of the winter, any loose young trees were heeled in again and subsequently the plants were weeded two or three times during the year, '... cutting off only the tall growing weeds'. On poor soils furse was sown with success: '... we commonly find the best plants in the strongest bed of whins. This shows how acceptable shelter is to the oak whilst young.' (A forerunner of tree shelters again.) Hunter says that 'on poor land Scots pine, was recommended as a nurse between the oaks as long as it is removed once protection is no longer needed ... when the trees are grown to a size sufficient for their protection, the firs [i.e. the pine] in the centre [of the wood] which I call the nurses, should be removed, otherwise they will injure the young oaks.' He also says that at Welbeck, beech, larch and Spanish chestnut were mixed with oak; '... in all the young plantations, the Spanish chestnuts keeps an equal pace, or rather outgrow the Oak.' Perhaps his are the first references to the standard techniques used today for establishing oak by nursing. There is still evidence in Clumber Park of these techniques having been used in the eighteenth century.

In 1778 Boutcher was a strong advocate of transplanting oak in the nursery but was adamant that it should be done properly to produce strong and vigorous plants. He was critical of many nurserymen who recommended that plants should be reared on poorer soil than that in which they were to be grown and that they should be sown thickly and left in the seed bed for two to three years. Although many nursery techniques had improved since the publication of Evelyn's first edition, Boutcher was aware that the high demand for nursery plants had led to some nurserymen not taking enough care; they were producing poor plants and 'as many purchasers not being skilful enough to estimate the value of a tree by any other standard than its height, without attending to the far more essential circumstances of its roots, thickness, and proportion' they were disappointed with the results. Of oak in particular he writes: 'No tree requires more address but none is more neglected.' To grow oak, Boutcher makes a point of starting with good acorns, discarding any that float in water. Today we would add that those that fall first tend to be malformed or empty, usually following the first frost. Sound acorns tend to fall a week or so later (Aldhous 1972). We would also support Boutcher's transplanting in the nursery as this encourages the development of a fibrous root system most suitable for planting out. Often this is done now by undercutting mechanically rather than actually lifting and replanting the plants.

Boutcher recommends that in the spring the acorns are sown in drills 18 inches apart at two-inch intervals. The following spring, the seedlings are cut four to five inches underground with a sharp spade and left until the next spring, when they are lifted. The straight seedlings are separated and planted in rows two feet apart at nine-inch intervals and the crooked ones in separate rows. The good seedlings can then be planted in the wood after two to three years more. The crooked seedlings after two years must be cut down to the ground and one shoot selected. After another two years these poorer oaks are ready for planting out. Boutcher was against dibbling the plants in as this constricts the fibrous root which the nursery man has been at pains to develop, a view endorsed by later authors. If larger trees were needed, he transplanted every two years, gradually increasing the space between the trees in the nursery. He planted in the spring as although 'most deciduous trees ... succeed best, being planted in autumn, the Oak is one exception to this rule, ... and grow[s] more freely, when transplanted in the spring.'

In 1789 we find Emmerlich in his *Culture of Forests* mixing in ash, birch and beech seed when acorns were sown directly into the ground. He states: 'The Beech, in particular, is the Oak's protector; for wherever an Oak and a Beech are seen standing together, they are both found in a thriving condition.' Previously, authors had concentrated on how to grow oak on the better soils, using ash, chestnut, hazel, birch and willow as underwood which could be cut for profit. Emmerlich's recommendation of sowing beech as underwood to oak is interesting, not because it was useful economically but for its benefit to the oak. Emmerlich had practised forestry on the continent where beech was an important component of the forest; he says he was 'formally employed by his late Prussian Majesty, as Forest Master and Manager of his Forests in Westphalia ... upon leaving his Prussian Majesty's service, I had the honour of being appointed to the similar office in this country, in the year 1775, by Lord North, the Prime Minister of Great Britain.'

It does not appear that Emmerlich's methods were taken up to any extent. In the New Forest in 1793 we find Nichols still stating that thorns provided a good nurse for oak in the Forest. However, Scots pine was introduced to the New Forest in 1776, presumably as a nurse on poor soils, but by whom is not evident. For obtaining natural regeneration Emmerlich writes: 'When the Manager and Director of a forest meets with a good year for seed, he may order more timber to be cut than he is immediately in want of, provided it is fit for cutting, but not before the seed is ripe and drop from the trees; as while the timber which is cut is carrying out of the forest, the seed is trod into the earth, and the next spring, plenty of it will come up.'

Until the mid-eighteenth century, many landowners planted up good agricultural land with oak plantations but the onset of wars before and during the Napoleonic period meant that the price of corn was high and it remained so until the 1840s (Newton 1859). As a result good land was ploughed to grow corn and was no longer available to grow trees. Attention was therefore turned to growing oak and other species on the poorer land, of which a large area was available. This shift, together with the decline in markets for coppice, led to oak being grown with conifers which provided income. Between 1730 and 1760 many nurseries were established (Brown and Nisbet 1894). Nicol in 1803 observed that plants were not expensive and that a wide range of species was available due to the demand. Linnard (1982) records Welsh landowners buying from nurseries outside Wales early in the eighteenth century. Scots pine was bought in 1722, spruce, silver fir and larch in 1778 and other conifers, chestnut and oak in 1794. Although like other authors he says that oak for good timber, especially for shipbuilding, should be grown on the best soils, there was a demand for oak of lesser quality for tan bark, pit props, fencing, charcoal and industrial distillation. On poor soil Nicol recommended planting oak with Scots pine but he was very much in favour of larch as a nurse on the slightly better soils. He also mentioned mountain ash (*Sorbus aucuparia*) in such situations for this purpose as at that time it produced a useful timber for tool handles and wheels. He thought that many landowners plant too many nurses and he would plant three to four nurses to one oak, the oaks being planted at nine-foot intervals. He points out that whatever the proportion of nurses to oak 'in no case however should the nurse be suffered to over-top or whip the plants intended for a timber crop.' Thus by the late eighteenth century the value of nursing oak was widely accepted. Many subsequent recommendations refer to various nursing techniques.

Planting out oak up to this time had been undertaken by trenching or pit planting. Trenching or double digging involved lines for the oak being dug with a spade or with a trenching plough, 30 feet apart and about three feet wide, though this must only have been undertaken on good soils. Oak was planted in these trenches 30 feet apart, sometimes more, and the spaces between filled up with ash, elm and other species. The more usual method was to excavate pits and when oak seedlings became cheaper they were planted much closer.

Like Evelyn before him, the importance of good soils in which to grow oak was emphasised by Marshall (1796). 'The Oak, in shallow barren soils, and in bleak exposed situations, cannot be raised with profit, as a timber tree' but cornland 'can seldom be converted to woodland.' He was also against staking young trees unless they are very large, planting firmly being more important. Of pests he stated: 'In raising a wood, from seed, it is not only necessary to fence against cattle and sheep but against hares also ... against rabbits, nothing less than death is effectual.'

Today, if oak is to be grown economically, and there is a tenfold difference between the value of low grade oak and first quality veneer butts (see Chapter 3), attention to local site and soil conditions is of paramount importance. Unlike many tree species, oak shows little regional variation in growth throughout Britain, being not greatly affected by altitude or rainfall. Local soil and site conditions, however, are critical for the production of good quality trees and timber. Blyth *et al.* (1987) warned that oak does not grow well on shallow, ill-drained and infertile soils or exposed sites. Soil requirements do differ between the two species: pedunculate oak requires a higher fertility and less acid soil but will tolerate rather wetter conditions than sessile oak; even so, sessile is planted more widely today because it often has a straighter stem and lighter branches. Kerr and Evans (1993) insist on the need for careful site selection, recommending that: 'Oak should be established on deep, fertile acidic clays and loams because these sites are optimal for the species and are believed to reduce the incidence of shake. [Whereas] Oak growing on light, freely draining typically stony or gravelly soils commonly produces timber which is shaken and cannot be used in any high quality application.' They go on to say that 'sessile oak tolerates less base rich soils than does pedunculate oak' and give a table specifying the soil requirements of the two species.

In the nineteenth century conifers became the accepted nurses for oak. Pontey in 1809 suggests not only planting larch as a nurse crop for deciduous trees, including oak but also advocates the use of Norway spruce. He says that conifers should be used as nurses for deciduous trees as conifer poles have more uses than birch and will bring in some early returns. Nicol and Sang (1812) used ploughing for areas where oak was to be planted on fields as 'oak requires and deserves a good soil'. On less workable soils pit planting six feet from centre to centre was used, placing the turf from one pit into the bottom of the next to provide a rooting medium. In many cases Nicol would use larch as a nurse but on poor soils he planted Scots pine first and added oak plants four to seven feet apart two or three years later. In his book he refers to deciduous trees as hardwoods and it appears that this term came into use about this time. Loudon (1838) states that Turner, the Deputy Surveyor of the New Forest in 1819, found Scots pine the best nurse for oak in the New Forest on poor soils.

Planting on poor, wet soils, besides requiring a change in nurses, also meant that provision of adequate drainage was important. The wet conditions also required a change in planting techniques, so Billington (1825) introduced a new method. He found that using pit planting on wet soils led to the holes filling with water and the trees did not grow. He therefore removed two turfs from either side of the spot on which the pit would have been and inverted them on the planting site. They were then left to rot before planting. In the spring the seedlings were planted in the turf and the roots had a dry medium in which to grow. The channels from which the turfs were taken helped to drain surplus water into excavated drains. In the Forest of Dean he planted oak in every tenth position and sweet chestnut in every hundredth, the sites being four feet apart. Ash, elm, beech, sycamore, fir (Norway spruce) and pine were planted between the oak and sweet chestnut. Both crop trees and nurses were planted at the same time. On poor and exposed ground 'the fir tribe seems best adapted for that purpose, if properly managed and taken out in time, otherwise they are the worst enemies.' (A lesson we have lost sight of today.) 'The growth of oak is astonishing when sheltered a little in their infancy, and until they are large enough to shelter each other'. Shelter from spring frosts was also considered important, to prevent damage. Evans (1984) points out that young oak leaves are very sensitive to frost and suggests that sessile oak may be more sensitive in this respect than pedunculate oak.

Like all authors, Billington stressed the importance of keeping the young oaks weed-free until they are above the ground vegetation as 'where the grass, fern, or other herbage has quite got over them, the grass falls down upon them ... and where the strong fern abounds it falls down with the first heavy snow [upon them]'. Both Billington and Nicol emphasise that care is required in the first few years after planting out from the nursery, to get good, straight, oak plants and they recommend shortening the side shoots to two-thirds their length to encourage growth into the leader. These shortened shoots are pruned right back later to keep the stem clean when there is sufficient growth and successive side shoots are treated in a similar manner.

Cruickshank (1830) used larch and Scots pine as nurses in Scotland and like Nicol his method was to plant the conifers first. When these were about four feet high he planted five acorns in each oak position as he did not believe in transplanting young oak trees. The conifers gave protection, especially from spring frosts. Two years after planting the acorns, surplus oak seedlings were removed and any competing conifers had to be sacrificed. This method was also used in the New Forest, the Scots pine being planted first, but good oak plants were used rather than acorns. About five years after planting the oak, the pine was gradually removed and sacrificed.

By 1838, Loudon was writing: 'Modern planters seem to be all agreed, that the best mode of producing shelter for the oak is, by first covering the surface with Scots pine, larch or birch; this practice seems to have originated at Welbeck.' Loudon goes on to say that 'Scots pine and spruce fir [Norway spruce] are preferable' as nurses.

In 1868 Grigor observed that the practice of planting conifer nurses first is not always necessary except on bare and exposed ground 'as the larch and pines advance more rapidly than the oak, and find shelter in a very short time, when the whole are inserted at once.' He was not in favour of sowing acorns but plants strong trees, which have first been transplanted in the nursery. He was also in favour of pit planting rather than expensive trenching, the pits being 18 inches square by 15 inches deep, dug some time before planting the oak trees. He considered that slit planting (a single slit made with a spade into which the young plant is thrust) which was also now used, although suitable for small conifer seedlings, was not so for oak which needed loose soil for the fibrous roots of the transplants to establish and grow. He stated: 'The oak is in general of slower growth than the others (ash, elm, sycamore) ... and requires rather more space to allow it to grow to maturity in its best form' and 'with shelter the young plant soon takes a powerful hold on the soil ... after being pretty closely sheltered, it often advances rapidly.' As the oak grows he recommended that the nurses near the oak need to have their branches cut back so as not to interfere with the oak and the oak plants need the side shoots shortened to encourage growth of the leader.

Methods of growing oak in the nursery had changed little by the mid-1800s and transplanting for good root growth had become accepted practice. Brown and Nisbet (1894), however, pointed out that in 'younger forests raised artificially by sowing or planting, a preference seems to have been given to the latter species [common oak, i.e. pedunculate] probably on account of the somewhat larger size of the acorns' whereas naturally regenerated forests are more usually sessile oak. He also pointed out that 'the danger of premature germination is less in the case of the British [pedunculate] than the Durmast

Oak [sessile], whose smaller acorns are more difficult to store safely through the winter months.' The acorns of pedunculate oak (Figure 3) are produced early in life after only ten years and the trees fruit heavily in mast years. The acorns are larger than those of sessile oak and fall more easily from the cup, so can be collected in large quantities off the ground. There was also the added consideration that: 'All the oak plantations made throughout Britain during the greater part of the last two hundred years in the State forests [Royal forests] ... as well as by private landowners were formed with the express intention of growing wood suited for the purposes of ship building' (Brown and Nisbet 1894) for which pedunculate oak was considered superior (see Chapter 5).

In the nursery Brown (1851) sowed the acorns thinly, not thickly as was often the custom, and recommended that the seed beds should be covered with nets or branches to deter vermin and that seedlings be transplanted at one year old and then planted out after two to four years, depending on their size. 'The Oak during the first year after being transplanted, makes very little progress in growth, but merely establishes its roots in the ground. During the second year it begins to send out new shoots and from the third year onwards it usually grows vigorously.' To prevent disease from building up in the nursery beds, he rotated the species of seedlings grown.

Another major development during the nineteenth century was the availability of wire for fencing; before this wooden fences and paling had been used as well as thorn hedges and earth or stone banks. Wire netting was mentioned as being available in 1832 for keeping rabbits out and soon afterwards wire fences of different strengths, including barbed wire (invented in America) were erected around both nurseries and plantations. Brown observes: 'In the matter of fencing ... this may be truly said to be the *iron age* for wire fences ... are setting aside most others.'

Towards the mid-nineteenth century the demand for 'crooked' ship timber, which required a long rotation to provide material with enough heartwood, declined. There was more imported timber available due to the repeal of the Navigation Act in 1850, which had required ships to be built of home-grown oak. Iron knees had replaced wooden ones, iron ships were being built, timbers were steamed into shape rather than 'grown'. Thus the wide spacing for oak trees recommended by the eighteenth-century authors for ship timber was being replaced by planting oak at closer spacing and the use of conifer nurses. Sessile oak then became more important because of its straighter timber, better tan bark and ability to grow on less fertile soils than pedunculate oak.

Trenching was still practised when oaks were planted at wide spacing but this became impractical as more oak trees were planted per acre. Selby in 1842 pointed out: 'The benefit of trenching ... previously to planting has been much insisted on ... we think, however, that those who speak so highly in its favour ... have been premature in their conclusions ... had they waited the result of 2, 8, or 30 years growth, their conclusions ... would have been very different from those drawn from the state of plants, as exhibited in trenched ground, of 8 or 10 years growth.' He quotes an example of trees grown in trenched ground and others grown in pits nearby. The trenched trees grew better until they were about fifteen years old, when the others caught up with them, and by thirty years there was little difference between them. 'Trenching, therefore, may be considered not only an expensive and unprofitable preparation for growing timber, but as money thrown away.'

By the end of the nineteenth century the method of raising oak seedlings in the nursery was established. The main change from Evelyn's recommendation that the nursery should face south was that it should face north or north-west to avoid frost damage. Oak plants were no longer given 'garden' treatment in the forest, which had been practical when there were only about 25 to 40 trees per acre but were instead planted in pits, on mounds, on raised turf or they were notch planted. All these methods gradually replaced expensive trenching, as much as anything because oak was no longer being established on deep, fertile soils which could be dug or ploughed easily.

It is interesting to see which of the recommendations reviewed above have survived to the present day and to consider what is advocated now in order to achieve satisfactory establishment of oak.

Of all the controversies between foresters in the eighteenth and nineteenth centuries, one stands out, whether to sow or dibble acorns directly in to the forest soil or to grow the seedlings in a 'seminary' (nursery) first in order to obtain a good fibrous root system rather than a single, vulnerable tap root, before planting out. As we have seen, these discussions were eventually resolved in favour of nursery production of good plants for planting out at a few years old. In these discussions the views of Evelyn and Batty Langley were paramount. Eventually the views of Nicol and Boutcher prevailed and with good reason.

Natural regeneration

Although natural regeneration of oak has been widely practised over several centuries in Europe, it has never been very successful in Britain; Evelyn (1662) did not even mention it. There are several reasons for this but the primary factor is probably consumption of acorns on the ground by small mammals, as oak flowers and produces good seed almost as regularly in Britain as in the warmer climate of central Europe. Watt (1919) suggested that the failure of oak regeneration in Britain is mainly due to predation of the acorns by animals and birds, damage to the foliage by oak mildew and defoliation by the larvae of *Tortrix* moths. He considered that successful regeneration was most likely in moist oak woods and less so on dry oak sites. The seedlings are also very susceptible to frost; a temperature of −6°C is sufficient to kill acorns (Jones 1959). In the New Forest, Small (1982) reports browsing of oak seedlings by deer as a major restraint and Voysey (1982) similarly reports damage by ungulates (deer and sheep) as major factors restricting oak regeneration in the Lake District.

Indeed, it was not until British forestry practice started to be influenced by continental, particularly German, practice that natural regeneration was seriously considered here for oak and other species. One of the earliest references to it is by Nisbet in his revision of Brown and Nisbet (1894): 'Natural regeneration has hitherto in Britain not been so much practised in high-timber forest as is the case on the Continent, and it is chiefly in Copse and Coppice that it has been made use of' (which is not a method of natural regeneration as understood today). He goes on to describe classical natural regeneration systems for Scots pine and oak, emphasising that if natural regeneration is employed for oak, the 'seedlings of light-demanding species, like Oak and Pine, become sooner intolerant of overshadowing than those of shade-bearing trees.' However, his is only a cursory discussion of natural regeneration, mainly of how it is used abroad and might be applied in Britain, before he moves on to lengthy and detailed prescriptions for planting. It seems then that natural regeneration did not prove satisfactory other than to a limited extent in the New Forest and Forest of Dean.

Nisbet went on to write several forestry texts of his own and in 1900, whilst still being mainly concerned with oak coppice, with creating high forest by singling coppice shoots and establishing oak woods by planting, he does give some consideration to natural regeneration but acknowledges that: 'Many ... oak woods are now found difficult to regenerate naturally.' He continues: 'Owing to the want of close cover the soil often gets overgrown with grass, or worse still, with moss; and then a satisfactory crop of self-sown seedlings cannot be reasonably expected. Soil preparation of some sort is in such cases absolutely essential to enable acorns and mast to germinate and establish themselves in the soil. Moreover, the change in the conditions between the olden and the present times must also be taken into account.' He tells us that: 'Most of the woods now mature date back to a period when cattle and swine were probably still largely driven into the oak and beech woods for grazing and pannage, and they were in the vast majority of cases, no doubt, the principal agents in obtaining a satisfactory regeneration.' He went on to describe in some detail methods of preparing the soil to receive and encourage the acorns to germinate and then emphasises the importance of removing the overstorey before the young trees become shaded. Finally he returned to the necessity of planting up the blanks with nursery plants and even recommends planting larch amongst the oak seedlings.

In 1911 Nisbet was writing again, this time with a forestry text book in response to the 'Afforestation Policy' of the Development Commission, the first proposal for a national forest policy in Britain. Here woods are classified as coppice, simple or with standards and as 'highwoods', the latter being regenerated artificially by clear felling and sowing or planting or partial clearance for natural regeneration in groups or by uniform natural regeneration. He considers that highwoods are 'the only way to produce long straight clean stems of oak' on rotations of 120 years or more. Though devoting most of his text to various methods of establishing and regenerating woods by planting, he does consider natural regeneration suitable for oak, beech and Scots pine as practised on the Continent and suggests that it could be more widely used in Britain. He tells us that: 'Natural regeneration of Oak in Britain was originally solely by means of enclosure, with prohibition of grazing; and this simple method, easy through acorns being usually plentiful every 3 or 4 years, still gives good results in both Oak and Beech woods in the forest of Dean' but does not go into further detail for oak, suggesting that natural regeneration of the species was never widespread in Britain.

Even though natural regeneration of oak is still not likely to be practised widely here today, there are occasions when it may be suitable and it is a silvicultural challenge that appeals to most foresters when the opportunity arises. How then can it be achieved with oak in British conditions? We have a good deal of guidance from up-to-date research and field observations, both on what to avoid and on how to achieve satisfactory natural regeneration of oak. Too often woodland managers or owners, on the strength of the appearance of a few seedlings, assume the wood can be regenerated by merely clearing around them but if the conditions are not exactly right, heavy weed growth, usually of bramble, will soon swamp the site.

Early in the twentieth century, Hanson (1911), writing about successful natural regeneration of oak in the Forest of Dean, warned about the problems of weed growth or a 'hard turf' which did not allow acorns to germinate and recommended light ploughing, not an easy operation in woodland. He recommended leaving 40 seed trees per acre (100 per hectare) under a shelterwood system and removal of the overstorey as soon as three years after sufficient seedlings were established because oak is a light-demander. He describes a large area in the Forest of Dean being regenerated in this way in the first decade of the nineteenth century. However, few attempts since have been so successful. He says that oak begins to produce good seed from 70 to 80 years and then every three to four years, though Savill (1991) says that good seed years can be as much as ten years apart. Matthews (1989) reports that good seed years of both oak species occur in England about every three to five years and Lines (1999), using Forestry Commission records, reports that 'Quercus robur mast years occur every two to six years; Quercus petraea every three to eight years.' Hart (1991) refers to a very abundant oak mast year in the Forest of Dean in 1899 when about 200 hectares were enclosed and oak regeneration appeared in quantity; the seed-bearing parents were gradually removed and gaps filled in with Norway spruce, sycamore and European larch. (Perhaps this is the area Hanson refers to.) By 1952 the oak had been underplanted with beech; Jones (1959) described the result as 'an excellent uniform crop of oak (and beech), equal to anything to be seen on the Continent of Europe.'

More recently, Small (1982) has also described the use of the shelterwood system in the New Forest to regenerate even-aged oak stands but even then with a good deal of enrichment by planting. Interestingly, he goes on to say that some of the most extensive natural regeneration of oak in the New

Forest has occurred outside the forest inclosures on surrounding 'heathland at the perimeters of the original high forest.' This demonstrates how difficult it is to get the light conditions right for oak within woodland and indeed it is common to see oak seedlings germinating in fields well away from mother trees, a phenomenon observed by earlier authors.

Savill (1991) warns that: 'Natural regeneration of oak is usually accomplished in Britain with difficulty, when it can be accomplished at all.' Although group systems are popular today for other species, he says that the group or selection systems of natural regeneration are unsuitable for oak as the seedlings need light early and are heavily defoliated by caterpillars if under an oak canopy. (Group systems consist of regenerating very small cleared areas; in contrast, selection systems retain the overall canopy.) He concludes that: 'Attempts to manage oak by selection or group systems (except by using very large groups) are doomed to failure, and the concept of an intimately mixed, all-age climax oak woodland is impossible.' He affirms that 'the uniform shelterwood system is the only suitable system.' Kerr and Evans (1993) also tell us that if natural regeneration of oak is to be practical, the shelterwood system is the most suitable because the seed is not carried by wind and the overstorey trees are needed to give shelter. Site preparation must be co-ordinated with mast years and the overwood needs to be completely removed by five to seven years – significantly longer than Hanson's recommendation – after the naturally regenerated crop is established. They agree with that author that there is evidence that sessile oak will stand more shade than pedunculate.

There is thus, today, a consensus that the only way to regenerate oak from natural seedlings is under a shelterwood system from which the overstorey seed trees are removed just a few years after the seedlings are established. Any form of group selection or continuous cover systems will not succeed with oak. (Continuous cover systems are similar to selection systems.) Seldom do the right conditions arise in Britain. The right conditions are: good seed trees, preparation of the site in a good mast year, lack of competing vegetation, absence of acorn predation, quick establishment of the seedlings and early removal of the overstorey; all this on a moist, loamy, rich soil. Without these conditions prevailing, only failure will result. Even then, if regeneration occurs, blank areas will need to be enriched (planted up) with nursery grown plants quickly before bramble and other growth dominates the site.

Tree shelters

All the eighteenth- and nineteenth-century authors emphasised the need for shelter for oak at planting time, first using other broadleaved trees and shrubs, often growing naturally on the site, then using conifers when they became available. It is not surprising therefore that the most significant modern development in the successful establishment of oak has been the introduction of the artificial tree shelter, following experiments started by Graham Tuley in 1979 (Tuley 1985). The principles underlying the use of the tree shelter are the same as those underlying the methods put forward by those experienced foresters who wrote so knowledgeably in the eighteenth and nineteenth centuries about growing oak. Young oak responds very well to being grown in tree shelters (Blyth *et al.* 1987) as it needs to be encouraged to grow upwards and requires overhead light but also side shade, otherwise it tends to be bushy in the early years. These conditions are provided by the tree shelter and there may be other benefits too. Evans (1984) points out that there are two periods of shoot growth in oak, May-June and July-August. The latter is 'lammas growth', that is a second flush of growth in mid or late summer, very common on oak. (The leaves are often red in colour, as they are when they first come out in spring. This is due to red pigmented anthocyanins which protect the DNA of the young leaf from the harmful effects of ultraviolet light.) Evans says: 'One effect of tree shelters is to stimulate lammas shoots with several occurring in one season' and explains oak's 'capacity generally to respond well to the technique.' Indeed, tree shelters produce a better overall growth response with oak than with any other species, more than doubling the rate of height growth in the first two to three years (Kerr and Evans 1993). This second surge of growth in mid summer is accompanied by a strong sap flow to be seen in early August on cut oak stumps, which bleed profusely at this time, whilst ash for instance, felled at the same time, exhibit no sap flow at all (Kerr and Evans 1993).

Oak and other light-demanders benefit from tree shelters in three ways and these have been reported by Potter (1991). Firstly, by a reduction of light as height growth is increased proportionally to reduction in light down to about 14 per cent of light transmitted through the shelter and then rapidly drops off below this. Secondly, stem diameter is not adversely affected down to about 55 per cent of full light but then drops off significantly below this light level. Thirdly, survival; this is not reduced by reduction in light until it is down below 90 per cent reduction.

Thus, we now know that reduction of light due to opacity of the shelter *increases* height growth of oak until 55 per cent of light is obscured (if darker, height growth falls off), whilst opacity up to 55 per cent reduction has no effect on diameter growth or rate of survival. Tree shelters therefore almost always improve survival rates; this is due to reduced water loss, both because transpiration is reduced and because some water vapour from transpiration condenses on the inside wall of the shelter and runs back onto the soil. Apart from the light effect, shelters also encourage height growth; in oak this is positively accelerated, because there is less movement of the young plants by wind so resources are devoted to height growth rather than thickening of the stem and roots to stabilise the young tree. Height of oak in shelters can be more than 100 per cent greater than that of unsheltered trees three years after planting; i.e. young trees in shelters are, after three years, more than twice as tall as those in the open. The enhanced height growth resulting from tree shelters, however, is short-lived and probably only advances canopy closure by one or two years but it is cost effective because it reduces the weeding period though not the need for initial weed control.

Tree shelters also show dramatic improvement in reduction of deer damage as well as browsing by hares and rabbits. In the latter respect the tree shelter was anticipated in America as early as 1892 by the 'Tree Protector' (Brown

FIGURE 4
This young plantation shows how well oak responds to the use of tree shelters when the site is suitable for the species. The nine-year-old sessile oak shown here were planted 'pure' (i.e. with no other species), three metres apart, and 1.2 m high tree shelters were removed two seasons previously. The excellent stem form shows little taper and is 10 cm below the crown but this is still somewhat bushy and has yet to develop a strong leader. Upward growth would be encouraged and the crown shape improved if western red cedar, a narrow, shade-bearing tree itself, were planted between the young oak and removed as poles after 20 to 25 years. This vigorous young stand is on a north-facing slope in warm, south-east Cornwall and was planted on the margin of a larger oak woodland: exactly the situation in which oak tends to regenerate naturally. Morval Estate, Cornwall.

E. H. M. HARRIS

and Nisbet 1904); a circle of cypress or cedar plastering laths held in twisted wire was placed round the young tree for the purposes of protection but enhanced growth was not claimed. 'The protector not only prevents sunscald on the trunk, but is an effectual preventative from rabbits and other rodents, as well as from whiffle-trees used in cultivation.' (Whiffle-trees are those blown by the wind.) Brown and Nisbet provide drawings of the construction and use of this device but there is no indication that it was widely adopted in Britain.

Tree shelters initially often result in a columnar rather than tapering stem on oak. The former is not as strong as the tapering shape which trees typically produce from the start when unprotected but as soon as the branches get out of the top of the shelter and wind starts to rock the young tree, the tree responds by developing thickening at the bottom of the stem. By the time the shelters deteriorate and break up (or need to be removed) there is no difference between the shapes of the stems of sheltered and unsheltered trees. Potter (1991) reports that after five years most trees have developed a strong enough stem to remain upright when the shelter is removed but if light levels are low (in a wood) trees require a longer period to attain stability. He says that oak emerging from tree shelters lack apical dominance and tend to a bushy appearance and multiple leaders but this is no more than occurs normally nearer the ground when trees are unsheltered and it is definitely easier to apply corrective pruning to them at this height.

Potter describes the tree shelter as acting as a 'solar still' with much of the moisture emitted by the tree and the soil condensing on the walls on a hot day. This reduces the drying conditions that occur on a warm summer day and this, together with reduced wind movement, increases photosynthetic carbon dioxide fixation provided the bottom of the shelter is in the ground. He says that: 'It appears that carbon dioxide originating from bacterial respiration in the soil is trapped in the lower part of the tube, an effect that is enhanced by sealing the shelter at the base by pressing it into the ground. As the gas moves up the tube by diffusion and convection it is rapidly consumed on contact with photosynthesising foliage ...' (Potter 1991).

Tuley (1985) in summarising his early experiments concluded that: 'Shelters are a way of making oak ... grow rapidly in height ... They greatly assist the establishment of young oak trees [and] reduce the number of expensive years when the trees must be weeded and protected against deer.' These views are as valid today as when shelters were first coming into wide use and they have undoubtedly become an invaluable tool in aiding the establishment of a difficult species.

Conclusion

It is clear that Harley's (1982) cautionary warning at the time when the planting of broadleaves, particularly oak, was becoming popular again, to be enshrined in the Broadleaved Policy of 1985, remains important today. He considers some of the silvicultural problems of growing oak and gives us several salutary warnings and useful guidance. He tells us that: 'There are many ... problems in growing good oak ..., with many ... expensive operations and with very few returns.' He warns us of: 'The impropriety of growing oak pure ... and the folly of planting oak under oak.' He points out that: 'The over-riding silvicultural characteristic of oak is its light demanding nature which raises problems both when grown pure and in mixture.' He goes on: 'Now, oak is a light demanding species which does not tolerate shade at any stage of its development, so satisfactory restocking with oak is not likely to be achieved except in the centre of large gaps. To plant oak ... into small holes in the wood is probably a complete waste of time even if it pleases the planters, and will delay the replacement of the crop.' Similarly, with regard to planting groups of oak in a matrix of other species, he warns that 'the small size of the groups necessitates early reduction of encroachment by the surrounding nurse crop and the two metres spacing needed to allow mechanical weeding requires even earlier attention to pruning the low branching oak.' Referring to the conversion of oak coppice to high forest, he says that 'selecting any maidens [seedling trees], singling the coppice stems on selected and sound stools and thinning gradually to develop high forest' is aesthetically pleasing – it is practised by the National Trust – but it takes 'a long time and the prospects of high quality timber eventually are not good.'

This then is how we should establish oak today, employing the tried and tested methods of the past and using proven modern techniques, in essence planting nursing mixtures and using tree shelters together with initial herbicide control of weeds. We will not succeed if we ignore the strong light-demanding characteristics of oak, particularly when it is young.

CHAPTER THREE

Management and Silviculture

....

The friendly pine the mighty oak invites.

Claudian

Before the Saxons

We have seen that management and the use of trees as a food and as a wood resource must have occurred quite early in Britain and that the techniques probably came with colonisation from Europe. Although burning woodlands and ring-barking trees for grazing were practised, the earliest form of positive forest management undertaken was almost certainly coppicing, when it was realised that many kinds of deciduous trees grew again from their cut stumps. As mentioned in the previous chapter, this was being actively practised in Britain over 5,000 years ago. The produce from coppiced stools provided wood of sizes that were easy to cut and handle, whilst the frequent cutting encouraged a large root system to develop which in turn led to vigorous re-growth. Pollarding, cutting off branches at about head height, was probably also practised early so that a supply of wood could be grown out of reach of browsing animals. Larger trees were felled for special purposes as they were needed, from the extensive areas of natural woodland.

As population pressure increased, the land was divided up between various tribes and some control over the allocation of forest resources took place. Large trees became more and more valuable as primary woodland was cleared, not only for timber but also as providers of animal fodder via the leaves and fruit. Ash and elm are very palatable for livestock, whilst acorns in autumn and oak twigs in winter also provided stock with sustenance. Oak boughs and twigs especially were used to feed deer in the Royal forests but not the leaves as there is too much tannin in them, unlike ash and elm leaves. In any areas of valuable woodland, other than coppice, the trees became the property of the land-owning classes, as they had abroad. There is reference in the Bible to Nehemiah asking King Artaxerxes in 384 BC for 'a letter unto Asaph, the keeper of the King's forest, that he may give me timber to make beams for the gates of the palace.' Roman texts of 138 AD were found inscribed on stone in the Lebanon showing that the forest had been marked out for the Emperor who claimed four species of tree for shipbuilding (Meiggs 1982). The growing and planting of trees was also practised early by rulers such as Cyrus in Babylon who laid out trees in the gardens in network formation or quincunx (Browne 1901).

FIGURE 5
Sessile oak woodland with beech understorey. The crown silhouetted against the sky shows the fan shape of sessile oak with the typical long bole suitable for planks.

E. H. M. HARRIS

Although Iron Age peoples had used wood for smelting as well as for other purposes and were able to fell large timber, the arrival of the Romans in Britain led to accelerated forest clearance, for both practical and political reasons. The felled timber was used for road construction, bridge-building, construction of forts and quays and for river piling. Later, timber was used in villas and other dwellings, for fuel and in the form of charcoal for metal smelting, especially lead, tin, iron, gold and silver, as well as in the manufacture of glass and the production of salt. There was thus a high demand for wood and extensive forest clearance and regeneration occurred. The Romans, as we have seen, were fully aware of coppicing systems in Italy and they used coppiced oak for vine poles and fencing. It is reasonable to suppose that oak coppice was also managed in Britain for these purposes as well as for charcoal for smelting. Oak bark was used for tanning. As mentioned in Chapter 1, even by Roman times large oak timbers were in short supply in England and when forts were dismantled, such timbers were taken away for re-use.

As well as coppicing, the Romans practised other forms of woodland management which constituted 'saltus' or pasture woods and mast woods. 'In Gaul two major forest systems were distinguished during the Gallo-Roman period; *silvae materiariae* [high forest] and *silvae caeduae* [coppice]' (Linnard 1982). No doubt the Romans applied the same distinctions in British woods. After the Romans left, oak mast woods were still a very important source of winter food for fattening pigs. Pannage – the right to feed pigs on acorns in a woodland – was the basis on which many woods were valued in the Domesday Book. The failures of the mast harvests in 1110 and 1116 and the resulting hardship were severe enough to be recorded in the *Anglo-Saxon Chronicle* (Savage 1995). How much pedunculate oak was actively encouraged for acorn production is unknown, but it is likely it was being favoured because it fruits much earlier in life than sessile oak and bears heavy crops of larger acorns, especially when the trees are widely spaced. Also the acorns, being on stalks, are more easily detached from the tree. A medieval manuscript (Figure 6) illustrates swineherds beating the acorns down with clubs for their pigs which are foraging beneath.

The Middle Ages

The few written records referring to woodlands that survive from the early medieval period relate mainly to warfare and forest clearance. However, controls existed in woodland: Evelyn quotes the laws of King Ine of Wessex in the mid-seventh century: 'If any one set fire of a felled wood, he shall be punished … and those who clandestinely cut wood … for every tree he shall be mulcted thirty shillings. A tree so felled, [oak for its acorns] under whose shadow thirty hogs can stand, the offender shall be mulcted three pounds.' These pannage laws were 'for the preservation of the forest, and regulating the right to keep swine therein' (Mosley 1910). Monasteries in the Anglo-Saxon period were granted considerable areas of woodland by various kings

FIGURE 6
Swineherds beating
oak trees to obtain
acorns as food for
their pigs, from
Queen Mary's Psalter,
1310–1320, now in the
British Museum.

DRAWING BY J. A. HARRIS

and in 852 the Abbot of Peterborough leased land back to the king on condition that 'each year into the monastery sixty loads of wood, twelve of brushwood, six of faggots' were provided (Savage 1995). Timber was granted by kings for the building of churches which according to Bede were built of oak with a thatched roof. Oak timbers were taken from the mainland to Iona across the sea to build the monastery in 680 (Anderson 1967). Hadfield (1957) relates that 'one authority goes so far as to suggest that English oak is not a native, but was introduced by the early farming monastic orders' but this is known now not to be the case (see Chapter 1). Anderson (1967) refers to old oaks at Cadzow: 'Some of these oaks are English oaks, supposed to have been planted by King David [of Scotland], first Earl of Huntingdon, about the year 1140'; he also quotes records of the Augustine friars planting sweet chestnut in 1280.

The Charter for the King's forests granted at Winchester in 1016 by King Canute (Lewis 1811) is now supposed to be a medieval forgery; it states: 'No man shall pull down highwood, or underwood, without licence of the chief men of the Forest ... if any man cut down a lofty tree, or any other tree, that beareth fruit for food for the beasts of the Forest, he shall pay 20s. to the King'.

Control of woodland was well-established by the time of the Norman Conquest and the Domesday Book in 1086 gives some idea of its uses and extent, which had fallen to 15 per cent of the land recorded (Hinde 1966). Coppice woods are also mentioned and in some places smelting continued to be carried out, requiring substantial quantities of fuel. Many of the woods were also valued as pannage woods; thus high forest was of particular importance. Pigs were fattened on the acorn crop in the autumn in pannage woods; in the New Forest they were allowed in for this purpose from 14 September to 11 November. This no doubt helped regeneration as the pigs and the wild boar would have turned over the soil in their search for food, thus providing a seed bed for acorns to germinate. In the winter, as well as for a period in spring when the deer were calving, grazing animals were excluded, so there was a chance for some natural regeneration to establish itself.

The Domesday Book shows that in England and Wales the King and his family held in demesne about 17 per cent of land recorded, the bishops and abbots of monasteries 26 per cent and 190 tenants-in-chief, 54 per cent (Hinde 1996). Most landowners leased the underwood and other rights in their woods to tenants but retained the ownership of the larger timber trees for their own use. Such timber was used for repairing castles, mills, buildings and ships and for gifts to monasteries and favourites. Hart (1966) lists gifts of oak trees and timber from the Forest of Dean made by the King to a variety of people for different purposes in the thirteenth century. Edward I in his Charter of 1280 intimates that timber trees belong to him, stating: 'Trees ... shall remain in the forest' and 'if any man shall be found felling an oak ... he shall be attached by four pledges' (Lewis 1811). In Scotland, other records show large oak trees

Oak
A British History

FIGURE 7
The boundary of a medieval oak woodland held in demesne by the king: King's Wood, St Austell, Cornwall. Note the boundary wall.

JEAN WILLIAMSON

being transported long distances for special purposes, such as 40 oak trees in 1291 from Moray to Dornoch for the cathedral there and 60 to Selkirk for the Abbey, and in 1296 40 oak trees from Moray to Arbroath Abbey (Anderson 1967). Oakwoods were still extensive in Scotland at this time and they were granted to subjects and monasteries by charters from the King. 'Although heavy oak mast years are of somewhat infrequent occurrence in Scotland, the pasturage of pigs and payment of pannage was more widespread than one might expect' (Anderson 1967). Anderson also gives many instances of pannage and pasture being granted from 1142 onwards to monasteries and others and also of rights to wood and timber. Pannage was also important from early times in Wales (Linnard 1982).

In Europe Roman forestry practices were without doubt continued in woodland belonging to monasteries and abbeys. St Benedict founded his first monastery at Monte Cassino in Italy in 529, not long after the break-up of the Roman Empire and no doubt the monks continued to tend the woods. Certainly by the seventh century the Benedictines 'had evolved good forestry rules and worked to a carefully developed programme of felling and planting' (Meiggs 1982). Ellenberg (1988) tells us that coppice-with-standards was practised in the Middle Ages in Europe.

Woodland management, which was practised by early British monasteries, was probably brought by monks from the 'mother houses' on the Continent. Contact between monasteries in Britain and on the Continent were frequent even before the conquest in 1066. Numerous visits and travel abroad by bishops and abbots are recorded in the Venerable Bede's history and in the *Anglo-Saxon Chronicle*. Meiggs (1982) mentions management by Benedictine monks in woods owned by an Italian monastery in the eleventh century; the woods continued under its ownership until they were sold to the Italian state in 1866. Linnard (1982) mentions that the Cistercians monks in the thirteenth century were 'leading exponents of forest management as they were on the continent'. He also draws attention to the account book of Beaulieu Abbey from 1269 to 1270 and the *Tabula Forestarii*, 'a guide book or set of rules governing forest yield, wood measurement, and specifications and prices of forest products. This is the earliest forester's *vade mecum* known in Britain. The main products were large timber, bundles of small fuel wood, bundles of vine stakes or hedge rods, faggots, billets for charcoal burning, charcoal, tanbark, and pannage payments ... The accounts show that very large quantities of forest products were harvested and sold ... Surveys of some Cistercian monastery woods at about the time of the Dissolution (1536–39) reveal age structures that betoken careful silvicultural management for at least a century. The surveys indicate that all three major silvicultural systems were in existence; high forest, coppice with standards, and simple coppice.'

Written records of forest management in Britain become more available from the thirteenth century onwards. From them it can be seen that the coppice and underwood were let out by landowners to tenants for a number of uses: fuel, charcoal, stakes, poles, rods, round and split timber, house materials, fencing, bridge building, tools and coffins. The species grown varied according to use and demand and coppice was by no means restricted to hazel which today is usually thought of as the traditional coppice species. The standard timber trees, mostly oak, growing within the coppice, were not harvested so regularly but taken out when needed; they were usually reserved by the landowner. In some cases the mature standard trees were de-branched where the underwood was valuable so as not to restrict the growth of the latter. Trees were also lopped illegally for fuel and de-branched to feed deer and cattle. The underwood was cut many times during the life of the oak standards; it helped to keep the lower part of these trees free of branches, thereby enhancing the timber value.

In more open pasture woods, the trees would have been open grown with heavy spreading branches to provide crucks for houses and later 'grown timber' for shipbuilding (see Chapter 5). The Royal forests contained many of these open grown trees as these forests were primarily to provide pasture for the deer which were hunted for sport and venison. The Welsh laws of the early thirteenth century refer to the King's forest in Wales and to 'preserved woodland' which was reserved for pannage and other forest products. Offences in the King's forest were subject to fines; court rolls of 1295 detail fines of *6d.* for cattle feeding in the forest and *12d.* for 'cutting down boughs of oak for oxen'. In a later court, fines were imposed for cutting underwood and rods: oak is mentioned as well as ash, hazel and crab apple (Linnard 1982). Estover rights (estovers) existed in many woods. These allowed officials and tenants to take firebote (fuel), housebote (for repairing buildings), ploughbote (for repairing implements), haybote (for hedges) and hedgebote (for repairs to gates and fences). These rights were often abused by illegal felling of oak trees and fines were imposed.

James (1981) records that in 1436: 'The great hard biting frost began the 7th day of December and endured unto the 22nd day of February next, which grieved the people wonder sore; and much people died in that time, for cold and scarcity of wood and cole' (cole at that time being charcoal, not mined coal). He also mentions that there was 'the great scarcity of woods that is happened since the time of the said King Edward the Fourth' [1461–63]. The shortage of fuel wood may in some part have been due to illegal felling, especially during wars, and the neglect of protecting felled coppice and woods as required. An Act in 1482 allowed an owner to fell his woods but he then had to enclose the land for seven years to protect the young growth. The shortage of wood may also be reflected by Rackham (1976) noting that in many medieval buildings the oaks used were small, about 25 to 70 years old, the King and other landowners keeping the best for other purposes, particularly churches and royal buildings. Rackham (1976) cites large oaks, some 40 feet in length, being used in the fourteenth century, for the construction of Ely Cathedral and some in stock 50 feet long at Westminster.

Rents and lettings were fixed periodically at manor courts and motes, where also infringements were dealt with. In the Duchy of Cornwall in the fourteenth century, letting or assession meetings took place every seven years. At these, people bid for rights to cut underwood, for pasture, to harvest furze and cut fern (bracken for bedding) and to cut turf for fuel. In a 1359 rental, the coppice was to be cut down and enclosed with a hedge 'so that beasts may not enter and do damage to the young growth'. A lease in the Duchy of Cornwall woods in 1663 reserved the oak timber for the Duchy. In the Duchy woods there was to be one felling in ten years and the woods were to be fenced 'to keep the springs from treading down, biting or harm by horses or cattle'.

Sixteenth-century silviculture

Much of the coppice and underwood in the South West went for smelting tin and soon came to be in short supply. Later, like all Crown leases in the sixteenth century, the leases extended to 21 years, but the number and timing of cuttings were controlled, different lengths of cutting applying in different places depending on species and site. Rackham (1976) notes that coppice rotations gradually increased in eastern England. For example, in Hayley Wood, they were seven years in the fourteenth century, 11 in 1584 and 15 by 1765. The reason for the different periods could hardly be the ageing coppice as fresh stools would have been introduced periodically by layering or natural regeneration, processes that had been in use for a long time. (Layering consisted of pegging down some stems so that they rooted and formed new coppice stools.) In the 1400s, fuel wood was scarce in severe winters. Rotations were short in order to supply enough fuel wood but by the mid-sixteenth century, mined coal was beginning to be used. Leases in Crown woods were extended to 21 years at this time with fellings specified and in some cases also tree-planting.

The increasing rotation length probably reflects a change in demand and therefore the species favoured; hazel, sallow, poplar and elm had been harvested on short rotations, whilst ash, chestnut and oak provided a better yield on longer rotations. Oak charcoal, in particular, became in demand for the rising industry of iron smelting in the sixteenth century and required trees of a particular size, usually felled at about 17 years, to produce billets of specified size for efficient conversion to charcoal. There was also the factor of tithes, which by the eighteenth century were payable on fellings under 21 years so that short underwood rotations meant paying more than one set of tithes during a 21-year period. Oak coppice felled for tan bark was usually grown on a rotation of about 24 years and had been used for this purpose since early times. Beech was not subject to tithes, and tithes were not payable if the tree was lopped (Evelyn 1786).

Evelyn (1786), Brown (1851) and others give the following oak coppice rotations: two to three years for making barrels (cooperage), for which oaks growing from the stools, five to ten feet high, were used for the binding hoops; four to six years for hop poles; to ten years for cordwood; 11 years for spars; 10 to 15 years for fencing; 16 to 17 years for smelting; 25 years for tan bark. Marshall (1815) gives a rotation age in the Midlands of six years to make crates for the pottery industry. For coppice, Tusser (1577) gives the following advice:

> Sell bark to the tanner, ere timber ye fell
> Cut low to the ground, else do ye not well
> In breaking save crooked, for mill and for ships
> And over, in hewing, save carpenter's chips.

In Holinshed's *Description of Britain* (1577) it is recorded that a wide range of species were growing in the woods in the sixteenth century: 'there is not anie wood, park, hedgerow, grove or forest, that is not mixed with diverse, as oke, ash, hasell, hawthorne, birch, beech, hardbeame, hull [holly], sorfe, quicken apse, poplars, wild cherie and such like, whereof oke hath alwaies the prehiminence, as most meet for building and the navie, whereunto it is reserved.' Holinshed also records: 'plantations of trees began to be made for the purpose of utility' in Henry VIII's reign. For 'within these fortie years we shall have little timber growing above forty years old; for it is commonlie scene that those young staddles which we leave standing at one and twenty yeeres fall, are usually at the next sale cut down without any danger of the Statute, and serve for fire bote, if it please the owner to burne them.' He also writes that 'everie man ... [who] enjoieth fortie acres of land ... might plant one acre of wood, or sowe the same with okemast, hasell, beech and sufficient provision be made that it may be cherished and kept.'

Hunter (1883) notes that in Scotland in 1457 an Act of James II charged freeholders that 'all tenants [should] plant woods and trees and make hedges' as well as working the produce because the lowlands had been cleared where formerly trees, including oak, had grown. In 1503 they were required to 'plant 1 acre of wood where there are no great woods nor forests'. In 1535 it was stated 'every man having an hundred pounds land of new extent, where there is no wood, plant and make hedges and haining, extending to three acres, and that the tenants of every merk land plant a tree.' Anderson (1967) also records plantations in Scotland in the early 1500s, whilst Manwood (1598) (quoted by Anderson 1967) makes a distinction between woods and forests, saying: 'where the Trees are scattering, and at such a distance that they do not touch one another, such places are properly called Woods' and 'Coverts are those Woods which are thickets, and full of Trees touching one another.'

In England and Wales, an Act of Henry VIII in 1543 was an important landmark in forest history as it attempted to establish a form of woodland management by law, applying to all woodlands. The aim was to provide a continuous supply of both timber and underwood. In the former oak featured prominently. This *Statute of Woods* made provisions that: 12 standils or storers of oak were to be left standing on every acre of coppice wood or underwood felled at 24 years or under and if there were not 12 of oak, the number had to be made up with other timber trees such as elm, ash, aspen or beech. Trees left from earlier fellings were to be retained to grow on for timber. All standard trees were to be left until they measured 12 inches square 3 feet from the ground. People not complying were to be fined. Coppices that were felled on rotations of less than 14 years were to be enclosed and fenced for 4 years, those from 14 to 24 years, to be enclosed and fenced for six years, those with standards over 24 years must leave 12 timber trees for a further 20 years and after felling the wood to be enclosed for seven years. Fines were to be imposed for each month this was not carried out after felling. In addition, any coppice woods of over two acres could not be converted into arable or pasture if more than two furlongs from a house. In 1570 the period of enclosure and fencing was increased in all cases by two years.

Thus coppice with standards was now fully established as the accepted form of management in an attempt to preserve oak timber trees. How effective the Statute of Woods was in practice is debatable; the iron masters in particular did not like having to leave standards over the coppice as this reduced the yield of the underwood and, as a result, timber trees were often felled for fuel or lopped and de-branched so heavily as to be useless (Hart 1966, Perlin 1989). This in turn led to further acts in 1558, 1581 and 1585 which prohibited the felling of timber trees (oak, ash and elm) for iron smelting within 14 miles of named rivers (transport of large naval timber was mainly by water at this time) and near certain places, and prevented the erection of new iron foundries. Many woods were taken away from the Church at the Dissolution and sold by the Crown. In contrast to the careful management of high forest and coppice by the monasteries, their new owners exploited them with no thought for the future and woods on fertile land were turned to arable land.

Although the destruction of woods for iron smelting is lamented at this period, the worst side of things usually gets the publicity. In fact, as Linnard (1982) tells us: 'The iron masters obviously had a vital interest in maintaining their charcoal supplies.' One ironmaster in particular, Christopher Darrell, is mentioned by Perlin (1989) as preserving his woodlands. Evelyn writes in 1664 of his father telling him 'that a forge, and some other mills, to which he furnished much fuel, were a means of maintaining and improving his woods; I suppose by increasing the industry of planting and care, as what he left standing of his own planting, inclosing and cherishing ... did ... sufficiently evince.' However, wood for making iron, copper, lead and glass was in short supply in England and after James I came to the throne in 1603, extensive exploitation of Scottish woods began (Anderson 1967); Irish woods too were felled (Perlin 1989). At the beginning of the seventeenth century there was little positive management in any of the Royal forests, the timber being removed in a haphazard fashion; trees that grew naturally into required shapes were selected when needed for particular purposes. The result was that much good timber was wasted and the rest not looked after as the welfare of the deer, pannage, grazing and the sale of underwood had always been more important.

During James's reign the first books which advocated planting oak trees were published in 1611 and 1613, written by Arthur Standish. As a result two Bills to preserve the supply of oak were presented to Parliament but both were rejected. One was an 'Act for the Better Breeding, Increasing and Preserving of Timber and Underwoods' and the other 'An Act For the Increase of Timber for Ensuing Times' (Perlin 1989). King James was concerned that so much wood was being used and he issued proclamations prohibiting the use of timber for firewood and for building houses. In 1615 a further proclamation was issued, forbidding the use of wood to make glass. This industry had arisen in Elizabethan times and provided window glass, now in great demand for houses and drinking glasses. For making glass, as with other industries, oak about twenty years old was favoured for making charcoal. From this time onwards, coal became increasingly used for fuel.

Evelyn and his successors

This was the position when various authors began to write about the need to prevent future timber shortage, particularly of specialised 'grown' oak for ships. Oak for this purpose needed a long rotation to provide timber with enough heartwood to grow large enough knees and other natural shapes. Against this background Evelyn put together *Sylva* (1664). Evelyn, when talking of the treatment of oak in the wood after planting, was thinking mainly about growing it for ship timber. This required a deep soil, fast growth and a long rotation of 100 to 120 years to maximise the amount of heartwood. His recommendation was to plant oak seedlings from the nursery 40 feet apart for the broad-crowned pedunculate oak, to allow the tree to spread and 15 feet apart for sessile oak, which is more upright and therefore required less space. At this time it was thought that the two species were merely varieties of *Quercus robur* and that sessile oak was more likely to be brittle and shaken (split). There was also much debate for many years over the perceived inferior value of sessile oak timber compared with pedunculate. It was believed that the long fibres of pedunculate oak when used for planking prevented cannon balls from penetrating the hulls of ships. It was a long time before it was realised that this property was actually related to how fast the trees had been grown. Because Evelyn was thinking of planting oak on good soils, he recommended that the underwood should be ash. Careful pruning of the oak (as the saplings were so far apart) and thinning of the underwood was also needed. Thinning of the oak was important when oak saplings were established from sown acorns. Transplanted young oaks would have been pruned in the nursery but Evelyn advised the removal of lower branches as it became necessary after planting in the wood. He quotes from Lawson (1597) who said that timber trees should be dressed (pruned): 'For believe me, I have tried it: I can bring any tree (beginning betime) to any form. The Pear and Holly may be made to spread, and the Oak to close.'

Evelyn does not spend much time on the management of coppice, presumably because it was so familiar to his audience and his message is mainly about planted woods, especially for ship timber. He mentions that woods for coppice, whether by planting or from acorns, should be ready for their first thinning at 14 years and the oak stools should be 20 feet apart. Oak grown for tan bark needs to be felled in May to June when the sap is rising and the bark then strips off easily. In contrast, oak for timber should be felled in the winter when the moisture content is low. The oak coppice should be divided into 80 parts and cut in rotation as often as required depending on the growth, with seed trees left at 20 feet apart for regeneration.

Hunter, in the sixth edition of *Silva* (1786), added some remarks on thinning: 'On the judicious thinning and cleaning of a young wood, depends much of the planter's success and profit; on which account all gentlemen who engage deeply in planting will find it highly necessary to appoint proper persons, whose office shall be solely confined to the superintendance of the woods. From a neglect in this particular, the hopes of half a century may be thrown away in a period of a few years.' Also in the 1786 edition of *Silva*, Hunter expanded on Evelyn's text with copious notes. When woods are established by ploughing and sowing acorns in fields where they are to form a wood, he recommends thinning the seedlings from a two feet planting distance to four feet at 12 to 14 years depending on the growth, removing every second plant. After about another seven years, the best trees are marked for timber 20 to 30 feet apart and the others cut down and allowed to sprout again as underwood, the produce so obtained being sold for poles. When the crowns of the timber trees meet, the underwood can again be cut and the stools removed as any subsequent underwood beneath them will be of little value. Hunter pointed out that woods grown near rivers reduce transport problems as it is easier to transport large timber by water than on the poor roads. He emphasised that planting good land will produce clean and fast growing trees, with a final crop of good timber.

At the end of the eighteenth century, fuel wood was still in demand and Hunter considered it profitable to grow coppice or 'springwood' between the oak where there was a market for it. By this time oak was usually grown on poorer land than that visualised by Evelyn. As a result treatment of the woods varied and the value of conifers as 'nurses' on poor land began to be recognised. Claudian's observation, quoted by Evelyn, 'the friendly Pine the mighty oak invites' was put into practice by the planting, particularly by the Earl of Haddington, of mixed woods of pine and oak in Scotland. Discussing Welbeck in Nottinghamshire, Hunter wrote: 'We plant about three or four hundred birches of the large size on an acre, and nearly the same number of the first-sized Oaks; we also plant here and there a Beech, larch, Spanish chestnut, ... We then proceed to plant plentifully of the second and lesser sized Oaks; and last of all a great number of the small birches ... these we remove to the succeeding plantation after the term of five or six years. Of the several sizes of the different kinds of trees we generally plant upwards of two thousand plants upon an acre of land, all in an irregular manner. After the planting is finished we then sow the acorns.'

When sown with birch, any birch interfering with an oak was de-branched. When the oak was about 14 feet high the birch was cut and the oak thinned from time to time, any dead branches being removed. The forester at Welbeck stated: 'We are cautious about [thinning] knowing well that if we can but once obtain a length of timber, time will bring it into thickness; therefore we let them grow very close together for the first 50 years.' On higher land at Welbeck, Scots pine was used as a windbreak round the edges of plantations and amongst the oak, the 'firs' being removed before they impeded the growth of the oak. Chestnut was found to keep pace with oak on lower land. These are some of the first references to nursing oak with conifers, a practice which was to prove beneficial and which is discussed later.

However, let us return to other authors writing after the first edition of the *Sylva* in 1664 when oak was still planted primarily for ship timber, both 'grown' timbers and planks. Moses Cook in 1617 was keen on pruning to produce a clean bole for planks. He pointed out that the side branches must be removed before they get too big to avoid large knots and pruning therefore needs to be carried out frequently until the desired height of timber is reached. He wrote: 'I wish I could persuade all Lovers of handsome Timber Trees at every Fall of their Woods, [the underwood] to prune all the Timber Trees: but then the Wood [underwood] must not stand too long before it is felled. You may prune off the Boughs of ten years growth very well, and so every ten years or oftener.' He added: 'take off the small Roots [epicormics] that are broke out on the side of your tree … two or three years together … till you have a Clear body' and then recommends slitting the bark above these shoots. He pointed out that a clean stem can also be obtained in other ways than by such artificial pruning: 'that is by Cattle cropping, by underwood or by standing close to one another.' His reference to cattle cropping is to trees in pasture that have clean stems up to the browse line, where cattle have removed all the young shoots that they can reach. The recommendation to slit the bark to prevent epicormics did not become common practice.

Bradley (1718) too advocated pruning and quoted Lawson (1597): 'How many forests and woods wherein you shall have for one thriving tree, four (nay sometimes twenty four) evil thriving, rotten and dying trees … and … thousands of bushes and shrubs! … and … those all [with] unprofitable boughs, cankered arms, crooked, little and short boles. The greater trees (those for timber, especially oak) if in the prime of growth they had been taken away close all but one top, and clean by the bulk … [would have] … put forth a fair, long and straight body for timber profitable, huge great of bulk, and of infinite last.'

Like other authors at this time, Bradley planted his oak (as groups of acorns, later singled) at wide spacing, 33 feet in his case, at 40 trees to the acre with ash underwood. Some of the latter, was ready to harvest in nine years after

FIGURE 8
Ring barking, as
advocated by Wheeler
(1747). '*a*. the place
where the first
approaching mortality
thereon usually
appears. *b-c.* the two
bark rings of the
Boughs debarkt. *d.*
Two small Boughs left
to arrest the
Ascending sap against
the next debarking
time appointed.'
DRAWING BY J. A. HARRIS

planting and again at 17 years for poles. At 25 years, the ash can be cut again and the oak is well grown but he is referring to good land which can be ploughed. On less deep soils other underwood that he would grow includes chestnut and hazel, the latter cut about every eight years.

We find Batty Langley (1740) recommending the artificial training of oak saplings for ship timbers and wheels: '... since crooked timber is of great value to the shipwright, wheelwright, and millwright, we may for such uses bend to such curves, as best fit their several purposes, as many young oaks, elms, beeches etc. as we please, fixing their heads bowed down, by twisting them to their next adjoining trees. But they should in general be bowed towards the south, because their sap will then have its natural attraction by the sun's heat and they will remain in their curved positions; whereas, when they are bent to the northward, they will, by the attraction of the sun, break loose, and become perpendicular again.'

He regarded the 12 standils per acre (60 feet apart) in Henry VIII's Statute and recommended by other authors as too few and specifies 27 or 30, when the oaks would be about 40 feet apart. To keep a length of timber, the small buds (epicormics) needed to be removed regularly. When cutting coppice, including oak, he advised cutting at 21 years to avoid paying tithes to the Church: 'have Patience till the 21 years are expired, and then to deal with the Country Parson as they please. But if you cut it before twenty years are over, you must comply' as tithes are due on each felling. For height growth on the oak he thought it important to remove the epicormic buds in spring. He would use ash as underwood to oak only on good soils as: 'To have a fine coppice of Ash we must make use of the best land we have.'

Ellis (1745) recommended hazel and sallow as underwood, to be cut every eight to nine years and ash at 18 years for poles, if planted with oak. At that time 'ground' oak (coppice) saplings were in demand for poles, cudgels, laths and barrel staves but later hazel became the usual underwood to grow with oak and much of it can still be seen today.

Wheeler in his *Modern Druid* of 1747 decided that pruning the lower branches of oak saplings was not the answer. He complained that he has followed Evelyn's and Cook's advice to prune the lower branches but then had the problem of epicormics: 'yet I found sufficient reason not

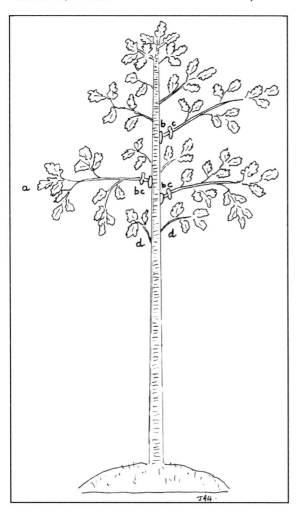

to repeat these trials … as so many ramiscules like Hydra's heads sprung out thereupon.' Rather than pruning close to the stem, Wheeler ring barked the side branches, starting with the lower ones. When the branch had died it was then sawn off near the stem. In this way he thought that the tree was less likely to be damaged than by pruning close to the stem as advocated by other authors. This may have had the beneficial effect of more rapid healing than pruning close to the stem, which Shigo *et al.* (1987) demonstrated as physiologically sound as recently as the 1970s. The method Wheeler developed to keep his oak clean consisted of sending a man up the tree to perform four tasks at once with a saw, knife and hammer. With the saw, the dead, ring-barked branches were cut between the rings but near the inner ring; with the hammer, small epicormic branches were literally crushed; with the knife, smaller branches were ring-barked and the bark of the trunk slit in various places (there was a belief that this helped the tree to grow as it was thought to be constricted by the bark). He repeated this operation two or three times on each oak tree in its early years (Figure 8).

Wheeler was against growing oak timber from old coppice stools ('grandfathers' heads') that had been 'cut down ten or a dozen times' as he felt they could not sustain the growth as well as those from a vigorous young stool. He was also sceptical about bending young oak trees for ship timber, either by tying the tree to others (a practice that seems to have originated in France) or by hanging a weight on the leader. He had tried bending very small oaks at the base with poor results and mentions that he thought the demand for grown timbers would decline as the Navy was now steaming timbers into shape. Good grown timbers were however worth a fifth more in value than straight timber. He was also critical of people who had begun to grow oak close together and were then not thinning them early enough but were opening them out suddenly to final spacing, with the result that epicormic growth was encouraged: 'That by the very reason of the means and manner of the former restraint they have laid on their young plants, they will at last produce vimenious lateral germans; when their final necessary distances from each other are allotted them … upon so great a change; Such is the unaccustomed influence of the sun upon their naked sides … so small and slender their heads … that the arbusculae will thereupon at last break out in their sides.'

Much later, Maw (1909) endorsed this view thus: 'With some trees, especially oak and chestnut, an unduly thick canopy will often cause, especially in the latter half of the rotation, the flushing of lateral buds along the stem and epicormic branches will be thrown out. The reason of this is because the crown is too small and the root system too vigorous'. He goes on to say that epicormics are also produced owing to the sudden exposure of thin and tender bark to sunlight. This observation by Wheeler and Maw is often confirmed today when close grown oak is suddenly opened out.

The Earl of Haddington (1761) was also not happy with the wide spacing of oak at 40 and 60 feet apart in new plantations, saying: 'It is certain if we should plant trees at that distance ... they might turn to bushes perhaps, but never come to that which is called a tree ... so I think, if oaks are planted at 20 feet distance, and other trees set amongst them, it may do very well'. He conceded that in the past you 'may see great trees stand so, yet it is more than probable these trees stood in a thicket, and the rest in time have been taken away.' The timber trees must not be allowed to fork and any epicormics must be removed by 'rubbing off the said buds in the spring'. Thinning could take place later if needed. Haddington's observations about young oak tending to be bushy and the wisdom of setting other trees amongst widely-spaced oak is a lesson we should not forget today. Oak is best grown in a matrix of other trees that shade its lower branches.

As far as producing crooked trees was concerned, Haddington said these could be obtained by allowing cattle to browse. He then quotes Bouffon who had carried out an experiment for producing crooked timber not using weights. 'In a copse I made the stems of several young trees be cut at different heights, *viz.* at 2, 4, 6, 8, 10 and 12 feet from the ground. I cut the top of the young branches which these cropped trees have produced. The shape of these trees became so irregular by this double operation that it is impossible to describe it'.

Emmerlich (1789) when growing oak had ash, birch and beech as underwood, the ash and birch to give a quick return. The beech underwood on poorer soils was to be cut at 15 to 20 years and then allowed to re-coppice under the oak. However, the beech would need control and Gilpin (1791), writing of the New Forest where beech was used with oak, quoted Evelyn's remark 'that every forest, in which oak and beech grow, ... will in the course of ages become entirely beechen' and 'Where goodly Oak grew, and were cut down by my grandfather almost a hundred years since, is now altogether Beech' (Gilpin 1791).

Knowledge of the physiology and growth of trees in the eighteenth century became increasingly scientific; it was, for example, no longer considered that the moon exerted the influence attributed to it previously. The problem of how sap behaved in the tree was still a subject of much speculation at this time. Nichols, however, in 1791 writing of oak in the New Forest, exhibits an understanding of tree growth which is not fully appreciated by some people even today. He stated: 'Trees of all kinds increase in their diameters by additional coats of new wood annually formed by the sap, between the bark and the coat of the previous year (by which the age of all trees may with certainty be obtained) and these coats never increase in thickness ... There is no expansion from the hearts of trees as some have imagined, of this opinion Mr Evelyn seems to have been ... Trees increase also, in height by the repetitions of new shoots, and these shoots never extend in length after being once formed; therefore according to this principle, trees do not increase in height, from their roots to the extremity of their branches, but from the extremity of their branches upwards ... This I know is contrary to common received opinion, which is that every part of a tree grows gradually in height from the root upwards.'

Nichols was adamant that: 'One of the most essential things to be observed in the management of oak woods, if the plants have been raised pretty close together as they always should be, they thereby support each other and are sheltered ... is, the judicious thinning of them from time to time until the trees are reduced to a proper number, and stand at a distance to grow to maturity.' He decided that they should be about 40 to 50 per acre, 30 feet apart, but they should be grown close at first so as to get a length of straight timber before being allowed to spread. Thus he used the trees to prune themselves rather than incurring the labour-intensive pruning and shaping advocated by most authors with fewer, widely spaced trees, or the later practice of growing oak with nursing conifers.

Marshall (1796) defined four types of woodland: simple coppice – with no timber trees – the absence of which is beneficial to the underwood; coppice with standards, where the effect on the underwood increases the more timber trees that there are; woody waste of rough, unmanaged woodland; and timber groves, which he considered both ornamental and useful where the trees are grown close together to produce straight timber. 'The timber grove is the prevailing plantation of modern time' (although we think of groves as small areas, Marshall uses the word for larger stands). He rightly pointed to the need for light and recommends that oak should be grown at wide spacing and that open woods are only suitable for growing oak when the trees should be 33 feet apart and that such woods can only be used for raising ship timber as 'no timber tree whatever, but the Oak, can be raised with propriety in open woods, and this, only, when a supply of ship timber is intended.' Such woods needed to be near water because of transport difficulties overland which were a problem until the coming of canals, railways and improved roads. These woods needed to be planted on good land as: 'The Oak, in shallow, barren, soils, cannot be raised with profit, as a [ship] timber tree.' The underwood grown with oak standards reflected the locality and demand; oak with hazel and ash was mentioned for Surrey, the produce used for hoops and stakes, beech underwood near ironworks for charcoal, chestnut and ash in Kent for hop poles. Even so, the underwood should be managed with the welfare of the (ship) oak paramount even if 'the coppice wood may not have reached the most profitable estate'; otherwise, if cutting is delayed, the oak will become too tall and slender and may fall over. At 15 to 20 feet the leader should be cut and the tree encouraged to spread. It was no good leaving the oak 'to fortuitous circumstances, and suffer them, by spreading too low, to destroy the underwood which surround them' and 'if straight timber is required, close groves ... are the fit places to raise it in.' 'Land, such at least as will grow ship timber with advantage, is become too valuable to be given up, in any case, to accident or neglect.' 'By freeing the stems of young trees from side shoots, and by keeping their leaders single, a LENGTH OF STEM is, *with certainty*, obtained; and, by afterwards checking their upright growth, and throwing the main strength of the head into one principal bough (by checking not removing the rest), a CROOKEDNESS of Timber is had, ... and what is equally necessary in SHIP TIMBER, a CLEANNESS and EVENNESS of contexture are, at the same time, produced.' Shaping of the tree when young (Figure 9) was considered very important as lopping large, old boughs and branches spoils the tree and encourages rot to enter. As other authors had recommended, oak could also be planted in hedges for ship timber; Marshall suggested they should be a rod (five and a half yards) apart.

By the end of the eighteenth century, a number of important changes had therefore taken place. Good soils for ship oak had been taken into agriculture and the growing of oak shifted to poorer soils. The value of small sized underwood had fallen because it was no longer required in the same quantities for fuel as a result of a rise in coal production for domestic, smelting and manufacturing use. Indeed, we find a tenant of the Duchy of Cornwall woods in 1747 asking for her rent to be reduced on the grounds that the value of the underwood had fallen because the tin was now taken to Wales for smelting with coal. The reduction in the demand for underwood led many landowners to use their 'copses' for game rather than produce. As a result, the oak timber crop now became the more important element of planting for producing profit, rather than the underwood. Oak plants had become cheaper and the seedlings began to be planted at closer spacing so that more oaks were grown per acre and then gradually thinned out. Sessile oak, with its upright habit compared to pedunculate, slowly became more important as it could be grown on poorer, lighter soils, of which a large acreage was now available. The timber was used for mining timber, charcoal, fencing and tan bark on shorter rotations (felling cycles) than ship timber, the bark of sessile being preferred for tanning. Sessile oak was not damaged by spring frosts as much as the earlier flushing (leafing out in spring) pedunculate oak.

FIGURE 9
How to bend young oak trees to form crooks, from Matthew (1831). The dotted portion is growth after bending.

DRAWING BY J. A. HARRIS

The nineteenth century

The demand for tan bark rose in Europe in the eighteenth and nineteenth centuries (Ellenberg 1988). Nichols in 1793 observes: 'The very great advance lately made on the price of Oak Bark, together with the increased demand for small Oak Timber, and the prices given by the Government for large timber not being sufficient to induce Gentlemen to let their trees stand till they become of a size for naval purposes, added to our improving state in agriculture, will, I fear, be the means of hastening the destruction of most of the Oak Trees in the kingdom, on private estates.'

The underwood now became a nurse to the oak rather than a crop in its own right with scattered oak standards and it was increasingly emphasised by authors that the management of the underwood was subservient to that of the oak. Landowners began to look for 'nurses' on the poorer soils that would also give a return when the slower growing oak was establishing. The use of conifers as nurses starts to be recommended by the authors of the early nineteenth century. In Wales, by 1800, oak was being planted at spacings of five feet and nine feet, with beech, larch and sycamore nurses (Linnard 1982). Nicol (1803) was advising that oak should be planted close (nine feet) as plants were now so much cheaper and that, depending on the soil, different species of nurse should be grown between at a ratio of 3 or 4:1 as there was now a wide range of nurse species available. He mentioned larch, Scots pine, Norway spruce, silver fir and American spruce (white and black); and of the hardwoods, sycamore, beech, hornbeam, ash and birch. He talked of intimate mixtures as: 'If the utility of nursing in the forest be admitted, it precludes the idea of grouping (species) at the time of planting; and if grouping at first be determined on, it precludes the idea of nursing at all'. Like all authors he puts an emphasis on correct thinning and advised: 'cut for the good of the timber to be left' (something that should be remembered more often today). He recommends that the side branches of the young oak need to be pruned back two thirds of their length to encourage the leader to grow upwards. His advice for thinning was 'to pay respect to the distance of the tops not to the roots of the trees'.

Sang edited a new edition of Nicol's *The Planter's Kalendar* in 1812. This contains interesting observations relating to current conditions, such as the high prices obtainable for tan bark in the seven years before 1812 and the increasing tendency to leave copses and woods for ornament and game rather than to manage them for produce. Neglect was evident and landowners are urged to attend to 'properly thinning out and cultivating plantations, and the reclaiming of neglected woods and copses'. It is in this book that Sang, a Scotsman, used the term *hardwood* for all broad-leaved trees, a term taken up by subsequent authors. This appears to be the first use of this term, which still causes so much confusion because not all broad-leaved trees have particularly hard wood. Sang also suggested that the conifer nurses should be planted two to three years before the oak.

FIGURE 10
Shaping planks for shipbuilding, from Matthew (1831). '*v*, *x*, *y* and *z* represent the most advantageous form of logs for cutting into planks. The straighter the log is [to] the plane of the saw, it is the more suitable, as the planks bends sufficient side-way by steaming; *v*, of considerable bend and taper, where the planks, when cut, have a bend edge-way is the most valuable; this form requires to be very free of knots. In straighter planks, *z*, cleanness from knots is not such a desideratum. *z* and *y* [may be] of any length; *x*, from 25–35 feet; *v* from 12–24 feet.'

DRAWING BY J. A. HARRIS

The use of conifers as nurses to oak was also put forward by Pontey (1809) on the grounds that two-thirds of available planting land was now sands and heaths and conifers thrive on poor soils. He mentioned the use of Scots pine, larch and Norway spruce: if the oak fails, there is still a profitable crop and conifer thinnings are of more value as poles than birch is as fuelwood. He considers that some people plant 'more principal than nurses and advises a ratio of 3 nurse plants to one oak.'

Billington (1825) who had worked in the Forest of Dean and at Chopwell in County Durham (and when writing was with the Earl of Haddington on his Tynningham Estate, East Lothian, in Scotland) was worried that in many cases the conifers then being used as nurses were not being taken out soon enough to allow the oak to grow, a lesson we have not yet learnt today. He said that, with the aid of conifer nurses, oak could be raised in many places if all are planted at the same time but the 'firs' (true firs, pine and spruce) must be removed gradually, 'the fir tribe ... if properly managed and taken out in time [is best], otherwise they are the worst enemies.' In the New Forest early in the nineteenth century, pine nurses were taken out early but later were left and allowed to get too big (Forestry Commission 1960). As well as conifers, Billington was also using sycamore, elm, ash and beech as nurses on lower ground.

Ideas, however, take time to establish and Cruickshank (1830) in Scotland was still convinced that oak ought to be raised in its final position from acorns

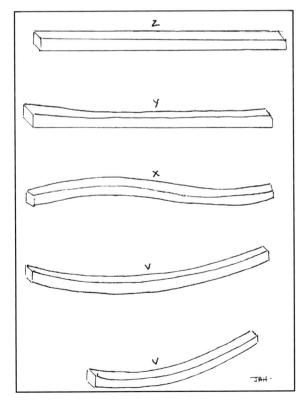

rather than transplants so that the tap root was not disturbed, although many before him had pointed out the heavy losses from vermin eating the acorns (and could have added how much better the roots are when first grown in a nursery). On poor and exposed soils he developed the technique of planting his nurse 'firs' (Scots pine and larch) first and when these were about five to six feet high, he formed patches in them, by removing any plants in the way, ten feet apart, in which he planted about five acorns. After two to three years the oak seedlings were singled and any competing nurses or interfering branches removed. All the nurses were taken out at 16 years. At five years, the oak was thinned and pruned. He emphasised that it was important to do this whilst the trees were young as: 'I could mention many plantations in which the oaks have been ruined by want of thinning alone.' Although he stressed thinning and says it should take place early when the branches begin to interfere with each other, he could not quite bring himself to sacrifice a good tree:

'sometimes it will happen that two fine trees interfere with one another ... in such a case, both the former should be allowed to stand'; a tradition and fault still perpetuated by many foresters today.

It is evident that by now various authors were concerned to find the best way to grow ship oak timber and how to produce it more consistently by pruning and artificial bending instead of allowing nature to do these things through wind and animal browsing. Crooked timber was still in demand and worth a lot more than straight timber. Matthew (1831) approached the problem from the shipwright's view-point: 'Trees intended for plank ought to be reared in close forest, or protected situation, drawn tall and straight, or what is preferable for a part, with a gentle regular bend, technically *sny*. It requires to be of clean solid texture, from 12 to 40 feet in length, and at least 8″ in diameter at the small end, or any greater thickness.' When cut 'the section to be in the plane of the curve the straighter the log is in the plane of the saw, it is the more suitable, as the planks bend sufficiently side-way by steaming.' With bent, curved timber, planks 'when cut, have a bend *edge-way*, [and] is the most valuable; this form requires to be very free of knots.'

Matthew considered that the timber needed to be cut into planks whilst green as this was easier and helped to prevent drought cracks. To train the growing tree, he divided the branches into leaders and feeders and shortens branches, leaving one overall leader.

However, Matthew stated that much excellent plank timber could be imported and it is better to concentrate on the more expensive crooked timber as: 'On the Continent of Europe, in the natural forest, it is chiefly the tops of old lofty trees which afford the crooks; in consequence, those we import, are for the most part, of a free, light, insufficient quality.' For crook timber, to be used for the floor and futtocks [foot hooks] and which must have little cross grain, young trees up to 15 feet high should be bent and fixed with rods. 'A fine regular curve may be obtained by bending the plant for several successive years, a little lower every year' and cutting any strong feeders, 'ship timbers being generally required of greater depth than thickness, that is, broadest in the plane of the curve, hedge-row is better adapted to growing them' 'The lateral spread of the roots in thickly planted rows being greater than the longitudinal, also tends to give elliptic bole ... Forests intended

FIGURE II
Training plank timber, from Matthew (1831). 'Divide all branches into leaders and feeders; leaders, the main of superior shoots, which tend to become stems, *A, a, a*; feeders, the inferior branches, *B, b, b*, should more than one leader appear from the time of planting, shorten all but the most promising one down to the condition of feeders.'
DRAWING BY J. A. HARRIS

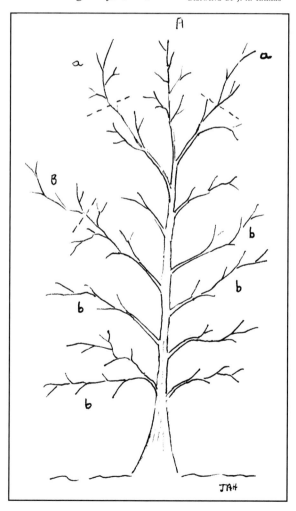

60

for ship timbers might be planted and kept in rows a considerable distance apart, with the plants close in the row, and thus acquire the elliptic bole.' He recommended double rows with glades between, when the trees would grow and bend away from each other. If planted in a triple row with glades between, with spruce or larch in the middle row, the outside oaks would bend away from the conifers which can then be removed once the oak 'had received sufficient side bias'. Knees could be obtained, especially in hedgerows, by allowing trees to divide into four leaders and to grow up. Knees and some crook timber could be cut out but the branches for the crooks must not get too large before use otherwise they would get damaged by wind. Good soils on which to grow ship timber were difficult to obtain at this time for plantations as agriculture was very profitable.

Up to the 1850s, the price of oak bark was high and many potential timber trees were sacrificed to obtain the bark rather than be allowed to grow to full size. The trees were often stripped of their bark in the spring and then left to stand and later felled in the winter. Monteath (1836) devotes much of his book to explaining how to raise oak by growing oak coppice, or as he terms it, 'natural woods'. The produce from these woods was mainly oak tan bark and Monteath showed how to obtain an annual income from such woods. How much 'natural wood' was planted at this time when prices were high and how much was existing coppice is difficult to evaluate now but that planted coppices were profitable is shown by his statement: 'To give one example ... [the owner] ... was cutting from the plant, in order to turn it into a natural coppice wood.' This was in Forfarshire; the wood had been planted in 1818 and was twenty years old. Hunter (1883) relates that on the Glenalmond Estate: 'The largest larch ... is a relic of the original stock, the old stock having been cleared out to make way for oak at a time when oak bark was of considerably more value than it is at present.'

To establish a 'natural wood' (coppice), Monteath recommended planting in pits six to eight feet apart mixed with larch, or without shelter in less exposed places. The planted area is divided into 24 hags (which will eventually be a coppice unit). When the oak is six to seven feet high the larch is cut out and the oak left close so that the saplings grow tall and straight. The first cutting should take place at 15 years and although this is early and the yield from the bark of less volume, it has the advantage that by this time the oak will have enough root growth and size of stool 'to carry two, three and four stems for the next cutting' ... when 'it will pay at least three times more ... This

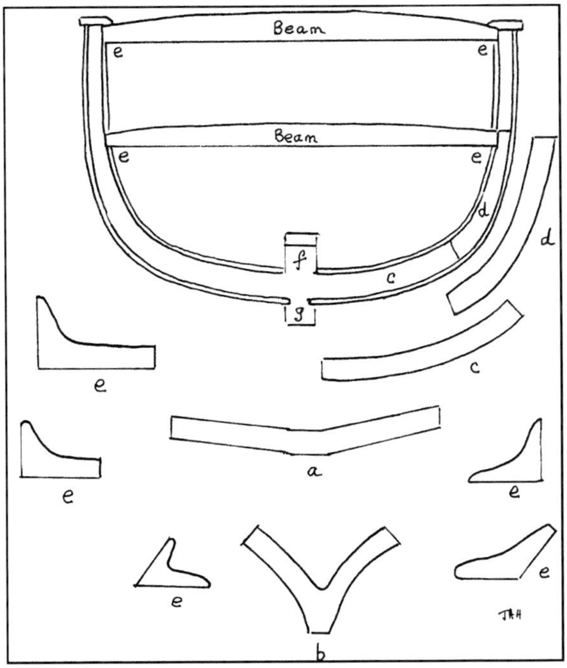

FIGURE 12
The structure of a
wooden vessel: cross
section at midships,
from Matthew (1831).
a. flat floor; *b.* rising
floor; *c.* first
foot-hook; *d.* second
foot-hook; *e.* knee; *f.*
keelson; *g.* keel.
DRAWING BY J. A. HARRIS

FIGURE 13
Trees for knees, from
Matthew (1831). 'The
main stem, either used
whole, sawn in two,
or quartered, will
form one wing of the
knee and the bent
branch the other.'
DRAWING BY J. A. HARRIS

will be found to be the most profitable of all planting, and the only method
by which a proprietor can have a regular annual return'. In Scotland, 'in every
place, excepting where there is a great proportion of bare rock, coppice oak
can be made to grow'; Monteath would plant acorns in rock crevices wherever
there was some soil. The optimum rotation for cutting the trees for bark was
about 24 years, at 30 years it was beginning to get 'corky' and was not so
valuable.

Although for timber, heartwood is needed, bark from young, fast-grown
sappy trees is better for tanning. Harvesting tan bark is carried out in the
spring, May to July, when the sap is rising; the bark is then easier to peel
off. A circular incision is made round the base of the stem to stop the bark
stripping down into the root and damaging the stool. Monteath preferred
harvesting the bark with a saw rather than an axe as then the stool is not
loosened so much. All the wood and bark needs to be removed away from
the hag by the end of July to allow some 'Lammas growth' in the year of
cutting. Any so called black wood, i.e. weed species such as birch, willow,
elder and hazel, were destroyed by peeling the bark round their roots. The
residual oak timber, with little heartwood, had limited value but was used for
poles, wheel spokes, other small items and, as burnt chips, for smoking fish.
In Wales it was used for mining timber (Linnard 1982). After cutting, the
stools were dressed with a special chisel, leaving the centre high to shed
rainwater. (Modern research however has shown that such careful preparation
of the stool is not necessary; a horizontal cut with a chain saw provides equally
satisfactory re-growth (Harmer 2001).) After two years, the new shoots on
the stools were reduced by thinning out and then again at about 12 years,
this time in May as the thinnings were big enough to take tan bark off. If
larger trees were to be grown, one-third of the stools were dressed for
underwood and the remainder, at about 25 feet apart, thinned to leave three

stems which were pruned up. The underwood stools were felled every 15 to 20 years. The bark, after being peeled in sections from the tree, was dried and sold. To avoid a lot of stool thinning, Monteith describes an experiment where he cut sections of bark out of the stool down into the earth. Shoots appeared where the bark had been left on and 17 years after he stated the experiment was growing well; this had meant no time was spent on thinning. In Scotland many oak coppices had been left unenclosed and converted to pasture so there was profit to be made by establishing new coppice. Most of the oak bark for tanning in the south of England was purchased from oak coppice grown in Wales.

Monteath gaves few new directions on raising ship timber beyond saying he was sure grown timbers were stronger than steamed ones and advocating pruning to get crooked timber.

Sinclair (1832) did not recommend growing oak for timber from coppice stools unless the shoots are straight and rise near the root. Later, Jones (1959) explained this, stating that with 'close cut stems ... many new stems arise from below ground level and form their own adventitious roots' thus giving a good reason for cutting low. Sinclair went on to say that saplings grown from stools that have been cut high do not grow as fast and are subject to rot and this 'is the chief cause of the unsoundness of coppice-reared timber, particularly at the root or butt end of the bole.' For good timber he considered that oak needs to grow rapidly as when fast and slow growing trees of the same species are compared, the fast growing tree produces 'wood of greater strength, toughness and durability'. Sinclair continued: 'The experiments of Professor Barlow on the strength of different woods confirm the above conclusions. The opinion of Thomas Andrew Knight F.R.S. on this important subject is that the toughest and most durable oak timber is obtained from trees of vigorous, rapid growth.' This may explain the prejudice against sessile oak timber, which was usually slow grown with close rings and though 'mild' and easier to work does not have the toughness of fast grown pedunculate oak. Even today the importance of rapid growth to produce wide rings and thus strength is often not understood: narrow rings which provide a more *workable* texture are frequently but wrongly associated with strength.

In 1838 Loudon published his comprehensive work on British trees and shrubs. At last, pedunculate and sessile oak were regarded as separate species and not forms of *Quercus robur*. The controversy over the relative quality of the timber was still being debated, that of sessile, usually slow grown, still being regarded as inferior, especially for shipbuilding. It was in this publication that attention was drawn for the first time to the many insects found on oak but these are looked upon as pests at this time. Oak 'is attacked by a far greater number of insect enemies than any of the other trees of this country ... we have the authority of Mr Stephens ... for stating that nearly half the phytophagous insects of England are either exclusively, or partially, inhabitants of oak ... Perhaps if we give 2000 as the number of oak feeders and their parasites, we shall scarcely run the risk of over-rating the quantity'; thus the origin of the overworked assumption today that oak is of paramount import-ance for insect conservation and biodiversity.

By the mid-nineteenth century further changes had taken place. The price of tan bark fell as the country was no longer at war and much bark was imported from the continent; also, tanning began to be undertaken by chemical treatment. The demand for 'ship' timbers fell dramatically as wood was replaced by iron in building ships from the late 1840s onward; already iron knees had gradually replaced wooden knees. The final blow to the Navy's wooden ships came in 1862 during the American Civil War when 'a naval encounter ... signalled the end of the long era of wooden ships in the Royal Navy' (James 1981). The use of timber for shipbuilding was limited to small river and coastal vessels and for the wide-ranging, fast sailing clippers carrying cargoes worldwide, which were not dependent on using coal like iron steam-ships, whose range was limited by the availability of coaling stations. The demand for old, long-rotation oak therefore gradually declined. The repeal of the Navigation Acts in 1850 meant that goods no longer had to be carried in British built merchant-ships. Ships could therefore be built abroad with foreign timber. Further blows to growing oak were the removal of import duty in 1846, which enabled timber and other goods to be imported more easily, especially from the New World, and the introduction of taxes on woods producing timber, mainly oak, ash and elm (Brown and Nisbet 1894).

By 1850 the price of oak bark had fallen by one-third from its peak and planting of coppice woods could no longer be recommended. Selby (1842) was already writing that oak coppice needed to be converted into timber if it was to be profitable. Brown (1851) also warned about planting oak coppice and was concerned that many owners were trying to convert old coppice to timber standards with poor results, as they had 'the mistaken view of taking as nearly as possible a full crop of coppice shoots from the stoles before converting them.' When cutting the coppice, shoots were singled on some stools 20 to 30 feet apart. This resulted in close grown shoots being suddenly exposed to the elements. 'I have seen this system practised in England; and from receiving such bad treatment, the trees, of course were in an unhealthy state ... The only sure way of converting a coppice plantation into healthy standing timber is this:- When the regular coppice [after felling] has been thinned for the first time, say at three years old, have in view the raising of a regular portion of the best shoots for ultimate timber; and with this view, thin out all the weakly shoots and such as are badly formed, and leave none but the choicest, and those rather thinner upon the stole, than if the plantation were merely thinned with the intention of its remaining under coppice.'

The retained shoots were gradually thinned to a single stem by twenty years. The advantages were: 'the trees are trained up gradually and naturally, and never suffer any check; second, A better selection can be made, from there being a continual choice of shoots at the command of the forester as they grow up at different stages; and, third, By this method of selecting and training up, the plants, or trees as we may term them, at nearly twenty years old, will be twice the size that others would [be] when merely chosen from the body of a thick coppice-wood and exposed all at once.' Such shoots should rise at the root of the stool and be pruned.

Until this time high forest oak was grown in Britain primarily as ship timber (see Chapter 5), for which natural bends and crooks were the primary objective. Authors now, in the mid-nineteenth century, recommended growing straight timber and it was advised that oak trees should be grown close until a certain length of bole was achieved. As long ago as 1728, Stoughton had remarked that 'one foot of timber near the root is worth three further up.' Main (1847) recommended that snags from dead branches should be pruned off and branches shortened to encourage growth into the leader. These shortened branches should later be pruned close when they were no longer important to promote growth but needed to be removed whilst still of small diameter. Brown (1851) pointed out that: 'Wherever a hardwood tree is drawn up rather closely among firs, with sufficient head room, it seldom produces many side branches' … pruning should only be used 'to clear from branches one-third of the height of the tree from the ground, in order to form a trunk'. The importance of thinning was again emphasised by all authors and the lack of it in many plantations deplored. Brown went on: 'The whole secret of training

up healthy plantations lies in the after management.' For hardwood trees, Brown thinned them so that they are 'half their height apart'. He emphasises that oak should not be pruned and thinned at the same time but that the pruning should be done at least two years before thinning to avoid too much exposure of the wounds.

We have seen that towards the end of the nineteenth century the demand for crooks for shipbuilding timber had declined. Although authors had been recommending that owners should concentrate on growing straight timber, little notice seems to have been taken, and Nisbet (1911) stated that there was great difficulty in finding enough suitable home grown straight oak timber to build the locks on the Manchester Ship Canal. Much American timber was being imported but Hunter (1883) and Brown (1894) both expressed the view that before long it would not be available. It was no longer the practice to plant oak at wide spacing which had meant expensive weeding and cleaning (Brown and Nisbet 1894) or to thin it to the wide spacing previously adopted for ship timber.

From 1872 to 1892 agriculture suffered a decline and arable land was 'falling down' to grass. In the previous decades, whilst agriculture was very profitable, woods had been neglected and used as game coverts. Many plantations suffered from animal grazing, the stock often being turned into young woods at about 25 years with resulting damage. From 1870 oak coppice declined too and many owners attempted to convert it to high forest. Brown and Nisbet (1894) warned that timber grown from old stools was not of such good quality as planted oak and such trees were often rotten at the base and slow grown as the stools lost vigour when they were about 85 years old.

Brown (1851) rightly drew attention to the different silviculture that is needed to grow oak successfully when he points out that, compared with other hardwoods, oak needs a lot more room and light to grow, especially in the later stages of the rotation. 'Thinning, in the rearing of oak plantations, must at all times be more severe than when thinning away firs from among the common kinds of hardwood. And, indeed, this particular forms the only difference worth mentioning between the cultivation of the oak and the cultivation of hardwood in general; that is, the oak trees, after they are once properly established in the ground, and brought into shape by a judicious pruning, must, through the whole course of their culture afterwards have more room and air than any other species of hardwood trees ... in every [other] respect oak plantations are to be managed upon the same principles as other hardwood ones.' In these few phrases, Brown captures the essence of growing oak and gives us the guiding principles to successful cultivation of oak today.

Nisbet (1911) recommended that oak should be opened out gradually: 'begin early but moderately and repeat frequently.' Tables had been produced which recommended mechanical thinning by numbers rather than looking at the requirements of trees and many authors were advocating low thinning, thus taking out only diseased and small trees. Brown (1851) however had already pointed out: 'There is no part of the forester's education more neglected than … a thorough knowledge of the size that trees ought to be, on a given situation at a given age.' He provides a table for oak showing the average diameter of oak trees on good, moderate and poor soils. The table shows that oak goes on increasing in diameter for longer on good soils, up to 120 years and more, whilst on poor soils it ceases growing at 80 years. In Brown and Nisbet (1894) it is stated that: 'Growth in girth is in all species of forest trees practically proportional to the growth in height, as they are each the expression of the vigour of the individual tree.' We know this to be misleading today because only height is an expression of vigour whilst girth is in inverse proportion to the number of stems.

These authors, following continental thinking at the time, were concerned that wide final spacing and light foliage of the oak would lead to soil deterioration and so advocated under-planting with beech at 70 to 80 years, thus following Emmerlich's comments on the use of beech with oak, a hundred years before (see Chapter 2). Brown (1851), having grown oak in mixture with larch and Scot's pine, removed all the conifers by the time the oak was 30 years old but this was later considered too soon. Nisbet (in Brown and Nisbet 1894), whilst much concerned with continental concepts and experience, such as sustained yield (a regular supply of timber without depleting the resource) and the concept of the 'normal forest' (one with all age classes represented), was looking more and more to conifers for profit, rather than hardwoods. Thus the long reign of the mighty oak as the principal timber tree, unless of prime quality for specialist purposes such as building restoration, furniture and the building of small ships, was over, although there was still a market for tan bark, fencing, pit wood and charcoal, giving way to imported hardwoods, exotic and more profitable softwoods and to modern technology.

In his chapter on Finance and Planning, Stebbing (1919) states: 'The greater bulk of the oak, ash, elm etc., utilised in this country will, as we have seen, probably be raised in the woods kept either for sport, shelter, or amenity purposes, and may to a great extent be left out of the question. It may be suggested, however, that a certain percentage of the better class oak soils in England should be confined to the growth of this species.' In the following decades, the growing of oak was mainly confined to private landowners. In recent years, interest in the growing of oak has returned, with the timber being required for specialist uses and for its conservation value.

Lessons in oak cultivation

Many lessons relevant today can be learnt from the writings quoted above of these nineteenth-century authors. They were aware of the silvicultural value of conifer nurses to ensure good growth of oak as soon as conifers became available from abroad, firstly European larch and then Norway spruce. Having obtained height growth by this means, they knew oak needs space to grow in order to get open crowns above the length of bole required. They were conscious of the importance of controlling epicormics by physical removal or

limiting their growth by shading the young stem and they gave attention to pruning. How does this all apply to the successful cultivation of oak today?

Early in the twentieth century Hanson (1911) pointed out that 'oak is not suitable for pure woods but it may be grown pure up to the fortieth year, when it should be underplanted with beech.' He goes on to say that 'in fact first-class oak timber can hardly be produced without an admixture of beech.' Matthews (1989) tells us that the famous Spessart oak of Germany is grown in mixture with beech to reduce epicormic growth, whilst in Hungary naturally regenerated pedunculate oak, which comes up with hornbeam and other broadleaved species, is cleaned to leave pure oak and the hornbeam is coppiced to form an understorey in order to control epicormics (Harris and Harris 1988). The hornbeam is finally cleared again towards the end of a 120 year rotation to provide a clean forest floor for the next generation of oak seedlings. This technique was adopted by the sixth Earl of Bradford on his Weston-Under-Lizard Estate, Shropshire, in the 1960s when two widely spaced oak plantations, established on agricultural land, were underplanted with hornbeam in order to control epicormic shoot growth. Both have done well, winning several woodlands awards; the underplanting has been entirely successful in suppressing epicormic growth and the form of the oak stems is excellent (Figure 15).

There is a tendency today, now that there is renewed enthusiasm for growing oak, to grow it pure but this is to ignore the lessons learnt in the past and evidence still surviving today in many of our woods. As Blyth *et al.* (1987) point out: 'The presence of an occasional conifer in a predominantly broadleaved woodland (and there are many examples for the observant) is a good indication that the woodland was originally a mixture. The conifers probably acted as a "nurse" for the broadleaves and were mostly removed in early thinnings.' Hart (1991) states that oak 'appreciates a nurse species, e.g. Norway spruce, European larch, western red cedar or beech' of which western red cedar (*Thuja plicata*) is often the best as it has a narrow crown unlikely to suppress the oak but casting a very dense shade, thereby reducing competing vegetation and controlling epicormics. Indeed, western red cedar has probably not been recognised widely enough as the excellent nurse for oak that it is and this may be because it was introduced rather later (in 1853) than most of the other tree species from the north western American seaboard and even then was regarded for a long time as an ornamental rather than a forest tree. One of the first trials of western red cedar as a nurse for oak was by the Oxford University Forestry Department in the University's Wytham Wood near Oxford, an old woodland site. Pedunculate oak was planted in three row/three row mixtures with European larch and western red cedar at five feet between the rows and two and a half feet apart in the oak rows. This close spacing by present day standards would have the effect of early suppression of the crop being nursed. Fifteen years after planting, Jones (1964) found that the western red cedar was usually three feet (one metre) taller than the pedunculate oak but that on the wetter sites the oak was taller than the cedar. On the same site at 15 years oak

FIGURE 15

Clean stemmed, widely spaced oak resulting from underplanting with hornbeam which has successfully controlled epicormic growth. This is a registered seed stand and has won several woodland competitions. The oak was planted in 1934 and is yield class 6, the highest but one yield class recognised for oak. The hornbeam underplanting was first carried out in 1965, with further underplanting in 1972/3; it is not clear from the records whether this was in a different area, or whether the original hornbeam had failed. Goosemoor Gorse, Bradford Estate, Shropshire.

P. E. J. CLERK

in line mixture with European larch showed significant suppression but much less so by the cedar. Jones also pointed to the economic advantage of very early returns from the sale of cedar foliage to the floristry trade.

Philips Price (1966) was another to draw attention to the value of western red cedar as a nurse for oak, finding it superior to Norway spruce for this purpose. Regarding a well-drained heavy soil in Gloucestershire, he wrote: 'I have planted this mixture quite extensively and find that the thuya [western red cedar] grows only slightly quicker than the oak, whereas Norway spruce has to be watched more carefully to prevent damage to the oak. Thuya timber is as good as larch and gives a useful return in thinnings, leaving the oak as a final crop.'

Whitfield Estate in Herefordshire has grown good quality oak since the twelfth century, mainly sessile oak. In the 1960s much was felled and young oak crops were established with a variety of conifer nurses, both in lines and in groups, of which western red cedar proved the most successful. A report of a visit of the Royal Forestry Society (Anon 1998) records that: 'The two species had grown very well together' and the cedar 'appears to reduce the … growth of epicormics on the oak.'

Darrah and Dodds (1967) reported on a series of field meetings held over a period of eighteen months in the 1960s by a group of silviculturists in Wessex (southern England). They were studying the growing of broadleaved trees in mixture with conifers because pure stands of oak (and beech) were no longer economic by themselves and yet oak and beech formed a large part of the landscape and many woodland owners wished to perpetuate them. Conifer 'nurses' were found to be 'especially valuable on difficult, exposed or frosty sites. Their faster rate of growth may also improve both the form and height growth of broadleaved species, and may help to suppress herbaceous weeds quicker.' They emphasised the importance of compatibility between the nurse species and the main crop, noting that 'the success of the mixtures [inspected] was largely dependent on the degree of compatibility between the broadleaved trees and the chosen conifers. The main criterion for a compatible conifer is that it should have a height growth comparable with but slightly faster than the broadleaved species on a given site. It should also be reasonably columnar in crown shape as well as being a good volume producer, and should be saleable in its early stages of growth. However: 'In the New Forest [they recorded] a vigorously branched provenance of Scots pine threatening to suppress completely oak on poorish sites.' On good sites 'Norway spruce seemed to be the most compatible tree with oak' whilst 'larch tended to outgrow oak'. They suggested that 'Lawson cypress and western red cedar are likely to prove compatible species with broadleaves, their height growth is similar and their soft columnar branching favourable.' They were impressed by 'a good example of an oak-red cedar mixture at Wytham, near Oxford.'

Darrah and Dobbs suggested that: 'Compatibility problems can be met by varying the pattern, and the type of mixture will substantially affect the reaction

FIGURE 16
Young oak trees lack 'apical dominance' (i.e. tend naturally to bushy growth when young) and although they need full overhead light (see Chapter 2), they benefit in the early years from side shade.
a. Bushy oak emerging from tree shelter without the benefit of nurses.
b. Poor oak not in tree shelters but merely in 0.6 metre plastic sleeves. These will struggle for many years and make no more than scrub.
c. A line mixture of larch nursing oak showing good upward growth of the latter.
d. Oak with broadleaved nurses (sweet chestnut and cherry). Evergreen conifer nurses would be better but this is in a Site of Special Scientific Interest where they would not be allowed so the chestnut will be coppiced before it casts overhead shade. It will continue as an understorey to suppress epicormics, whilst the cherry will mature in another 30 years, leaving widely spaced oak to grow on and add girth to about 100 years.
E. H. M. HARRIS

71

between the broadleaved and the conifer species.' Of many stands visited 'they found five row oak—two row Norway spruce, and ten row oak—three row Norway spruce mixtures have given rise to promising crops' and 'a one row oak—two row Norway spruce mixtures was very successful.' They continued: 'The commonest mixture is the three row—three row one, and several good examples of this type were seen, particularly the oak-Norway spruce mixture.' Of group mixtures they said, although theoretically the best method, 'it is statistically improbable that the central tree will be the best tree, and final spacing will inevitably differ considerably from the theoretical ideal.' They concluded that: 'Over a very wide range of conditions, Norway spruce is a most compatible species with oak. It provides a flexible, easily managed mixture, and the thinnings are readily utilizable at all stages.'

Almost twenty years later, Savill and Evans (1986) also concluded that oak requires fairly dense stand conditions to ensure the development of a reasonably formed stem as well as upward growth. They go on to say that growing oak in mixture with carefully chosen conifers or natural broadleaved re-growth, should always be used and that Norway spruce and oak have similar early growth rates and thus are suitable to grow together; for example, one row of oak in three of spruce or two rows of oak in three, four or five rows of spruce. However, Joyce (1998) observes that in Ireland several oak/Norway spruce mixtures from the 1930s to 1950s have failed because the spruce almost always suppresses the oak. Evans (1984) though made the interesting observation that oak/Norway spruce mixtures are not successful in western Britain because there the spruce grows too fast (achieving yield class 14 or above) due to the wet conditions and suppresses the oak, whereas in the drier east of Britain, Norway spruce grows more slowly at yield class 10 or 12 and is then an ideal nurse for oak. This explains Joyce's findings.

Sometimes oak is planted in groups of nine in a matrix of conifers but although this avoids the striped appearance of lines and increases the proportion of conifer and thereby enhances the early yields, the oak is more easily suppressed if thinning is not timely and the thinning itself is more difficult to carry out. Harris and Harris (1997) favour line mixtures and suggest that: 'Line mixtures are a particularly good way of growing oak because young oak trees lack "apical dominance" (the tendency to grow upwards), and easily become bushy.' They go on to describe other mixtures, including a complex mixture of 'rectangles of 12 or up to 20 oak in a matrix of Norway spruce' as a way of increasing the proportion of early saleable material.

Although epicormics are more common on pedunculate oak than on sessile (Evans 1984) and the latter species is planted more widely today, they remain a major detraction to timber quality so far as its structural use is concerned. Evans considers that different provenances of sessile oak vary in this respect, indicating some genetic control but that epicormics are best limited by dense stand conditions as frequent, light thinnings reduce the problem. However, 'pippy oak', in which many small knots from epicormic shoots are displayed, is sought after for decorative turnery work but has poor working qualities (see Chapter 4). Trees exhibiting this valuable defect are often found in hedgerows.

Kerr and Evans (1993) also consider epicormics a major defect of oak and say they can be discouraged by allowing a dense understorey of shade-tolerant species to develop. They state: 'There is some evidence that sessile oak has a lower incidence of epicormics than pedunculate oak,' going on to say: 'To grow high quality oak the encouragement of an under-storey of beech, hornbeam, small-leaved lime or hazel should be part of the overall silvicultural plan ... The shading effect of the understorey will not affect the initiation of epicormic shoots but will reduce their survival and vigour'. Young epicormics can be rubbed off in June. Evans (1984) experimented with chemical and mechanical methods of epicormic control but these methods did not prove satisfactory; he states that green pruning remains the only option.

On epicormics, Savill (1996) makes the interesting observation that: 'Many of the behavioural traits of *Q. robur* and *Q. petraea* are characteristic of trees of warmer climates' and cites, amongst other things, 'the ability to produce epicormics, which is an adaptation to fire.' He goes on to say that 'they also come into leaf too late to make use of the growing season, and even are commonly damaged by frosts and the large fruits are readily killed by desiccation as well as frost.'

Oak timber had many uses in the past, as we have seen, and was accordingly valued. Today the uses of oak are more limited, so we need to grow it well and of high quality if its slow growth to maturity is to be justified. Much oak is being planted today that will almost certainly fail. There is no need for this if the guidance of modern authors, based on up to date research and well conducted field trials, is followed.

Savill (1996) states that: 'Oak which has grown very slowly, with annual rings less than one millimetre wide, is weak and brittle, because it is composed almost entirely of springwood, made up of large diameter vessels [sap conducting tubes]. It is very light when dry. The later formed summer wood gives oak its strength. Hence, the faster oak is grown, the stronger it is.' Kerr and Evans (1993) emphasise that 'oak varies greatly in quality, depending on straightness of grain and presence of knots, epicormics, internal splits, stain etc., with the best timber commanding a price ten times that of the poorest. Oak is more variable in character than most woods, with British timber typically heavy, strong and tough from vigorous growth trees; that from old or slow grown trees is softer and milder.' They say that the timber of the two oak species is indistinguishable to the naked eye and Evans (1984) states that the two British oaks 'produce nearly identical timbers'.

Hart (1991), using information from Henry Venables Limited of Stafford, ranks the value of standing parcels of oak timber in five quality categories from low grade pallet material (one value unit), through fencing oak (two units), beam quality (two and a half units), first quality butts (six units) to veneer butts (ten units). This emphasises the importance of growing good quality oak because similar comparisons for ash and beech veneer butts are only five and a half times and two and a half times respectively the value of ash and beech pallet wood.

Oak is particularly prone to shake (internal structural failure causing the timber to fall apart when sawn up) which appears on felled trees as 'star shakes' radiating from the centre or 'ring shakes' running round an annual ring but which cannot be identified from the outside of a standing tree. They are not the same thing as drying cracks, which are not a major defect (Figure 18). The tendency to shake is shared only with sweet chestnut. Many theories for its cause were advanced in the past. It has long been thought to occur more frequently on light, sandy or stony soils and to be noticeably less in oak grown on heavy clays and clay-loams if they are deep and moist. Uneven growth rates following sudden opening up of the canopy may also predispose oak trees to shake (Kerr and Evans 1993). Henman and Denne (1992) emphasise the need to maintain an even growth rate in order to reduce sudden changes in growth ring width. Only recently is light being shed on the problem which gives us some guidance on how to avoid shake. Henman (1984) found that shake occurred most commonly on dry sites, suggesting that water shortage caused the problem, at least on trees with an inherited tendency to shake. Savill (1996) found that early wood vessels with a larger diameter than the average predisposed trees to shake but pointed out that vessel size is strongly inherited in oak. He and Mather (1990) found that trees that come into leaf late also have the largest springwood vessels and are the most prone to shake. This is a big step forward in the resolution of a long standing problem which has not been understood before and they suggest that it should now be possible to recognise trees prone to shake and remove them in early thinnings.

Broad (1998) expresses the view that storing oak 'in the log' before sawing reduces the tendency to shake but he does not support this with any evidence. This view would seem to be at variance with Savill's work quoted above.

The old foresters paid a lot of attention to shaping and pruning oak. Originally, as we have seen, this was to encourage the growth of crooks and bends for shipbuilding. Later they pruned the trees up to obtain long, straight timber and that is still the usual requirement for oak today. Labour costs were of course much lower; pruning of anything but the best oak today cannot be justified but where high quality oak is to be obtained, we must give just as much attention to pruning as in the past. The nineteenth-century writers emphasised the importance of early pruning to rectify the tendency of young oak to a bushy habit. We now describe this as 'formative pruning' with the aim of encouraging upward growth. If there is no dominant leading shoot, 'singling' is also required to obtain a single straight stem of at least five metres (Kerr and Evans 1993). This is followed by 'high pruning' with the aim of producing a clear stem of five to six metres, and thus a high quality butt log. This may have to be done in a series of operations in order to avoid loss of increment due to the reduction of the photosynthetic area if the live crown is reduced to less than one third of the height of the tree at any time during its growth. Kerr and Evans (1993) provisionally recommend that oak is pruned in December but report that the Forestry Commission has ongoing studies to confirm this. There is no clear guidance from the past on the best time to prune oak. Nicol and Sang (1812) favour January and February and then September to November with the emphasis on September.

CHAPTER FOUR

Past and Present Uses

....

> After oak timber is made perfectly dry, and placed in
> a free open air, it will endure for ages.
>
> *Nichols*

For several hundred years, oak occupied a unique position in supplying Britain with timber and other secondary products. It was fortunate that oak was naturally widespread in the woodlands of the British Isles. Oak timber is strong, hard and heavy, the heartwood is very durable when seasoned and the tree can grow to a considerable size. Uses included bark for tanning, charcoal for smelting and distilling, fuel for domestic and industrial purposes (such as smoking foods to preserve them, lime burning, salt production and glass making) and food for animals, especially pigs and deer. Acorns were also used by humans for both food and a coffee-like drink. The wood was used for a wide variety of purposes: building (castles, churches, guildhalls, other public buildings, shops, houses); for ships, docks, bridges, piling, weirs, mills and mill wheels (wind, river, tide and cider mills); forge beams (according to Evelyn these were seven and half yards long and four square feet at the end); other beams, barns, stables, cattle sheds, roof shingles (Figure 17), pales, fencing, mining timber, cooperage (including wine casks); laths, studding, wattle, clapboard (used both vertically and horizontally); wainscots, panelling, staircases, flooring, furniture (particularly tables, chairs, bed heads and chests); coffins, wheel spokes, pins, pegs, spars, baskets, poles and cudgels. Ink was made from oak bark and oak galls, whilst tannin was used as a mordant (fixing agent) for dyes. A brown dye was made from oak and when combined with copper, a blue dye. Combination with other salts produced black, purple or yellow dyes. Oak bark was also used in pottery glazes.

Large timbers were provided by old oak trees, which, when growing in wood pasture, also provided mast (acorns) for animals as the trees were far apart and so flowered well. This was a very important use of the forest up to Tudor times. Pure oak coppice and coppice with standards (coppice of various species such as willow, hazel and ash which complemented the use of oak in many crafts) were the main source for the uses requiring both small and large trees. Oak coppice was the main source of oak charcoal, used for smelting metal ores from early times and it provided bark for tanning leather and sails. Different products were obtained from oak coppice of various ages and it was managed on different rotations: two to three years for cooperage (hoops), four

FIGURE 17
Splitting oak shingles.

to six years for hop poles, 10 years for fuel (cordwood), from 10 to 15 years for round fencing material, 11 years for thatching spars, 16 to 17 to make charcoal for smelting, 24 to 25 years for mining timber and tan bark, 25 to 30 years for spelk baskets (see below) and cleft stakes. Cordwood was cut into four-foot lengths and a cord was four by four by eight feet and thus comprised 128 cubic feet. Faggots and billets were usually three feet long. By the end of the eighteenth century other timbers from abroad began to replace oak in building and in furniture making; by the mid-nineteenth century it was no longer so essential for building ships.

The wood and bark of oak contains tannin which reacts with iron and causes staining. Iron fittings, for example door hinges, are corroded by contact with oak because the tannin, in which oak is very rich, reacts to form tannic acid which attacks the iron. Historically, when iron was the only material suitable for door furniture (hinges, handles etc.) leather was sometimes used between the iron and the wood to prevent the iron from being broken down by this chemical action. At Capel St Mary in Suffolk, rather gruesomely, the leather used behind the hinges is reputed to be from the tanned skin of a Dane, possibly a prisoner of war from a Viking invasion.

Cleft oak

Many of the uses of oak depended upon the ease with which the wood can be split and the great strength and durability that it exhibits when cleaved, or riven, rather than cut with an edge tool or sawn. Splitting occurs more easily in oak than in most other species due to the large medullary rays that run out radially from the heart. These show clearly as 'silvery grain' in quarter sawn oak panelling. When the wood is cleaved apart in the plane of the rays, the rays provide a line of comparative weakness along which the fibres separate. Cleaving, or riving, is most easily carried out in summer when the sap is up. Cleft timber is strong and durable because the wood cells (tracheids) along the line of cleavage are forced apart instead of being cut through (as they are by sawing), resulting in a smooth surface without weak points through which decay can enter. Tabor (1994) describes this well: 'When a pole is riven, the wood fibres are parted from one another along their length. A few are torn, and raised as spears, but the face of a cleft presents a ribbed-rough surface of remarkable continuity, following

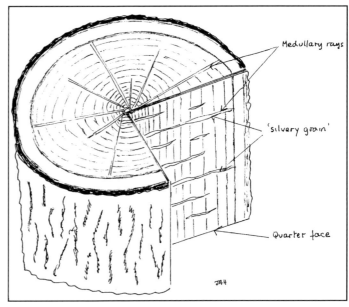

every curve and fold of the pole's growth, even around knots. Because the wood vessels have not been cut across, exposing their open ends, this surface is uniquely waterproof, and explains why cleft poles in oak or chestnut have stood in damp shade on park banks for over three-quarters of a century. Further, since they follow the natural flow of the grain rather than cutting across it as do sawn lengths, there are few points of weakness that might fracture under stress, and indeed the very process of riving frequently reveals weaknesses that sawing would not.'

This process is of great antiquity, as Tabor goes on to explain: 'A flint with sharpened edge can start a split in a green hazel rod as well as a billhook, so small cleft wood has been a valuable resource since probably the Neolithic period.' This must have applied to oak as well as hazel and indeed there is evidence that oak, almost certainly some of it cleaved, was used in the Sweet Track in Somerset 6,000 years ago (see Chapters 1 and 3). Cleft oak was also used to build early ships (see Chapter 5).

Wooden wedges were used to split the larger oak logs for constructional use and to make various artefacts. These were used rather than iron wedges because they were more suitable for separating the fibres along the natural lines of cleavage caused by the medullary rays and thus produced flat, parallel-sided timbers, whereas iron wedges would tear the fibres. Wooden wedges (often of oak too) were certainly being used for this in Medieval times and probably much earlier. Probably the earliest written reference to cleft oak is in Homer's *Odyssey* where the homestead of Eumaeus, the swineherd, is described: 'As an additional protection outside he had fenced the whole length from either hand with a closely set stockade made of split oak which he had taken from the dark part [the heartwood] of the logs.'

Cleft oak has always provided good stakes for fencing and other similar

FIGURE 18
a. *opposite* The medullary rays – which run radially through the timber and in which the products of photosynthesis are stored – are displayed particularly well in oak. Quarter sawing exposes the radial face, and the medullary rays show as 'silver grain', seen typically in oak panelling. Cut 'on the quarter', the thin pieces used for panelling shrink less than timber which has been cut 'through and through'.

J. A. HARRIS

b. Star shake in the end of an oak log. See p. 74.

JEAN WILLIAMSON

uses. Before pressure impregnated preservatives were available for all species of wood, the natural durability of cleft oak meant that oak stakes were the most long-lasting. Manufactured out of 20 to 30 year old coppice stems, the usual dimensions were five feet six inches in length with a six-inch face on the widest side (after the removal of the non-durable sapwood) and pointed. The best stakes were produced from logs from which the sapwood had been removed, or allowed to rot away before the logs were cleft, as it is only the heartwood of oak that is durable and which cleaves so well. Oak paling, with stakes set closely together, was used around early deer parks. Larger material was also cleaved for construction timbers where a flat, sawn surface was not needed, such as wattle and daub houses. Smaller logs were cleaved for light gates and sheep hurdles when these were not made of woven hazel wattle and sometimes also, for cleft pale fencing, though this was more often sweet chestnut. Rail fencing from cleft oak is sometimes seen today, particularly around horse paddocks; it is used in order to avoid damage to valuable animals from wire but it is expensive.

The fact that oak could be cleft was important to many rural industries throughout the ages and was the foundation of the long standing and once very important craft of the 'cooper', who for many centuries manufactured a wide range of the only containers then available: wooden barrels and casks. These were only slowly replaced by iron and steel and, comparatively recently, by other forms of packaging. Wooden barrels were usually made of oak; they were constructed out of cleft staves and oak's durability made it ideal for the purpose. 'Cooperage' was the most intricate of all woodland crafts as not only the skill of cleaving was needed but judgement also of the size of each cleft or stave required for the particular size of barrel and the careful shaping of the staves to fit tightly together. The cask or barrel had to be watertight if intended for liquids and often of an exact internal size as it was usually used as a measure of the contents. Barrels also had to be strong, particularly when used for fermenting alcoholic liquids, and able to withstand prolonged, rough, use.

Jenkins (1965) tells us that: 'The craft is one of great antiquity; there are references to it in the Bible, it was known in Ancient Egypt, while it is probable that the Roman invaders brought it to this country. Like so many other crafts, the art of cask-making disappeared with the departure of the Romans from this country, but it was again re-introduced by the Anglo-Saxons. By the close of the Middle Ages, the cask was the standard package in most European countries, and the craft of coopering was very widespread. On board ship, for example, almost everything was stored in casks ... It was customary to load ships in British ports with a large number of roughly shaped staves. On the outward journey to some far corner of the globe, the coopers would be busily engaged in making casks in which the cargo of sugar, wine or spirits would be stored for the return voyage.' Indeed, the cooper was such an important person on board ship that he was paid as well as all the officers other than the captain, at the same rate as the mates and the ship's surgeon. Thomas (1997), writing of the middle of the eighteenth century, reports that:

'On all vessels, coopers were well paid, because of the need to carry so much water: 300 barrels, say.'

In 1501, the Cooper's Company received its Charter of Incorporation, though the earliest reference to a company was in 1298. In 1501, however, a beadle was employed by the Company to search for unauthorised practices, one of which was the making of casks in a brewery. It was not until the late eighteenth century that brewers were allowed to make casks on their premises, but by the end of the nineteenth century master coopers were rare and the majority of workshops were to be found in breweries (Jenkins 1965).

Jenkins goes on to describe how barrels were made. 'The manufacture of a tight barrel starts in the woods where oak trees averaging two hundred years old are selected and felled. These are cut with cross-cut saws to roughly the lengths required for staves. The logs are then quartered with beetle and wedge and further broken down to the required shape with a long-handled fromard. They are then shaped roughly with a draw knife, and cut to the exact length of the required stave. The rough staves are then thoroughly dried by piling in the open for a length of time, which varies according to moisture and temperature conditions. So far, preparing the staves has been the province of the woodland worker, and it is not until the rough staves are dried down to a uniform moisture content, that they are taken to the cooper's workshop.' Here the staves were shaved to their final shape, placed inside an iron hoop and an ash truss was forced down over them to give the required shape. The staves were then steamed to soften the fibres and bent into the final shape. The whole was then held over a small fire to dry out the staves and set them in position. The heads, one at each end, also of oak, were then fitted.

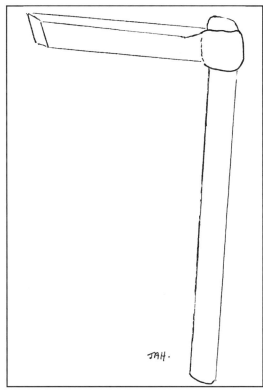

Continuing, Jenkins explains that: 'Different qualities of wood are required for different classes of work. For example, porosity is essential in some wine casks to allow for the passage of air through the wood to assist fermentation. For spirits the wall of the cask must be so tight that neither water nor alcohol can escape and for this reason cleft staves along the radius of a tree are used; the natural concentric rings of the tree making the barrel perfectly tight.' Edlin (1944) describes this more fully, referring to the preparation of staves for brandy barrels: 'For this purpose, large, clean-grown butts are needed, and the sapwood and inner heart are both discarded. The outer heartwood is sawn across to the desired length, and split radially into as many segments as possible – each segment containing at least one unbroken medullary ray, since it is the cells of these that prevent the escape of water and

81

alcohol. The segments are shaped and shaved to exact dimensions, and when used in the barrel they lie at right angles to their original position in the tree – i.e. with their long axis tangential instead of radial.'

The most skilled cooper's craft was 'wet cooperage' for the manufacture of tight casks to hold liquids, for which the staves must fit exactly together. For this only oak was used, much of it white oak from New England once this was available. As high quality material was needed, much was also imported from the Continent when supplies of good English oak began to run out. Latham (1957) quotes Chaloner's catalogue of 1865 reporting imports of barrel staves from the Austrian oak forests and white oak staves from the United States. Explaining that 'the medieval word "barelholt" means barrelstave', he quotes a 1390 customs entry reporting '"Barelholts" ... formed part of the cargo of the ship *Haricog* of Hamburg, unloading at Newcastle.'

Jenkins (1965) tells us that: '... by far the most specialised and common [form] is wet coopering, the manufacture of tight casks to hold liquid substances. The work is very careful and exact, for not only must the staves fit exactly together, but the cask must be strong enough to bear the strain of fermenting liquids and resist rough handling during transportation by sea and land. The only timber used in wet coopering is oak.'

The construction of casks intended for dry materials was less exacting than 'wet coopering'. Such products as flour, tobacco, fruit, vegetables and china were transported and stored in 'slack barrels'. Tabor (1994) tells us that: 'Unlike their iron-bound watertight brethren, the looser staves of slack barrels were bound with wooden *hoops* made in the copse. Today, very few slack barrels are made, and those mainly in halves for use as flower tubs.' The hoops were usually made of ash or hazel but were sometimes made of riven oak. Sturt, writing in 1923, recalled how, from 1884 onwards, paint for his family wheelwright business came in tins and drums 'instead of the barrels in which these materials were formerly packed' as: 'The wood-worker who made barrels was going ... and the tin-worker was coming [in] ... or at any rate his ancient provincial skill was falling obsolete ...'

The wheelwright was in demand in the past for building farm wagon frames and wheels until the middle of the twentieth century and for the wooden wheels of other vehicles. The hub of the wheel was shaped out of well seasoned oak or elm and the spokes were shaped from cleft oak. The outer part of the wheel was of ash, protected by a metal tyre. This was placed over the rim whilst very hot and cooled rapidly with cold water so that it contracted quickly to give a tight fit. The spokes were not sawn but were of cleft oak for strength. Oak for this purpose was felled in the summer when the sap was up and the wood easier to cleave. The wood from trees felled for tan bark as especially suitable for this purpose as after the bark had been harvested in the late spring the trees had to be removed to allow the coppice to grow that year. The wood for the spokes was then seasoned before being shaped for use. Venables (1974) describes how: 'All through the first war my company had two men cleaving oak spokes for artillery wagon wheels. After that war one of them went on cleaving spokes and, from the off falling smaller pieces, ladder rungs, for many years. The other man switched over to splitting and dressing cleft oak fencing rails and pales. When they retired they were not replaced. Oak spokes were no longer required and cleft oak fence pales are now only produced by one or two specialist firms.'

Sturt (1923) records that 'the "felloes", wooden sections of the rim of a wheel, were often made of oak and the spokes: 'were invariably oak, chiefly because oak alone, of the suitable English hard-woods, could be cleft instead of sawn. It mattered, with spokes. A cut across the grain, on a saw-bench, might have produced a cross-grained spoke that would be liable to snap shamefully. Therefore the spokes were never sawn. And since only oak would cleave, properly cleft oak was always used. But the cleaving had to be done in the summer, while the wood was full of sap and would "run" from end to end. Cleaving was a job for the woods therefore; woodmen with beetle (pronounced bittle) and wedges usually had first handling of the beautiful yellowish parallel grain for spokes, that split so easily yet was tough as wire the other way.'

Another use to which riven oak was put was in the production of 'spelk' or 'spale baskets', also known as 'swills' and 'wiskets'. Oak spelk baskets were bowl-shaped and two to three feet across. Like barrels and casks, they were a widely used form of container but for carrying rather than storing and thus of a more temporary nature. Most were made of willow but oak spelks were strong, durable and tougher than osier baskets due to the closeness of the weave achieved by the use of the very thin material that it is possible to manufacture from oak. Their construction depended upon the ease with which oak could be cleaved. They were very resistant to damage because the thin slivers of oak from which they were made set into the strong shape of a basket when they dried out after manufacture and because they were constructed of pliable material. Unlike willow baskets, the manufacture of which was widespread, oak spelks were chiefly made in the Furness district of Lancashire and in the Wyre Forest in Worcestershire. They were also used in the Midlands and the north of England right up to the middle of the twentieth century, for carrying a variety of farm produce, for shell fish and for cotton waste.

Great skill and dexterity were needed to make spelk baskets and a full seven year apprenticeship was usual. The interwoven laths or 'spelks' of which they were made were manufactured from straight, coppice grown oak of 25 to 30 years growth, free from knots and about six inches in diameter, such trees usually being grown primarily for tan-bark. After felling and removing the bark the poles were seasoned out of doors for some time before being cut into four- to five-foot lengths.

FIGURE 20
A beetle: a heavy, wooden-headed mallet used with wedges to cleave and split.

DRAWING BY J. A. HARRIS, AFTER TABOR (1994)

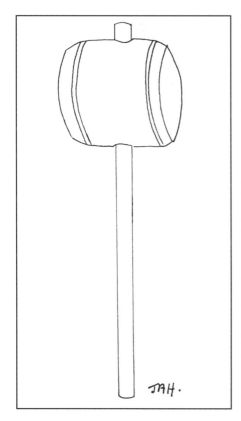

These short poles were immersed in boiling water in metal tanks heated over burning shavings for several hours. Whilst still hot, they were quartered by cleaving through the centre with a beetle and wedge to provide symmetrical sections. These quarters were split again into thin strips (spelks), not more than a sixteenth of an inch thick and of uniform width and thickness throughout their length. This was done by first starting the froe (like a flat bladed short handled adze), or sometimes a billhook, to split the wood and then working it down whilst twisting it from side to side to separate the fibres. The spelks, held in a shaving horse, were carefully trimmed with a spokeshave. The oak ribbons thus produced were put in water again whilst being fixed to the 'bool' or rim, which was often of hazel but sometimes oak, to form the warp of the interwoven basket. The basket shape was achieved by placing the longest ribbons in the middle and successively shorter ones to the outside. The weft was then formed by weaving thinner, shorter ribbons of wood, known as 'chissies', through the warp.

The carpenter's wood

The village carpenter used oak for a wide variety of purposes, including making ploughs, farm implements, domestic products and furniture, as did the wheelwright. Indeed, oak was his principal timber because of its durability, though elm, ash, and for high quality indoor goods, walnut, were used too. The village carpenter Walter Rose (1943), wrote: 'The oak most suitable for our work was large-grown mellow butts, large enough to cut down the centre and quarter the two halves afterwards – that is, to saw them into board or plank with the flat side on the pit'. He goes on '... many [trees] were crooked; they would have been more suitable for the wheelwright, who was usually glad to secure small strong wood suitable for the curves of carts and wagons. It sometimes happened that a piece of timber in our yard, too crooked for us carpenters to use, would be purchased by the wheelwright because he saw in the natural contour just what he wanted, a curve difficult to obtain'.

In many cases the village carpenter was also the builder and undertaker and no doubt could make a child's cot as well as he could a coffin and in so doing, provided for the needs of his customers from the cradle to the grave. Rose vividly describes what the craftsman sees in his wood and how trees were cut up. 'The quality of wood has a mesmeric influence on the craftsman. The large butt or stack of sawn plank to him is promise of usefulness and beauty. When my father looked at the oak butts for sale he always kept in mind what use he would find for them. This large mellow butt would be reckoned large enough to split (saw) down the centre and quarter-up for coffin and other boards. Another, younger and of much smaller circumference, would be suitable for rails and slats of field gates. In a stumpy butt, with large branches spreading off not far from the base, he would see four large gate posts, the spread of the branches to form the portion that would go into the ground. From a few lots he would turn aside and not trouble to measure them, seeing

FIGURE 21
A disused sawpit. The
large, two handled
saw is part way
through an oak log
held by an iron dog,
lying on bolsters over
the pit; the bolsters
would be moved as
the sawing proceeded.
Cutting lines were
'struck' top and
bottom with a cord
soaked in lampblack.
The top sawyer was
responsible for
sharpening the saw
and directing
operations. The under
sawyer had to 'throw'
the saw up and pull it
down on the cutting
stroke, whilst the
sawdust poured over
him.

E. H. M. HARRIS

in them sizes and shapes unsuitable for our work. These he would leave for
the wheelwright to buy.'

Oak is very strong and this characteristic has led to many other uses. The
great strength of oak was utilised to its full in the windmills that ground corn
for centuries to feed generations of people. Positioned to catch the wind, their
structure required tremendous strength in the oak beams, braced together by
curved stays but most of all supported by the central post, usually 30 inches
square at the base and made of a solid oak tree (Rose 1943). He states: 'I
always felt that the service fulfilled by these beams, those strong stays and that
large post, was worthy of oak'. In water mills the cogs (teeth) on the wheels
were usually made of beech but oak cogs were also used, because oak is more
durable, on the driving pit wheel which often ran partly in water (Rose 1943).

One of the most unusual uses of oak timber was by John Harrison in the
seventeenth century, who later became famous for his novel clocks designed
to keep time accurately for long periods at sea and therefore make it possible
for the first time to measure longitude accurately. Harrison was the son of a
carpenter and apprenticed to that trade but as a local bell ringer, he was asked
to design and build a clock for the tower on the stables at Sir Charles Pelham's
Brocklesby Park Estate in north Lincolnshire, near his home. For this he
invented and incorporated a wooden 'movement' in lignum vitae, a naturally
oily wood, to overcome the problem of friction, which tended to slow clocks
down, as this did not need lubrication. Harrison was also anxious to avoid

the use of iron and steel, obviating rust in the damp conditions, so he used oak for the teeth of the gear wheels of the stable clock and for the gear wheels themselves. Oak was used rather than metal which would have expanded and contracted with temperature changes, thereby altering the speed of the clock and thus making it lose or gain time. He carefully selected suitable wood from radial cut (quarter sawn) planks which provided parallel grain for the oak teeth 'radiating from the center of the wheel to the tips of the teeth' (Sobel and Andrewes 1998), i.e. in the strongest orientation. 'Harrison constructed his wheels so that the teeth had a radial grain to give them the required strength and overcome the possibility of breakage' (Sobel and Andrewes 1998). These authors also tell us that: 'Harrison further guaranteed the wheel teeth their enduring structure by selecting the oak from fast-growing trees, ... Such trees yield lumber with a wide grain and great might, ... Elsewhere, wherever Harrison was willing to sacrifice strength for a lighter-weight material, as in the central portions of the wheels, he turned to slow-growing oak; ... The body [of the wheels] was taken from a plank running through the center of the trunk, in order to prevent the wheel from warping; ... The wood was so well seasoned and carefully chosen that even after 250 years, the wheels are almost as good and true as they were when made'. The stable clock at Brocklesby is still running after nearly three centuries.

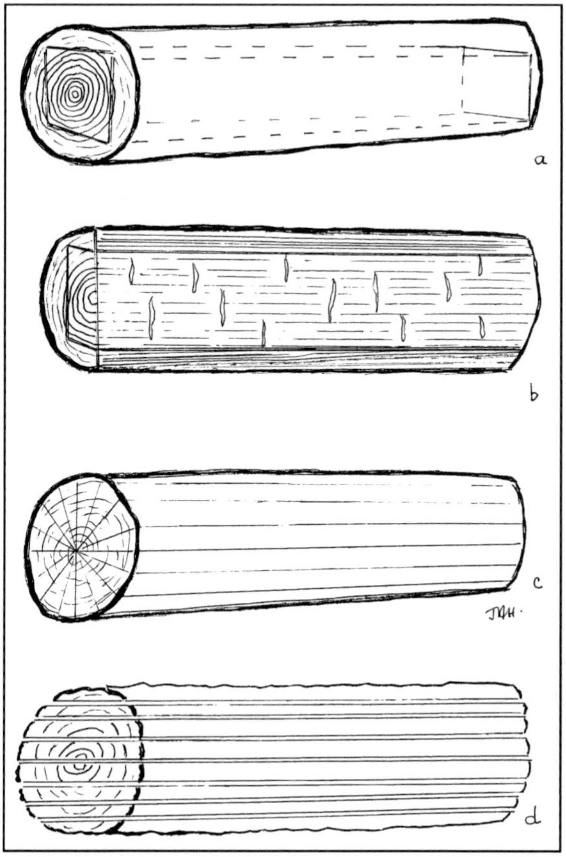

In some parts of England, particularly in the south-eastern counties, oak was used for roof coverings after it had been split into thin pieces, similar to slates, known as shingles. These were shaped so that they were thicker and rounded at the outside end and were fixed with oak pegs (Brown 1997). Since these were light in weight, the roof timbers could be reduced in size. In the course of time, however, shingles were replaced by tiles and slates. Shingles were also used for covering church spires and were still being used late in the twentieth century in parts of Kent and Sussex. This craft had survived from the first century AD, as 'riven oak shingles for roofing hovels were being made in the southern counties of England' at that time (Tabor 1994).

FIGURE 22
The conversion of oak for building timber: *a.* a squared beam for posts, wall plates and beams; *b.* a halved beam; *c.* a quartered log cleft for studding, bracers, rafters and joists. *d.* a log sawn 'through and through' for planking.
DRAWING BY J. A. HARRIS AFTER BROWN (1997)

Buildings

Oak was used as beams and posts of buildings, castles, churches and other structures from early times. Smaller trees were barked and used whole though often the sapwood was not removed and attack by wood boring beetle larvae soon followed, first in the sapwood and then spreading into the heartwood. Large trees were squared with an adze. The squared beam was either used whole or halved. Large beams could be seven and a half yards long and four foot square at the end. Trees were also quartered to provide smaller material.

In early construction, posts were set into the ground and small whole timbers used. Some of the halls (upper-class dwelling houses were single large rooms) in Saxon times in England were quite substantial. A description of an early Scandinavian hall is given in Beowulf (Huyshe 1907). Here the building 'was rectangular; its roof was supported by four rows of pillars, of which the two outer rows were close to the walls ... so that the Hall was divided into a nave and two side aisles.' The wooden church at Greensted-juxta-Ongar in Essex is the earliest surviving building, dating from AD 835. 'The nave is built of split oak logs (staves) set vertically and jointed together by oak tongues let into grooves' (Brown 1997). The wooden tower is roofed with shingles.

Two methods of construction were employed in later buildings. In the first the frame of the building was like a box, later set on a sill. The second was the use of 'crucks'. These were naturally curved timbers set up in pairs, like an inverted Y which supported the ridge of the roof. Matching pairs were obtained by splitting the tree in half. Additional strength was obtained by linking the crucks together. Joints were all pegged with oak pegs. Such crucks were also used for early doorways. Cruck construction was used in many buildings but most have now survived only in cottages and barns. The crucks were set up either at ground level or on a wall.

In both types of building, the wall space was originally filled with 'wattle and daub'. Upright studs or staves were fixed into horizontal members which were usually of hazel, cleft oak or chestnut. The wattle or wickerwork was woven between the studs and could be hazel, ash or riven oak; this provided a base on which to apply the daub. The daub itself was applied in layers from both sides; it consisted of wet clay mixed with hair, straw and dung. Lime was added for strength. The outside was waterproofed with a lime wash or plaster of lime, sand and hair (Brown 1997).

Ordinary labourers lived in small houses built of a variety of tree species. With the increased prosperity in the sixteenth century, there was more demand for oak buildings. Holinshed (1577) noted that: 'In times past men were contented to dwell in houses builded of sallow, plumtree, hardbeame and elme, so that the use of oke was in manner dedicated wholie unto churches, religious houses, princes palaces, nobleman's lodging and navigation: but now all these are rejected and nothing but oke anie whit regarded.' Leland, travelling in Britain between 1535 and 1543, recorded during his visit to Yorkshire that 'the hole town of Doncaster is builded of wodde and the houses be slated: yet there is plenty of stone.'

Although stone became the building material for the walls of cathedrals, churches, monasteries, castles and other important buildings, timber, usually oak, was used in the construction of the roof. There are many records of large

oaks being used in such buildings from the thirteenth century onwards. Outstanding examples are the magnificent hammer beam roof of Westminster Hall which dates from 1394 and the roof of the Merchant Adventurers' Hall in York which was built between 1357 and 1368. Latham (1957) tells us that: 'Much of the oak for the Palace of Westminster built at the end of the fourteenth century for King Richard II was procured from woods near Farnham, in Surrey where trees were not only felled, but also wrought into the staunch timbers required for the roof of the Great Hall and other rooms. In 1395 an order was made for thirty strong "waynes" to convey the timber from Farnham to Kingston, from which place they were brought down the river Thames to Westminster.'

'Next to stone, oak was the chief glory of Gothic buildings' (Hennell 1943). Hennell goes on: 'The roof of Westminster Hall, of length 238 feet and 68 feet in span, which was begun in 1394, is the largest and the greatest triumph of mediaeval carpentry which England has ever possessed. It was built of Sussex (*sic*) oak. It was formed of thirteen roof-trusses, each with a pair of hammer-beams and hammer-posts, of which a single timber weighs three-and-a-half tons and must have required an oak of four feet diameter'.

At Hays Barton, East Budleigh in Devon, the birth-place of Sir Walter Raleigh in 1552, there is an oak beam 80 feet in length which must now have been *in situ* for at least four and a half centuries.

Oak was used not only in the construction of ecclesiastical buildings but also in their decoration and furnishings. The shrine of Edward the Confessor in Westminster Abbey, for example, was built of oak. Pews or benches began to be placed in churches in the middle of the thirteenth century and these were invariably of oak. From 1603 churches were required to provide pulpits.

FIGURE 23
Opposite and right:
The magnificent, 600-year-old oak roof of Westminster Hall, built for Richard II by Hugh Herland, is the earliest surviving example of hammer-beam construction. It has survived many threats: Guy Fawkes in 1605, a fire in 1833, the Fenians in 1885, the Luftwaffe in 1941, and an IRA bomb in 1979. Detailed carvings of flying angels decorate the beam ends.

FIGURE 24
The Great Barn at
Buckland Abbey,
Devon. This fifteenth
century, arch-braced
roof is of massive
proportions and
strength; it covers a
building 159 ft long,
32 feet wide and 40
feet high. The
construction is of oak,
held together by
mortise and tenon
joints with wooden
pegs.
NATIONAL TRUST

Other church furniture and fittings were often made of oak, including altars, lecterns, reading desks and rood screens. Lych gates too, at the entrance to the church where the coffin was rested, were often constructed of oak.

Before the widespread use of window glass, window spaces were filled with lattices which let in some light and up to 'early Tudor times [they] had often been filled up with "wicker" or fine rifts of oak in chequerwise' (Trevelyan 1944). These must have been very thin pieces of cleft oak, in this case used not for its durability but because it was possible to separate the fibres by cleaving them into thin 'slivers'.

In the past, timber which was used inside houses was believed to 'harden' due to the smoke which permeated the premises. Holinshed (1577) considered that this improved the health of the occupants as well as the strength of the timbers. 'For as the smoke in those daies was supposed to be a sufficient hardening for the timber of the house; so it was reputed a far better medicine to keep the goodman and his familie from the quacke or poss, wherewith as then, verie few were oft acquainted.' Oak was also thought to be more resistant to fire than other timbers and: 'In re-building London, after the fire in 1666, no other timber than oak was allowed to be used in roof, door, window frames or cellar floor of any house' (Eleventh Report of the Commissioners 1792). Inns, market halls, almshouses, shops and houses built in oak still survive, some of them from early times. Examples can be found throughout Britain.

In Tudor and Stuart houses, oak was used extensively. By this time many houses had second storeys which projected over the street. As well as oak being used for flooring and staircases, oak panelling replaced tapestry as a wall covering. This was often carved with vertical folds to resemble folded linen or was more elaborately decorated. Oak panels were also used for paintings. Oak floorboards were cleft and sawn as was the panelling. Chairs, tables, sideboards, bed heads, chests and Bible boxes were all fashioned in oak. 'Period furniture reveals to those who handle it the character of life when it was made. The oak furniture of Elizabeth's reign represents the happiness of the people in its profusion of carvings, many of which are amusingly grotesque. The Gothic character of that which preceded it – of which genuine specimens are rare – may denote the influence of the Church on domestic life. Almost all the early furniture that has survived is made of oak. The oak furniture of the Puritan (or Cromwellian) period, in its solidarity and the restraint of its ornamentation, corresponds well with the severe and restrained outlook on life; it is in direct contrast to the flamboyant pieces made subsequently to the Restoration' (Rose 1943).

Charcoal, tanning, transport

The rise of industry and trade in the sixteenth century meant drastic inroads into the country's stock of oak, especially for charcoal used in the iron industry, so much so that felling of oak for such purposes was forbidden within 14 miles of a waterway (which made the transport of large timber comparatively

easy) in order to preserve it for the construction of ships. Charcoal manufacture was an old industry and one of the main secondary uses of oak, the other being tan bark. Both these uses depended on the utilisation of oak on a coppice rotation of 25 to 30 years for bark and 15 years for charcoal. Although any species can be charcoaled, oak was considered the best for smelting iron. Oak billets were cut into three foot lengths and stacked round a central pole. Smaller pieces were stacked lengthwise on the outside edge. The whole was then covered with turf and the central pole removed. Hot charcoal was dropped down the central hole and the stack carefully tended to get an even burn. In contrast, modern iron kilns need far less tending. The larger pieces of charcoal went for smelting and the smaller for domestic fuel. Thus the rapid rise of the iron industry in Tudor times devastated many oakwoods (see Chapter 3).

Oak tan bark had also been harvested for centuries; the best bark was obtained from trees coppiced at 25 to 30 years when the bark was easy to strip and gave a better overall yield than older trees. In times of shortage, bark could be used from any oak tree but the tannin content was lower in older trees. Nisbet (1911) gives the following figures: 14 to 16 year old oak bark contains 15 to 20 per cent tannin, older stems fall to eight to ten per cent, whilst coarse bark from old trees only yields five to eight per cent. The bark was stripped with a special tool, two horizontal incisions being made and the bark stripped between by making vertical incisions. This was then stacked under cover to dry so that the tannin was not leached out. At the tanneries, the bark was ground and added to water to make a liquid in which hides

FIGURE 25
Charcoal burning in the seventeenth century. This drawing, from John Evelyn's *Sylva* (1670), shows three stages in the construction of a charcoal kiln. In the centre, initial preparations are carried out; on the left is the complete kiln before covering it with earth, and on the right is the kiln after firing.

FIGURE 26
Bark stripping. A
team of eight pose
beside an oak from
which the lower six
feet of bark have
already been removed.
The remainder will be
stripped after the tree
is felled. The date is
around 1905.
INSTITUTE OF
AGRICULTURAL HISTORY,
UNIVERSITY OF READING

were soaked. Rose (1943) describes the preparation of tan bark as practised
into the early twentieth century. 'The stripping of the bark was a simple
process and was done directly after each tree was felled, before the larger
branches were cut off. With a light axe we cut the circumference round at
distances of about two feet, and also made one longitudinal cut into which
we inserted the barking iron, a simple iron tool with heart-shaped end on a
wooden handle. This enabled us to remove a complete shell of bark all round
the large branch on which we were working. The bark shells were then stacked
on end in shocks to dry before being sent to the tanyard'. This industry was
finally overtaken by chemical methods of tanning.

The coming of the canals provided access to woods from which it had
previously been difficult to transport timber. One of the first canals to be
built was the Bridgewater Canal between Manchester and Worsley, the main
part of which was opened in 1765. During the following seventy years, more
than thirty canals were built in England and these all used timber in their
construction, much of it oak. Lock gates had large balance beams, sluices and
paddles to maintain water levels. Swing bridges enabled people to cross the
canal and the narrowboats and barges too were built primarily of oak.

Towards the end of the eighteenth century, steps were taken to improve
the country's roads, many of which were little better than tracks and almost
impassable in wet weather. Prominent in this work were the inventor of
macadam roads, John McAdam (1756–1836) and Thomas Telford (1757–1836)
who built roads, bridges and canals. Oak was used for bridges, fencing and

toll gates. It was difficult to find large oak trees by the eighteenth century but there were still some large trees that had not been felled because of the difficulty in transporting them before the advent of improved roads and canals. In 1789, Gilbert White described large oaks which had grown near Selborne: 'On the Blackmore Estate there is a small wood called Losel's, of a few acres that was lately furnished with a set of oaks of a peculiar growth and great value: they were tall and taper like firs, but standing near together had very small heads – only a little brush without any large limbs. About twenty years ago the bridge at the Toy, near Hampton Court, being much decayed, some trees were wanted for the repairs, that were fifty feet long without a bough, and would measure twelve inches diameter at the little end. Twenty such trees did a purveyor find in this little wood, with this advantage, that many of them answered the description at sixty feet'.

During the nineteenth and twentieth centuries the supply of oak for the increased demands of the population and for shipbuilding was insufficient so oak had to be replaced by other timbers. Softwood, from coniferous trees, which could be nailed easily and was lighter, replaced it in building work and imported hardwoods, such as mahogany, were used in furniture. The use of iron to build ships meant that oak was no longer important to the Navy and merchant shipping (see Chapter 5). Whilst the traditional use for tanning remained important until the twentieth century, when chemicals replaced oak bark, a few tanning firms still remain today that use oak bark for high quality leather production and there is still a demand for mining timber, albeit much reduced.

Uses of oak today

Today oak is still in demand for good quality fencing, boat restoration and repair (see Chapter 5), coffins, house restoration and repair projects; oak beams being in particular demand for the latter. Many old barns are also being restored. For instance, at Braintree in Essex, the Wheat Barns are some of the finest surviving medieval buildings of cruck construction. Much of the oak for these works comes from private estates who have looked after their oak trees.

Oak is widely used in the historic houses belonging to the National Trust and on the Trust's properties for gates, farm buildings *et cetera*. Oak is also widely used in church restoration; for example, the church at Lydford in Devon was restored in the late nineteenth and early twentieth century. The roof is of oak and all the pew ends have Biblical and ecclesiastical figures carved on them. There is also an intricately carved oak rood screen. At Lansallos church near Fowey in Cornwall there are particularly fine examples of intricate carving on the oak pew ends dating from 1475.

Oak beams have been replaced in the cathedrals at Lincoln and St Albans cathedrals recently and extensive restoration was undertaken at York Minster after the fire there in July 1984. For this green (unseasoned) oak was employed so that the joints would shrink on drying and tighten up in use in the

FIGURE 27
Opposite and overleaf. Carved oak pew ends in St. Petrock's Church, Lydford. *a.* Saint Alphage, Bishop of Winchester in 984, bordered with a scroll of oak leaves and acorns. *b.* The Venerable Bede holding a quill pen and book, bordered with tulips; *c.* David Livingstone preaching, bordered by palm leaves; *d.* Jonah, holding the ship from which he was cast, bordered with mice and water rats.

E. H. M. HARRIS

traditional way. Both green and seasoned oak were used for the extensive restoration at Windsor Castle following the devastating fire in 1992, the former for a newly designed ceiling in St George's Hall. Oak was also used for the floor in the Hall, the balcony and the vaulted ceiling in the Lantern Lobby (Plate 4), which was rebuilt using first grade English oak laminated onto other timbers, as were the eight oak columns there.

Green oak was also used recently in a huge building designed along the lines of a traditional tithe barn and is claimed to be the largest green oak structure to be built in Britain for over three hundred years (Miles 1999). Taking two years and 21,000 man hours to construct, it was completed in 1998 using 350 oak trees (10,000 young oak trees were planted to replace them) and is an entertainment complex at Highfield House in Warwickshire.

At Portcullis House, the new offices for Members of Parliament built in 1999, solid English oak was used for both the furniture and panelling. Oak was used for the restoration of the hammer-beam roof of Westminster Hall, one of the earliest buildings with such a roof; the beams are about three feet by two feet and 20 feet long. In 1996 a closely accurate replica of the Shakespearian Globe Theatre 300 yards from the original site in Southwark, London, was begun; it was opened in 1999. It reproduces the original construction of a 20-sided polygon, each column constructed from a single oak tree. It is framed in oak, each joint being individually pegged and with wattle and daub between. All is green oak and is an example of perfection in timber framing, the timber being supplied from all over the country.

The present use of oak in shipbuilding and the restoration of old boats is dealt with in Chapter 5. Oak is also again being used for good quality furniture, such as that produced in the workshop of the 'Mouse Man' (Robert Thompson's Craftsmen Limited) at Kilburn in Yorkshire and for reproduction furniture. Born in 1876, Robert Thompson was the son of a joiner and wheelwright. He was impressed by the quality and intricacy of the medieval oak furnishings in Ripon and York Cathedrals and determined to spend his life bringing back the spirit of craftsmanship in English oak. For this he sought out traditional tools and learnt how to use them. When he took over his father's workshop he developed a style of furniture following the English traditions of the seventeenth century and from the start, never used anything other than English oak. Carving in oak became very important to him and he insisted on seasoning his timber naturally rather than in a kiln, a practice which the firm continues today. He was soon engaged to furnish many churches in the style that had attracted him initially and for which his firm became well known, all the time with oak alone. He developed a technique of finishing the surface of his furniture with an adze, a medieval tool used in

FIGURE 28
Seagull House Barn:
contemporary use of
green oak by
Carpenter Oak
Limited. The
company specialises in
the design, building
and erection of new
green oak frames for
modern and
traditional buildings.
COUNTRY LIVING

FIGURE 29
Using an adze in the
Kilburn workshop of
Robert Thompson
Limited, to give a
traditional finish to an
oak coffee table top.
TESSA BUNNEY

the past for roughing out ship timber and this remains a characteristic of the firm's furniture today under the management of his grandsons and great grandsons. His trade mark carved on every piece was a mouse, each individually carved (Plate 5). The company he founded still uses it today.

Brown, bog and pippy oak

Besides being prized for its attractive figure displaying characteristic medullary rays, there are two unusual and valuable forms of oak, 'brown oak' and 'bog oak'. These result from discoloration of the wood, which enhances its decorative quality for interior work and furniture. Very occasionally 'green oak', discoloured by a fungus, is used for figurative work. Evans (1984) states: 'Brown oak is rare and is much sought for panelling, cabinet work and other furniture uses.' It is a deeper, red-brown colour than normal oak and is darker, with a more golden lustre, than walnut. Brown oak occurs as a result of a pigment from a large bracket fungus (*Fistulina hepatica* or beef steak fungus) that grows on the tree and penetrates much of the sapwood. It normally attacks the lower part of the stem (Morris and Perring 1974). The fungus appears to be indigenous in Britain but is largely confined to England. Brough (1947) tells us that 'only one authentic specimen has been recorded as found in Scotland' and it occurs mainly in 'the midland and southern counties'. Brown oak is also known as 'pollard oak' because the fungus frequently enters the sapwood after pollarding (Forest Products Research Laboratory 1952). *Fistulina* is a weak parasite, attacking the living sapwood but without destroying it completely and remaining to colour the wood when the latter turns to heartwood. The attack does not significantly reduce the strength of the timber but makes it too valuable as a decorative wood for it to be used for constructional purposes, as it is particularly valuable for veneer and inlay work. Although not much used today, it is obtainable but at about three times the price of normal oak timber. The village carpenter Walter Rose (1943) describes the appeal of brown

FIGURE 30
The underside of this oak fruitbowl shows 'pippy' figure, formed by adventitious buds and the distorted grain around them.

G. E. HARRIS

99

oak as one who has worked with it: 'If the tree is left [before felling] until a slight decay commences at the base beautiful variegated streaks of rich brown colour that permanently tone the centre of the tree will result. In rare cases this quality (known as 'brown figured oak') is of extreme beauty, like unto the streaks of a ripe apple or the flaming rays of the setting sun. But actually it is the first stage of decay, and such figured wood should not be used out-of-doors or where it will have to bear great strain. But for interior work in churches and furniture it cannot be surpassed. Work made in such wood is beautiful by nature and should not be darkened or treated with oil or polish'.

Bog oak is also normal oak timber, given a special colour in this case by long submersion in waterlogged anaerobic conditions. It is dark, almost black in colour, sometimes with a greenish tinge and exhibiting a characteristic silky sheen. True bog oak is obtained from logs which have lain in the anaerobic conditions of peat bogs for at least 4000 years and are the remains of oak trees that died as a result of climate change (see Chapter 1). This caused a rise in the water table, killing the trees, which then fell into bogs. The black staining of the wood is due to a reaction between iron in the ground water and tannins in the wood, which has both darkened and toughened it. Bog oak usually comes from 'buried forests' covered by peat formation. It occurs most commonly in Ireland but also in the north and west of Britain. A list of oak trees recorded in Scottish bogs can be found in Anderson (1967). Bog oak recovered from Borth Bog in Wales has been carbon-dated at 6000 years old. Large trees have been found in the East Anglian Fenland, where 'radio-carbon dating of their outer rings shows that they were killed around 4,500 years ago, a date conformable with their association with Neolithic artefacts' (Godwin and Deacon 1974). In many deposits where bog oak occurs it is associated with oak artefacts made by prehistoric man who also used oak for dwelling construction, trackways, palisades, boats, looms, tubs, shields and firewood in the Neolithic, Bronze and Iron Ages. Similar use continued in the Anglo-Saxon, Norman and Medieval periods. Like brown oak, bog oak has been used as inlay in furniture and cabinet work, contrasting it with white-coloured holly wood and sometimes with cream-coloured sycamore, first by the Tudors and then in the eighteenth and nineteenth centuries. It is not easily obtained today.

Another unique feature of oak that is exploited for its decorative effect in veneers, more often nowadays in turned oak bowls, is 'pippy oak'. This is oak timber in which numerous small knots are displayed, creating attractive features in the wood. The knots arise from numerous small, adventitious buds, normally dormant in the bark but in this case stimulated to develop by sudden exposure of the stem of a mature tree to light, or sometimes, in a hedgerow tree, to constant nibbling off by farm stock which then stimulates more adventitious buds to develop. In oak these aborted buds are particularly numerous and according to Thomas (2000) 45 to 70 per cent of the buds produced each season do not mature and become enclosed within the wood as it develops.

Even the by-products of working with oak can be utilised. Oak chips were used, and still are in a small way, for curing fish by smoking over an oak chip fire, whilst Sturt (1923) records selling oak sawdust cleared out from below a saw pit: 'Being from dry timber, and mostly oak, it was useful for bacon-curing, and I used to sell it for that purpose at fourpence the sack.' Thus we see/ that oak and its timber have had a particularly important place in British history, because of its special characteristics. It is still a special tree today, with a promising future (see Chapter 7).

FIGURE 31
Epicormic growth on a hedgerow oak. The stem is exposed to full light, resulting in a profusion of leafy twigs sprouting from adventitious buds under the bark. Sudden exposure to increased light often has this effect.

N. D. G. JAMES

101

FIGURE 32
A mature oak felled
for timber.

JEAN WILLIAMSON

CHAPTER FIVE

Shipbuilding

....

Heart of oak are our ship,
Heart of oak are our men.

David Garrick

Oak timber, due to its strength, durability, workability, cleavability and abundance in historical times, was of prime importance in shipbuilding. Albion (1926) tells us that: 'In all maritime countries, oak was considered the ship timber *par excellence*'. Oak was the principal timber used for ship and boat construction from early times. The British Isles were no exception and it was used extensively for all types of vessels. Although the many early references to the timber used in shipbuilding do not always state the species of tree, the term 'ship-timber' is assumed to mean oak. There is much archaeological evidence for the use of oak in the earliest ship building and new examples are being found all the time.

From prehistory to the Middle Ages

Greenhill and Morrison (1995) designate four types of early boats: rafts, skin-covered boats such as the coracle, bark boats such as the North American canoe and log boats from which subsequent boats were derived. The earliest log boats were single hollowed out logs; later side planks were added to the central log to provide freeboard. Over 320 such boats have been found in the British Isles. The three Ferriby boats found between 1937 and 1963 on the Humber were originally dated to about 1700 BC but recent work employing improved carbon dating puts them further back at 1880, 1940 and 2030 BC (*Classic Boat* 156). They are the earliest example yet found with planks sewn together. One of these boats had cleaved planks 52 feet long, fastened together with yew bindings. Oak laths on the joints held in moss caulking. A similar boat found at Brigg in Lincolnshire (dated 800 BC) also had sewn oak planks with moss caulking. A recent find at Dover (dated to 1350 BC) currently being thoroughly examined, will add to knowledge of the construction of an actual boat. It has been possible to determine that axes and adzes were used in the construction, and controlled splitting and cleaving of quite large oak logs was achieved. Cleft material was commonly used as it is comparatively waterproof (see Chapter 4). The adze was used to shape both large baulks of timber and the outside of the hull when complete. It is estimated that this boat was

15 metres long and that a single oak tree split in half forms the two timbers either side of the keel. The planks of the boat were bound together by yew withies and made waterproof with beeswax and moss. 'The Dover boat is simply the most intact complex piece of Bronze Age woodwork ever found in Britain if not North West Europe' (Goodburn 1996).

About 300 BC oak 'was used for their ships by the Veneti, a Gallic tribe living in Brittany but strength in the Atlantic was more important than speed' (Meiggs 1982). In 56 BC Caesar describes the Veneti as a powerful maritime tribe with a large fleet of ships, trading and allied with Britain. Caesar states: '... sailing in a wide ocean was clearly a very different matter from sailing in a land-locked sea like the Mediterranean ... The Gauls' own ships were built and rigged in a different manner from ours. They were made with much flatter bottoms, to help them to ride shallow water caused by shoals or ebb tides. Exceptionally high bows and sterns fitted them for use in heavy seas and violent gales, and the hulls were made entirely of oak, to enable them to stand any amount of shocks and rough usage ... We could not injure them by ramming because they were so solidly built ... they could bring to in shallow water with greater safety and when left aground by the tide had nothing to fear from reefs or pointed rocks' (Handford 1953).

In 1910 a Roman merchant ship was excavated in the Thames; it was solidly built entirely of oak and of carvel construction, with planks fixed edge-to-edge, butted together and nailed to an internal frame (which was built first) rather than overlapping. The ship is thought to have been a trading vessel and is 70 feet long, dated to about 300 AD. Two further ships, also constructed in oak, were found in the Thames in 1958 and 1962, both dating to the second century AD (Bass 1974).

The Anglo-Saxons and Vikings favoured clinker built boats with overlapping planks nailed along their edges. The Nydam Oak Boat found in Jutland is built of oak felled between 310 to 320 AD. It represents a type of boat used by the Anglo-Saxons at that time. It is clinker built, completely of oak and is a rowing boat rather than one that was paddled and sailed. The Nydam Boat demonstrates 'a breakthrough in technical achievement ... the key features of this vessel being the construction in oak of the frames, the planks and the prow, and the use of clenched iron nails in the fastenings' (MacDonald 2000). Saxon ships about the fifth century 'we are told by Aneurin, a Welsh bard, "were single-masted, carrying one square sail. They had curved bottoms, and their prows and poops were adorned with the heads and tails of monsters"' (Loudon 1838).

The ship found at Sutton Hoo in Suffolk dates from about 625 and is thought to be the burial place of Raedwald, King of East Anglia. It was 89 feet long and 14 feet wide. It appeared to have had no sail but had places for forty oarsmen and was clinker built, fastened with iron rivets. It was similar in construction and shape to the Viking longships of the same period (Carver 1998). A half scale replica of this ship has been built called the *Sae Wylfing*. As this ship had large stern frames to support a side rudder, the replica was

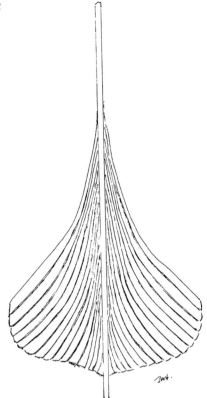

a

rigged with a square sail of Roman pattern. She sails well and proves that the original Sutton Hoo ship could have sailed at speeds up to 10 knots (Gifford and Gifford 1996).

Graham-Campbell and Kidd (1980) describe the well-researched Gokstad Viking longship which was used when raiding, dated to between 895 and 900. 'The Gokstad ship was removed from its bed of blue clay, which had been its protection in the ground, and can now be seen, reconstructed, in the Viking Ship Museum in Oslo. Apart from the mast and the decking (made of pine), most of the ship was built of oak with the keel consisting of a single timber, nearly 58 feet long. Greenhill and Morrison (1995) add that it was clinker built of radially split planks. These planks were fastened into shape whilst green and unseasoned, when they would still have been flexible, thus making them easy to bend. A group of five early eleventh century Viking ships was raised in 1962 from Roskilde Fjord in Denmark; two longships, two cargo ships and a smaller boat. One of the longships was '95 feet long and built of oak' (Graham-Campbell and Kidd 1980). Greenhill and Morrison (1995) add that this ship was built of oak which had originated from Dublin and

b

FIGURE 33
a. The Gokstad Ship.

J. A. HARRIS, AFTER
GRAHAM-CAMPBELL AND
KIDD (1980)

b. A replica of the Sutton Hoo ship, the *Sae Wylfing*.

J. A. HARRIS

105

had probably been built there, where there was a well established Viking settlement. The Viking form of construction and shape persisted in the fishing boats of the Shetlands up to the end of the nineteenth century, grown oak being used for the stem and frames (Mansfield 1996).

Fighting ships in England first became important under King Alfred (849–901) in response to the threat from the Vikings. The Anglo-Saxon Chronicles describe how: 'Alfred learnt from his enemies'. In the entry for 896, the Chronicles describe the new ships designed by Alfred: 'Then King Alfred commanded long ships to be built against the … ships [of the Vikings]. They were nearly twice as long as the others; some had sixty oars, some more. They were both swifter and steadier, also higher than the others; nor were they in the Frisian manner or the Danish, but as he himself thought might be most useful' (Savage 1995).

If Alfred followed the Viking method of construction he will have utilised similar materials, particularly oak, as it would have been readily available in large sizes in his kingdom of Wessex. A trading vessel found at Graveney in Kent, dated to the early tenth century, was a sea-going boat. It was clinker built with massive oak frames and used for heavy cargoes (Greenhill and Morrison 1995).

The Vikings continued to ravage the English coast throughout the tenth and eleventh centuries. The Anglo-Saxon Chronicle entry for 1008 states: 'the King [Aethelred] bade that all over England ships were to be made constantly, that is, that three hundred and ten hides [of land owned] provide one warship' (Savage 1995). As these ships were made locally it is reasonable to suppose that oak was mainly used. In the times that followed ships were built for trade rather than for defence and in 1066: 'It was only with difficulty that he [Harold] was able to assemble men and vessels along the Channel coast' (Savage 1995) to repel the Norman invasion. An idea of the sort of ships used at this time can be obtained from the Bayeux Tapestry (which depicts the Norman invasion) showing trees being felled, planks that have been cleaved, certainly of oak, being shaped and ships being built.

Ships became more important for trade after the Norman Conquest, especially for the export of wool and cloth. In times of war they were conscripted for defence and transport, each town or area supplying a specified number of vessels. Only a few ships were owned by the King and these were hired to merchants in times of peace. From the Forest of Dean there is a record of timber being sent to Bristol for the King's galley in the thirteenth century. One oak tree to make a boat was given to: 'The woman looking after the ferry at Newnham' in 1238 (Hart 1966). Oak timber from the Dean was also used to repair castles, when large logs were often transported by boat as this was more practical and far less costly than overland transport. Around 1300, Caernarvon Castle was maintained with oak felled from the Conwy Valley and Cheshire. In 1185 a fleet of ships carried timber from Chepstow to Kenfig Castle in Glamorgan. In 1430 oak timber was required to repair the King's barge at Carmarthen (Linnard 1982). In the fourteenth and fifteenth centuries shipbuilding in the West Country became important for trade and exports from Plymouth and other ports increased considerably (Finberg 1969). Protection of trading vessels over these centuries was therefore important, requiring control of the seas and 'Edward III's new gold coinage (1327–77) represents him standing armed and crowned in a ship' (Trevelyan 1952). This ship is similar to that in the Bayeux Tapestry and is clinker built, presumably of oak planks, with a single mast. This type of ship was known as a 'cog'. The clinker method of construction continued until the fifteenth century, when a change was made to carvel built ships, with more than one mast and a superstructure. 'These developments produced the large 'carracks' of the period 1460–1560 and in turn the sixteenth-century galleons' (*Country Life* 1978).

In 1413 Henry V ordered larger ships to be built like those of Castile and Genoa, including the *Trinity*, the *Holy Ghost* and the *Grace De Dieu*. The last was burnt out after being struck by lightning in the Hamble river in 1439 and was excavated in 1933. This ship had a keel of 112 feet, was clinker built with three over-lapping layers of short planks fixed with oak treenails (see below) and caulked with moss and pitch. 'It was the largest ship built in England until the reign of Charles II' (Abell 1948). Williamson (1959) states: 'in that large size the [clinker] method proved inadequate to provide a sea worthy hull.' In 1506 the King of Scotland built the *Great Michael* which '... was of so great stature and took so much timber, that she wasted all the woods in Fife which were oak wood' (Charnock 1800–2). She is recorded as being 240 feet long and 36 feet wide.

Tudor shipbuilding

From 1485, when Henry VII came to the throne the Tudors brought comparative peace to England. Henry VII had owned few ships and only built four during his reign, relying on using merchant ships and hiring others from abroad in times of war. By this time the oak forests, 'decimated by Roman iron smelting centuries before, had long since regenerated' and 'no lack of timber was felt or feared' (Perlin 1989). Perlin also states: 'During the sixteenth century the size of warships increased dramatically to enable them to carry their many and large and heavy cannons.' Building in timber, however, places constraints on the size of ships that can be built and much larger ships were only possible when different materials, such as iron, could be used in their construction.

Albion (1926) says that 'even when Henry VIII came to the throne, England had an ample supply of wood.' Much was exported as firewood and Boulogne was supplied with wood for 'ships, storehouses and faggots' (Perlin 1989). Albion states that 'the last twelve years of Henry's reign (1535–47) saw more oaks cut than in an ordinary half century hitherto.' On the Cotehele Estate owned by the Edgcumbe family on the Cornish bank of the Tamar, records show that all the mature oak was cut by order of Henry VIII.

During Henry VIII's reign, England began to manufacture goods and develop as a marine power. With increased trade, more and more merchant ships were needed. In 1532 a merchant and shipowner, Nicholas Thorne of Bristol, requested '200 oaks from the Forest of Dean towards building a ship' (Hart 1966). The growing scarcity of shipbuilding timber gave rise to the Statute of Woods (1543) which was directed at reserving woods for timber and applied to the whole country (see Chapter 3).

Henry VIII found it necessary to build up his navy to protect shipping and to keep the Channel open for trade. In the dry dock at Portsmouth, built by his father Henry VII, several new ships were built. These included the *Mary Rose* in 1509 and the *Harry Grace à Dieu* in 1514. This building programme required a considerable amount of oak.

The *Mary Rose* was Admiral Howard's flagship for many years and was refitted in 1536. She capsized in 1545 and has now been salvaged by The Mary Rose Trust. Her hull provides much information concerning the structure of ships of that time. 'The main hull is carvel-planked externally with oak planks placed edge to edge and securely fastened to the frames with wooden treenails' (Rule 1986). Treenails are: 'Cylindrical wooden pins used to fix a ship's planks to its frames. They swell with moisture when the ship is afloat, thus making a firm fitting' (*Country Life* 1978).

'Most shipbuilders purchased treenails, or trenels – round or 16-sided seasoned oak nails between 12 and 36 inches long, used to fasten the plankwood – in bulk from manufacturers. Most of the Hampshire builders bought treenails from specialist makers in Owslebury, a village east of Winchester' (Holland 1971). 'To fasten the plank wood 'treenails' – trenels – were used. These were turned from oak and made up 36 in. long and two inches diameter and as short as 12 inches and one and a quarter inches across. Sutherland says that the value of the largest size was £12 per 1000, of which the wood cost £10 10s. They were made of sound and seasoned timber, cut from the top part of the tree, so as to be free from knots and sap. Great skill was needed to drive them and the size of the 'auger' was a matter of concern. Sutherland remarks that 'an Augre of one inch and Half Diameter is suitable to drive a Trenel of one inch and ¾ Diameter' (Abell 1948).

Johnson (1996), discussing traditional wooden boat construction, writes: 'First come the trenails, or 'tree nails' – wooden dowels that were driven into tight holes and then wedged at each end. The trenail was usually cut from a well dried, tough and resilient wood – oak or larch (though only under water), ... Ideally, a trenail was split from the balk rather than sawn, so that the grain remained long and didn't run out at the sides of the trenail.' However, trenails lacked the strength and ability of nails and other metal fastenings to draw timbers together.

The threat of war and the fact that England imported arms and hired ships from abroad forced Henry VIII to start producing arms as well as ships at home. Iron masters were by then exploiting the oakwoods of the Sussex Weald and the first cannon was produced in 1543. From then on the arms industry developed rapidly and by 1549, fifty three forges and furnaces were operating and had made England self-sufficient in arms. The blast furnaces used charcoal from the oakwoods and it is calculated that '117,000 chords of wood each year' were used. The residents of Lamberhurst complained that the forge in their area had destroyed 'the most part of all the oaks standing ... Oak, especially from Sussex was preferred by the shipwrights' (Perlin 1989). Thus the requirement of oak for the Navy was in direct conflict with the iron masters who wanted it to produce charcoal.

A regular importation of masts began under the Tudor kings with the building of larger ships. Albion (1926) tells us that: 'In the early fifteenth century there were imports of masts and "spars de firr" [probably Scots pine].' ... the "oaken masts" which had served for the earlier ships were inadequate for the Navy which came into being with Henry VII and his son ... there were foreign masts in the *Harry Grace à Dieu*.

To build a ship required vast amounts of oak timber and much of it had to be obtained from mature trees to get the required shapes in the heart-wood, known as 'compass timber': 'Wood that is naturally curved or bent, and can therefore be used for various parts of a ship's construction' (*Country Life* 1978). Compass timber, also called 'grown timber', was so called because the limbs of suitable oak trees grow to all points of the compass and thereby provide wood of the right shape for the knees and bends required. Most authorities calculate that one to two tons of timber were required to build one ton of ship. 'Timber was usually measured in loads, one load being the amount that could be drawn by one horse cart, or the equivalent of forty cubic feet or one ton weight' (Holland 1971). In 1593 'just repairing four Royal Navy ships required 1,740 mature oaks, or about 2,000 tons of oak wood. To build a large warship took about 2,000 oaks which had to be at least a century old ... thus stripping at least 50 acres of woods. The great rise in shipping necessitated the felling of large quantities of oak, especially in Sussex' (Perlin 1989).

At Henry's death in 1547 the Royal Navy had been built up to '70 vessels of which 12 were between 250 and 700 tons' (Abell 1948). The increase in shipbuilding slowed down under Edward and Mary and it was not until Elizabeth became Queen in 1558 that interest in the Navy revived. At her accession, the Royal Navy only had eighteen ships over 100 tons which were serviceable, the rest having fallen into disrepair due to using unseasoned oak, probably containing sapwood. As many goods were now manufactured in Britain, trading was becoming much more important and many merchant ships were built. Control of the seas became necessary to avoid the numerous privateers of the time who plundered cargoes. In the first year of her reign an Act was passed restricting the use of timber for iron smelting and to conserve oak timber for ship building 'iron workers were prohibited from taking trees more than a foot in diameter within fourteen miles of the sea' (Albion 1926).

As well as rebuilding the Navy, incentives were provided for ships to be built privately in order to increase the number of commercial ships that could be used in time of war; it was also stipulated that ships built in England could not be sold to foreign owners. Anyone building ships over 100 tons received a subsidy; imports and inshore trading had to be carried out only in English ships. By 1592 'there were 177 ships built in England greater than 100 tons' (Perlin 1959).

In 1578, John Hawkins was given the task of reorganizing the Navy. He made changes in ship design and, drawing on his sailing experience abroad, they were built much longer and lower in the water than previously. The superstructure, especially the large forecastle, was dispensed with, enabling the ships to sail to windward. The smaller, second-rate ships (400 to 500 tons) were easier to manoeuvre than the heavier first-rates (over 600 tons). Under Hawkins ships were built of various sizes, the largest of which was the *Ark Royal* (800 tons). From this time the design of fighting ships changed little during the remaining era of sailing ships. By the time of the Armada in 1588, out of the 197 ships taking part in the battle, only 34 were naval vessels.

By the end of Elizabeth's reign in 1603, the total naval tonnage was 17,110 tons. This compared with 12,455 tons when Henry VIII died (1547), 11,066 tons at the end of Edward VI's reign (1553) and 7,110 tons when Mary died (1558) (James 1981). For every ton of finished ship two tons of green oak was needed; thus this represented 34,220 tons of oak wood used for naval ships in Elizabeth's reign. This does not take into account the amount used for the expanding merchant fleet and the numerous small boats used for coastal trade, fishing, river trade and ferries, most of which were built on their local rivers, mainly of oak. The ships of the East India Company, founded in 1600, were large and armed so that they could defend themselves on long voyages. Again in times of war they could be used as warships.

In the middle of Elizabeth's reign concern began to be expressed over the wanton destruction of the remaining oak forest. This was due to the high demand for smelting, charcoal, glass making, domestic fuel, building (many merchants who had made fortunes were building elaborate houses using oak for construction and containing decorative oak panelling and furniture) as well as for shipbuilding. To bring in money, Elizabeth had sold licences for extensive cutting rights in the Royal Forests and this reduced the timber available to the Navy from this source. In 1580 Lord Burleigh, the Lord High Treasurer, investigated the amount of oak being felled, legally and illegally, and was concerned enough to order 'thirteen acres of Cranbourne Walk in Windsor Park to be sown with acorns. This is credited as the oldest regular and authenticated plantation that can be shown and 50 years later it had developed into a wood of some thousands of tall young trees' (Albion 1926).

Stuart shipbuilding

Little, however, was done in practice to halt the felling of oak in Elizabeth's reign and James I (1603–25) continued to grant cutting licences in the Royal forests. As fears were being expressed on the amount of oak timber remaining for naval ships, in 1608 James ordered a survey of the Royal forests to see what he could sell. The survey stated that 500,000 loads of timber were available for naval purposes (Abell 1948). If the survey had been acted upon and the Royal forests had been properly managed, a sufficient supply of oak timber could have been maintained but instead it was squandered through inefficiency and wanton felling. In addition to building new naval ships, repairs had to be carried out on existing ships. The East India Company also needed as much timber to build one of their ships as the navy and 'between 1675 and 1680 it built some sixteen large ships with burdens up to 1300 tons' (Abell 1948). The oak used in these ships was the best as 'in Stuart times the East India Company owned some thirty great vessels for the voyage round the Cape ... [the] great ships that survived were so strongly built of the best English oak as to be able to face the high seas for thirty or even for sixty years' (Trevelyan 1944).

Charles I (1625–49) continued the exploitation of the Royal Forests as he needed money. Many Royal forests were sold off, including Feckenham in Leicestershire, Selwood in Wiltshire and part of Rockingham, Northamptonshire. In a bid to further increase revenues, Charles tried to extend the boundaries of some of the Royal forests. These policies were unpopular and when he wished to build more ships, including the large *Sovereign of the Seas*, timber had to be sought as far away from Woolwich as Sherwood Forest in Nottinghamshire and Chopwell Wood in County Durham.

The *Sovereign of the Seas* was the largest ship to be built since Henry VIII's *Harry Grace à Dieu*. Her keel was reputed to be 126 feet long. It was laid down in 1637 and the ship remained in service until 1696. She was of 1,522 tons burden and her builder, Phineas Pett, selected the timbers in the forest, mainly from Chopwell Wood. For this he employed moulds (templates) so that the timber of the right shape could be cut on site. It was then transported to Woolwich and assembled. This procedure avoided the wastage which was inevitable when whole trees were transported as on arrival at the dockyard, many were found to be unsuitable or rotten and knees and other components were cut to shape instead of using grown timbers, producing a weaker construction. By selecting in the forest, unsound wood could be rejected, reducing the cost of transport and making full use of the wood purchased. However, this involved experienced shipwrights selecting the timber in the forest. Most of the time it was easier to cut down the trees and ship them to the dockyards, as all this could be done with unskilled labour. The care taken in building the *Sovereign* meant that she was in service for sixty years and might have lasted longer if she had not been destroyed by fire at Chatham in 1696 (Loudon 1838).

Most oak timber for shipbuilding was transported by water on slow sloops known as 'timber hoys', which navigated along the coast to the dockyards. These were easily overpowered and 'the Turks captured timber cargoes bound from Dean Forest to Plymouth in the reign of Charles I' (Albion 1926). In many areas, most of the oak near rivers had been cut and it therefore had to be transported overland. This was much more expensive and raised the price of oak as transport could only be undertaken in dry weather; wet conditions made haulage too difficult. Loads were often abandoned for the winter and could be in transport for two years or more. As a result much large oak, suitable for ship building, was cut up as it was too costly to transport. The horse drawn cart could carry about a ton per load but larger logs needed extra pulling power. For the 'great keelson of the *Sovereign of the Seas*, described in 1637: 'One great piece of timber, which made the keelson, was so great and weighty that twenty eight oxen and four horses with much difficulty drew it from the place where it grew, and from whence it was cut, down unto the water side ..., A century or two later, the Navy would gladly have made twice that effort if such logs had been available' (Albion 1926).

During the reigns of James and Charles, overseas trade increased and as well as trade to the east, trade to the west opened up. One of the most important areas was the Newfoundland cod fishery which expanded rapidly and many ships were built by private owners to take part in this trade. This was particularly true of the West Country and ports such as Plymouth and Dartmouth sent many ships on this enterprise, some of which were built locally on West Country rivers. In 1615 'a 100 ton ship with 40 men' was the standard size and 'in 1634 to 1637 there were said to be 500 English ships in the trade' (Williamson 1959). By the end of these two reigns, the shortage of oak timber for ship building was again acute and was reflected in rapidly rising prices.

The Civil War (1642–49) followed, when both the Royal forests and private estates belonging to Royalist families were denuded of their timber. Royalists were heavily fined and they 'often had to fell their oaks to meet the unusual penalties. By 1644, the Earl of Thanet alone had lost from his estate timber to the value of £20,000 – enough to build at least ten ships of the line.' In addition, the Navy was allowed 'to take whatever oak they needed from the Royal Forests, parks and chases' (Albion 1926). In the Forest of Dean 'fifty thousand trees have been destroyed since 1641' (Perlin 1989). In 1655, Hartlib wrote: 'Yet at this time it is very rare to see a good timber tree in a wood' and 'we fell continually and never plant or take care for posterity.'

During the Commonwealth (1649–60) the fleet needed to be built up again to protect trading interests in the Channel as Royalist ships were attacking and pirating cargoes from overseas, thereby undermining the economy. The Dutch too were becoming trade rivals and this led to the Dutch Wars. 'The tonnage of the fleet was raised 2½ times in 11 years' (Abell 1948) and at the Restoration of Charles II in 1660 was '57,463 tons' (James 1981). The supply of timber for these ships was easily obtained from confiscated Royalist estates and Royal forests. In the Forest of Dean at Lydney, frigates were built in 1656 and 1660 and other ships were repaired (Hart 1966).

By 1660, when Charles II was restored to the throne, oak timber had become expensive and was in short supply. Now serious thought had to be given to providing a future supply of naval oak timber and: 'The Navy Board ... appealed to the Royal Society for advice' (Albion 1926). This was given by Evelyn in 1664 in *Sylva*. As a result, private people began to plant trees and Charles II interested himself in the supply of naval timber. Six years later Evelyn (1670) wrote: 'There is not a cheaper, easier, or more prompt expedient to advance Ship timber, than to solicit that in all his Majesties Forests, Woods and Parks, the spreading oak ... be cherish'd.' The Royal forests had all been exploited and the Forest of Dean had been devastated by felling for smelting, domestic purposes and shipbuilding. In 1668 an Act stated '11,000 acres of waste land were to be enclosed at once and planted with oak' and another Act for the New Forest in 1698 stipulated that 2,000 acres 'be set with young oaks at once and 200 acres a year for twenty years' (Albion 1926). These plantings were not however continued by later governments and although there were still 68 Royal Forests, only three were of importance for shipbuilding supplies: the Forest of Dean, the New Forest and Alice Holt Forest. The Dean had long been famous for its oak and it is said that on one of the Armada ships 'orders were found for the destruction of oaks in Dean as a blow to England's sea power' (Albion 1926).

James II (1685–88) continued to expand the fleet but the pressure on the woods eased a little due to the increased use of coal for heating and smelting. There was however still competition for shipbuilding timber from the increasing merchant fleet as trade overseas was expanding. In the 1680s oak timber from the Gwydyr Estate in North Wales was sawn into planks and floated down the River Conwy. Some of it went to local shipbuilders but most was supplied to Liverpool shipwrights (Linnard 1982).

Towards the end of the seventeenth century any ship timber within twenty miles of a river had been exploited but oak was still available if a sufficient price was paid to include transport overland. The Great Fire of London in 1666 meant there was further demand for oak timber as it was ordained that: 'When rebuilding London after the Fire in 1666 only oak was allowed to be used for Roofs, Doors and Windows' (eleventh Report of the Commissioners). Oak plank was in very short supply for shipbuilding and was brought from Ireland and imported from Poland. In addition to felled timber, much was lost to severe storms. Hart (1966) records a storm in 1634 which blew down 1,000 trees and another in 1662 which destroyed 3,000 oaks in the Forest of Dean. The great storm of 1703 was recorded by a number of authors, including Evelyn (1706), who wrote: 'I still feel, the dismal groans of our forests, when that last dreadful hurricane [happening on 26 November 1703] subverted so many thousands of goodly Oaks, prostrating the trees, laying them in ghastly postures, like whole regiments fallen in battle ... The public accounts return no less than 3,000 brave oaks in one park only of the Forest of Dean blown down; in the New Forest in Hampshire, about 4,000 and in about 450 Parks and Groves, from 200 large trees to 1,000 of excellent timber. Sir Edward Harly had 1,300 blown down, myself above 2,000.' In the same gale the navy lost about 70 ships out of 130 lying off Portsmouth.

After the Dutch wars, many naval ships were damaged and unserviceable but there was not enough good timber, especially compass timber, available of the large sizes needed for repairs. The Navy also needed to build new, large ships and the scarcity of compass timber became critical. Suitable trees had to be sought out by the shipwrights and purchased in small quantities, one of whom wrote: 'Called on the widow Gulledge and marked out several pieces of compass timber which we bought of her' (Albion 1926). However, much of this hard won timber was wasted as it was not seasoned properly and as a result the new ships did not last. In 1684 Pepys found 'new ships ready to sink at the moorings, timbers rotted everywhere and the holes patched over as if they had just returned from battle, though many had never even gone to sea ... The green [unseasoned] timber was undoubtedly largely responsible' (Albion 1926). The shortage of large oak trees during the late seventeenth and through the eighteenth century (especially between 1730 and 1785 when the Navy experienced real problems with rotting ships) made it difficult to obtain the size of grown timbers in heartwood alone of the right shapes required for the frames of large ships. The problem was not so acute with smaller vessels, which could obtain enough heartwood from the timber of smaller trees; these could also be seasoned more easily. Timbers for the larger ships were therefore in some cases cut into the shapes required, instead of being obtained from timber that had grown in that form (Nichols 1791). However, cutting across the fibres not only provided areas where water could penetrate but also gave a weaker structure (see Chapter 4). In addition, sapwood was almost certainly incorporated, especially when timbers were squared in the forest for ease of transport (Nichols 1791), which would initiate rot. As a result, many ships were no longer composed of properly seasoned 'heart of oak'. Incorporating sapwood and unseasoned timber would lead to rotting and must explain why some ships had a very short working life, whilst others, properly constructed of seasoned heartwood, were in service for many years, as the *Sovereign* had been. When the demand for ship timbers was high, trees were felled all the year round but summer-felled oak needs longer to season and this may not always have been done properly.

Oak planted by landowners in response to Evelyn's *Sylva* from 1664 onwards were not always looked after and also needed a rotation age of 120 years to provide trees large enough to contain sufficient heartwood for the framing of ships of the line. Mature trees were thus in short supply at the end of the seventeenth and first part of the eighteenth century. As a result, trees were probably felled prematurely to meet the demand for grown timbers of the required size and sapwood was undoubtedly incorporated. Compass timber, previously from the larger limbs, was also obtained from the crowns of trees which contain a higher proportion of sapwood and some was imported. As Matthew noted in 1831: 'On the Continent of Europe it is chiefly the tops of lofty old trees which afford the crooks; in consequence, those we import are for the most part, of free, light insufficient quality'.

FIGURE 34
Oak for the Royal
Navy: the frontispiece
to James Wheeler's
The Modern Druid
(1747). In the centre is
an oak bearing a
heavy crop of acorns.
On the right,
Britannia sits holding
an oak seedling in her
hand while in the
background, ships of
the fleet are
assembled. The Latin
inscription translates
as 'the glory and
protection of Britain.'

The eighteenth century saw further increase in overseas trade and thus the
development of ports along the south coast. 'In the late eighteenth century it
was estimated that on one average day there were 1,400 vessels large and small

FIGURE 35
Felling and selling oak timber, from Moses Cook's *The Manner of Raising ... Forest Trees* (1717). The owner and his agent discuss the price with the timber merchant. The crooks at the opposite ends of the two butts in the foreground are most probably for ship's timbers.

lying in the Port of London' (Williamson 1959). Many of these were small vessels built on their home rivers and trading to London with coal, fish and grain. Large merchant men traded with the East Indies, the West Indies and

America. 'In the century after the Restoration the [East India] company's trade multiplied fourfold, and after that there was a runaway increase, with China and all the tropic east added to India as the field of business' (Williamson 1959). The East India Company ships were large, up to 1,300 tons, armed, and required nearly as much oak in building as an equivalent naval ship but had fewer ribs. Naval ships were also built away from the Royal dockyards on the Thames, especially at Portsmouth, Southampton and Plymouth; the latter port expanded rapidly at this time.

The planting of oak, which had received encouragement under Charles II with the publication of Evelyn's *Sylva*, slowed down and the policy was not pursued. The shortage of timber meant that in areas that were still coppiced, the oak standards that were supposed to be left for naval timber were felled on shorter rotations than was required for ship-timber and used for charcoal, buildings and smaller ships, often because of the difficulty of transporting large trees overland. Gilpin (1791) describes this: 'Some of the noblest oaks in England were at least formerly found in Sussex. They required sometimes a score of oxen to draw them, and were carried in a sort of wain, which in that deep country is expressively called a tug. Two or three years was not an uncommon space of time for a tree to spend in performing its journey to Chatham. One tug carried the load but a little way, and left it for another tug to take up. If the rains set in, it stirred no more that year; and, sometimes, no part of the next summer until it was dry enough for the tug to proceed. So that the timber was generally pretty well seasoned before it arrived at the king's yard'. By the middle of the century more ships were required urgently for the Navy, especially during the Seven Years War (1756–63) and the high price of oak meant that many woodland owners were persuaded to sell their old oak trees. The building of canals from 1755 onwards enabled more inland woods to be exploited, especially towards the end of the century. By 1763 'many of the counties had only a quarter, or even a tenth, of the woods they possessed forty years before' (Albion 1926). Linnard (1982) tells us that 'from 1754 to 1760 over £50,000 worth of forest oak was cut on the Gwydyr Estate and floated down the Conwy. The War caused a general shortage of naval oak timber throughout England and Wales.'

Between 1730 and 1785, many of the ships built for the Navy had a short life with extensive rot, similar to the problems reported by Pepys in 1684. The causes of this have been put down to various factors. Some authors (Rackham 1980, Whitlock 1985) have claimed that there was no shortage of timber at this time but all the contemporary writings and concerns do not support this. There was no shortage of oak wood as such, though for shipbuilding, particularly the larger ships, not just any tree could satisfy the rigid specifications required by shipwrights for different parts of the ship. Each ship built was an individual so that the constituent parts were selected with care. Not only that but individual trees provided timber suitable for a number of ships. For example, the famous Golynos Oak was purchased for the Plymouth Dockyard in 1810 and provided the following timber: 'The main trunk was cut into quarter boards and Cooper's stuff; the Limbs, one upper piece stem for a one hundred gun ship, one ditto fifty guns, one other piece seventy-four guns, three lower futtocks each one hundred guns, one fourth futtock one hundred guns, one ditto seventy-four guns, one ditto forty-four guns, one floor timber seventy-four guns, one second futtock one hundred guns, and about twenty knees, all of which were large enough for the Navy' (Jones 1933). Marshall (1796) states that two-thirds of the timber required to build a ship is compass timber and one third is straight timber. Compass timbers had to bend in the right direction naturally, to be free of large knots and to contain enough sound heartwood. To obtain the large sizes the trees had to grow fast for 100–120 years in good soil. They were sometimes de-branched to supply fuel, to feed the deer or to encourage coppice beneath to grow. However, this practice encouraged heart rot, which rendered the trees of no use as compass timber. The 8th Report of the Commissioners stated: 'The lopping of trees for browse for the deer, we conceive to be one great cause of the decrease of timber *fit for Naval use.*'

Trees were also subject to other damage such as 'shake' (Figure 18) giving defects in the timber, so that the number of trees recorded on a site bore no relation to the timber that could be used. In addition, if suitable trees were felled badly the timber was rendered useless and great care had to be taken to fell suitable trees. In the New Forest in 1758 when the Langley Oak was felled: 'The knees and crooks were cut off one by one, whilst the tree was standing, and lowered by tackles, to prevent their breaking. The two largest arms were sawed off at such distances from the bole as to make first rate knees; scaffolds were then erected, and two pit saws being braced together, the body was first cut across, half through, at the bottom, and then sawed down the middle, perpendicularly, between the two stumps of arms that had

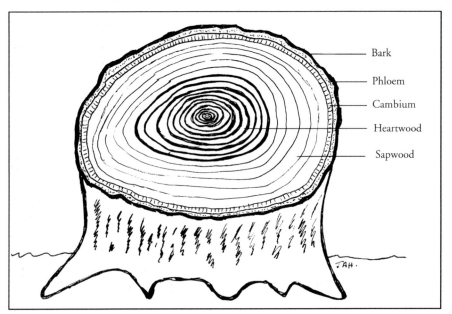

— Bark

— Phloem

— Cambium

— Heartwood

— Sapwood

FIGURE 36
A diagrammatic cross-section of an oak tree, showing the position of the dead heartwood, sapwood and the other living parts of the trunk.

J. A. HARRIS

been left, at the end of one stood a perpendicular bough, bigger than most timber trees. To prevent this being injured, a bed was made of hundreds of faggots, to catch it when it fell' (Loudon 1838). The Golynos Oak mentioned above was also felled carefully, the valuable limbs first being cut off and the brushwood from the tree 'was placed as a bed, to prevent the Timber from bursting in falling' (Jones 1933).

By the mid 1700s, the Navy was obtaining some of its crooked timbers by steaming them into shape. Wheeler in 1747 comments, 'since the invention of crooking ship timber by fire, natural bent timber has been a falling commodity ... Yet do not such builders pretend, that which is artificially crooked by fire, is equal in strength to what is so grown – I may call naturally this way ... but it must be owned every sort of that kind grows still scarcer, more especially the most desirable knee timber'. Nichols (Purveyor of the Navy at Portsmouth Dockyard) also points to timbers being cut to shape as he writes (1791) 'for I have known a great deal of timber much injured in its conversion by cutting it off to improper lengths, and giving it that form by hewing, which nature had never given it.' The shortage of compass timber meant that it became imperative to plant oak to replenish the woods. 'In 1759 the Royal Society of Arts determined to encourage proprietors to plant timber trees by offering gold and silver medals for the largest plantations of each kind of tree every year' (Albion 1926).

Nichols also commented on the shortage of naval oak in the New Forest and advocated proper management. 'Several of the woods in the forest, are almost ruined for want of this necessary work of thinning them.' He considered that with proper management there could be sufficient oak to supply the dockyards, especially if the final number of trees per acre was raised from 10 to 40 or 50; this was in contrast to the traditional method of coppice-with-standards in which fewer trees were left. He was also concerned that much timber was wasted as it was not properly seasoned and this resulted in early rotting which meant extensive repair work. This was often carried out with green timber which only made things worse. Nichols advocated slow seasoning, leaving the sapwood on to begin with so that the heartwood did not dry out on the surface too quickly. 'It is well known that oak timber of a good quality, when worked and placed so the air may act freely on it, and not too much exposed to the inclemency of the atmosphere, whether it be felled in the winter or the spring, will endure time immemorial.' Timber was also seasoned in salt water to remove the sap. In his observations on the Nature of Sap of Oak Trees (1793), Nichols observes: 'For want of examining ... the Sap of Oak trees, and the progress of its decay ... some have been led to imagine that by trees laying for any length of time the Sap increases in its thickness [i.e. becomes heartwood] ... but this is absurd and contradicted by experience; ... It will perish and moulder away, as the sap of oak trees always do ... Every experienced ship-builder or carpenter well knows, that wherever any Sap is worked with the heart of Oak (as it sometimes is), it will ultimately tend to weaken and injure the building wherin it is used; for however fair and well it may appear at first, it will most assuredly decay in a short time.' Matthew (1831) also observes 'the sap-wood, in all cases (except in those small craft used in carrying lime, which preserves it from rot) being worse than useless; by its decay not only weakening the vessel from the want of entireness of the timbers, but also acting as a ferment to further corruption.' He recommended taking logs whole out of the forest as 'the centre planks can thus be much broader than after squaring the log' (to make transport easier). When a log is squared, some sap is left on it and this 'when left on the side of the plank in the vessel ... is only useful to the shipwright, as it decays in two or three years and demands an expensive repair.'

Nichols also advocated building ships under cover to minimize the effect of rain water keeping the wood damp and initiating rot. To offset this he states that: 'If ... passages were made between all the broad surfaces that were brought into contact (which was a practice in use formerly, and called snail creeping) ... For it is found that after Oak timber is made perfectly dry, and placed in free open air, it will endure for ages ... The reason why small ships last so much longer than large is the Timber of which they are built is so much less and of course easier and sooner seasoned.' The original dry-dock at Devonport Dockyard (Plymouth), built in 1791, was the first to be covered with a roof. It was built in oak, resembling a ship up-side-down and was rebuilt (in softwood) in the 1980s as part of the restoration of the historic William Yard. Later other dry docks at Devonport were covered, thus: 'Between 1816 and 1830 the slips were covered in as were the North Dock and the New North Dock. The covering of the slips and docks was an effort to protect ships from the deterioration imposed upon them by the weather. New ships often rotted upon the slips before they even touched the water and financial implications alone were serious. In those days it took about 2,000 trees to build a 74-gun ship and the value of the hull alone of a three decker was not less than £100,000.' (Dicker 1969).

Nichols found that because of the shortage of compass timber, shipwrights preferred to have timber delivered to the yards in a rough state so that they could more easily select what they wanted. He visited various shipyards to find out exactly what shipwrights needed, including Mr Adams at Buckler's Hard in 1791. 'I called on Mr Adams, the ship builder at Buckler's-hard, who I believe has built more men of war for Government than any other private builder in the kingdom. I asked him some questions concerning the mould [shape] of timber in the woods, in the different parts of the country, for the several purposes of ship building. He said that it was impossible to be done, (it is to be observed that Mr Adams is allowed to have been one of the best converters of timber in the trade;) and that he always wished to have his timber brought to his yard rough hewed, as in that state he could take every advantage in converting it to the best and most profitable uses; ... tho' frequently from great distances by land, at a very heavy expense.' Other shipwrights that Nichols interviewed were of the same opinion and preferred to select what they wanted from the rough logs as compass timber was so difficult to obtain. In 1789 and 1790 Nichols had standing trees stripped of their bark to provide a source of seasoned oak treenails.

The ships being built in the mid-eighteenth century had changed little in general design from those of Elizabethan times. Some figures give us an idea of the vast quantity of timber incorporated in British ships at the height of Britain's imperial expansion. The larger ships had four decks: the hold, orlop, gun and main decks. In 1759 a ship carrying 74 guns with a 166 foot gun deck and whose burden was 1,610 tons required the following timbers for its construction. Straight oak 720 loads; compass oak (any timber that curved five inches in 12 feet) 1890 loads; knees 150 loads; 'thick stuff' (planks over four and a half to 10 inches thick) 410 loads; thinner or cut oak plank (two to four inches thick) 300 loads: out of a total including other timbers (elm and fir) of 3,700 loads, thus 94 per cent was of oak. A load was about 50 cubic feet, rather more than a ton in weight. Another ship built in 1760 required 2,810 loads of oak out of a total of 3,010 loads of timber. In the latter: 'The main timbers, with knees, took up some 75 per cent of the total, the thick stuff over 14 per cent, and the planking 10 per cent … oak formed nearly 95 per cent of the total figure' (Abell 1948). A 120 gun ship needed 6,000 loads of oak timber, an 84 gun ship, 4,400 loads and a frigate, 2,400 loads (First Report of the Select Committee 1849). In addition, large numbers of oak treenails were used to fix the planks. In 1788, there were 413,667 tons of naval shipping, in 1792, there were 79,913 tons of East India Company shipping and in 1790 the tonnage of merchant shipping was 1,480, 990 (Nichols 1793).

Oak trees needed to be grown in different ways depending on whether the end product was for compass timber or planks. For compass timber open grown oak was used, such as those growing in wood pasture or hedges. They had to be at least 120 years old to provide the sizes needed with enough heartwood. Trees for planking could be harvested earlier and were grown close together to provide the straight timber needed for planks. Planking was used whilst green so that it could be bent to shape whilst being fitted on the frames.

In the late eighteenth century the East India Company was still competing for timber with the Navy and their ships used as much as the smaller naval warships. The Company was able to bid higher prices for better timber than the Navy and the Company ships were constructed carefully so that they lasted considerably longer. 'On several occasions, the East India Company was ordered to reduce the size of the timber used in its ships, and in 1771, it was ordered to suspend construction until its tonnage was reduced to a specified level' (Albion 1926). The surveyor of the Company at that time was Gabriel Snodgrass and he was the first to use iron for the knees of the ships instead of compass timber. He also advocated a change in the shape of the hull, which by being less rounded, would not require so much timber. To protect the hull timbers, copper sheathing was introduced. 'In 1761 the outer skin was coated with thin sheets of copper to prevent "fouling" … in the Tropics … This practice of sheathing vessels … in the Tropics was in use until recent times' (Abell 1948).

Merchant shipping was using three times the amount of oak as that used in the naval dockyards because the various navigation acts of Charles II stipulated that trading vessels should only be built in Britain. Most of the smaller merchant ships were built in northern ports, the southern ports concentrating on naval ships. The smaller naval ships were built at suitable sites along the coast on contract but the larger ships and East India Company trading vessels were mainly built by the big naval dockyards, mostly on the Thames. Smaller ships were built in suitable places along the riverside or on the shore. Between 1650 and 1814 over 150 were launched from yards in the Southampton area using New Forest oak. Many were trading ships but contracts were also taken for naval vessels to provide Nelson's oak-walled sea power. The *Agamemnon*, built at Buckler's Hard in Hampshire in 1781, was one of Nelson's favourite ships. Attention was given to reducing decay in oak hulls in order to save timber and by 1771, ships had to 'stand in their frames' for a year before being planked up in order that the framing wood had time to season and planking timber was placed in stacks for some six months so that a current of air passed between them. Experiments were conducted to compare the durability of winter- and spring-felled oak. It is recorded that, following this experiment, two ships built of winter-felled oak required few repairs for twenty years in comparison with those built of spring-felled oak in which the sap had risen and which had not been given time to season properly. The sloop *Hawk* was built with one side of winter-felled and the other of summer-felled oak. When taken to pieces, the officers could not decide which was which so all must have seasoned properly (First Report of the Commissioners 1787) but there is no record of the length of time allowed for seasoning. Much of the timber used for shipbuilding had previously been felled in the spring because when the sap was up it was easier to strip the bark for tanning, this being a valuable by-product.

Experiments were also carried out at New Park in the New Forest to assess the relative value of pedunculate and sessile oak, there being prejudice towards the latter; the long fibres of fast grown pedunculate oak were believed to be effective in reducing the impact of cannon balls. The results do not appear to be available. A ship called the *Vindictive* was later built of mixed timbers for the purpose 'of trying the relative strength of both of them' but no results appear to have been recorded (First Report of the Select Committee 1849).

These reports were made to assess the supply of oak available at various times. Albion (1926) states: 'Commissioners of Land Revenue were appointed in 1787 to investigate the condition of the Royal Forest and other crown lands ... their seventeen reports are excellent sources for the history of England's forest policy.' As well as all the former competing uses for oak timber, oak trees were now being felled to convert woodland to growing corn as this was more profitable. The Commissioners of Land Revenue in 1788 stated: 'The oak, to become a great timber, requires the strongest and deepest soil, which being also the most profitable for agriculture, is the least likely to be employed by individuals in raising timber.' Large oak trees and compass timbers were virtually unobtainable as many hedgerow trees had been felled and removed to make large cornfields. These reports also highlighted the drastic fall in oak reserves in the Royal forests and they recommended that

PRIME MAIDEN
Timber, and Pollards,
IN FARWAY, DEVON.

FOR SALE

AT AUCTION,

BY MR. HUSSEY,

AT THE GOLDEN LION INN, IN HONITON,
On MONDAY, the 26th Day of JANUARY, Instant,
AT 3 O'CLOCK IN THE AFTERNOON,

117 Maiden Oak, Elm and Ash, TIMBER

TREES,

And 200 Oak & Ash POLLARDS;

As they stand numerically marked with WHITE PAINT, on *Cotshayes, Edhill, Widcombe and Lambrooke Estates, and Ball and Arrish Coppice,* situate in the Parish of FARWAY; in the following Lots:

MAIDEN TREES.

On Cotshayes.

LOT.		NO.		
1.	Ten Maiden Oak	1	to	10
2.	Five Ditto	11	to	15
3.	Ten Maiden Ash...........	1	to	10
4.	Ten Ditto.................	11	to	20

On Edhill.

5.	Ten Maiden Oak	1	to	10
6.	Ten Maiden Ash	1	to	10
7.	Ten Ditto	11	to	20
8.	Seven Ditto	21	to	27
9.	Five Maiden Elm ...!.....	1	to	5
10.	Five Ditto	6	to	10
11.	Five Ditto	11	to	15
12.	Five Ditto	16	to	20

On Widcombe.

13.	Twelve Maiden Oak	1	to	12
14.	Ten Maiden Ash	1	to	10

On Lambrooke.

15.	One Maiden Ash	1		
16.	Two Maiden Elm	1	to	2

POLLARDS.

On Ball and Arrish Coppice, in Widcombe aforesaid

LOT.		NO.		
17.	Ten Oak Pollards	1	to	10
18.	Ten Ditto	11	to	20
19.	Ten Ditto	21	to	30
20.	Ten Ditto	31	to	40
21.	Ten Ditto	41	to	50
22.	Ten Ditto	51	to	60
23.	Ten Ditto	61	to	70
24.	Ten Ditto	71	to	80
25.	Ten Ditto	81	to	90
26.	Ten Ditto	91	to	100

On Widcombe, and Ball Coppice.

27.	Ten Ash Pollards	1	to	10
28.	Ten Ditto	11	to	20
29.	Ten Ditto	21	to	30
30.	Ten Ditto	31	to	40
31.	Ten Ditto	41	to	50
32.	Ten Ditto	51	to	60
33.	Ten Ditto	61	to	70
34.	Ten Ditto	71	to	80
35.	Ten Ditto	81	to	90
36.	Ten Ditto	91	to	100

The above Timber is of great Lengths, large Dimensions, very superior in Quality, well situated for Carriage, and is well worth the attention of *Ship and House Builders, Coopers, &c. &c.*

☞ *For Viewing the same,* apply to Mr. EDWARD THOMAS, CARPENTER, in FARWAY *aforesaid.*
Dated Gittisham, January 13th, 1829.

FIGURE 37
A nineteenth-century notice of oak for ship timber and other trees to be sold at auction.

7,000 acres of oak should be planted in them for the future. It was also recommended that other timbers should be used for ship building.

The government was slow to act on these recommendations and it was not until 1808 that an official planting policy was adopted; by then the supply of oak from the Royal forests had virtually ceased. This policy was too little and too late, although planting went ahead in the Royal forests but by the time these trees would be mature, wood in ships would have been replaced by iron as a construction material. Most of the timber used was now coming from private estates. The Third Report of the Commissioners of Land Revenue in 1788 stated of the 25,000 loads used by the Navy each year, 23,000 were supplied by individuals and only 2,000 from Crown Forests. Many private owners, who had continued to sow acorns and plant trees, now had access to canals which provided cheap transport and 'in 1804 a total of 1,157 oak trees in the parishes of Llantrisant and Llanwonno [in South Wales] were advertised for sale in London and Swansea papers in the following terms; "the above timber is of the best quality, and fit for the Naval Engineer and other purposes that require timber of the largest dimensions, is situated within from one quarter or three miles of the turnpike road and canal to Merthir and a part of Cardiff"' (Linnard 1982).

The interest taken in the nurture of woodlands was evident in the number of publications on forest practice that now appeared. The emphasis was naturally on providing oak timber for ship building and Nichols (1793) advocated the planting of English oak rather than sessile oak. Wheeler (1747) writes of methods to train oak to shape which do not seem to have been satisfactory. This subject was enlarged upon later by Monteath (1820) who advocated pruning the leader to encourage side shoots. Tying down the leader was another method suggested. This subject is dealt with more fully in Chapter 3. In 1796 Marshall wrote in his *Planting and Rural Ornament*: 'When we consider the number of the Kings ships that have been built during the late wars, and the East Indiamen, merchant ships, colliers, and small craft, that are launched daily in different parts of the Kingdom, we are ready to tremble for the consequences.'

Because of the oak shortage, experiments were carried out by various people trying out new methods of construction and materials. Sir Robert Seppings in the late nineteenth century introduced various modifications which strengthened the wooden frames of ships and prevented 'hogging'; the dropping of the ends of the ship relative to the middle (Bradford 1966). This was effected by cross ties and extra filling between the oak frames. The shape of the stern and bow was also altered. These changes allowed the length of vessels to be increased. Six experimental ships were built by Bentham about the same time in an attempt to economize on the amount of oak utilised. His ships had straight sides and the bow and stern were identical. A saving of over 30 per cent of the timber normally required was achieved as straight oak planks could be used. These ships were wholly built of oak (Holland 1971). Frigates were also built of fir but these did not prove durable. In 1820 a frigate was built of larch, which was called the *Athol*, after the Duke of Athol who had planted extensive larch plantations. This ship gave good service.

The shortage of English oak in the nineteenth century meant that ship builders began to look abroad for shipbuilding timber. The repeal of the Navigation Acts and removal of import duty meant that the range of woods available increased rapidly. Oak planking was replaced by pitch pine and trading ships were now built abroad, teak being a favourite timber for hulls. Many other tropical timbers, such as mahogany, were utilized for various parts of the ship and English oak was used less and less. The railways also made the transport of timber easier from importing ports to the shipbuilding yards.

The decline of oak shipbuilding

With the coming of steamships, oak gave way to iron in their construction. However, in 1835, the first large steam ship, the *Great Western*, designed by the famous Victorian engineer Brunel, was built of wood and contained oak ribs close together, with iron and wooden diagonals for strength. She was in service for twenty years. The pioneering work of Brunel showed that iron ships were fast, durable and could be much larger. In the construction of iron ships, there was not the limitation on size exercised by wood and the availability of coal in the north meant that building of iron ships developed there. The navy then began to build the foundations of the modern fleet. The success of the 'iron clad' ships, the *Merrimac* and the *Monitor*, in the American Civil War in 1862, meant that the days of wooden fighting ships were over. Oak therefore lost its position as the paramount shipbuilding material. Apart from its use in the fast clipper ships which were able to trade world-wide without the need to re-fuel like steamships, its use was confined to fishing vessels, smaller trading boats and pleasure craft built in local yards on the rivers. Examples of such craft are: 'The "peter" boat ... the oldest Thames craft, built in large numbers and ranging from 12–28 feet for fishing with nets and long lines, mainly in the salt water tideway, though smaller ones fished well upriver, netting for eels, smelt and other fish. Peter boats were beamy and clinker planked on sawn frames ... Construction was almost totally of oak ... The workaday rowing boat of the Thames into the late nineteenth century was the wherry ... they were clinker planked on oak sawn frames ... Planking was often pine on oak side knees and floors' (Leather 1998).

The last type of working boat to be built in wood was the sturdy Bristol Channel Pilot cutter, recently described by Stuckey (1999), and designed to 'keep the sea' in all weathers in what is perhaps the windiest and most tide racked estuary in Britain, through which large quantities of shipping entered the Port of Bristol. To earn their living, the pilots had to stay at sea off Lundy Island or further out to sea in all weathers in order to meet the incoming shipping. Though dating back many centuries, by the early nineteenth century a special type of craft, known locally as a cutter, had been developed and was probably the most seaworthy type of vessel afloat. They were largely built of oak for strength and the durability that the timber could provide but Muir (1938), who sailed in one as a temporary hand in the pilot service and later restored two as yachts, described how unsuitable oak was for the top-sides planking. 'The wind had taken off a little but the seas were still enormous, bearing down on us in such over-whelming masses that again and again I felt sure she could not rise to them in time to prevent them from breaking on our decks and driving them in. One nuisance was that our top sides were leaky, and for the first time we had to use the pump to free her from the considerable amount of bilge water that had collected. This is one of the great drawbacks of oak top sides. Although this wood has great strength and durability it is a most unsuitable material for use in a position where it is alternately wet and dry. The wood swells with the damp and contracts with the dry exposure and spews the caulking very quickly. All the cutters I examined suffered from this defect, but the owners stuck to oak as the only wood that stood up to the rough work they were called upon to endure.'

One of the last ships to be built of oak in Britain was the *Discovery* for Scott's first expedition to the Antarctic from 1901 to 1904. When it was decided to undertake the expedition, Scott and his supporters gave detailed consideration to the type of ship required, finally deciding upon a traditional English 'whaler' hull shape, thereby drawing on the experience of the whaling trade. She needed to both 'sail the high seas and push forcefully through the looser ice-packs' (Scott 1905). Wood, in fact English oak, was decided upon despite the lapse of many decades since this material had been replaced by iron and steel. When asked his reason for this, Scott explained that steel 'is in constant need of repair; nothing but a wooden structure has the elasticity and strength to grapple with thick Polar ice without injury.' He wrote: 'The art of building wooden ships is now almost lost to the United Kingdom; probably in twenty or thirty years' time a new '*Discovery*' will give more trouble and cost more money than a moderate-sized war-ship. This is natural enough: it is the day of steel, of the puncher and the riveter; the adze and the wood-plane are passing away. It must become increasingly difficult to find the contractors who will undertake to build a wooden ship, or the seasoned wood and the skilled workmen necessary for its construction.' Scott describes the demise of wooden ship building as 'a strange ending to an industry which a century ago produced those stout wooden walls that were the main defence of the kingdom'.

When tenders were sought for the building of the *Discovery*, only one yard was found with recent experience of building in wood. 'In March 1900 the keel ... was laid, ... and ... the massive oak frames ... raised ...' The ship had a displacement of 1,620 tons, length of 172 feet and breadth of 34 feet. The frames of solid English oak were very close together to provide strength in the pack ice and were eleven inches thick. The bows too were strengthened with 'a network of solid oak stiffeners [to] give to this portion of the vessel a strength which almost amounted to solidity. No single tree could provide the wood for such a stem [bow], but the several that were employed were cunningly scarfed to provide the equivalent of a solid block' (Scott 1905).

An important part of the Expedition's scientific work was magnetic observation to be taken during the voyages to and from the Antarctic. The wooden ship had an advantage here and great care was taken to remove all metal objects from the vicinity of the 'Magnetic Observatory' when measurements were being taken.

There was a good deal of criticism of the design and construction of the hull of the *Discovery* at the time but her success for the unique task she was designed to execute vindicated her. Scott said that the Ship Committee and designer 'had provided us with the finest vessel which was ever built for exploring purposes'; a fitting epitaph for the last wooden ship of this size to be built in England.

There were of course a few smaller river trading vessels still being made but this ceased about the time the *Discovery* was built; one of the last was the *Garlandstone* constructed on the river Tamar between 1903 and 1909 by James Goss, largely of oak. She was 'the last wooden merchant sailing vessel, save one, to be built in southern England. Her frames were made entirely of English oak ... coming originally from woods in the Pilton area [North Devon]' (Greenhill 1982). She was a coastal 'outside' trading barge, one that went out to sea, of 76 tons and 76 feet length (Plate 6).

During the 1939–45 war, oak was once again in demand, this time for the construction of mine sweepers, as a wooden hull did not attract magnetic mines. 'The stem and stern posts and the keel, the floors and "grown" frames, the beams, and knees and shelves were all of oak, as was the "thickstuff" for the wales at the bilge and for the sheer strakes ... most of the builders of East Anglia built their vessels of oak throughout' (Abel 1948).

The contemporary revival

Today most wooden shipbuilding is for restoration or for pleasure craft. The renewed interest in the 'tall ships' has lead to the repair of old vessels and the building of new ones. Oak is still the preferred timber for part of the construction and restored boats are re-built mainly in oak. The yachting press, particularly *Classic Boat*, regularly features restoration projects and almost always oak is used for the main structural timbers.

The increasing interest in the restoration of classic craft since the 1970s has called for small, specialized parcels of oak again. In the south west and along the east coast in particular, there has been an active interest in boat restoration. Authentic techniques and more importantly, authentic materials are used, the most important of which is oak. Its use is only limited by availability of suitable supplies, particularly of knees and bends, so much so that keen amateur restorers scavenge West Country oak woods for them. Most restoration is of small fishing or trading craft for personal pleasure but there are an increasing number of larger, professional projects to restore ships for cadet sail training, adventure cruising holidays and display at historic and maritime museums. One of the latter is the *Garlandstone*, previously mentioned, now on display at Morwellham Quay in Devon, which has been restored by Tomi Nielson & Co. of Gloucester, using large quantities of oak from the Forest of Dean for the massive frames, knees and deck beams (Plate 6). The English oak originally used in the construction of the *Garlandstone* included the frames, seven-inch thick floors, eight-inch square deck beams as well as oak lodging and locking knees supporting the beams. She also has a fiddlehead at her bow of carved oak leaves and acorns.

On a more modest scale and entirely with private means and a lot of hard work, the Tamar barge *Lynher*, built in 1891 also by James Goss, has also been restored at Morwellham Quay. She was only 29 tons and 51 feet long, typical of many of the small craft that carried building stone, farm produce and other goods on the Tamar and other West Country rivers. Her frames have all been restored with locally grown oak (Plate 6).

Some years earlier and on the same river, the smaller 'inside' barge (one that did not trade outside Plymouth breakwater) *Shamrock*, built in 1899 at Stonehouse, Plymouth, was restored by the National Maritime Museum using entirely traditional materials and is on display at the National Trust's Cotehele Estate on the Cornish bank. *Shamrock* is 32 tons and 57 feet long with 35 oak frames restored as they were originally.

On the East Coast, *Valkyrie II*, a typical east coast fishing smack of 39 feet, as used on the Essex Blackwater river, was built at Brightlingsea in 1896 to a high standard by the well known builder of that time, T. Aldous, and was restored by Sarah and Dave Johnston in the early 1980s. New frames were made of three-inch thick oak and shaped by adze, a traditional ship-wright's tool which works particularly well on oak. The original deck beams were of one and half inch oak, as were the knees, the replacements were often cut out around knots to get the necessary natural curve of a grown knee. Solid oak was also used for the breast hook in the bow and the cleats; many of the latter are the originals which were reusable, testifying to the durability of oak.

These are only a few examples of the many wooden ship and boat reconstructions that have brought oak to the fore once again, albeit in small quantities, on our rivers and coasts. Many amateur sailors prefer it aesthetically to modern materials and value it as a durable material in constantly wet conditions.

Replicas of well-known ships of the past have been built, though not necessarily using traditional materials. The Icelandic *Islendingur*, a sailing replica of the Goktsad Viking ship mentioned earlier in this chapter, was launched in 1996. Other Viking replicas have sailed the old Viking routes in Russia. The famous ship found at Sutton Hoo in Suffolk has also been built as a half-scale replica, the *Sae Wylfing*, detailed earlier in this chapter. Also launched in 1996 and authentically built in traditional materials with oak carvel planking at Bristol is *The Matthew*, commemorating John Cabot's ship of the same name. *The Matthew* sailed from Bristol only five years after Columbus in 1497 with 'letters patent' issued by Henry VII, to look for 'New

Founde Land'. A replica of Drake's *Golden Hind* is another ship that has been successfully sailed across the Atlantic.

Oak had another use in the days of sail other than as timber. This was to tan or 'bark' sails. Oak bark was a vital ingredient in the tanning process because of its high tannin content. It was called 'tanner's bark' and cost £20 a ton to the fishermen of Cumloden on upper Lochfyneside in 1818 (Ostermann 1997). Very early sails were made of felted wool and then later of hemp or linen when oak bark was used to preserve them from damp, mould and rot. This practice continued up to the 1940s. Fishing ports in the past were crowded with red and brown dyed sails and up to the Second World War the tanned sails of the Thames barges were still to be seen in the river and over the Essex marshes. 'In Brixham in south Devon sails were "barked" with oak, a half to one hundredweight being used for a suit, boiled in water overnight, poured hot into a tub with red or yellow ochre, a hundredweight of tallow and a bucketful of Stockholm tar. The mixture was "payed" into the sails hot' (Ostermann 1997). In his *Sailing Drifters*, Edgar J. March, quoted by Ostermann (1997) describes how the hemp nets of the Mount's Bay fishery were 'steeped in oak bark collected from nearby woods'.

Oak still has, therefore, a part to play in future shipbuilding and restoration; well-built vessels of oak will, no doubt, outlive many of their modern counterparts.

CHAPTER SIX

Myths, Symbols
and the Age of Oak Trees

Straight Lelius from amidst the rest stood forth,
An old centurion of distinguish'd worth:
An oaken wreath his hardy temples bore,
Mark of a citizen preserved he wore.

Lucan

Of all the trees that grow in Britain oak holds a unique position. Not only is it considered to be the most important broadleaved species in forestry but it is also an attractive and long-lasting hedgerow tree. Its economic importance in the past has also made it important culturally, as part of legend and tradition. The oak has been called 'The King of the Forest', 'The Monarch of the Forest', 'The Pride of the Forest', 'The Glory of the British Navy' and 'The Stay of the Nation'. It provided the 'wooden walls' of Britain and to Chaucer it was the 'bildere oak', whilst to Spenser it was 'the builder oake, sole king of forests all'.

The oak and the druids

The oak tree is associated with various gods, including Jupiter (synonymous with the Greek god Zeus), the god of thunder, who lived in an oak and Saturn (also known as Baal, the Celtic god of fire associated with the sun), who was worshipped as an oak. 'The Celts worshipped Teut under the form of this tree; and the ancient Britons regarded it as a symbol of their god Tarnawa, the god of thunder' (Loudon 1838). The association of oaks with thunder is connected with the creaking and groaning when a large tree is felled. Whitlock (1985) quotes John Aubrey, writing in the seventeenth century: 'When an oak is felling, before it falls it gives a kind of shreikes or groanes that may be heard a mile off.' There was too, the fact that the twisting arms of old trees bore a resemblance to forked lightning.

FIGURE 38
One of the Gog and Magog oak trees, Wick, Glastonbury, Somerset. Appendix A, Number 237. They were probably dead in the summer of 2003.
JEAN WILLIAMSON

The oak was also a symbol of the circle of life and death and represented fortitude and strength. The Celtic calendar contained thirteen months, measured from one full moon to the next and oak gave its name to the month of 'Duir', which spanned June and July (Whitlock 1985). As trees were felled and groves of old oaks were left, these assumed religious significance, as groves of old trees do nowadays in, for example, Japan and China. Perhaps, too, the

131

timber circles which preceded stone circles took over the role of oak groves. This concept has been strengthened by the discovery of the 'Seahenge' timber circle on the seashore in Norfolk, dated to 2049 BC. This timber circle enclosed a dead 167-year-old oak tree in the centre, buried up-side-down, which obviously was of great significance (Bayliss *et al.* 1999).

According to Frazer in his great work on ancient myth (Frazer, 1930) the Druids, practising their religion in Britain before they were conquered by

F. Hayman inv.^t et del.   A. Walker sc.

The Druids, or the Conversion of y^e Britons to Christianity

FIGURE 39
A fanciful representation of druidism by the eighteenth century artist Francis Hayman. The druid in the oak is collecting mistletoe as the bishop arrives to convert the people to Christianity.

132

the Romans in the first century AD, held oak trees to be sacred. Their religious cults and practices were bound up to a large extent with oak and mistletoe (*Viscum album*), the golden bough. In Welsh, the word for druid is *derwydd* which, it is understood, is derived from *derw* – an oak tree. Wistman's Wood on Dartmoor, consisting of distorted, ancient-looking oak trees, has rather fancifully been put forward as a Druid grove (Plate 1 and Figure 1).

Nothing was more sacred to the Druids than mistletoe provided that it was found growing on an oak; such areas were set apart as hallowed groves. In these the priests conducted their religious ceremonies and performed their mysterious rites, some connected with the belief in the transmigration of souls, some of which included human sacrifices. It was their belief that when a mistletoe grew on an oak, it was of heavenly origin and was a clear indication that the tree had been favoured by the gods. The way mistletoe grows ensures that it has never been in contact with the earth and consequently it was endowed with celestial and mystical powers. Amongst these it was supposed to cure epilepsy, heal sores, tumours and ulcers, quench fires and enable women to conceive (Frazer 1930). Such properties, coupled with the fact that it was only rarely found on oak, gave rise to an elaborate ceremony whenever it was gathered. It is significant, according to Loudon (1838), that apple trees were grown near sacred oak groves. Mistletoe grows freely on apple and would therefore be more likely to transfer to oak nearby, or it could be that it was transferred to the oak by artificial means.

The first consideration of the ceremony was that the mistletoe could only be gathered on the sixth day of the moon, that is six days after the new moon had appeared and strict customs had to be observed before the proceedings could begin. Special baskets made of oak twigs, 'similar to that still carried by Jack-in-the-Green on May-day' (Loudon 1838), contained the mistletoe and were carried by the priests. The priest who was to perform the rite had to be dressed in white and provided with a gold sickle, knife or shears with which to cut the mistletoe. A white cloth, onto which the cut mistletoe would fall, had to be held beneath the oak to prevent the former from coming into contact with the earth. At the same time, two white bulls would be brought to the appointed place to be sacrificed (Frazer 1930).

The seeds of mistletoe are covered with a glutinous substance which stick them to birds' bills. To clean its bill, a bird wipes it on the branch of a tree, leaving behind the seed. Several suggestions have been made to explain why mistletoe is not usually found on oak. On trees with soft bark the seed sticks and establishes itself more easily than on the hard, furrowed bark of oak. Perhaps more important is the thickness of oak bark, as the seed needs to root through into the living phloem under the bark. This will be much easier on thin barked trees; for instance, poplar commonly carries mistletoe in France. Mosley (1910) refers to the view that the tannic acid in oak bark may be unfavourable to the establishment and development of the seed. Several bird species feed on mistletoe, especially the mistle thrush (*Turdus viscivorus*), which is sometimes known as the 'mistletoe thrush'.

TABLE 2: Mistletoe Oaks (listed by county)

County	Location	Year Recorded	Source
Berkshire	Windsor Forest	—	Maxwell
Devon	Near Plymouth	1870	Woolhope
Devon	Plymouth, beside S. Devon railway	1884	Elwes
Gloucestershire	Badham's Court, Sedbury, Chepstow	1870	Elwes
	Near Cheltenham	1873	Elwes
	Frampton-on-Seven (10m. SW of Gloucester)	1870	Woolhope
	as above	1904	Elwes
	Sedbury Park near Chepstow	1870	Woolhope
Gwent (Monmouthshire)	The Hendre, Llangattock, Lingoed (4m. NE of Abergavenny)	1870	Woolhope
	as above	1870	Elwes
	Penperlleni, Goytre (6m. S of Abergavenny)	1844	Mosley
	St Dills or Dials Farm, Monmouth (1m. SW of Monmouth)	1853	Mosley
	Near Usk	1860	Mosley
Gwynedd (Anglesey)	Plas Newydd	1857	Elwes
Hampshire	Hackwood Park, Basingstoke	1870	Woolhope
	as above	1873	Elwes
Herefordshire	Bredwardine (2m. W of Staunton-on-Wye)	1870	Woolhope
	as above	1870	Elwes
	Haven Farm (3m. NW of Mortimers Cross)	1870	Woolhope
	as above	1870	Elwes
	Eastnor (2m. SE of Ledbury)*	1838	Loudon
	Eastnor	1866	Woolhope
	as above	1870	Elwes
	Near Ledbury	1831	Loudon
	Moccas Park, Bredwardine	1904	Elwes
	Stoke Edith Park (7m. E of Hereford)	1910	Mosley
	Tedstone Delamere (3m. NE of Bromyard)	1866	Woolhope
	as above	1870	Elwes
	Woodbury Wood	1904	Elwes
Kent	Lee Court	1873	Elwes
Norfolk	Alderley	1866	Elwes
	Shottesham	1866	Elwes
Nottinghamshire	Sherwood Forest	—	Maxwell
Surrey	Bedlam's Court, Sunbury Park	1873	Elwes
	Burnifold Farm, Dunsfold	1870	Woolhope
	as above	1873	Elwes
	Seven miles from Godalming	1843	Mosley
	as above	1860	Elwes
	Richmond Park	—	Maxwell
Worcestershire	Knightwick Church (5m. E of Bromyard)	1873	Elwes
	Lindridge (5m. E of Tenbury Wells)	1873	Elwes
	Stoulton	—	Maxwell

Note: * According to Hadfield (1974) this tree still had mistletoe growing upon it in 1972.

Oak trees which are host to mistletoe are usually referred to as 'mistletoe oaks'. It was considered very unlucky to fell such oaks and disaster was predicted to befall anyone who was so foolish. The selective list of 'mistletoe oaks' (Table 2) has been collated from Loudon (1838), The Woolhope Naturalists Club (1870), Elwes and Henry (1907), Mosley (1910) and Sir Herbert Maxwell.

Fire was also important to the Druids and they were supposed to have control over it. Once a year, people had to put out their fires and have them re-lighted from the sacred fire kept by the Druids. Loudon (1838) relates that: 'This was the origin of the Yule log, with which, even as late as the commencement of the last century, the Christmas fire, in some parts of the country was always kindled; a fresh log being thrown on and lighted, but taken off before it was consumed, and reserved to kindle the Christmas fire of the following year. The Yule log was always of oak; and the ancient Britons believed that it was essential for their hearth fires to be renewed every year from the sacred fire of the Druids.' There were other festivals which included sacred fires, using oak logs, such as the Beltane festival at the start of the agricultural season on May 1st. May Day was connected with fertility rites, which included dancing round the Maypole and the selection of a queen and a king. 'The King was a tree spirit, the spirit of the oak, and appeared on May Day clad in oak greenery. By medieval times he had become known simply as The Green Man, or Jack-in-the-Green' (Whitlock 1985). Another festival was that of Lammas or Loafmas, when the first corn of the harvest was made into bread and consecrated. It was originally connected with the sun god Lugh and was celebrated on 1st August. This was carried on into Christian times. It is from this festival that the term 'Lammas growth' is applied to the late summer second flush of leaves which occurs more commonly on oak than on most other species.

Oak and the landscape

The religious symbolism of oak carried on long after the coming of Christianity and the oak is found in carvings in many churches (Plate 8). Hadfield (1974) writes: 'Again and again the decoration of these [roof bosses] consists of oak leaves – apparently a relic of old pagan traditions discreetly placed high up in the roof. Likewise, they are found in another secretive feature – the undersides of misericords. Foliated masks of 'green men' are not uncommon as decorations on capitals and ... oak leaves, almost invariably with accurate representations of acorns are found in every English cathedral and many churches. The remarkable fact is that almost always they are unmistakably pedunculate.' Perhaps it is relevant that this oak was more important than sessile for pannage to fatten pigs to tide the population over the winter. Pevsner (1945) notes that the carvings of foliage in York Minster and Southwell Minster, the latter near Newark, are particularly fine.

The numerous towns and villages with oak in their names reflect the importance and widespread acknowledgement of the role of oak in everyday life and may indicate where tracts of important oak woodland still remained. Names beginning with ac, ack, aik and ak, as for example Acton (London), Acklam (North Yorkshire), Aikton (Cumbria) and Akeley (Buckinghamshire) all originate from the word oak. More easily recognised are names with the prefix or suffix oak or oke, such as Oakengates (Shropshire), Okehampton (Devon), Okeford Fitzpaine (Dorset), Sevenoaks (Kent) and Matlock (Derbyshire). Less obvious is Eakring (Nottinghamshire), meaning the place where oak was growing in a circle or a ring. Place names which contained 'derw' (Celtic for oak) indicated oak, such as Derwent (Cumbria) – the place where there are many oaks near a river. The Oaks Estate near Epsom gave its name to the famous horse race, 'The Oaks', for three-year-old fillies, started in 1779.

As woodlands were felled, individual oak trees in the landscape became prominent landmarks in the countryside. Many provided meeting places or trysting places. At Tara, in Eire, the ancient kings met under an oak. Gatherings known as the Folkmeet met under oak trees. Later, shire oaks marked places where shire boundaries met and where Shire Courts were held. Boundary oaks helped to define land ownership and were often pollarded to rejuvenate them; they appear frequently in old deeds. Crosses of stone and (often oak) trees marked cross-roads, for example, Cross Oak Road at Berkhamstead in Hertfordshire. Many of these were gallow trees under which criminals were tried and hanged, being left as an example to passers-by. Gospel oaks (Plate 7) were so called because passages from the Gospels were read under them when the minister and his parishioners were 'beating the bounds' of the parish, usually at 'Rogationtide' three days before Ascension Day. Robert Herrick recorded this custom in a poem:

> Dearest, bury me
> under that Holy oke, or Gospel Tree;
> where, though thou see'st not,
> Though may'st think upon
> me, when yor yearly go'st procession.

Before the advent of Christianity, couples were married under oak trees. Later, although the practice was banned by the Church, after the marriage service couples might go and dance three times round an oak tree 'as ancient custom decreed' (Whitlock 1985). Marriages were also celebrated under oak trees in Cromwell's time (Clarke *et al.* 1987).

'Bull oaks' were old hollow oak trees and were used to provide shelter for bulls and other livestock. They were also used as prisons by local landowners. Such hollow oak trees were also used to shelter officials collecting dues on the turnpike roads; they were then known as Turnpike oaks (Whitlock 1985). This author also relates details of Dancing Trees, many of which were oak trees. He quotes Baring-Gould, who in the 1890s wrote about the Meavy Oak in Devonshire (Plate 7, Figure 40): 'This tree till within this century was, on the

FIGURE 40
The Meavy Oak.
N. D. G. JAMES

village festival, surrounded with poles, a platform was erected above the tree, the top of which was kept clipped flat, like a table, and a set of stairs erected, by means of which a platform could be reached. On the top a table and chairs were placed, and feasting took place.' Whitlock further writes: 'A certain landowning family [the Fulfords] held its land on condition of dining once a year on top of a Dancing Tree at Dunsford (Cheriton Cross), also in Devonshire. At Trebursaye, in the same area, the dancing was discontinued when a woman fell off the platform and broke her neck. Thereafter her ghost haunted the place until exorcised by the rector of Launceston.'

Many oak trees also became associated with events and people; these, together with the oaks mentioned above, are listed in the Appendix with the details known about them.

Oak trees were therefore always an important part of the landscape. In the eighteenth century they became an important component of the 'natural' landscapes created by Bridgman, Kent, Brown and Repton on many landed estates. Before their time, areas around houses had been formalised and regimented, laid out with avenues and rigid planting patterns. Oak was not often used as an avenue tree but fine examples still exist, for example, at Powderham Castle in Devon, Croft Castle in Herefordshire and at the Speech House in the Forest of Dean. Walpole (quoted in Marshall 1796) wrote: 'the tide turned ... Bridgman, the next fashionable designer of gardens, was far more chaste ... he banished verdant sculpture and did not even revert to the square precision of the fore-going age ... though he still adhered much to straight walks with high clipped hedges, they were only his great lines: the rest he diversified by wilderness, and with loose groves of oak ... but the capital stroke was (I believe the first thought was Bridgman's) the destruction of walls for boundaries and the invention of fosses ... an attempt deemed so astonishing that the common people called them Ha! Ha's! to express their surprise at finding a sudden and unperceived check to their walk ... The sunk fence ascertained the specific garden ... and the contiguous out-lying parts came to be included in a kind of general design ... At that moment appeared Kent ... He leaped the fence and saw that all nature was a garden ... the pencil of his imagination bestowed all the arts of landscape on the scenes he handled. The great principles on which he worked were perspective, and light and shade. Groups of trees broke too uniform or too extensive a lawn; evergreens and woods were opposed to the glare of the champaign; and where the view was less fortunate, or so much exposed as to be beheld at once, he blotted out some parts by thick shades, ... where any eminent Oak, or master Beech, had escaped maiming ... all its honours were restored to distinguish and shade the plain ... It was fortunate for the country and Mr Kent, that he was succeeded by a very able master' [this was Lancelot 'Capability' Brown].'

Kent also 'planted' dead trees to 'naturalise' his compositions. In Kent's time and the years following when Brown and Repton were active, many parks and gardens were fundamentally changed in appearance following Kent's lead. Individual trees were used in the foreground of the view from the house, often in parks grazed by deer and other animals. Oak, especially pedunculate oak, lent itself well to this situation with its spreading habit, stout limbs and rounded outline; it was described as 'the most picturesque tree' by Gilpin in his *Remarks on Forest Scenery and Other Woodland Views* (1791).

Because oak is so long-lived, it was able to provide a focal point in the landscape for a very long time. Further from the house, clumps were used to draw the eye in particular directions or to hide or accentuate objects further away. Careful placing of clumps provided a contrast with the background. Where large woods dominated the skyline, a few large clumps in the foreground led the eye to the distant woods, often of oak and beech. Clumps could contain different species and different ages of trees in their composition; evergreen conifers with dense foliage and upright outline contrasted with the softer outline, colour and shape of the hardwoods. These included oak, contrasting in shape and colour with other species, as it comes into leaf later and keeps its leaves longer in the autumn than other hardwood trees. The foliage is 'lighter' in texture and the reddish Lammas growth in August gave a splash of colour and new leaves when other species were looking 'worn'. Gilpin (1791) writes: 'We can bear the glow of the distant beechwood, where it contrasts at hand by a spreading oak, whose foliage has yet scarce lost its summer tint.' Clumps were sometimes planted with the aim of leaving one tree eventually but often the 'nurses' were not removed, negating the original plan (Gorer 1975).

Further away from the individual trees and clumps in the foreground, in the distant view, the landscape designers paid attention to the background of their 'living paintings'. Thus the skyline was given an irregular outline by mixing oak with beech and other trees. In the autumn the gold of beech was accentuated by the contrast with the still-green oak leaves which later turned brown. Brown was said to copy nature so closely that 'his works will be mistaken' as natural.

To achieve the effects they desired quickly, the landscapers made use of trees already present as well as creating instant features by planting large trees lifted from elsewhere. Main (1828) describes trees from 15 to 40 feet high being transplanted using a 'low oaken sledge' on to which the root ball was rolled; the sledge was then dragged by horse to the planting site. Trees were also moved on special carriages. Such planting was often successful as long as the relocated trees were kept well watered. The creation of these 'natural' landscapes attracted painters to record the scenes, of which oaks were often an important component, old and misshapen oaks attracting their particular attention.

Customs and kings

Oak trees provided a focus for other uses and customs. Wreaths or garlands of oak leaves and acorns had special significance. In Imperial Rome, wreaths or 'chaplets' of oak leaves were placed on the heads of those who had distinguished themselves in battle or the service of the State. Roman coins depict various Emperors with such chaplets. Evelyn (1664) notes that the chaplet or civic coronet referred to by Pliny, 'might be composed of the leaves or branches of any oak provided it were a bearing tree and had acorns upon it.' Oak leaves were thus as important as the laurel and palm in signifying esteem and success. The poet Andrew Marvell (1621–78) wrote:

> How vainly men themselves amaze
> To win the palm the oak or bays.

Shakespeare, in *Coriolanus*, at the beginning of Act I, Scene 2, has Volumnia telling Virgilia: 'To a cruel war I sent him, from whence he returned, his brow bound with oak.'

The oak was thus associated with important people in classical times. It came to be regarded as a national symbol of the British character owing to its ruggedness and durability; the specific name of pedunculate oak, *robur*, means strong and rugged. Smeaton, who designed the third Eddystone lighthouse off Plymouth after disasters had befallen the first two structures, took 'as his model the trunk of an oak, which so seldom succumbs to the tempest. This work was commenced in 1757 and finished in 1759, and the success with which it has braved the storms of 100 winters is sufficient proof of the skill of its projecter' (Murray 1859). The original tower, no longer in use as a lighthouse, now stands on Plymouth Hoe.

King Arthur, the legendary King of the Britons or *Cymri*, supposedly resisted the Saxons who drove him and his followers into Wales and the West Country. He is said to have established an order of chivalry, known as the Knights of the Round Table, as all were of equal status when sitting at it. The usual custom at that time had been for leaders to sit at a high table, one standing on a platform, above the rest of the knights. The huge circular oak table, 18 feet in diameter, that has hung in the Castle Hall at Winchester for several hundred years, was said to be Arthur's Round Table, but in 1991 tree ring dating showed that it was probably made about 1290, in Edward I's time (Hammond 1991).

Later kings were also associated with oak trees. The old church at Greensted in Essex has a Bible and prayer book the covers of which were made from the oak tree under which Edmund the Martyr was killed in 870 during the Danish invasion. 'The tree grew at Hoxne, in Suffolk and had become a giant nearly 20 feet round when it fell a hundred years ago. Tradition had long fixed on this as Edmund's tree, and it is remarkable that when the tree fell a Danish arrowhead was found in the trunk. The arrow is still in existence' (Mee 1940).

In the fifteenth century, Henry VI is supposed to have hidden in an oak tree near Ireton Hall, in Cumbria, after the battle of Muncaster. Similarly, after the battle of Worcester in September 1651, Charles II escaped capture when fleeing from Cromwell's army by hiding in a hollow oak tree at Boscobel House, 22 miles east of Shrewsbury (Stamper 2002). The tree there, now known as the 'Boscobel' or 'Royal Oak' is not the original tree but a replacement. It was probably planted at the Restoration in 1660: the original tree had been destroyed by people taking away souvenirs to their houses in the belief that this would protect them from storm damage. The story handed down is that the King was given peasant's clothes by a woodcutter, who tried to guide him to Wales but he was cut off by Cromwell's troops at the Severn. He then went to Boscobel, where he hid in the hollow oak tree by day and under an attic floor at night. He continued to wander for 43 days, part of the time disguised as a servant to an eloping couple, passing by Stonehenge and eventually reaching Shoreham in Sussex dressed in groom's clothes. From there he took ship and fled to France.

This story became very popular and the event is commemorated on 'Oak Apple Day' or 'Royal Oak Day'. This is held on 29 May and is both the date that Charles II was born and also the day on which he returned from France in 1660 to be restored to the throne. The day was designated by Parliament in 1664 as a day of thanksgiving for the restoration of the monarchy. Until early in the nineteenth century, Royalists wore oak leaves or oak apples (oak galls) on this day. The reddish young oak leaves were girls' leaves and the more mature green leaves were worn by the boys. Sometimes the leaves and oak apples were gilded. The custom was for people not wearing oak leaves or apples to be punished by being pelted with eggs or kicked or punched. In some areas, the punishment for not wearing the oak was to be stung with nettles. Perhaps fortunately, all these activities lasted only until midday. As well as individuals, houses, pubs and church gates were adorned with oak branches. At the Royal Hospital, Chelsea, the statue of Charles II, the founder, was decorated with oak boughs. In Northampton, children wore gilded sprigs of oak and the verger of All Saints Church there adorned the local statue of Charles II with oak leaves. This was in gratitude for his gift of 1000 loads of timber from the Royal Forest of Whittlewood to restore the wooden houses of the town and the church, razed to the ground by a great fire in 1675. Mosley (1910) tells us that railway trains in the north early in the twentieth century were decorated with oak leaves and ploughboys put sprays of oak leaves on their horses' bridles.

There are several other memorials to Charles II connected with this story. A salver or stand for a tankard, turned out of the wood of the original Boscobel oak, is in the Bodleian Library in Oxford and was a gift to that institution from a member of the family that assisted Charles to escape. The Barber-Surgeons Company of London has a silver parcel-gilt cup, the stem and body of which are in the form of an oak tree. Bells in the form of acorns hang from it, whilst the cover depicts the crown of England. It was made at Charles'

FIGURE 41
'The Royall Oak of Brittayne': a Royalist broadsheet from the period of the Commonwealth (1649–1660). Oliver Cromwell, the barbarian destroyer of the Golden Age, demolishes the British Constitution, represented here by the oak tree with its splendid fruits. The pigs being fattened represent the common people, and the soldiers of the new Model Army are busy overthrowing established social values. Oak has been used symbolically throughout British history.

request and presented by him to the Company. A memorial plate or charger was produced, marked C.R.2 and dated 1682, decorated with a border of stylised acorns. Charles also had a medal struck on the installation of his son as Prince of Wales, which featured a royal oak under a prince's coronet. The popularity of the story is also shown by the number of public houses with the name 'Royal Oak'. It was at this time that the oak became a symbol of loyalty to royalty and the nation. The name *Royal Oak* was also given to certain ships in the Navy.

Oak Apple Day itself, however, almost certainly reflects earlier traditions. At Castletown in Derbyshire, the Garland King and Queen ride through the village on Royal Oak Day but this tradition appears to predate Charles II. The tradition of naming King and Queen Oaks may reflect earlier celebrations. The 29 May was also regarded by country people as the end of the bird-nesting season and it was considered unlucky to rob nests after this date. Robbins (1992) gives a number of customs associated with 29 May, including a festival at Groveley in Wiltshire connected with wood-gathering rights and the commemoration at Durham of the battle of Neville's Cross in 1346, when the Scots were defeated by the English. Several other festivals are connected with this day.

Oak trees were named after other monarchs, such as Queen Elizabeth's Oak, and after important people. It is said that many of the oak trees growing in the grounds of Lady Jane Grey's estate in Leicestershire were pollarded (beheaded) on the day she was beheaded in 1554 (Clarke *et al.* 1987). There is a Chaucer's Oak, under which he is thought to have written some of his works. There was also the 'foul oak' near Hatcham, where the poet was robbed in 1390 for the second time in one day (Pollard 1919). In similar vein, there is a Shakespeare's Oak, under which the bard is thought to have written some of his plays. Many other oaks are associated with people. Oak trees continue to be the preferred tree for planting ceremonies today.

Symbols and sayings

Many honours and awards still link the oak tree with royalty and to the nation. Membership of the Order of Merit can be either military or civil: the respective badges are distinguished by crossed swords or oak leaves. In the armed forces and the merchant navy, the emblem of an oak leaf is worn on certain medal ribbons. Bronze oak leaves denote a 'mention in dispatches', a King's or Queen's Commendation for brave conduct and also for distinguished services in the air. The oak also features in the uniform and accoutrements of senior officers in the Services. Oak leaves, with in some cases acorns, are worn on the peaks of caps and were applicable on gorget patches. The ceremonial pattern sword carried by general officers incorporates oak leaves in the design of the hilt, whilst the enlarged end of a sword knot is known as an 'acorn'.

The oak, its leaves or acorns are featured in the design of regimental and other badges in the British Army, though some of these are now obsolete because regiments have been amalgamated or suspended. The badge of the Cheshire Regiment has an acorn with oak leaves as its centre-piece and its regimental journal is the *Oak Tree*. The badge of the Suffolk Regiment (now part of the Royal Anglian Regiment) was supported on either side by oak leaves and acorns. The right-hand portion of the wreath surrounding the badge centre of the Royal Army Chaplain's Department comprises acorns and oak leaves. Other regiments also have badges with acorns and oak leaves.

Oak leaves and acorns are depicted on some coins of the realm. The shilling and sixpence of 1831 carried a design with a wreath of oak leaves, together with olive and laurel leaves. The sixpenny and threepenny coins, issued from 1927 to 1936, depicted acorns and oak leaves on their reverse face. In 1991, the coins of Maundy Money still included a wreath of oak leaves. When pound notes were replaced by pound coins in 1983, four different designs were approved for the four constituent parts of Great Britain. The coin for England shows an oak tree encircled with the Royal Diadem; it was first produced in 1987 (Figure 42). Some cities have oak depicted in their seals, such as the

FIGURE 42
The reverse of the 1987 English pound coin, showing an oak tree encircled by the Royal diadem.

THE ROYAL MINT

143

Common Seal of Coventry of 1349 (Clarke *et al.* 1987). Oak leaves have also appeared on a number of postage stamps.

Many other instances of oak used as a symbol can be found. In 1936 the National Trust held a competition for a design to identify their properties; one showing oak leaves and acorns was chosen and is still widely used, whilst The Royal Oak Foundation is the National Trust's United States membership affiliate. In heraldry, oak trees, leaves or acorns are incorporated into the arms of individuals or corporate bodies. The arms of the Royal Forestry Society of England, Wales and Northern Ireland incorporates three oak trees bearing acorns and the Society's badge is an oak tree surmounted by a crown. Flowers of oak, which signify hospitality, are sometimes used as a symbol (Mosley 1910). In the Tynwald, the parliament of the Isle of Man, the oath of allegiance is taken whilst holding a staff of oak. This has replaced the original which was made of willow.

It is not surprising, therefore, that there are many sayings about this well known tree. The most obvious one, which used to be known to every country-born child, is:

> Ash before oak in for a soak;
> oak before ash, in for a splash.

However, other versions are known which are contradictory, such as those given by Mosley (1910).

> Oak before ash
> Have a splash;
> Ash before oak
> There'll be smoke.

and:

> When the oak comes out before the ash,
> There'll be a summer of wet and splash;
> When the ash comes out before the oak,
> There'll be a summer of dust and smoke.

John Dryden's poem about the lifespan of oak is often quoted:

> The monarch oak, the patriach of trees
> Shoots, rises up, and spreads by slow degrees
> Three centuries he grows, and three he stays
> Supreme in state, and in three more decays.

Shorter sayings about oak include: *Born of an oak*, a term applied to foundlings, as such children were often left in hollow oak trees; *sporting one's oak*, closing the outer oak door to one's room in an Oxford college; *sporting the oak*, displaying oak branches to show loyalty to the Crown, especially on Royal Oak Day; *mighty oaks from little acorns grow; heart of oak are our ship; heart of oak are our men* (heart of oak meant a 'stout, courageous spirit'); *Stag-headed,* a term given to dying oaks, whose branches resemble a stag's antlers (Figure 44, p. 150); *hey derry down*, thought by some authors to mean 'in a circle, the oak move around'; *fairy folk, live in old oaks*. Robin is an old fairy name and many of the stories about Robin Hood are associated with oak trees. Another belief in the past concerned the barnacle goose, ('bairn' – a child, 'acle' – oak), which was believed, before bird migration was understood, to have hatched from barnacles growing on rotting ships' timbers.

As well as being celebrated in literature, the oak tree is a dominant subject in many paintings (Clarke *et al.* 1987). Some of these depict oaks which have suffered from wind and weather and those which had been struck by lightning (Shakespeare's 'oak cleaving thunderbolt' in *King Lear*). In the past, because oaks were associated with the god of thunder, such trees were considered to have special properties and pieces were placed on houses to give protection in ensuing storms. In 1935 Bower published a table for the years 1932 to 1935 showing that pedunculate oak was struck about fifty times more often than sessile oak. This, however, would not be a species difference but would be due to the more isolated situations in which pedunculate oak is grown, such as in hedgerows and pasture. In support of this, it is significant that ash and formerly elm, too, were frequently struck; they grow in similar situations.

The Dutch painters of the seventeenth century painted dramatic seascapes and great sailing ships in oil on oakwood panels (Cordingly 1998). This is another example of the advantages of oak which can so easily be cleaved into thin slices of equal thickness and as minimum shrinkage occurs along the radius of the log when the wood dried (see Chapter 4). There are examples of such marine painting on oak panels in the Greenwich National Maritime Museum.

Oak bark, leaves and acorns were considered to have a medicinal value in the past, though the effect of some of the uses are questionable; they included controlling diarrhoea, preventing inflammation, stopping bleeding, curing rheumatism and killing intestinal worms. Oak bark, owing to its tannin, provided a substitute for quinine. A mixture of acorns, oak bark and milk was an old country remedy used to reduce the effect of poisons and infections in the digestive tract (Miles 1999). It was also believed that lying in the shade of an oak tree cured paralysis and other conditions.

Another unusual use of oak depended upon the fact that soil influences how a tree grows and that plants are able to tolerate unusual conditions, in some cases accumulating elements in their tissues. The following account from a manuscript in York Minster is quoted by Temple (1998): 'Sir Thom. Challoner Observed the Leaves of Oak Trees were (*sic*) the Mines are, to be of a deeper green than elsewhere and the Boughs more spreading the Boles Dwarfish but strong having little sap, and not deep rooted ... on which he conceited there was included some valuable minerals especially Alum.' This was in about 1600 and Sir Thomas had observed oak growing near alum mines in Italy. As a result of his observation, the first alum mines in England were found on his property in Yorkshire. Alum is a double sulphate containing both the elements of potassium and aluminium combined with the sulphate radical. All these chemicals would affect tree growth.

The age of oak trees

Finally we turn to the question of age, as great age is often attributed to oak trees. Thus the age of oak trees has long been a matter of interest and one of the most persistent beliefs about oak is that it is a very long-lived tree, rivalling yew in this respect. Oak certainly does live longer than most other trees but although a few single oak trees may indeed be quite old, this is by no means true of all large oak trees. Many are comparatively young but are particularly vigorous or in the most vigorous stage of growth. Mitchell (1966) found that 'fully crowned trees are usually not older than 300 years, after which the crown dies back, and only the very biggest pollards may exceed 700 years in age before rapidly disintegrating.'

Nichols, writing in 1791 about oak in the New Forest, was the first to describe how a tree grows. He realised that an envelope of wood was put on all round the tree every year, thereby increasing its diameter annually. 'Trees of all kinds increase in their diameters by additional coats of new wood annually formed by the sap, between the bark and the coat of the previous year (by which the age of all trees may with certainty be obtained) and these coats never increase in thickness.' We now describe this regular addition of new wood as annual growth rings. They are added all over the woody part of the tree; the trunk (bole), the branches and twigs. These rings are quite distinct in oak but on a large tree that is growing slowly they are narrow (because a larger circumference has to be covered each successive year), close together and often difficult to see. However, the tree has to be cut down to see them, so ageing famous trees in this way is not always practicable.

Loudon (1838) wrote about oak in Volume III of his comprehensive *Arboretum Fruticetum Britannicum*, which we have already quoted extensively. A short but particularly interesting passage discusses: 'The Rate of Growth of Oak' in which he considers the size of nine trees of known age in the New Forest, four of them of 60 years old and five of 120 years. From these and other records, he found a relationship between the circumference of the tree and its age when grown 'in a good soil and situation'. He found that his four 60 year old samples grew at an average of $5\frac{1}{4}$ inches in circumference in eight years (i.e. $\frac{2}{3}$ of an inch per year) and the 120 year old samples average $3\frac{3}{4}$ inches in eight years (i.e. $\frac{1}{2}$ inch per year), all measurements taken at six feet from the ground. He concludes that: 'The growth of a middle-aged oak is generally from $1\frac{1}{3}$ to 1 inch in circumference yearly; between its twentieth and its hundredth year, it sometimes exceeds this measure, and in its second century, falls within it; but, as the solidity of the shaft consists less in its length than the square of its diameter in the girthing place, a small addition to the diameter there enlarges the square abundantly. Wherefore, though the

PLATE 1. Wistmans's Wood on Dartmoor: an ancient oak woodland in an upland setting consisting, surprisingly, of pedunculate rather than sessile oak.

PHOTOGRAPH: JEAN WILLIAMSON

PLATE 2a. Oak woodland from which timber has been extracted by horse to avoid damage to the ground flora. Recently planted with sessile oak in tree shelters and a matrix of Scots pine and other nurses, the latter too small to see amongst the flowers.

PHOTOGRAPH: J. A. HARRIS

2b. Prime oak logs extracted to ride side for sale.

PHOTOGRAPH: E. H. M. HARRIS

PLATE 3. One of the venerable oak pollards in the park at Chatsworth, Derbyshire, dating from the late medieval period.
PHOTOGRAPH: RICHARD PURSLOW

PLATE 4. The modern use of oak for restoration work in the Lantern Lobby, Windsor Castle, following the fire of 1992. 25 ribs come out of each of the eight columns to form the vaulted ceiling above the balcony.

PHOTOGRAPH: HENRY VENABLES

PLATE 5. The trademark of Robert Thompson Limited, being carved into an oak coffee table top.
PHOTOGRAPH: TESSA BUNNEY

PLATE 6. The early twentieth-century Tamar Barge *Garlandstone* and (in the background) the late-nineteenth-century *Lynher*, undergoing restoration at Morwellham Quay on the bank of the Tamar in Devon. West Country oak was used extensively in both boats: for the keel, the keelson, frames, knees, the stern post, beam shelves, horn timbers, stanchions, covering boards, deck beams, carlins, coamings and for the rudder.
PHOTOGRAPH: MOREWELLHAM AND TAMAR VALLEY TRUST

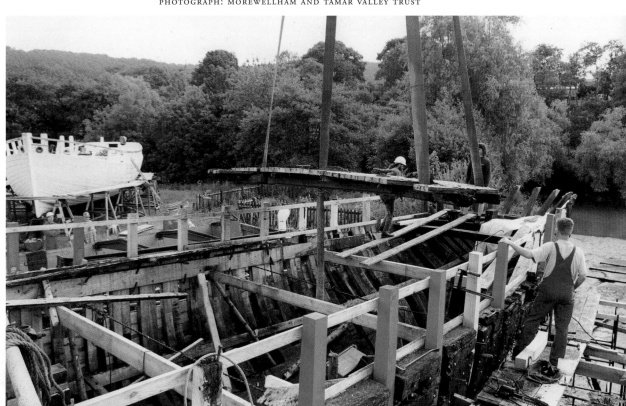

PLATE 7. The Meavy Oak, Tavistock, Dartmoor, Devon. The tree is reputed to be 800 years old and was used as a 'dancing tree'. Though much of the heartwood is gone, the tree still supports a healthy crown.

PHOTOGRAPH: JEAN WILLIAMSON

PLATE 8. The Green Man, with oak leaves and acorns, at the north end of the rood screen at St Melangell's Church, Pennant Melangell, Llangynog, Powys.

PHOTOGRAPH: MICK SHARP

PLATE 9. The Major Oak at Birklands Wood, Sherwood Forest, Edwinstowe, Nottinghamshire. The most impressive tree on the Robin Hood tourist trail actually commemorates one Major Hayman Rooke, an antiquarian who wrote about Sherwood Forest in the 1790s.

PHOTOGRAPH: JEAN WILLIAMSON

PLATE 10. The visual contribution of oak to the British landscape is immeasurable. Oakwoods in autumn colour, Dinorwic Slate Quarries, Llanberis, Gwynedd.

PHOTOGRAPH: MICK SHARP

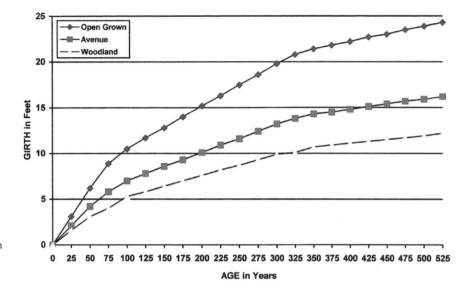

FIGURE 43
A graphical illustration
of Mitchell's formula
for ageing oak trees.

circumference from the 100th to the 150th year may not increase so fast as it did to the 100th ...'

Alan Mitchell (1966), who made a detailed study and meticulously recorded data of many trees throughout Britain during his professional forestry career, followed up Loudon's formula and considered ten oak trees aged from 26 to 238 years in locations ranging from the south of England to Wales and central Scotland. He also considered five trees recorded by Elwes and Henry in 1906 and from these data concluded that 'vigorous, large-crowned trees are likely to be 7 to 9 feet in girth at 70 years and 10 to 13 feet at 100 years; further growth is usually not far from one inch a year until over 20 feet in girth, and thereafter as long as the crown is largely maintained, the annual increase averages nearly three quarters of an inch, but under half and inch on less good sites.'

Later Mitchell (1974) pointed out that neither height nor spread of a tree is a reliable guide to age 'but the circumference of the bole of any tree must increase in some measure during every year of its life. The age of a tree is thus some function of the circumference alone.' Measuring 'the circumference (girth) ... at 1.5 metres (5 feet) from the highest point of the surrounding ground' and for trees with a full crown, he refined his 'rule of thumb' thus: 'Young oaks on a good site often grow 1.5–2 in (inches) a year for their first 60–80 years. From then on until they are 20–22 feet (6–6.6 m) in girth they maintain the "standard" rate [a rate of one inch a year]: Thereafter they slow further, the decrease depending on the loss of leafing crown. They seldom survive with a slower rate than one inch in 5–6 years.' This 'rule of thumb' applies to open grown trees; those in an avenue or slightly hemmed in will grow more slowly and Mitchell says, will be about two-thirds of this size, whilst in a wood the circumference will be about half. From the graph above it can be seen how open grown oak trees increasingly diverge in diameter growth from that exhibited by trees growing in close proximity to others.

Mitchell's formula can be represented in tabular form, from which the likely age of an old oak tree can be estimated, thus:

TABLE 3: Mitchell's formula for aging oak trees

AGE	Open Grown		Avenue		Woodland	
	Inches	*Feet*	*Inches*	*Feet*	*Inches*	*Feet*
25	37.5	3.1	25.0	2.1	18.7	1.6
50	75.0	6.2	50.0	4.2	37.5	3.1
75	112.5	9.4	75.0	6.2	56.2	4.7
100	126.4	10.5	84.3	7.0	63.2	5.3
125	140.3	11.7	93.5	7.8	70.1	5.8
150	154.2	12.8	102.8	8.6	77.1	6.4
175	168.1	14.0	112.0	9.3	84.0	7.0
200	182.0	15.2	121.3	10.1	91.0	7.6
225	195.9	16.3	130.6	10.9	97.9	8.2
250	209.8	17.5	139.9	11.6	104.9	8.7
275	223.7	18.6	149.1	12.4	111.8	9.3
300	237.6	19.8	158.4	13.2	118.8	9.9
325	252.0	21.0	168.0	14.0	126.0	10.5
350	257.0	21.4	171.3	14.3	128.5	10.7
375	262.0	21.8	174.7	14.5	131.0	10.9
400	267.0	22.2	178.0	14.8	133.5	11.1
425	272.0	22.7	181.3	15.1	136.0	11.3
450	277.0	23.0	184.7	15.4	138.5	11.5
475	282.0	23.5	188.0	15.7	141.0	11.7
500	287.0	23.9	191.3	15.9	143.5	11.9
525	292.0	24.3	194.7	16.2	146.0	12.2

Note: These are merely average measurements giving an estimate of a large oak tree's likely age.

Mitchell (1966) also drew attention to the effect of pollarding, a common practice in the past on oak and, as he points out, 'most of the biggest famous oaks are either pollards or have grown in a similar way, in that by the height of ten feet their boles divide into numerous main limbs.' He writes that 'maiden oaks with single boles of 20 feet or more in length are extremely rare at big sizes, and this may be because the value of the timber mitigates against their remaining for their natural span', pointing out that pollarding encourages regeneration of the crown so such trees are likely to be more long-lived and have large-girth boles.

Mitchell applied his principles to three contrasting famous trees, the Knightwood Oak in the New Forest, the Major Oak in Sherwood Forest (Plate 9) and the Newlands Oak in the Forest of Dean. The first was a full-crowned tall tree lacking historical measurements but as it still had a complete crown he judged it to be relatively young. Applying his formula, he thought it no more than 300 years old and perhaps less than 250. The Major Oak at this time had an enormous branch-spread but was dying back; it had been measured in 1906. Mitchell calculated it then to have been 340 years, i.e. about 400 years in 1966. Mitchell reported on it again in 1996 and his account is an example of how important it is to look critically at a tree rather than to assume great age from the appearance alone. He wrote: 'The most famous surviving oak is probably the Major Oak in Sherwood Forest near Ollerton in Nottinghamshire. It is nowhere near the biggest, nor can it be the oldest, but one is assured by locals that it is both. It is a pollard at eight feet with one great branch leaning out and leaving only five feet of bole. The central branch of the outer four is vertical and accounts for the tree having been sometimes said to be a maiden, but the others are grossly thick too, and arise from an ugly swelling above a poorly shaped bole with a narrow opening five feet tall.' He concludes that: 'Although ugly in some details, the tree has grandeur ... From early measurements ... its age can be estimated fairly closely as around 480 (*sic*) years.'

The Newlands Oak was also measured in 1906 and had been photographed in the previous century. In 1966 Mitchell estimated it to be 'rather over 750 years ... but may be around 1000 years.' He went on: 'Only a few churchyard yews can claim to equal this ...' He concludes: 'In general it may be said that oaks with wide, but complete, undamaged crowns are unlikely to be much older than 300 years however big they are, and that thereafter crowns die-back and break off, but except in a few old pollards they are likely to be dead long before 700 years; rare survivors lasting perhaps 200 years more. Survival in a shattered or branchless state is relatively brief.'

Large, apparently old, trees, then, are often not as old as is frequently claimed for them. Of the list of named oak trees forming Appendix A, there are few reliable records of age but, as Mitchell says, many have fictitious ages attached to them. Sometimes they may be replacements carrying the name of their predecessor, such as the Hunter's Oak at St Dominic in Cornwall; for others it is hard to say what is the original tree, particularly if hollow and new growth, albeit from the same root system, has grown up around a hollow core.

It is of course only the wood (xylem) that may be old. The bark and phloem (conductive tissue) outside the wood, having the respective functions of protecting the tree and conducting the sap-rich food down from the photo-synthesising leaves, do not last so long and give no indication of age. The wood when young and alive (sapwood) conducts water from the roots to the live crown but then thickens and dies, in oak becoming darker and very durable heartwood, giving immense structural strength to the standing tree. It is this that endures for many decades, being added to year by year (at first as sapwood) and from which a felled tree can be aged.

The Forestry Commission (1998) has taken Mitchell's work forward and made use of more recent data. Although looking at veteran trees as a whole, much of the research was done on oak in England. This was summarised by White (1995) who pointed out that: 'Accurate age estimation depends on making the right assumptions about the past growing conditions.' For instance, 'there may be evidence of large low branches or their scars which would indicate open growing conditions from the time the tree was young' whilst 'a long branch-free stem on a now isolated tree might indicate that it began life and developed in woodland'. He notes that 'on a good site the optimum ring area in oak is reached when the stem diameter at breast height [1.3 metres or 4 feet 3 inches from the ground on the highest side of the tree] is around 64 cm' [79.2 inches]. This is rather earlier than Mitchell suggested for

FIGURE 44
Stag-headed oak trees
in Sherwood Forest.
Their condition may
be due not to old age
but to altered water
table levels.
MICK SHARP

open-grown oak, which, according to him, reaches this diameter at 50 years or soon after, but is close to his 'avenue or slightly hemmed in' trees which reach this diameter at about 75 years. White (1975) goes on to say 'this feature has remained constant for virtually all (post-glacial) time. Even counts on "bog oaks" several thousand years old are fairly true to form, showing ring width decline only after this size.'

To demonstrate this in practice, Mitchell's formula and the Forestry Commission method have been applied to an isolated oak tree standing alone in pasture land at Harewood in Cornwall, producing an interesting result. The tree has a clear bole with no signs of previous branches for 3 metres (ten feet) and then spreads out into a broad, healthy crown carried on heavy branches, all arising at much the same point. It is not a tall tree at 14.3 metres (47 feet) (see photograph below). In 1999 the girth at breast height was measured as 2.9 metres (9 feet 6 inches). Applying Mitchell's formula (for open-grown trees) it would be about 75 years old but the Forestry Commission method makes it nearer 123 years (for an open-grown tree on a good site) or 136 years if on an average site. This gives a planting date (or natural seedling) of 1924, if 75 years old, or at the very earliest, 1863. However, the tree shows clearly as an isolated tree in a photograph of about 1880, in which it is some two miles from the camera so is already fairly large and indeed appears much as it does today. The land the tree is growing on, known historically as The

FIGURE 45

A pedunculate oak of
about 275 year
growing in isolation in
pasture on The Plain
at Harewood,
Cornwall. The clean,
10 ft (3m) bole carries
a short, spreading
crown of heavy
branches, indicating a
tree that started life in
woodland. It has
made little upward
growth since its
release from woodland
conditions at about
60 years of age.

E. H. M HARRIS

Plain, is rough pasture in the nineteenth-century photograph and was part of
the Harewood Estate, for which records exist. Going back further, in 1593 The
Plain carried oak woodland which was let to Sir Francis Drake, no doubt to
repair his ships at nearby Plymouth. It is not suggested that the tree is a
remnant of this woodland but the next record, in 1754, is of the then owner
planting 'many trees' and a map of the time shows them on The Plain though
without reference to species. There is then a record of felling following a land
sale in 1815, from when The Plain became permanent pasture, as it is today.

Could this tree be a remnant of the crop felled in 1815? Mitchell's formula
and the Forestry Commission method do not at first sight seem to confirm
this as they indicate a planting date of between 1863 and 1924. However, a
tree planted in 1754 would be 245 years old in 1999. If it is assumed that it
was a woodland tree, both Mitchell's formula and the Forestry Commission
method suggest that a tree with a girth of nine and a half feet in 1999 would
be about 275 years old. Perhaps it continued to grow well when first isolated
at 61 years by the removal of the rest of the wood but a tree already of this
age is very unlikely to change its pattern of growth dramatically to exhibit
the growth rate typical of a tree isolated throughout its early life. This then
suggests that the tree is indeed a remnant from the 1754 plantation and indicates
how the history of a tree can sometimes be ascertained by these ageing methods
based on predictable annual growth patterns of oak trees but also illustrates
that ageing by girth alone can have its pitfalls.

CHAPTER SEVEN

The Role of Oak in the Future

Wae's me, wae's me,
The acorn's not yet
Fallen from the tree
That's to grow the wood,
That's to make the cradle,
That's to rock the bairn,
That's to grow a man,
That's to lay me.

George Meredith

Today oak has a paramount place in nature conservation and this function is likely to become increasingly significant. The numerous 'enemies of oak' sustained by oakwoods, recorded by the Victorians and regarded as pests then, now have a conservation value. The light foliage of oak woodlands and the wide spacing of the trees at maturity maintain a good ground flora, as well as insects and bird life. Old oak trees in open pasture with decay sustain some rare insects and lichens (Harding and Rose 1986). Areas such as Windsor Park, Moccas Park and Shute Park are important in this respect. *The British Oak*, edited by Morris and Perring (1974), gives a full account of the value of oak to conservation. Knowledge of the past management of oak helps us to understand how to maintain the wildlife that it sustains. It is for this reason that coppicing is now being practised by many wildlife trusts and attempts are being made to revive the charcoal industry and to utilise the produce. Interest is also being revived in other woodland crafts as it has come to be realised that oak woodlands need management for their survival and for the wildlife that uses them; merely leaving woods unmanaged diminishes the numbers and variety of plants and animals that they can sustain.

It is often claimed that native oak, even very local provenances of oak, should be the only sources of seed for use in Britain. The claim is that only very local strains of a tree species can properly provide for the range of other species dependent upon it, particularly insects and fungi, and on oak there are numerous rare species growing on the tree or on rotting oak wood. This claim that native provenances are essential in this respect, however, has never been firmly substantiated and should not be taken too far.

Although there is a long history in this country of ornamental and fruit tree species, and more recently of north-western American conifers, being

FIGURE 46
Bethesda woods,
Gwynedd.

JEAN WILLIAMSON

153

introduced by the use of imported seed, this does not apply to such a great extent to oak. Lines (1999) investigated the records of oak seed imports for the 70 years from 1920 to 1990 which are held by the Forestry Commission and found that over this period 89 per cent of the acorns used for state and private planting were from home-collected sources. This is the same for the two species of native oak, both pedunculate and sessile. In 26 of the 70 years

FIGURE 47
Sneyd Wood, Sutton Bottom, Forest of Dean: a fine pedunculate oak woodland planted in 1929. The tree the figure is beside has a quarter girth of 26 cm (11.25 inches) at 1.5 m (5 ft), which indicates that the stand is probably yield class 8 – the highest yield class of oak.

no oak seed was imported at all and in several years there was very little. In every year from 1921 to 1955 some home grown acorns were collected and only in 1923 and 1941 was this less than 1000kg.

Lines also points to a tradition, of at least 200 years standing, for private woodland estates to collect their own seed for sowing in estate nurseries. Quoting from Forestry Commission annual reports, he writes: 'During the early years of the Forestry Commission, it is clear that a major effort was made to obtain as much (beech and) oak as practicable from home sources and to rely on imports only when sufficient seed was not available at home'. He concludes: 'For oak, nearly 90 per cent of the material passing through the Forestry Commission supply chain (which includes supplies to private planters) between 1920 and 1990 was collected in Britain and was, therefore of British provenance.'

Conservation in woodlands, however, is not the subject of this book. We have written of it elsewhere (Harris and Harris 1997) and there are many useful reports and papers on conservation in which the role of oak features prominently.

As we have suggested (see Chapter 4), one of the attractions of growing oak comes from the timber produced by it, both its special characteristics of strength and durability and its particular beauty. For these reasons, oak timber has a special place in Britain, both in the past as a timber of paramount importance but perhaps also in the future for specialised uses, for example in quality furniture and as such is already finding an increasing demand as standards of living, and thus of disposable income, rise. Oak has a future in the home, the office, in public buildings as a decorative material and in restoration.

Will oak also play a part, albeit very small, in the reduction of global warming by carbon sequestration? All trees carry out this function to some extent by absorbing atmospheric carbon dioxide during the process of photosynthesis, which can be summarised as:

$$CO_2 + \text{sunlight} + \text{mineral salts from the soil} = \text{energy stored in plant food} + \text{oxygen.}$$

As Cannell (1999) points out, this only represents a temporary reduction in atmospheric carbon dioxide, during the time that the carbon is held in the living tree, until the trees die and decay, are burnt or are manufactured into short-lived products such as paper or building boards. It is only when the timber of the felled tree is put to some long-term use, such as in furniture, that the carbon locked up as the tree grows is retained outside the atmosphere semi-permanently.

Cannell suggests that when the use to which the timber is put lasts as long again as the life of the tree, then significant removal of carbon dioxide from the atmosphere occurs. 'If harvested wood is included, then most carbon is stored in the forest-plus-products by harvesting at the time of maximum mean annual increment (65 to 100 years according to site), provided that the

average lifetime of the wood products is equal to, or exceeds, the length of a rotation.' Taking the average life of an oak tree as one hundred years, then for significant carbon storage, the furniture made from it must also last at least one hundred years. Of all the timbers in use, oak probably lasts longest in this form owing to the durability and beauty of the furniture made from it. Oak thus perhaps contributes more than most tree species to a containment of increasing carbon dioxide levels in the atmosphere. Cannell emphasised that the trees need to be widely spaced to encourage 'free growth' in order to absorb the maximum amount of carbon dioxide from the atmosphere. He calculated that an oak tree can be expected to accumulate 'about 2.9 tons of carbon after 100 years, averaging 29kgC per year and requiring 38 (widely spaced) trees to absorb the emissions of an average car over the 100 year period.' He also calculated that it would require something like 12.6 million hectares of oak woodland to absorb the carbon emissions from the UK's 23 million cars. This area is hardly a realistic proposition but at least one can enjoy a nice new piece of oak furniture knowing that it is making a very small contribution to reduction of global warming, though it must be kept for at least one hundred years to do so!

It is to be welcomed that the area of oakwood has increased in Britain since the early twentieth century despite the excessively heavy felling of all woods necessitated by both World Wars. Since the formation of the Forestry Commission in 1919, the area of 'high forest' oak woodland (i.e. woodland other than forms of coppice) has increased, mainly on land other than that planted by the Forestry Commission supported though by Forestry Commission grants and favourable tax allowances.

Thus there is still a lot of oak woodland in this country, much of it in small, isolated woods. Not all is of high timber quality because of the heavy exploitation in both World Wars. Much is of coppice origin and under-managed. Nevertheless it is an important wildlife and conservation resource as well as being significant in the landscape and some will continue to provide valuable oak timber into the future.

Looked at in more detail, the first Forestry Commission Census of Woodlands, dated 1924, recorded that 48 per cent of the woodland area of Britain was high forest but at that time the 'scrub' classification included 'dwarf oak', particularly in west Wales. Of the high forest, conifers already dominated, making up 47 per cent; hardwoods formed 32 per cent, the balance being mixed stands (21 per cent). Of the hardwoods, much was over-mature. Coppice and coppice-with-standards, the latter mainly oak, predominantly in England, formed 18 per cent of total woodland area and scrub formed an additional 11 per cent, the remainder being felled or devastated woodlands (resulting from the wartime requisitions) and amenity woods. Thus in 1924:

- 48 per cent of the woodland area was high forest (1,416,890 acres)
- 18 per cent was coppice and coppice-with-standards (528,680 acres)
- 11 per cent was scrub (330,703 acres)

The total woodland area in 1924 over 2 acres in extent was 2,958,672 acres, including woodland bare of trees at the time of survey, giving 5.3 per cent of the land area of Britain as woodland of some form.

Species distribution and percentage was not recorded in the 1924 woodland census but the report stated that: 'The reserves of mature hardwood (mainly oak), which were not drawn on to the same extent during the war, are considerable although the average quality is not good. There is a great lack of young hardwood plantations. Oak planting in particular has gone out of fashion in favour of conifers. When the existing mature and semi-mature oak woods have disappeared, as they are steadily doing, the supply of home-grown oak will become negligible.' It goes on to say: 'The unprecedented war fellings swept away the bulk of the best coniferous timber, the best ash and much of the good oak.'

Comparison with later censuses can only be general as the survey methods varied but by 1947, in spite of the gloomy predictions about the plight of oak in the 1924 census, it was stated 'that the apparent decline of oak (and beech) had been arrested and reversed during the last 30 years'. The 1947 Census surveyed woods of 5 acres and over, recording nearly 3.5 million acres in total, i.e. 6.1 per cent of land area of Britain. Almost one quarter of this was pure broadleaves and 10 per cent coppice (mostly in England), with scrub a further 15 per cent. The report stated that '... in Great Britain as a whole the most important species in High Forest is oak, with 431,495 acres, or 24 per cent. of the total High Forest area, ... this despite the increase in coniferous planting'. This figure excludes woods under 5 acres so it is a conservative estimate so far as oak is concerned. As can be seen from Table 4, the area of oak High Forest had risen considerably from that recorded in 1924, probably due to oak coppice being 'stored', i.e. singled and grown on.

TABLE 4: Status of Oak in Britain (acres)

Forest category	1924 Census	1947 Census	1979 Census	1995–99 Census
Broadleaved high forest	443,354	754,936	—	–
Mixed high forest	301,695	166,066	—	–
Broadleaved & mixed	745,049	921,002	—	395,360
Mainly broadleaved	682,465*	843,852	1,394,112	2,399,341
Oak high forest	341,232*	431,495	424,815	551,033
Oak as % of broadleaved & mixed high forest	50%	50%	31%	
Oak as % of total forest area	12%	13%	9%	
Volume of oak	—	—	32,893,800 cu metres	–
Vol. of non-woodland oak	—	—	8,818,000 cu metres	–

* Individual species are not recorded by area in the 1924 Census. To arrive at an estimate for oak high forest for 1924 the following calculation has been employed. Using the proportions recorded in 1947 for the total of mixed and broadleaved high forest (754,936 + 166,066 = 921,002 acres) and mainly broadleaved high forest (843,852 acres) gives 682,465 acres of mainly broadleaved high forest in 1924. 50 per cent of this has been taken to give the area of oak, estimated thereby at 341,232 acres. 1995–99 data from *Forest Statistics* (2001).

The Census report of 1947 included the map reproduced as Figure 49 and stated that oak 'is seen to occur to some extent in all but a few of the northern counties, and to be by far the commonest High Forest tree in many of the southern ones. This predominance is most noticeable in a belt stretching across the heavier soils of the south Midlands.' It goes on to say that: 'Observations made in the course of the Census survey confirmed the generally western distribution of sessile oak, which however, was found to extend eastwards on most of the lighter and more acid soils. Planted oak proved to be almost entirely of pedunculate or hybrid origin.'

Thus at 1947:

- 52 per cent of the woodland area was high forest (1,788,799 acres)
- 10 per cent was coppice and coppice-with-standards (349,994 acres)
- 15 per cent was scrub (496,951 acres)

The 1979–82 census extended the recorded areas down to half an acre as well as to non-woodland trees. The woodland cover of Britain had risen to 9.4 per cent (2,108,000 hectares or 5,206,760 acres), 27 per cent of this being broadleaved high forest but now only 2 per cent was coppice. It recorded a fall-off in hardwood planting after 1960. The report concluded that 'on balance the total area of broadleaved woodland was much the same as in 1947. However, its composition has certainly changed … (with) … less of oak but more sycamore, ash and birch than in 1947.' The area of oak high forest had fallen by 6,680 acres since 1947 but oak remained the dominant species in England, at 16 per cent of high forest there. Oak as pure coppice was no longer significant but still occurred in coppice-with-standards, amounting to 27,172 acres. There was also 12 per cent oak scrub (44,593 acres). Of the non-woodland trees oak exceeded all other species.

Thus at 1979:

- 89 per cent of the woodland area was high forest (4,646,628 acres)
- 2 per cent was coppice (96,656 acres)
- 7 per cent was scrub (366,133 acres)

Looked at another way, the importance of oak is also borne out by the volume recorded in the report which showed that oak high forest provided the greatest timber volume of all species at 32,893,800 cubic metres, contributing 36 per cent of total broadleaved volume and 17 per cent of the total standing volume of the country's timber resource. Of non-woodland trees, oak had remained static from 1951 to 1980, providing an additional volume of 8,818 cubic metres. The total standing volume of oak therefore exceeded by a long way that of any other species, the next highest being Sitka spruce at 28,187,000 cubic metres.

The most recent figures, from 1995–1999, show that the area of oak high forest has continued to expand in the last years of the twentieth century.

What is the future for oak? If we are to grow oak timber of quality we need to improve the sources seed is collected from. A project that will surely be significant in the longer term was the concept of Dr Neil Paterson, inaugurated under the title of 'The National Hardwood Project' at a conference in 1980 (Harris 1981). This was set against the background at the time (and which has continued) of increasing interest in growing more hardwoods, particularly oak, that could substitute for imported tropical hardwood timbers. Paterson proposed clonal reproduction of material from the occasional high quality trees that already occur in our woodlands and which are acclimatised to British conditions.

The Project has developed into important work now going on jointly at the Oxford Forestry Institute and at Horticultural Research International at East Malling in Kent, under the British Hardwoods Improvement Programme, to breed improved oak (and five other species) from selected prime trees. Material from selected mother trees is being grown in seed orchards and will be micro-propagated from the best of the seed orchard trees in order to speed up the availability of improved oak stock. There are two principal objectives of the oak project within the Programme, the first to increase the proportion of recoverable timber per hectare and the second to improve the quality of timber produced. If successful, it is hoped that this will lead to an increase in the area of oak being grown in lowland Britain. The Programme does not distinguish between *Q. petraea* and *Q. robur* as their timbers are indistinguishable but about equal quantities of each are under trial.

Forest-grown trees rather than open-grown parkland trees are used as the source for propagation material as the former have already gone through a more rigorous selection process in competitive forest conditions. Thus *dominant*, mature forest trees are sought.

The wood properties looked for in the trees selected are a low number of sapwood rings (which is an inherited character) and reduced susceptibility to

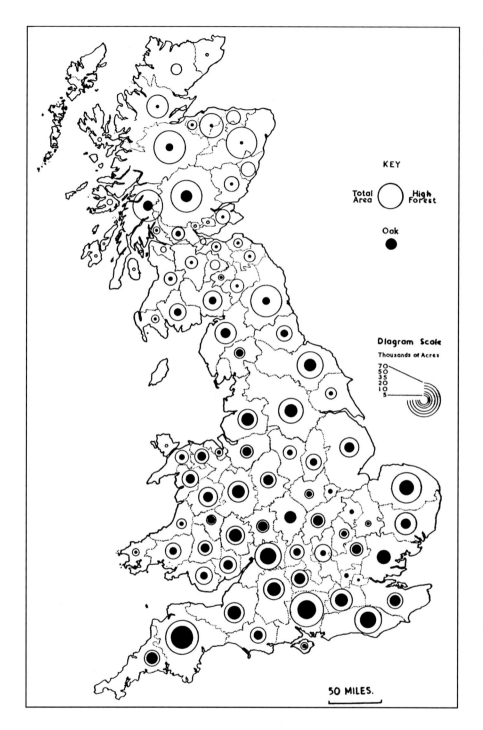

KEY

Total Area — High Forest

Oak

Diagram Scale
Thousands of Acres
70
50
35
20
10
5

50 MILES.

FIGURE 49
The distribution of
oak high forest
in 1947.

CROWN COPYRIGHT,
REPRODUCED WITH
PERMISSION OF THE
FORESTRY COMMISSION

shake. The latter is linked to early wood vessel diameter; large early wood vessels give a greater tendency to shake (Savill 1996). Good characters to be perpetuated are: straight stem; improved length of first-class utilisable timber; absence of stem fluting; absence of spiral grain; absence of basal sweep and reduction in tendency to epicormics. Most trees have been selected from the English Midlands.

Thus the future for oak, both as a tree and in the form of timber, is bright, though it may not be planted as widely as in the past. Oak woods and old oak trees will be increasingly important as a conservation resource. Oak timber, especially high quality material from well managed woodlands, will substitute to some extent for tropical timbers and will find an important place for specialised uses, for quality furniture and for other wooden artefacts. For such uses, oak needs as much careful management as it was given in the past. The new plantations of oak (and other hardwoods) must not be left unmanaged, as they often have been in the recent past, as this will result in wood fit only for the fire and reduced conservation value due to lack of thinning.

From its lowest ebb in the 1960s when oak timber was worth no more than one shilling per cubic foot (£7.82 per cubic metre) oak has seen a steady revival and this can be expected to continue commensurate with rising standards of living and increased spendable income. To achieve this, however, oak timber must be of the highest quality as there is little place for second grade material, except perhaps as flooring blocks. To achieve this oak requires to be grown on the best sites and with full use of the modern techniques now available, such as tree shelters and the initial use of herbicides to aid establishment. This will enable a revival, though never on a large scale, of the growing of oak but only if the lessons of the past described here in Chapters 2 and 3, together with modern techniques, are understood and practised. Oak is a tree that requires quality management and a high input of technical expertise; without these, few woods of ecological value and able to produce utilisable timber will be achieved. It is reassuring therefore that the area of oak woodland remaining in Britain today is considerable and is likely to remain so.

It is appropriate to quote the words of one whose life was making things from timber, particularly oak, the village carpenter, Walter Rose (1943). He wrote with feeling about the oak trees he gave a second life to and his sentiments are as appropriate today as when he expressed them fifty years ago. 'Every right-minded person deplores the ruthless felling of trees. At the same time, sight of the pitiable remains of once noble oaks (there are some in Windsor Great Park), fragments of trunks from which every branch has been torn by gales – left there to perish – compels the tender thought that the tree of beauty, after fulfilling its years of life, might better have given another period of usefulness, another period of order and charm. The once noble oak, felled at the right time, might have been transformed by hand of man into the roof of a hall, or the fittings of a church, or the staircase of an ordinary house, or panelwork for its walls; then its usefulness and beauty would have continued (in another form) for centuries as a delight and inspiration to the beholder.'

Oak will surely remain a tree which is prized and will continue to have a special place in Britain. As the concept of this book was that of the late

N. D. G. James, it is appropriate to conclude with a poem from his anthology *A Book of Trees* published by the Royal Forestry Society in 1973.

*Oak
A British History*

When We Are Lowly Laid

Sing for the oak-tree,
    The monarch of the wood,
Sing for the oak-tree,
    That groweth green and good;
That groweth broad and branching
    Within the forest shade,
That groweth now, and yet shall grow,
    When we are lowly laid!

The winds came, and the rain fell,
    The gusty tempests blew,
All, all were friends to the oak tree,
    And stronger yet it grew.
The boy that saw the acorn fall,
    He feeble grew and gray;
But the oak was still a thriving tree,
    And strengthened every day.

Mary Howlett, 1799–1888

A List of Historic and Named Oak Trees in Britain

Oak trees have always held a special place in our history and it was for this reason that the late N. D. G. James compiled a list of named and historic oak trees in Britain. He built upon the records of the eighteenth and nineteenth centuries when a great interest was taken in special trees and researched many old books to record the status and history of the oak trees described during that period. He also collected information from other sources, such as the records of the Woolhope Club, which was active in the Welsh borders in the late nineteenth century. He then searched the modern literature and contacted many individuals and organisations about named oak trees. Subsequently, he visited several of the trees between 1989 and 1992 to verify their existence, to photograph them and record their condition. Whilst about two-thirds of the following list is compiled from information collected by him before his death in 1993, the rest have been added since.

This is the most complete list of British named oak trees, past and present, and as such deserves publication as a comprehensive list which, though inevitably incomplete, can be added to. The list may also stimulate interest in some of these old trees and their historical connections. As many are in parks and on private land, permission to visit them often needs to be sought.

Although some of the trees in the list are named because of their size, the aim is not to record them for this reason but because they have been named. (Recording large trees, including oak trees, is undertaken by the Tree Register of the British Isles.) There are many fine oak trees throughout the British Isles that are not named, the majority in England and Scotland with fewer in Wales and Ireland. Loudon (1838) gives details of the old estates and parks which had fine oak trees then, many of which still exist, whilst Hunter (1883) recorded estates in Perthshire with large oak trees.

Named oaks fall into a number of categories reflecting the reasons for describing them. These include boundary oaks, gospel oaks, shire oaks, oaks which were meeting places such as where the hunt met, oaks where weddings took place, oaks marking sites such as cross-roads (these could also be gibbet oaks), oaks used as a lookout post, oak trees associated with people, events (such as Coronation oaks) or legends. Old hollow oak trees were used for housing animals (bull oaks), hiding places and for festivities (for example dancing trees). Other oaks were named because of their shape or because they were particularly fine trees. Many of the oak trees with historical associations no longer exist but trees raised from their acorns have been planted as replacements and have been recorded as such.

The following records include the name, alternative names, county, location, national grid reference (in some cases only an approximation), status, details and bibliographic references.

A note on the abbreviations

For distances, m. denotes miles. References are given after Ref:, in the form Author (publication date, page number). Where the tree is illustrated elsewhere, the reference is in bold. Ordnance Survey Grid References are given as Grid ref: SO 2645 and are either 4 or, where possible, 6 figure.

1. Abbot's Oak, The. (I). Bedfordshire. Woburn Abbey Park. Grid ref. SP 966323.

Robert Hobbs (Abbot of Woburn) and other clerics were hanged on this tree by order of Henry VIII having spoken publicly against the King's marriage to Anne Boleyn and for not acknowledging the King's supremacy. Ref: Loudon (1838) Vol. III p. 1753. Anon. (1853, 44). Mosley (1910, 57). Wilks (1972, 77). Brewer's Dict. (1983).

2. Abbot's Oak, The. (II). Warwickshire. Kenilworth. Grid ref. SP 278710 (Oaks Farm).
   Ref: Hewins (1945, 6).

3. Abbot's Oak, The. (III). Clwyd. Basingwerk Abbey, Greenfield. Grid ref. SJ 1977.
   Girth 18 ft (Camden 1806). Ref: Camden (1806).

4. Abolition Oak, The. See Wilberforce Oak.

5. Acton Round Oak. Shropshire. On the highway between Weston and Wenlock. Grid ref. SO 6395.
   Girth 28 ft (Morton 1986). Pollard. Probably a boundary tree in Shirlett Forest. A document of 1256 mentions an oak tree called 'Ronsak' i.e. Round Oak (Morton 1986). Ref: Morton (1986, 39–41). **Morton p. 41.**

6. Adam And Eve. (I). Hampshire. Minstead: On E side of lane from Minstead Village to Newtown – just below Manor Farm. Grid ref. SU 279109.
   Alive 1991. Ref: Letter, Hants C.C. 16/11/1991.

7. Adam and Eve. (II). Herefordshire. Lugg Meadows, Moreton-on-Lugg. 3 m. N of Hereford, on E of A 49 road. Grid ref: SO 514455 (approx).
   Eve measured 25 ft in girth. Used as hut for navvies when the Shrewsbury and Hereford Rly was being built. After line opened it was used as the Stationmaster's residence and later as a lamp room. Ref: Elwes and Henry (1907). **Elwes and Henry (1907) Vol. II p. 314.**

8. Addlestone Oak. See Crouch Oak.

9. Ale Oak. Shropshire. Nr Mainstone. 7 m. WSW of Bishops Castle; 1½ m. NW Newcastle (in Clun Forest). Grid ref. SO 224840. Marked on map.
   The name is a corruption of 'hale', a Saxon boundary word. This is probably the Border Oak in Loudon. Ref: Loudon (1838, 1778). Hewins (1945, 11). Morton (1986, 39).

10. Alfred's Oak. See Magdalen Oak.

11. Allerton Oak. Also known as Court Tree. Lancashire. Calderstones Park, Liverpool. Grid ref. SJ 3986 (Allerton).

Sessile oak. Alive 1991. Ref: Wilks (1972, 243). White (1991).

12. Amy Tree. Cornwall. St. Mellion: 5 m. WNW of Tamar Bridge, Saltash. 3 m. SE Callington on A338. Grid ref. SX 389656 (St Mellion Church).
    Ref: Wilks (1972, 245).

13. Apostles Oak. See Rock Oak.

14. Arley Oak. Cheshire. Arley Hall. Grid ref. SJ 6780 (Arley Hall).
    Alive in 1938. A former squire of Arley squeezed eleven boys into the hollow tree and paid them one shilling for doing it (Mee 1938). Ref: Mee (1938, 20).

15. Arondell's Oak. Cornwall. 'The Parke of Lanhadron'. Lanhadron Farm is 2 m. SE of Sticker and 2 m. NNE of Mevagissey. Grid ref. SX 995476.
    Felled 1730s. Lanhadron Park belonged to the Arondell family. This oak was famous for its variegated leaves and several trees were propagated from it and grown elsewhere (Thurston 1930). Hunter (1883) records a variegated oak at Freeland, Perthshire. Ref: Hunter (1883). Thurston (1930, 186–7).

16. Ashton Oak. Devon. Loudon states it was 'about 4 m. from Chudleigh'. Its description would indicate it was about ¼ m. NW of Higher Ashton Church, near a brook. Grid ref. SX 853848 (Approx).
    In 1805 was 16 ft girth at 4 ft and 20 ft at ground level. 75 ft to the first branch. In 1837 was sold to be felled for 60 guineas (Loudon 1838). Ref: Loudon (1838) Vol. II pp. 1837–8. **Loudon (1838, 1836).**

17. Aubrey's Oak. Hampshire. Malwood Castle, 1 m. SW of Cadnam and on S side of A31. Grid ref. SU 277122.
    Alive in 1991. Ref: Letter, Hants C.C. 16/11/1991.

18. Augustine's Oak. (I). Oxfordshire. Wychwood Forest. Grid ref. SP 3519.
    This tree was on one of the sites claimed as the meeting place of Augustine with the British bishops. Finberg (1976) states that this tree marked the border between the territories of the Saxons and Britons (Christian Hwicce). Ref: Finberg (1974, 40).

19. Augustine's Oak. (II). Kent. Ebbsfleet about 3 m. SW of Ramsgate. Grid ref. TR 335625 (Ebbfleet House) or TR 344637 (of St A's Well).
    An oak marking a preaching place of St Augustine. Ref: Mosley (1910, 54).

20. Avington Oak. See Gospel Oak. (I).

21. Baginton Oak. See Gospel Oak. (V).

22. Bagot's, Lord, Walking Stick or Sir Walter Bagot's Walking Stick. Staffordshire. Bagot's Park, 4 m. S of Uttoxeter: 2 m. N of Abbots Bromley. Grid ref. SK 090275 (Bagot's Park).

Hayes (1822) stated that in 1794 it was 16 ft circ. at 6 ft: 35 ft of clear bole then 40 ft of branches. This tree was in the old Forest of Needwood. Ref: Hayes (1794, 125). Elwes and Henry (1907) Vol. II p. 317. Hewins (1945, 7).

23. Bale Oak. Norfolk. 7 m. NE of Fakenham: 3 m. NW of Melton Constable. Grid ref. TG 010368 (Bale).

Existed until middle of nineteenth century. Girth 36 ft: was dead and hollow (Wilks 1972). This tree was probably a boundary oak and the name a corruption of the Saxon word 'hale', a boundary word. Ref: Wilks (1972, 197).

24. Barbados Oak. Berkshire. Windsor Great Park. Grid ref. SU 9672 (Windsor Great Park).

Alive in 1991. Ref: White (1991).

25. Bard's Tree, The. Invernesshire. Dalilea House, Moidart. West of Loch Shiel. Grid ref. NM 7369.

Alive in 1972. Planted in 1745 by Alasdair Macdonald; presumably to commemorate the landing of Charles Stuart in the area. Ref: Wilks (1972, 46).

26. Barjarg Oak. Dumfries. Nithsdale, Barjarg. Grid ref. NX 8890 (Barjarg Tower).

Girth 17 ft in 1796 (Loudon 1838). Ref: Loudon (1838, 1772).

27. Barnes Oak. See Keeper's Oak.

28. Barras Oak. Cumbria. Nr Dalston. Grid ref. NY 3750 (Dalston).

Marked on pre-war maps but no longer exists. Near a dyke, the openings of which were protected by 'bar houses'. Richard, Duke of Gloucester is said to have hidden in it to escape the Scots (Holdsworth 1990). Ref: Holdsworth (1990, 4).

29. Bate's Oak. See Betsy's Oak.

30. Bear's Oak. See Sydney's Oak.

31. Beauty Oak. One of the three Fredville Oaks (Beauty, Majesty, Stately). Kent. Fredville, Nonnington, 7 m. SE Canterbury. Grid ref. TR 256512.

Visited by Mr D. Drew Aug. 1991: He measured the girth as 24 ft and reported that the top had gone. Beauty, Majesty and Stately are within 100 yards of each other. In 1838 the tree was 16 ft in girth (Loudon 1838). Ref: Strutt (1830, 52). Lauder (1834, 254). Loudon (1838, 1762). Plumtree (1999).

32. Bedford's Oak. Essex. Havering-atte-Bower. 4 m. E Chigwell; 5 m. W Brentford. Grid ref. TQ 517920 (Bedford Park).

In 1907 Elwes visited this tree. He says that it was '27 feet in girth, decayed'. Ref: Elwes and Henry (1907) Vol. II p. 324.

33. Beelzebub (Oak). Sussex. Petworth House Park. 6 m. E of Midhurst: 5 m. NW of Pulborough. On parish boundary on Guildford Road NE of lower Park called Limbo, near farm and car park. Grid ref. SU 976218.

Alive in 1991. About 200 years old (Chance 1991). There is a plaque on the wall adjacent. Ref: White (1991). Letter, Mr. Chance 7/11/1991.

34. Beggar's Oak. Staffordshire. Bagot's Park, 4 m. S of Uttoxeter: 2 m. N of Abbots Bromley. Grid ref. SK 090275 (Bagot's Park).

Alive in 1972. Pedunculate oak. Girth 27 ft 3 ins at 5 ft (Loudon 1838). The roots above ground provide a seat which wandering beggars used. One story relates that one stormy night Lord Bagot refused a beggar alms and a curse was laid on him that his first born would not thrive. It is also recorded that the tree was a meeting place for deer stealers and robbers in Needwood Forest. Ref: Strutt (1830, 16). Loudon (1838, 1769). Selby (1842, 256). Lauder (1883, 254). Elwes and Henry (1907, 317). Hurst (1911, 819). Hewins (1945, 6). Wilks (1972, 248). **Loudon fig. 1614.**

35. Bell Oak. Hampshire. Burley Lawn. Grid ref. SO 2103.
Ref: Hardcastle (1951).

36. Bellman's Oak. Gloucestershire. Forest of Dean: High Meadow Woods 200 yds NE of Reddings Lodge which is 1 m. N of A 4136 road at Staunton. Grid ref. SO 548138.

Shown on 1922 map. A marker oak. Ref: Standing (1986, 13).

37. Belvoir Oak. Co. Down. Belvoir Park, between Belfast and Lisburn.

Loudon (1838) states that the original tree was 28 ft in girth and much decayed. This oak was taken as the crest of the family at Belvoir. Another oak near the Motte is known now as the Belvoir Oak. Ref: Loudon (1838). Browne (2000). **Browne (2000, 18).** The original photograph is owned by the National Museum.

38. Benjamin's Oak, Sir. Also known as Sir Benjamin Tichborne's Oak and The Tichbourne Oak (II). Hampshire. West Tisted: 4½ m. ESE of New Alresford: 4 m. SW of Four Marks. Grid ref. SU 653290.

The tree in which Sir Benjamin Tichbourne is supposed to have hidden from Cromwell's troopers after the battle of Cheriton in 1644. Ref: Wilks (1972, 58).

39. Bentley Oak. Also known as the Holt Forest Oak. Hampshire. Alice Holt Forest. Grid ref. SU 7844 (Bentley, Alice Holt Forest).

Girth 34 ft at 7 ft in 1759 (Loudon 1838). Ref: Gilpin (1791, 121). Rooke (1790, 15). Hayes (1794, 127). Loudon (1838) Vol. III, pp. 1761, 1764. Ablett (1880, 167).

40. Bessies Oak. See Betsy's Oak.

41. Betsy's Oak. Also known as Bessies Oak or Bates' Oak. Sussex. Parham Park which is 3 m. SSE of Pulborough; 7 m. SE of Petworth and 1½ m. W of Storrington. Grid ref. TQ 060143 (Parham House).

Only a small stump remains (Aug 1992). Under this tree Queen Elizabeth I rested on her way to 'Coudray' (Victoria County History 1907). The name 'Bates' Oak' is said to refer to one Bates who fought at the Battle of Agincourt. V.C.H. (1907) Sussex Vol. II. Ref: Visited by Mr D. Drew in August 1992.

42. Betts Pool Oak. Staffordshire. Bagot's Park, 4 m. S of Uttoxeter: 2 m. N. of Abbots Bromley. Grid ref. SK 0928 (Bagot's Park).

A hollow stump in 1838 (Loudon 1838). A bull oak. Ref: Loudon (1838) Vol. III p. 1769.

43. Big Bellied Oak. See Decanter Oak.

44. Big Ben. See Danbury Oaks.

45. Big Oak. (I). See Whitfield Oak.

46. Big Oak. (II). Oxfordshire. Henley-on-Thames (Wilks p. 59). Grid ref. SU 750820 (Henley).

It is said that Charles I escaped from Oxford in the Civil War disguised as a servant and hid in this oak. Ref: Wilks (1972, 59). Whitlock (1985, 104).

47. Big Oak. (III). See Lydham Manor Oak.

48. Billy Wilkin's Oak. See Wilkin's Oak, Billy.

49. Binley Oak. West Midlands. On the Brinklow road in Binley, Coventry, on the right hand side towards Coombe. Grid ref. SP 3778 (Binley).

Struck by lightning in early twentieth century and the site is now built over. Ref: Clarke *et al.* (1987). **Clarke *et al.* p. 19.**

50. Birchland Oak. See Shambles Oak.

51. Birnam Oak. Neil Gow's Oak. (II). Perthshire. On the south bank of R. Tay immediately behind Birnam Hotel at Murthly 5 m. SE of Dunkeld. Grid ref. NN 0938. (Murthly).

Girth: 18 ft at 5 ft (Hunter 1883). Remnant of the great Birnam wood. Neil Gow, a well known musician, is said to have slept under this oak after a drinking bout in a smuggler's den nearby. This led him to compose 'Neil Gow's Farewell to Whisky'. Ref: Hunter (1883, 73–4).

52. Bixley Oak. Norfolk. Armingland (present name Arminghall) 3 m. S. of Norwich. Grid ref. TG 2504 (Arminghall).

Girth: 17 ft 2 ins at 5 ft in 1841 (Grigor 1841). Ref: Grigor (1841, 270).

53. Blackmore Hill Oak. Northamptonshire. Salcey Forest in the Blackwood Quarter. Grid ref. SP 802522.

Alive in 1991. Ref: Forestry Commission (1991).

54. Blenheim Oak. Kent. Plaxtol. Grid ref. TQ 6053.

Replaced by young tree in 1967. This tree was planted in the grounds of Plaxtol Primary School to replace the original tree which had to be felled.

55. Blind Oak of Keir. Dumfriesshire. Nithsdale. Grid ref. NX 8593 (Keir Mill).

Girth 17 ft 2 ins at 4 ft 5 ins from the ground in 1810. This oak is mentioned in the title deeds of the estate in 1638 (Loudon 1838). Ref: Loudon (1838) Vol. III p. 1772.

56. Bloody Oak. The. Co. Armagh. At Salter's Grange off the Armagh to Loughgall Road.

The tree still stands on the Bloody Loaning, a lane leading to a ford over the Callan river where a massacre took place. 'Here on 14th August 1598 Marshall Bagenal, in charge of the English forces based at Newry, was marching to the relief of a hard pressed English Garrison at Portmore. His force was completely overwhelmed and he was slain with 2000 of his men at the Battle of the Yellow Ford' (Browne. D. 2000). Ref: Browne (2000). **Browne (2000, 32, 33).**

57. Boar Stag Oak. Worcestershire. 'In a field near the Severn, below Holt' (Elwes and Henry 1907). Holt is 1 m. SW of Ombersley. Grid ref. SO 835623 approx.

In 1867 it was 34 ft in girth at 3 ft agl. Thought to be 800 yrs old (Elwes and Henry 1907). Ref: Elwes and Henry (1907) Vol. II p. 314.

FIGURE 50. *Clockwise from top left*: The Bonnington Oak – a Law Day Oak (62); The Coplestone Oak (133); The Forester's Oak (214) – site of a Forest Court.; Gog Oak (235). N. D. G. JAMES

58. Bocase Tree. See Bowcase Oak.

59. Boconnoc Oak. Also known as King Charles Oak. (II). Cornwall. Boconnoc Park 3 m. E of Lostwithiel, 5½ m. ENE of Fowey. Near the gate of Rockwood Grove, leading to the Parsonage; near the war memorial. Grid ref. SX 140600.

The original tree is no longer there but a replacement has been planted. The Park belonged to the Mohun family when Charles I set up his standard by this tree, which had variegated leaves (see Arondell's Oak). Legend states that the leaves turned white when a shot was fired at the king, which missed him and made a hole in the tree. In March 1783, the upper part snapped off, the stump remained until 1930. Ref: Polwheles (1826). Thurston (1930, 187–8). Wilks (1972, 57–8).

60. Boddington Oak also known as the Cheltenham Oak, The. Gloucestershire. Boddington Manor Farm, Boddington, 4½ m. S of Tewkesbury and ½ m. S of A4019 (Cheltenham-Coombe Hill). Grid ref. SO 894252.

Bore acorns 1783, burnt down 1790. Small trunk remained 1807. Girth 54 ft at the base (Selby 1842). Ref: Rooke (1790, 15). Gilpin (1791, 121). Loudon (1838) Vol. III p. 1760. Selby (1842, 253). Ablett (1880, 171). Elwes and Henry (1907, 320). Wilks (1972, 29).

61. Bolton's Oak. Hereford and Worcester. Whitfield Park. Grid ref. SO 424335.
    Ref: White (1991).

62. Bonnington Oak. See Law-day Oak.

63. Boscobel Oak. Also known as the Royal Oak. (II) or Royal Boscobel Oak. Shropshire. About 200 yds S of Boscobel House which is 3 m. W of Brewood and 3 m. NE of Albrighton. Grid ref. SJ 838080.

Not the original (which was dead 1706) but a replacement from an acorn off the original tree. This was the oak in which the Penderell family hid the king (Charles II) after the battle of Worcester. At the Restoration, pieces were cut from the tree and carried away as souvenirs. Saplings raised from this tree were planted by Charles II in St James Park and the Botanic Gardens at Chelsea. A sapling raised from the replacement tree was planted here to celebrate Queen Victoria's Diamond Jubilee. Ref: Loudon (1838) Vol. III p. 1768. Anon (1853, 51–3). Ablett (1880, 172). Johns (1903) Elwes and Henry (1907, 325). Mosley (1910, 49–51). Hurst (1911, 189). Hewins (1945, 9). Wilks (1972, 43–4, 59–64). Brewer's Dict. (1983).

64. Bostock Oak. Cheshire. At Bostock Green, 3 m. NW of Middlewich and 3 m. SSE of Northwich. Grid ref. SJ 6769. This tree was planted to mark the centre of Cheshire. Ref: Mee (1938, 75). Wilks (1972, 241).

65. Bounds Park Oak. See Bounds Oak.

66. Boundary Oak. Berkshire. Near Bound Oak Cottage, Swallowfield, 6 m. N of Hartley Wintney and 2 m. SSW of Shinfield. Grid ref. SU 720645 (Swallowfield).
    Ref: Wilks (1972, 22).

67. Bounds Oak. Also known as the Bounds Park Oak. Kent. Bidborough, 2 m. SW Tonbridge. Grid ref. TQ 5643.

Felled about 1961 after housing development altered the water table. Replacement planted. Girth 22 ft at 2 ft in 1838 (Loudon). Visited by Mr D. Drew in Aug. 1991 and information was provided by him. Ref: Lauder (1834) Vol. I p. 255. Loudon (1838, 1837). Wilks (1972, 37–8). Bean (1976) Vol. III p. 508.

68. Bourton Oak. Gloucestershire. 'East side of the road to Stow' near Bourton-on-the-Water in grass field adjoining road and S of entrance road to Heath Hill Farm. Grid ref. SP 181229.

Pendunculate oak. Girth 22 ft 6 ins in 1906 (Elwes and Henry 1907). Girth 31 ft 4 ins in 1992 (James). Pollarded many years ago. Property of Mr R. M. Brooks, Heath Hill Farm. Ref: Elwes and Henry (1907) Vol. II pp. 317, 321. Visit by James 1992. **Elwes and Henry plate 93.**

69. Bowcase Oak. Also known as the Bocase Tree. Northamptonshire. 1½ m. N of Brigstock and adjoining E boundary of Harry's Park Wood. Part of the old Rockingham Forest. Grid ref. SP 950878.

Original oak felled. A young oak c. 6 ft high has been planted to replace the original one. The Bocase Stone was erected many years ago to mark the site of the old tree. The title reads 'In this plaes grew Bocase Tree'. The name is said to come from 'bocas' which was a meeting place in Norman times where forest rights were determined. Also that archery was practised here and bowcases were hung on it. More recently, a meeting place for the Pytchley Hunt. Ref: Loudon (1838) Vol. III p. 1766. 'Northamptonshire Past & Present' Vol. III p. 72. Visit by James. 1991. **Photographs James 24/10/91.**

70. Bowthorpe Oak. Also known as the Great Oak (XI). Lincolnshire. Bowthorpe Park Farm, Witham-on-the-Hill, 6 m. NNE of Stamford: 3½ m. SW of Bourne. Grid ref. TF 0516.

Pedunculate oak. Girth: 39 ft 6 ins (James 1991). Estimated age: 550–600 yrs. The largest *Q. robur* in Britain (Mitchell 1982). 'Lincolnshire's oldest and largest oak' AA road Book (1965). In 1768, a floor, table and benches were installed in the hollow tree by George Pauncefoot. It has also been used as a calf pen and pigeon loft. Ref: Mosley (1910, 68). Mitchell (1982, 271). Mitchell (1991, 88). Tree Register Newsletter (1992–93). Packenham (1996). **Packenham (1996, 174)**.

71. Bradgate Oaks. Leicestershire. Bradgate Park. Grid ref. SK 5112.

A number of old oaks growing amongst rocks. The Park is the birthplace of Lady Jane Grey. On the day of her execution it is said many of the oaks in her palace grounds were beheaded (pollarded). Ref: Hewins (1945, 14). Roberts (1890, 21–8). Clarke *et al.* (1987).

72. Brees Oak. Warwickshire. Beausale, near Kenilworth. Grid ref. SP 2470. (Beausale).

Named after the Rev. W. Bree, landscape painter. Ref: Clarke *et al.* (1987).

73. Brewer's Oak. (I). Shropshire. Brewer's Oak Farm 1¾ m. NNE of Shifnal Station. Grid ref. SJ 758114.

The name has two versions; it is associated with the suicide of a man named Brewer, or is called after a farmer Brewer who saved the tree from being felled. Whether this was the same person is not known. Ref: Hewins (1945, 9–10). Wilks (1972, 89).

74. Brewer's Oak. (II). Surrey. '400 yds from the Boundless and Brook turning off the A3 road to Hindhead'. (Wilks). Grid ref. SU 899377.

Ref: Wilks (1972, 201).

75. Bristol's, Lord, Walking Stick. Suffolk. Ickworth Estate, Horringer, 2 m. SW Bury St Edmunds. Grid ref. TL 815615 (Ickworth Park).

Girth: 24 ft 3 ins or 7.4 m. (James 1991). Ref: Letter, National Trust 10/6/1991. Visit by James 1991.

76. British Honduras Oak. Berkshire. Windsor Great Park. Grid ref. SU 9672. (Windsor Great Park).

Ref: White (1991).

77. Broad Oak. (I). Shropshire. On northern outskirts of Shrewsbury: on A528 ½ m. S of Albrighton and 1 m. E of Battlefield. Grid ref. SJ 498173 (Buildings marked Broadoak on map).

A very large oak in the nineteenth century. Ref: Hewins (1945, 10). Morton (1986, 58). **A drawing by P. Van Dyke-Brown in the Lower National Gallery at Cradley, near Malvern.**

78. Broad Oak. (II). Lancashire. Winwick Hall. Grid ref. SJ 6092 (Winwick).

Girth 17 ft at 1 ft, 30 ft high, spreading over 90 ft. Ref: Loudon (1838, 1840).

79. Broadstones Oaks. Gloucestershire. Staunton, Forest of Dean. Grid ref. SO 537124.

Two oaks stand on the boundary of Hadnock Chase and Staunton Manor. 3–400 years old. The boundary is also a parish, county and a national one. Ref: Standing (1986, 7).

80. Brockenhurst Oak. Hampshire. Brockenhurst (New Forest) nr the Church. Grid ref. SU 305018 (the Church).

Ref: Hurst (1911, 190).

81. Brockley Hall Oak. Somerset. Brockley Hall. Grid ref. ST 4666 (of Brockley).

Girth 36 ft. Ref: Loudon (1838, 1838).

82. Bucklebury Oaks. Berkshire. Grid ref. SU 5570.

A line of great oaks along the Bucklebury road. The finest trees in Berkshire. Ref: Rodgers (1941, 44).

83. Budby Oak. Nottinghamshire. At Thoresby Hall, near the lake. Grid ref. SK 6869 (Budby).

Ref: Hewins (1945, 15).

84. Bull Oak (I). See Salcey Great Oak.

85. Bull Oak (II). Also known as the Wedgenock Park Oak. Warwickshire. 3 m. NW of Warwick Station in Wedgenock Park. Grid ref. SP 257690 (Bulloak Farm).

Fell in 1930s. Girth 37 ft at 6 ft, 40 ft at 1 ft in 1838 (Loudon). Wedgenock Park was established in the reign of Henry I. A hollow oak. Ref: Strutt (1830, 22–3). Loudon (1838) Vol. III p. 1779. Lauder (1883, 257–8). Hurst (1911, 190). Hewins (1945, 6). Wilks (1972, 199). Whitlock (1985, 110). Morton (1986, 6). **Strutt (1830, 22). Loudon Vol. III fig. 1616.**

86. Bulthy Oak. Shropshire. Bulthy 7½ m. E of Welshpool about ½ m. N of Shrewsbury-Welshpool road A458. Grid ref. SJ 319135 (Bulthy Farm).

Ref: Hewins (1945, 11).

87. Bunyan's Oak. Also known as John Bunyan's Oak. Bedfordshire. Sampshill, a hamlet near Hartington: Hartington is 3 m. W of Barton-le-Clay and 2 m. NE of Toddington. Grid ref. TL 051321 (Upper Sampshill Farm).

John Bunyan said to have held services beneath this tree. Ref: Wilks (1972, 78). **Wilks (1972, 79).**

88. Burden Oak. Gloucestershire. Millway Grove ½ m. NE of English Bicknor Church, Forest of Dean. On SE of English Bickner to Lydbrook Road. Grid ref. SO 587165.

Sessile oak. Still alive 1991. Girth 18 ft 10 ins. Ht 83 ft. 30 ft to first branch. (Standing 1986). Age *c.* 300. Named after Rev. John Burden who became Rector of English Bicknor 25 June 1844. When Milway Grove was clear felled in 1950s the Rev Walker purchased it for £5 to save it (Standing 1986). Ref: Standing (1986, 8). **Hart (1966) frontispiece.**

89. Burton Overy Oak. Leicestershire. Grid ref. SP 6798.

An oak tree planted at the Restoration from an acorn off the Boscobel Oak, in the grounds of Burton Overy rectory. Ref: Hewins (1945, 15).

90. Butcher's Shambles, The. See Shambles Oak, The.

91. Button Oak. Shropshire. In village of Button Oak on Bewdley-Buttonbridge road B4194 3 m. NW of Bewdley Station in Wyre Forest. Grid ref. SO 753 779.

A pub called the Button Oak is near the original site of the oak. One of the 'Bewdley' oaks. Ref: Hewins (1945, 11). Morton (1986, 50).

92. Byron's Oak. Nottinghamshire. Newstead Abbey, near Nottinghamshire. Grid ref. SK 5454.

Planted by Byron in 1798 when he inherited the Abbey. Later, in 1807, on revisiting the tree he found it neglected and wrote a poem about it. A later owner of the Abbey, a Colonel Wildman, 'was going to fell the oak but learning of its association spared it and looked after it'. Ref: Mosley (1910, 57).

93. Cadenham Oak. See Cadnam Oak.

94. Cadnam Oak. Also known as the Cadenham Oak. Hampshire – New Forest. Said to have been in Copythorne not Cadnam (Whitlock 1985). Grid ref. SU 2913 (Cadnam), SU 315142 (Copythorne).

It was a pedunculate oak. Early flushing (Wilks). The leaves usually appeared on 6 Jan. the old Xmas Day (Whitlock 1985). Ref: Gilpin (1791, 165). Loudon (1838, 1761). Selby (1842, 245). Anon (1853, 171–3). Lauder (1883, 247). Hurst (1911, 190). Wilks (1972, 206). Whitlock (1985, 106). Letter Hants C.C. 16/11/1991.

95. Caerhyder Oak. Also known as the Coronation Oak. (III). Monmouthshire. On N side of road opposite Pencraig Farm house, ¼ m. S of Llanhennock (1½ m. NE of Caerleon). Grid ref. ST 356924.

The oak is still there but completely dead (James April 1992). Girth 24 ft 10 ins at 6 ft, 45 ft at ground (Wade 1931). Girth 27 ft 2 ins at 5 ft agl. Difficult to girth (James 1992). 38 ft 6 ins at 1 ft (Linnard 2000). A hybrid oak (Wade 1931). Celebrations were held under this tree in 1837 when Queen Victoria ascended the throne. Ref: Wade (1931, 134). Hyde (1977, 122). Hando (1944). Visit by James 1991. Linnard (2000, 126). **Photographs James 21/10/1991.**

96. Calthorpe Oak. See Cowthorpe Oak.

97. Canterton Oak. See Rufus Oak.

98. Capon Tree, The. Also known as The Kepping Tree or The Trysting Tree (Lauder). Roxburghshire. Beside Jedwater, Jedburgh 'in a meadow near old Castle of Ferniherst about 1½ m. above the town' (Loudon 1838). 'At Prior's Haugh' (Wilks 1972). Grid ref. NT 6520 (Jedburgh).

Sessile oak. In 1893 it was 22 ft 7 ins girth at 'narrowest part'. It divides at 6 ft into two stems girthing 16 ft 2 ins and 10 ft 9 ins (Elwes and Henry 1907). On Marquis of Lothian's estate. Girth 26 ft 6 ins in 1991 (Mitchell) but in poor condition. This tree was a place where the Border clans met. Capon is from the Scots word 'kep' = to meet. Ref: Loudon (1838) Vol. III pp. 1772–3: Grigor (1841, 270). Selby (1842, 255). Lauder (1883, 252). Michie (1888, 239–41). Elwes and Henry (1907, 329). Wilks (1972, 200). Mitchell (1991, 88). **Michie p. 241. Selby p. 255.**

99. Castle Hill Oak. (I). Nottinghamshire. Bothamsall. Grid ref. SK 6773 (Bothamsall).

An old oak on a mound with a dry moat. Ref: Hewins (1945, 14).

100. Castle Hill Oak. (II). See Umbrella Oak.

101. Castle Oak. Sussex. Knepp Castle.

Girth 207 cms at 1 m (1996). Ref: Johnson, Owen (1998).

102. Cawthorpe Oak. See Cowthorpe Oak.

103. Cecil Oak. Sussex. In Petworth Park, 6 m. E of Midhurst. Grid ref. SU 9721.

Pedunculate oak. Said to date from *c.* 1600; planted to commemorate a marriage into the Cecil Family. The tree lost limbs in storm of 1987 but was still alive in 1991. A plaque has now been removed. Ref: White (1991). Letter from Mr. Chance 7/11/1991.

104. Cefnmabli Oak. Glamorgan. On the boundary between Glamorgan and Monmouth. Grid ref. SO 223841.

Fell 1779. In 1739 recorded as having 66 ft of clean stem. When the tree began to decay it was capped with lead to preserve it. Linnard (2000, 124).

105. Central Oak. See Centre Tree.

106. Centre of England Oak, The. See Lillington Oak.

107. Centre Tree, The. Also known as the Central Oak. Nottinghamshire. In Birklands (Wood) 1¼ m. NW of Edwinstowe: 2¼ m. E of Warsop. Grid ref. SK 607676 (marked on O.S. map).

Named for its central position in the drive to Welbeck. This tree was said to be halfway between Thoresby and Welbeck, from which Robin Hood's paths radiated through the Forest of Sherwood. Ref: Hewins (1945, 14). Wilks (1972, 170–1).

108. Chair Oak, The. Northamptonshire. Grid ref. SP 8051 (Salcey Forest).

Ref: Loudon (1838).

109. Champion, The. Montgomeryshire. Powis Castle, Welshpool. Grid ref. SJ 2206.

Fell on a still evening 13 April 1939. Girth 24 ft, 110 ft high Linnard (2000). Ref: Elwes and Henry (1907, 309). Hyde (1977, 122). Linnard (2000).

110. Chandos Oak. Also known as the Michendon Oak. Middlesex. Michendon House, Southgate 8 m. N of London. Grid ref. TQ 3093.

Sessile oak (White). Girth 18 ft at 1 ft (Loudon 1838). Ref: Strutt (1830, 12–13). Loudon (1838) Vol. III p. 1756. Selby (1842, 256). Lauder (1883, 255). Hurst (1911, 190). Wilks (1972, 92). Mitchell (1974, 271). White (1991). **Strutt p. 12. Loudon fig. 1601.**

111. Charles II Oaks. See Three Brothers. (I).

112. Charles' Oak. Gloucestershire. Parkend, Forest of Dean. Grid ref. SO 624081.

Three oaks, 350–400 years old. Labelled G50, G51 and G52. In 1986 G52 had a girth of 20 ft 12. Said to date from the time of Charles II (Standing 1987). Ref: Standing (1987, 26).

113. Chatsworth Oak. Derbyshire. Chatsworth. Grid ref. SK 2670 (Chatsworth).

Planted by Princess Victoria before she became Queen.

114. Chaucer's Oak. Also known as the King's Oak. (I).

Berkshire. Donnington Castle Park, 1¾ m. NNW of Newbury Station. Grid ref. SU 460390 (Donnington Park).

This tree is said to have been planted by Chaucer, or he may have written some of his works beneath it. 'It was 50 ft to first branch and 5 sq ft at the butt end, all clear timber' (Loudon 1838). Ref: Evelyn (1670, 153). Langley (1740, 186). Gilpin (1791, 134). Loudon (1838) Vol. III p. 1754. Ablett (1880, 167). Hewins (1945, 15).

115. Cheltenham Oak. See Boddington Oak.

116. Chenies Oak, The. Buckinghamshire. Chenies, 4 m. E of Amersham. Grid ref. TQ 0198.

Loudon (1838) quotes 'is an old tree which was going to decay in reign of Queen Elizabeth [I]' but says that when farm yard was formed close by the resultant manure revived it. Ref: Loudon (1838) Vol. III p. 1756.

117. Cheriton Cross Oak. Cheriton Bishop, Dunsford, Somerset. Grid ref. SX 775929. A dancing oak formally marking the boundary of the Great Fulford Estate.

118. Chertsey Oak. Surrey. Chertsey. Grid ref. TQ 0466.

Steps lead to a former tree top platform (Whitlock 1985). Ref: Whitlock (1985, 107).

119. Chingford Oak. See Fairmead Oak.

120. Christ's Oak. See Lady Oak. (I).

121. Church Path Oak, Northamptonshire. Salcey Forest – Wakes Coppice. Grid ref. SP 801525.

Fell January 1996 after a hard frost. A seedling from the tree has been planted as a replacement. Pedunculate oak. Girth 19 ft 4 ins at 5 ft agl. (James 1991). Estimated to be c. 470 years old–AD 1521. A plaque reads 'Salcey Forest, Church Path Oak'. William Henry, the sixth Duke of Grafton was accustomed to rest under this tree on his way to and from Piddington Church. Ref: Wilks (1972, 172). Visit by James 1991. **Photographs James 24/10/1991.**

122. Churn Oak. Also known as The Old Churn Oak. Nottinghamshire. Warsop. Grid ref. SK 5765.

123. Cliff Oak, The. Also known as the King Tree. (II). Staffordshire. Bagot's Park. 4 m. S of Uttoxeter. 2 m. N of Abbots Bromley. Grid ref. SK 090275 (Bagot's Park).

Felled in 1933. The wood was used for panelling in the Queen Mary. Ref: Wilks (1972, 248).

124. Clipstone Oak. See Parliament Oak.

125. Cockpen Tree. See Major Oak. (I).

126. Codshall Oak. Staffordshire. Codshall Wood. Grid ref. SJ 8305 (Codshall Wood).

An old oak which was Parish property in 1945. A relic of Brewood Forest. Ref: Hewins (1945, 8).

127. Coltsthorpe Oak. See Cowthorpe Oak.

128. Colwall Oaks. Also known as the Colwill Oaks. Worcestershire. Colwall. Grid ref. SO 7541.

Fine oaks. One had a girth of 23 ft in 1945 (Hewins 1945). Ref: Transactions of the Woolhope Club (1867). Hewins (1945, 12). **Transactions of Woolhope Club (1867, 3).**

129. Colwill Oaks. See Colwall Oaks.

130. Compton House Oak. Dorset. Compton House. Grid ref. ST 5917.

Girth was 21 ft (Loudon 1838). Ref: Loudon (1838, 1837).

131. Conqueror's Oak. See King Oak. (VIII).

132. Copford Oaks. Essex. Copford Plain, Copford 4 m. WSW of Colchester. Grid ref. TL 9222.

Ref: Hurst (1911, 52, 63, 190).

133. Coplestone Oak. Devon. On triangle of grass at entrance to St. Mary's Church, Tamerton Foliat, now adjoining the northern limits of Plymouth. Grid ref. SX 472608.

Girth: 15 ft 2 ins at 5 ft agl. but one burr may have affected measurement (James 1992). Completely hollow, charred inside. A plaque reads: 'The Coplestone Oak dates from the sixteenth century'. The oak is where John Coplestone killed his godson. He escaped hanging by surrendering 13 Cornish manors to the Crown. Ref: Mee (1938b, 411). Visit by James 1992. **Photographs James 6/4/92.**

134. Copt Oak. Leicestershire. Charnwood Forest. Grid ref. SK 4812.

Marks the centre of the old Charnwood Forest (Rodgers 1941). Ref: Rodgers (1941, 97).

135. Coronation Oak. (I). Co. Londonderry. Derry City, in the grounds of Aberfoyle House.

Planted for Queen Elizabeth's Coronation in 1953. Ref: Browne. D. (2000, 25).

136. Coronation Oak. (II). Co. Derry. In the centre of Eglington.

Planted for the Coronation of Edward VII in 1902. Grown from an acorn from an oak in Windsor Great Park. Ref: Browne (2000, 25).

137. Coronation Oak. (III). See Caerhyder Oak.

138. Coronation Wood. Sussex. Hastings. Grid ref. TQ 823122.

Oaks were planted in Alexandra Park to commemorate George VI's Coronation raised from acorns from old trees in Windsor Great Park. Ref: Johnson, Owen (1998).

139. Coughton Court Oak. Warwickshire. North of Alcestor. Grid ref. SP 0760.

Girth 30 ft (Hewins 1945). Ref: Hewins (1945, 6).

140. Council Oak. Wiltshire. Coate Water Park, Swindon. Grid ref. SU 176823.

Alive Dec. 1991. Referred to in *Bevis* Jefferies (1932). Ref: 'Bevis' Jefferies (1932, 149–151). Letter, C. Caistor 16/12/1991. **Drawing by E. H. Shepard p. 151. Jefferies (1932).**

141. Court Oak. Essex. Great Leighs at Moulsham Hall. Grid ref. TL 7317.

Ref: Mee (1940, 166).

142. Court Tree, The. See Allerton Oak.

143. Cowarne Court Oak. Herefordshire. Cowarne Court. Grid ref. SO 615465.

Ref: Transactions of the Woolhope Club (1872, 16). **Transactions of the Woolhope Club (1872). p. 16.**

144. Cowper's Oak. Also known as Judith Oak or Yardley Oak. Northamptonshire. Was on S boundary of large woodland area in southern part of Yardley Chase in section named Church Slade. 5 m. from Weston Lodge. Grid ref. SP 862536 (or thereabouts).

Dead in 1969 and was removed. A replacement tree has not survived. Girth 24 ft 1 in at 6 ft agl. height 31 ft (Loudon 1838). Said to have been planted by Judith, William the Conqueror's niece (see Judith Oak). A favourite walk of the poet Cowper was to this oak. Ref: Loudon (1838) Vol. III p. 1765–6: Selby (1842, 254). Letter from Mr Pearson (1991) Agent at Castle Ashby.

145. Cowthorpe Oak. Also known as the Calthorpe Oak (Strutt) or Cawthorpe Oak (Ablett): or Coltsthorpe Oak (Lauder) and Father of The Forest. Yorkshire. Village of Cowthorpe is 3 m. NE of Wetherby and 2 m. W of Marston Moor. Grid ref. SE 427524 (Cowthorpe village).

One of the largest oaks ever to grow in UK: 78 ft girth at gl. (Selby 1842). In 1911 the tree was still alive when it was 48 ft at 3 ft (Hurst 1911). Ref: Rooke (1790, 15). Gilpin (1791, 121). Hayes (1822, 127). Strutt (1830, 34).

Loudon (1838) III p. 1771. Grigor (1841, 268–9). Empson (1842). Selby (1842, 254). Burt (1860, 65). Ablett (1880, 170–1). Lauder (1883, 260). Mosley (1910, 69–72). Hurst (1911, 85, 191). Wilks (1972, 249). Brewer's Dict. (1983). **Strutt p. 34. Loudon figs 1620, 1624. Empson frontispiece.**

146. Crad Oak. Gloucestershire. Forest of Dean – Sallow Vallets Inclosure. In a conifer plantation on W side of track running S from Sallow Vallets Lodge. Grid ref. SO 607140.

Probably planted about 1682. Tree almost dead in 1986: struck by lightning c. 1959–60. List of girths from 1830–1986 given by Standing (1986). Girth 12 ft 4 ins in 1830, 16 ft 8 ins girth in 1961. There was an oak in this vicinity in 1282 and it was noted as a 'mere' point (meer, a Saxon word = Boundary) between the bailiwicks of Ruardean and Dean Magna. Some natural regeneration from the oak grows nearby. Ref: Standing (1986, 8).

147. Creeping Oak. Wiltshire. Savernake Forest. 5 m. SE of Marlborough. Grid ref. SU 2265 (Savernake).

So called as one of the main boughs rested on the ground and appeared to creep along. Ref: Strutt (1830, 30). Loudon (1838, 1771). Hurst (1911, 191). **Loudon figs 1618, 1632.**

148. Cressage Oak. See Lady Oak. (I).

149. Crimea Oak. Northamptonshire. Althorp Park: on SW side of road from main west entrance road to a group of agricultural buildings and opposite these buildings. Grid ref. SP 679647.

Pedunculate oak. Girth 22 ft 7 ins at 5 ft agl. (James 1991). A fine maiden tree. In 1890 a stone nearby said 'This wood was planted by Robert, Lord Spencer in the year of our Lord 1602–1603. Ref: Mitchell (1890) Transactions of R.S.F.S. Vol. XIII pt I p. 86. Elwes and Henry (1907, 321). Mitchell (1996, 316). Visit by James 1991. **Elwes and Henry Vol. II plate 94. Photographs James 25/10/1991.**

150. Croft Castle Oak. Herefordshire. Croft Castle, near Leominster. In a disused quarry adjoining the Park, about 130 yards south of Sir Williams's Oak. Grid ref. SO 448653.

Sessile oak. Girth 12.39 metres in 1987 (National Trust) Girth 40 ft 5 ins at 5 ft (James 1991). This tree was measured by N.T. in summer 1991. The average of four girths between 4–6 ft was 42 ft 6 ins. The tree is heavily burred. Possibly the largest in the County. Ref: National Trust. Visit by James 1991. **Photographs James 23/10/1991.**

151. Cromwell Oak. Wiltshire. Melksham: on N side of Melksham to Devizes road (A365). Just past a lay-by. Grid ref. ST 918624.

Ref: Wilks (1972, 199–200).

152. Crossed Oak, The. Nottinghamshire. Sherwood Forest. Grid ref. SK 646645 (Rufford Abbey).

This oak marked the boundary of the Rufford Abbey lands. Ref: Clarke et al. (1987, 39).

153. Crouch Oak. Also known as the Addlestone Oak or Queen's Oak. (I). Surrey. Addlestone 1 m. W of Weybridge. Grid ref. TQ 0464.

In the fourteenth century, Wycliffe preached under this oak. Queen Elizabeth I is said to have feasted under it. Ref: Burt (1860, 64–5). Hurst (1911, 191). Wilks (1972, 30).

154. Crowleasowe Oak. Shropshire. Crowleasowe Farm, near Bitterley. Grid ref. SO 5577 (Bitterley).

Girth 10.97 metres (36 ft) in 1983 (Morton 1986). On the fringe of the old Clee Forest. This ceased to be a Royal Forest in 1155 and then became part of the Clifford Estate. Ref: Morton (1986, 43).

155. Crump Oak. Herefordshire. Near Kington. Grid ref. SO 3554 (marked on the map).

Ref: Transactions of the Woolhope Club (1870, 292).

156. Crumpler's, Samuel Oak. Dorset. Lytchett Matravers. Grid ref. SY 9495.

The tree marks the spot where farmer Samuel Crumpler was killed by his bull in 1849 at the age of 55 years. Buried by his family under the tree, his sons carved the shape of a coffin into the bark, which is periodically re-cut by his descendants who visit the tree annually. Ref: Stokes and Branchflower (2001).

157. Cuckoo Oak. (I). Shropshire. Cuckoo Oak, east of Madeley. Grid ref. SJ 6904 (Madeley).

The oak tree was fenced off by the villagers of Madeley to prevent the cuckoo from flying on to Dawley. Ref: Hewins (1945, 11).

158. Cuckoo Oak. (II). Staffordshire/Shropshire Border. Kingswood. Grid ref. SJ 8402.

Two large trees known as the Cuckoo Oaks. Ref: Hewins (1945, 11).

159. Cuckoo Oak. (III). Nottinghamshire Sherwood Forest. Grid ref. SK 5958 (Sherwood Forest).

160. Culford Oak. Suffolk. Culford. Grid ref. TL 8370.
Ref: O. Rackham (1994).

161. Cultoquhey Oak, The. Perthshire. Cultoquhey, near Crieff. Grid ref. NN 8621.

An oak near the house was grown from an acorn 'off the great oak in Knolle Park, Kent' in 1851. Ref: Hunter (1883).

162. Dalston Oak. Cumbria. 'A house in Dalston' Grid ref. NY 3750 (Dalston).

Girth 14 metres (Holdsworth 1990). Pollarded and heavily burred. On a mound. In 1867 said to be the largest oak in Cumberland. Ref: Holdsworth (1990, 4).

163. Damory's Oak. Dorset. Near Blandford. Grid ref. ST 8806 (Blandford).

Blown down in 1703 and felled 1755 (Johns 1847). Girth 68 ft at gl and 12 ft at 17 ft agl (Gilpin 1791). Suffered great damage in violent storm of 1703 (Gilpin). Sold and cut up for firewood in 1755 when it was 68 ft girth (Selby 1842). During the Civil War, an old man lived in the oak and sold ale. Ref: Gilpin (1791, 142). Loudon (1838, 1758). Selby (1842, 254). Johns (1903) Vol. I p. 76. Ablett (1880, 172). Wilks (1972, 31). **Hutchins (1800) Vol. I.**

164. Danbury Oaks. Essex. In Danbury Park between Chelmsford and Maldon; 4 m. from centre of Chelmsford and on S side of A414. Grid ref. TL 7805 (Danbury).

One of the oaks, called Big Ben, was 33 ft at 5 ft in 1911 (Hurst 1911). Ref: Hurst (1911, 106, 120, 191). **Hurst (1911, 140, 158).**

165. Darley Oak. Cornwall. In the front garden of Darley Farm farmhouse – at Darleyford on Launceston–Liskeard road B3254. Grid ref. SX 276732.

Girth approx 21 ft at 5 ft agl. Much of western portion of bole has gone (James 1991). In 1876 the hollow oak was used for pleasure parties. Seven stone steps lead to a look-out point. Ref: Thurston (1930, 191). Visit by James 1991. **Photographs Thurston p. 192. James 25/9/1991.**

166. Decanter Oak. Also known as the Big Bellied Oak. Wiltshire. Savernake Forest. Grid ref. SU 2464 (Savernake area).

Named from its unusual shape. Ref: Rodgers (1941, 60).

167. Derwen Cenbren Yr Ellyll. See Nannau Oak.

168. Devil's Stone Oak, The. See Shebbear Oak.

169. Domesday Oak. (I). Somerset (Avon). Ashton Court 1 m. SW of Clifton Suspension Bridge: 1 m. NE of Long Ashton near Bristol. Grid ref. ST 557718 (Ashton Court).

Said to be 700 years old in the Gardening Supplement to the Independent of 13/3/1994. Ref: Wilks (1972). **Wilks opp p. 220.**

170. Domesday Oak. (II). Also known as the Goodcheap Oak. Kent. Goodcheap Farm, Hinxhill, 2 m. NE Ashford. Grid ref. TR 047434.

In the past, four men ate supper in this oak. In 1953, saplings were raised from this oak. One was planted in the nearby secondary school grounds in 1958. Ref: Bunce (1959, 171). **Bunce (1959) in Q.J.F. p. 171.**

171. Domesday Oak. (III). Devon. Blue Hayes, Broadclyst. Grid ref. SX 9897 (of Broadclyst).

Blew down in 1990. Girth then 16 ft. Ref: Letter from J. Gill (1991).

172. Doodle Oak. Essex. Hatfield Forest (in north-west portion). Grid ref. TL 2309 (Hatfield).

Last bore leaves in 1858. A stump remained for many years. A young tree growing near may be a coppice shoot. Site marked by concrete pillar bearing inscription. Loudon (1838) gives girth as 42 ft at base in 1813, but previously above 60 ft. In 1949 a ring count on the stump came to 850. Ref: Loudon (1838) Vol. III p. 1759. Elwes and Henry (1907, 324). *Country Life* (1949). 'Trees of a Royal Forest'. *Country Life* (1950) 'Oaks of a Royal Forest'. Rackham (1989). Letter from M. Atkinson dated 20/12/1991. **Loudon Vol. III p. 1759: Young (c. 1790). Houblon (1907).**

173. Double Oak. Northamptonshire. Grid ref. SP 8051 (Salcey Forest).

174. Double Tree, The. Hampshire. The New Forest near the Rufus Stone. Grid ref. SU 270125 (the Rufus Stone).

Alive in 1991. Twin oaks. Ref: Letter, Hampshire County Council (1991).

175. Druid Oaks. (I). Northamptonshire. Southwick Wood, near Oundle. Grid ref. TL 005936.

Old hulks in 1991. Ref: Forestry Commission (1991).

176. Druid Oaks. (II). Shropshire. Oakly Park, Bromfield, nr Ludlow. Grid ref. SO 4876 (Bromfield).

Nearly all these oaks have gone. A former park (Morton 1986). Ref: Morton (1986, 43).

177. Drumin Oak. Tyrone/Londonderry Border. In the walled grounds of Killymoon Castle.

Girth 25 ft 6 ins. The biggest oak in Northern Ireland. It is claimed that King William tied his horse to it. Ref: Browne (2000, 70).

178. Dryden's Oak. Northampton. Blakesley: 3½ m. WNW of Towcester: 4¾ m. NW of Silverstone. Grid ref. SP 626503.

On the death of his father in 1654, John Dryden

(1631–1700) succeeded to a small estate at Blakesley. Ref: Chambers Biographical Dictionary (1956, 314). Wilks (1972, 245).

179. Dryton Oak. Shropshire. Eaton Constantine. On the lane that leads from the B4380 to the Eyton-on-Severn racecourse. Grid ref. SJ 5906 (Eaton Constantine).

Girth 8.53 metres (28 ft) in 1983. Ref: Morton (1986, 64). **Morton p. 48.**

180. Duke of Gloucester, The. Gloucestershire. Razies Bottom, (The Razies) Ashwicke Hall, 1½ m. SE of Marshfield and 3 m. N of Batheaston. Grid ref. ST 795721.

Girth 14 ft and a clear trunk for 25 ft (Loudon 1838). Ref: Loudon (1838) Vol. III p. 1760.

181. Duke of Portland's Walking Stick. Also known as The Duke's Walking Stick. Nottinghamshire. Welbeck Park. Grid ref. SK 564742 (the Abbey).

Original tree felled 1790. Girth 21 ft at gl and 14 ft at 3 ft. 111 ft high in 1790 (Loudon 1838). A similar tree nearby was given the name, Young Walking Stick. It was 95 ft high, girth 5 ft at 3 ft and 110 years old (Loudon 1838). Ref: Rooke (1790, 6–7). Hayes (1822, 125). Loudon (1838) Vol. III p. 1766. Elwes and Henry (1907, 322). Wilks (1972, 171). White (1991). Packenham (1996, 25). **Rooke plate 1. Loudon fig. 1607.**

182. Duke of Suffolk's Oak. Warwickshire. Astley Church, near Astley Castle. 'Two bow shots SW of the church'. Grid ref. SP 3189 (Astley).

The tree in which the Duke of Suffolk tried to conceal himself when the Wyatt rebellion failed (1554). A table and chair found in the hollow oak are kept in the Castle. Ref: Hewins (1945, 6).

183. Duke's Vaunt Oak. Wiltshire. Savernake Forest. On the northern boundary of the Parish of Burbage, half a mile from the A4. Grid ref. SU 2565.

Girth 30 ft in 1802. The name is from the Protector Somerset (Regent for Edward VI) who owned Savernake and who took a pride in this oak. Probably an old boundary oak. Ref: Rodgers (1941, 60).

184. Duke's Walking Stick, The. See Duke of Portland's Walking Stick.

185. Dumb-bell Oak. Hertfordshire. In the grounds of Haileybury College. Grid ref. TL 358108 (Haileybury Quad).
Ref: Wilks (1972, 25).

186. Dunmow Oak. Nottinghamshire. On the edge of Sherwood Forest. Grid ref. SK 5958 (Sherwood Forest).

Associated with Robin Hood. Maid Marion, the Countess of Huntingdon is buried here. Ref: Roberts (1890, 120).

187. Dunson's Oak. Oxfordshire. Shipton-under-Wychwood. Grid ref. SP 2717 (Shipton-under-Wychwood).

The tree has the initials H.D. and T.D. carved on it. Harry and Tom Dunson were eighteenth-century highwaymen captured near the tree and taken to Gloucester and hanged. Their bodies were brought back from there and hung on the tree. Ref: Timpson (1987).

188. Eagle Oak. Hampshire. New Forest: Knightwood Enclosure. Grid ref. SU 256061.

Pedunculate oak. This oak was so named as an eagle was shot in it about 1850. Ref: Rodgers (1941, 49). White (1991).

189. Eardisley Great Oak. See Eardisley Oak.

190. Eardisley Oak. Also known as The Great Oak (II) or Eardisley Great Oak. Herefordshire. Lower Welson, ¾ m. W of Eardisley and 5 m. S of Kington. According to Hewins it was on Hurstway Common. Grid ref. SO 299497.

Girth 30 ft 3½ ins at 5 ft agl. A fine tree in good condition (James 1991). Ref: Burt (1860, 65). Purchas and Ley (1889). Hewins (1945, 12). Wilks (1972, 201). Visit by James 1991. Photographs James 23/10/1991.

191. Earl of Thanet's Hollow Oak, The. See Hollow Oak, The. (I).

192. Eastern Oak. Hampshire. Possibly at Boldrewood, New Forest (Wise 1863, 16). Grid ref. SZ 2408 (Boldrewood).
Probably a boundary tree. Ref: Wise (1863, 16).

193. Edgewell Oak, The. See Edgewell Tree, The.

194. Edgewell Tree, The. Also known as The Edgewell Oak. Near the Castle of Dalhousie. On B704 near Bonnyrigg. Grid ref. NT 3465.
Alive in 1920 (Frazer). Ref: Frazer (1930) Vol. II p. 166.

195. Elderslee Oak. See Wallace Oak.

196. Elderslie Oak. See Wallace Oak.

197. Elfin Oak, The. London. Kensington Gardens. Grid ref. TQ 27778 (Kensington).

Exists as a dead stump. The tree destroyed by lightning in 1898. Subsequently elves, fairies and witches carved on stump by Ivor Innes. These were restored by repainting by Spike Milligan about 20 years ago. Surrounded by a protective iron palisade.

198. Elizabeth Oak, The. (I). See Queen Elizabeth's Oak (II).

199. Elizabeth Oak, The. (II). See Queen Elizabeth's Oak (V).

200. Ellerslie Oak. See Wallace Oak, The.

201. Eve Oak. Herefordshire. Moreton Station, North of Hereford. Grid ref. SO 5144 (Moreton).

Ref: Transactions of the Woolhope Club (1872). **Transactions of the Woolhope Club (1872, 1).**

202. Fair Oak. (I). Hampshire. Near the Old George Pub. Grid ref. SU 494185.

Fell in 1842. A young tree now grows about ten yards from the Old George. An annual fair was held here. A seat was made from the wood of the tree and is in Winchester Cathedral. Ref: Letter. Hants. C.C. (1991).

203. Fair Oak. (II). Glamorgan. Llantrisant, near Cardiff. Grid ref. ST 3996.

A boundary oak. Ref: Linnard (2000, 121).

204. Fairlop Oak. Essex. In Hainault Forest. Grid ref. TQ 453908 (Fairlop).

Was set on fire in 1805 and fell 1820. 48 ft in girth at ground level (Loudon 1838). An annual fair was held here and a man called Day served bacon and beans to the public from it. The pulpit and reading desk in St Pancras Church was made from the wood of this tree. Ref: Gilpin (1791, 141). Loudon (1838) Vol. III p. 1759. Johns (1847) Vol. I p. 74. Anon (1853, 136). W. H. Ablett (1880, 171). Mosley (1910, 61). Hurst (1911, 191). Wilks (1972, 176). Brewer's Dict. (1983). Whitlock (1985, 109).

205. Fairmead Oak. Also known as The Chingford Oak. Essex. At or near Chingford 4 m. S of Waltham Abbey. It stood in Epping Forest. Grid ref. TQ 893 (Chingford).

Dead in 1911 and burnt to the ground in 1955. Girth 30 ft in 1907 when much decayed (Elwes and Henry 1907). Hurst (1911) described it as a huge tree which had been pollarded. It is said that Henry VIII waited to hear the guns of the Tower of London announce the execution of Anne Boleyn beneath it (Whitlock 1985). Its branches were said to resemble a lightning flash. Ref: Elwes and Henry (1907) Vol. II p. 324. Hurst (1911, 190). Wilks (1972, 90). Whitlock (1985, 105).

206. Father of The Forest. See Cowthorpe Oak.

207. Felon's Oak. Somerset. ½ m. S of Rodhuish and at N entrance to Croydon Hall: 1¼ m. due S of Carhampton (on A39). Grid ref. ST 018388 (Named on O.S. map).

New tree planted c. 1987. 70 year old tree felled c. 1986 which in turn had replaced an even older tree. Present young tree was about 9 ft high on 2 July 1991 (James). The last person hanged on tree was said to be a sheep-stealer in 1821. Ref: Wilks (1972, 82). Letter from Somerset County Council (Environment Dept) 20/8/1991. Visit by James 1991. **Photographs Country Life by J. D. V. Ward. James 2/7/1991.**

208. Fingringhoe Oak. Essex. 4 m. SE of Colchester. Grid ref. TM 0220 (Fingringhoe).

Girth 43 ft 6 ins 2½ ft above the ground and 18 ft 9 ins at 7 ft, 3 Sept. 1910. (Hurst 1911). Ref: Hurst (1911, 34, 83, 192). **Hurst opp. p. 34 (Summer) and p. 83 (Winter).**

209. Fisher's Oak. Kent. About 17 m. from London on the Tunbridge Road (Loudon 1838). Grid ref. TQ 5355.

'Of enormous bulk. The part of the trunk now remaining is 24 ft in compass.' (Loudon 1838) The name is from a schoolmaster who, with his pupils, greeted King James here. Ref: Loudon (1838) Vol. III p. 1762.

210. Flittern Oak. Also known as the Flitton Oak. Devon. In a small triangle of trees surrounded by a bank, at the entrance to Flittern Barton, 1½ m. NW of North Molton. Grid ref. SS 714310. (Named on the OS map).

Sessile oak. Girth 28 ft in 1991 (James). It is now a hollow shell and one branch is propped up. 46 ft girth according to Selby (1842). Charles II is said to have hidden in it. Ref: Loudon (1838) Vol. III p. 1757. Selby (1842, 254). Visited by James 1991. **Loudon fig. 1592. Photograph James 1991.**

211. Flitton Oak. See Flittern Oak.

212. Forest Giant. Gloucestershire. Forest of Dean: Churchill Inclosure: on W side of track from Churchill Lodge to Parkend School. Grid ref. SO 627085.

Sessile oak. Girth 18 ft 9½ ins in 1986 (Standing 1986). Age over 300 yrs in 1990. Ref: Standing (1986, 5).

213. Forest Oak. See Quatford Oak.

214. Foresters Oaks. Monmouthshire. Wentwood: on NE side of road from Usk to Llamair Discoed and ¼ m. N of Wentwood Reservoir. Grid ref. ST 429939.

A circle of trees where foresters courts were held twice a year, when a jury of estate owners who had been granted rights, presided and dealt with interference to the deer, martens, hares, foxes, hawks, bees and fish. The vicar of Caerwent preached a sermon and as a fee received housebote and hay-bote. People were hung on these trees. The last person to be hung was in 1829 for sheep stealing. Ref:

Linnard (1982). Hando (1944). Visit by James 1991. **Linnard (1994, 31). Photographs James 9/4/92.**

215. Forestry Commissioner's Oak, The. Also known as Lord Robinson Oak.

216. Forrard Oak, The. Surrey. Witley 3½ m. SSW of Godalming and 6 m. NNE of Haslemere. Grid ref. SU 945396.

Pedunculate oak. An early flushing oak, hence the name. Ref: Wilks (1972, 206). Bean (1976) Vol. III p. 508. Whitlock (1985, 107). White (1991).

217. Foster's Oak, Simon. Nottinghamshire. Sherwood Forest: 2 m. W of Ollerton and 'near the Major Oak'. Grid ref. SK 627676 (the Major Oak).

Ref: Elwes and Henry (1907) Vol. II p. 322. Wilks (1972, 170).

218. Fredville Oaks. Also known as The Great Oaks (Strutt) See under individual names, Beauty, Majesty, Stately. Kent. Fredville, Nonnington 7 m. SE of Canterbury. Grid ref. TR 256512.

See Beauty, Majesty and Stately. Ref: Strutt (1830, 52). Loudon (1838, 1762). Lauder (1883, 254). Hurst (1911, 192). Plumtree (1975). Bean (1976) Vol. III p. 508. Pakenham (1996).

219. Freeland Oak, The. Perthshire. Freeland House, nr Forgandenny. Grid ref. NO 0818 (Forgandenny).

A variegated oak. Ref: Hunter (1883).

220. Frenchman's Oak. Hampshire. 2 m. SW of Winchfield (which is 1½ m. SSW of Hartley Wintney) and 1 m. NE of Odiham. Grid ref. SU 749522.

Alive in 1991. During the Napoleonic Wars, French prisoners were kept at Odiham. The officers gave their parole not to escape and were allowed to walk one mile from the village to this oak. Ref: James (1991).

221. Frodesley Oak. Shropshire. At Frodesley Lodge. 200 m up the side of Lodge Hill, close to Hoar Edge and the Causeway. Grid ref. SJ 5101 (Frodesley).

Girth 25 ft 6 ins in 1946, 27 ft in 1986 (Morton (1986). Frodesley Lodge was a seventeenth-century hunting lodge. Ref: Morton (1986). **Morton p. 46.**

222. Gallows Tree. Shropshire. At Prees Higher Heath on Gallows Tree Bank. Grid ref. SJ 5636.

In 1533 Richard Clowes robbed and murdered an Irish traveller here. Clowes was tried and hung in 1583 and his body nailed (gibbeted) to this tree (Morton 1986). Ref: Morton (1986, 58).

223. Gamekeeper's Oak. Also known as The Gamekeeper's Tree. Nottinghamshire. Welbeck Park. Grid ref. SK 564743 (Welbeck Abbey).

Girth 33 ft at ground level (Loudon 1838). 'In this tree, the gamekeeper secretes himself when he shoots the deer; and there makes a small aperture on the side opposite the entrance for his gun: on the inside is cut the date 1711' (Loudon 1838). Ref: Rooke (1790, 8). Loudon (1838) Vol. III p. 1766. **Rooke plate 4.**

224. Gamekeeper's Tree. See Gamekeeper's Oak.

225. Garter Oak. Perthshire. In the Horse Park, Dalguise House, 4 m. N of Dunkeld. Grid ref. NN 9947 (Dalguise).

A former laird of Dalguise sold the coppice but asked that this tree should remain in exchange for a pair of garters, which were then worn with knee breeches. His offer was accepted by the buyer of the coppice, hence the name of the tree (Hunter 1883). Ref: Hunter (1883, 68).

226. Giant, The. Montgomeryshire. Powis Castle, Welshpool, a few 100 yards across the approach road from the East. Grid ref. SJ 215064 (Powis Castle).

Sessile oak. Girth 33 ft 9 ins in 1961 (Linnard 2000). The largest oak tree in Britain i.e. with the largest trunk, and probably one of the oldest living oaks in Britain (Mitchell 1996). A hollow pollard. About 450 years old. Ref: Hyde (1977, 122). White (1991). Mitchell (1996, 309). Linnard (2000, 126).

227. Gibbet Oak, The. (I). Shropshire. Near the Horeshoes Inn on the A5 between Telford and Shrewsbury. Grid ref. SJ 579095 approx.

The notorious Bolas brothers were hung and gibbetted here on 4 September 1723. 'A report from 1814 ... tells of the nails from which the rotting bodies were hung still visible in the trunk of the oak' (Morton 1986). Ref: Morton (1986, 58).

228. Gibbet Oak, The. (II). Worcestershire. Kyrewood Estate: ¾ m. NE of Tenbury Wells. Grid ref. SO 606680 (Kyrewood House). Ref: Elwes and Henry (1907). Vol. II p. 313–14.

229. Gladstone Oak. Somerset. Holnicote 2 m. E of Porlock: 100 yds S of National Trust Estate Office. Grid ref. SS 911462.

Girth 10 ft 6 in at 5 ft agl. (James 1991). A well grown healthy tree at the foot of which is following plaque 'PLANTED BY/WILLIAM EUART/GLADSTONE/26 JAN 1877'. The estate at that time was owned by the Acland family. Ref: National Trust. Visit by James 1991. **Photographs James 2/7/1991.**

230. Glendower's Oak. Also known as Owen Glendower's Oak; Shelton Oak; Great Oak (X); Grete Oak; and Owen Glendower's Observatory. Shropshire. Said to be at junct. of Oswestry road (A5) and Welshpool road (A458) but 50:000 map shows 'The Oak' ¾ m. SW of this jct. Grid ref. SJ 465133 (road Junction). SJ 456125 (the Oak on map).

Girth was 40 ft. The dead trunk was removed in 1950 for road improvements. A sapling from this tree planted nearby at the A5/Welshpool junction, another at Dingle in Shrewsbury. Hewins (1945) says that this oak grew 'in the grounds of Shelton Priory'. Tradition states that Owen Glendower watched the battle of Tewkesbury (1403) from this oak. He was unable to cross the ford at Shelton with his men as the river was in flood and so could not assist Percy (Hotspur) against Henry IV. A title deed of 1543 mentions the 'Grete Oak'. In 1840 a bear was kept in it. Ref: Strutt (1830, 42.) Loudon (1838, 1767). Grigor (1841, 268). Anon (1853, 47). Ablett (1880, 169). Lauder (1883, 255). Mosley (1910, 61). Hurst (1911, 192). Hewins (1945, 9). Wilks (1972, 59). Brewer's Dict. (1983). Morton (1986, 57). **Loudon fig. 1611. Morton p. 57.**

231. Goblin's Hollow Oak. See Nannau Oak.

232. Godfraysok. See Godfrey Oak, The.

233. Godfrey Oak. Also known as Godfraysok. Gloucestershire. Grid ref. SO 6108.

A boundary oak. Ref: Hart (1966, 59).

234. Goff's Oak. Also known as Gough's Oak. Hertfordshire. Village of Goff's Oak is 2½ m. WNW of Cheshunt station and 5 m. ENE of Potters Bar station. Grid ref. TL 326033 (Goff's Oak village).

Girth 32 ft (Loudon 1838). Collapsed in 1950, replaced by a young tree *c.* 1951. A Plaque on the site gives the history. The tree was reputed to have been planted in 1066 by Sir Theodore Godfrey (or Goff'by), a Norman knight who came over with William the Conqueror. Ref: Loudon (1838) Vol. III p. 1762. Hurst (1911, 192). Wilks (1972, 26).

235. Gog. (I). of the Yardley Chase Oaks. Originally 2 oaks Gog and Magog (latter gone). Northamptonshire. Chase Park Farm 1½ m. SSW of Yardley Hastings. Grid ref. SP 852550.

Girth 27 ft 8 ins at 5 ft agl. Completely dead (James 1991). In 1838 Loudon records that Gog was 28 ft 5 ins at 6 ft and 72 ft high, Magog was 30 ft 7 ins at 6 ft and 66 ft high. These trees, together with others in the area, are said to have been planted by Judith, the niece of William the Conqueror, who lived here. She married the Earl of Northumbria and Huntingdon and after his execution for treason inherited his estate of Huntingdon about 1072. Ref: Loudon (1838) Vol. III p. 1765. Lauder (1883) Vol. I p. 259. Wilks (1972, 38). Visit by James 1991. **Loudon fig. 1765. Mitchell (1966). Photographs James 24/10/1991.**

236. Gog. (II). Staffordshire. Mavesyn Ridware; 3 m. SE of Rugeley and 4 m. NW of Lichfield 'Close to the River Trent' (Hewins). Grid ref. SK 082169 (Mavesyn Ridware Church).

Felled in the 1880s. Associated with an encounter between the Maversyn and Handsacre families in 1403. This oak was one of two. See Magog. (II). Ref: Hewins (1945, 8).

237. Gog and Magog oaks. Wick, Glastonbury, Somerset. Grid ref. ST 518396. Moribund 2003.

238. Golynos Oak. Also known as The Welsh Oak. Monmouthshire (Gwent). On the site now occupied by the Club House of the Newport Golf Club at Rogerstone. This is ¾ m. SSW of hamlet of Golynos (ST264504). The Club House is on the site of an earlier house known as Great Oak. Grid ref. ST 268893.

Felled 1810 and went to the Plymouth Dockyard. For details of the use of the timber see Ch. 5 and Stone (1933). 400 rings were counted in the trunk. The Chartists met under this tree in 1836. Ref: Burt (1880, 168). Mosley (1910, 68). Stone (1933, 151–2). Hyde (1977, 122). Linnard (1982, 83). **Print from the 'Western Mail' 21/8/1912 in Oates.**

239. Goodcheap Oak. See Domesday Oak. (II).

240. Goodmoor Oak. Worcestershire. Wyre Forest near Far Forest to Kinlet road: situated between Cherry Orchard House and Stepping Stones House. Grid ref. SO 723761 (approx).

Girth at 6 ft agl was 15 ft 6 ins on 20 Oct 1968 (Hickin 1972). Ref: Hickin (1972, 7–8). **Hickin p. 8 – Line drawing.**

241. Gospel Oak. (I). Also known as the Avington Oak. Hampshire. Hampage Wood 4 m. NE of Winchester: 2½ m. WSW New Alresford. Grid ref. SU 544312.

This oak is still marked on 1:50,000 OS sheet dated 1988 although Wilks states it 'fell about 1893'. Hampage Wood was cut down by Bishop Walkelin to be used for Winchester Cathedral. He obtained leave from William I to cut down as much timber as he could in four days and nights. By collecting all the unemployed men to work, he felled everything except the Gospel Oak! The tree was a rallying point for the Puritans in the seventeenth century. Ref: Wilks (1972, 243).

242. Gospel Oak. (II). Suffolk. Polstead Hall Park. Just outside the Churchyard. 12 miles SW of Ipswich. Grid ref. TL 9938 (Polstead).

A young oak has been planted to replace the original which collapsed in 1956. Girth 66 ft (Mosley 1910). Said to be where the Gospel was preached to the Saxons. Ref: Mosley (1910, 64). Hurst (1911, 7). Wilks (1972, 22). **Hurst p. 7. Wilks opp. p. 113.**

243. Gospel Oak. (III). Suffolk. Holyoak Farmyard, Coombs 1½ m. S of Stowmarket Station. Grid ref. TM 050565.

Dead tree was still in existence 1972. Ref: Wilks (1972, 244).

244. Gospel Oak. (IV). Suffolk. Lavenham. Grid ref. TL 915495.

Burnt or struck by lightning 1944. Ref: Wilks (1972, 244).

245. Gospel Oak. (V). Also known as the Baginton Oak. Warwickshire. Stoneleigh. On a mound near the village. Grid ref. SP 3271.

Fell in 1872. It marked the parishes of Stoneleigh and Baginton (Burt 1860). One of the trees where passages of the Gospel were read when marking the Parish bounds. Ref: Strutt (1830, 32). Loudon (1838) Vol. III p. 1771. Burt (1860, 77). Hurst (1911, 192). Clarke *et al.* (1987). **Loudon fig. 1617.**

246. Gospel Oak. (VI). Shropshire. High Ercall, near Shrewsbury. Grid ref. SJ 5917 (High Ercall).

Used as a preaching site by the Methodists until 1855 as at that time they were forbidden by the landowner to hold services in their houses. Ref: Morton (1986, 58).

247. Gough's Oak. See Goff's Oak.

248. Grafton Oak. Herefordshire. 2¾ m. SE of Much Dewchurch. Grid ref. SO 445289.

249. Great Britain Oak. Berkshire. Windsor Great Park. Grid ref. SU 9672 (Windsor Park).

Alive in 1991. Ref: White (1991).

250. Great Oak of Newland. See Newland Oak.

251. Great Oak, The. (I). Also known as Newton St Petrock Oak. Devon. In centre of Newton St Petrock, near the Church. Grid ref. SS 411122.

Girth at 5 ft agl 19 ft 4 ins. in 1992. Much of the tree is hollow (James 1992). 'On a patch of green by the roadside stands a great twin oak, a veteran 20 ft round and growing hollow with age' (Mee 1938). Ref: Mee (1938b, 292). Visit by James 1992. **Photographs James 2/3/1992.**

252. Great Oak, The. (II). See Eardisley Oak.

253. Great Oak, The. (III). See Panshanger Oak. Hertfordshire.

254. Great Oak, The. (IV). See King of Thorpe, The.

255. Great Oak, The. (V). Clwyd (Denbighshire). Pontfadog (Near Glyn Ceiriog). Grid ref. SJ 234382.

Sessile oak. Reputed to be the oak with the largest girth in Britain at 37 ft but in poor condition and equalled now by a tree at New Bells Farm, Haughley (Mitchell 1996). Ref: Mitchell (1996).

256. Great Oak. The. (VI). See Great Yeldham Oak.

257. Great Oak, The. (VII). See Magdalen Oak.

258. Great Oak, The. (VIII). Hampshire. Leweston, near Stockbridge. Grid ref. SU 3535 (Stockbridge).

Girth 22 ft. Ref: Letter, Hants. C.C. (1991).

259. Great Oak, The. (IX). Hampshire. Oakley. Grid ref. SU 5650 (Oakley). Ref: Letter, Hants County Council (1991).

260. Great Oak, The. (X). See Glendower's Oak.

261. Great Oak , The. (XI). See Bowthorpe Oak.

262. Great Oaks, The. See The Fredville Oaks; Beauty, Majesty and Stately.

263. Great Welsh Oak. See Millenium Derwen.

264. Great Yeldham Oak. Also known as The Great Oak. (VI). Essex. Great Yeldham. Grid ref. TL 760383.

Still there as a dead tree in 1991. In 1910 the girth was 28 ft 6 ins at 4 ft (Hurst 1911) The oak nearby was planted to commemorate the marriage of Edward VII in 1863. Ref: Hurst (1911, 44, 192). Wilks (1972, 70). **Hurst p. 44. Photographs A. Sullivan 1991.**

265. Greendale Oak. Also known as the Grindal Oak. Nottinghamshire. Welbeck Park (5 m. SW of Worksop). This oak is c. ½ m. SSE of Welbeck Abbey. Grid ref. SK 567735.

Girth was 35 ft when a passageway was cut through the oak for a carriage to drive through to win the 1st Duke of Portland a wager in 1724. A cabinet was made from the timber thus removed and is in the Abbey. It became the custom of successive dukes to drive through the archway with their brides soon after the marriage ceremony. Ref: Evelyn (1670) 2nd edn p. 157. Batty Langley (1740, 193).

Rooke (1790, 9–10). Strutt (1830, 38). Loudon (1838, 1766). Anon. (1853, 47). Ablett (1880, 172). Lauder (1883, 258). Elwes and Henry (1907, 322). Mosley (1910, 63). Hurst (1911, 192). Hewins (1945, 14). Wilks (1972, 171). Whitlock (1985, 109). Packenham (1996). **Rooke plate 5. Packenham p. 126.**

266. Grete Oak, The. See Glendower's Oak.

267. Grimstone Oak. (I). Essex. Epping Forest. Grid ref. TQ 413981. (Epping Forest Conservation Centre).

Commemorates G. S. Grimstone, cricketer and Verderer of Epping and Sussex Forest. Ref: Wilks (1972, 246).

268. Grimstone Oak, The. (II). See Oxhey Oak.

269. Grindal Oak. See Greendale Oak.

270. Grindstone Oak. Surrey. Nr Farnham. Grid ref. SU 8446.

Girth 48 ft. Ref: Loudon (1838).

271. Grindstone Oak. Also known as the Holt Forest Oak. (II). Hampshire. Hurst (1911) states 'Holt Forest Hampshire'. Loudon (1838) states 'near Farnham'. Holt Forest here presumably means 'Alice Holt Forest'. Grid ref. SU 805435 (Holt Pound Enclosure).

Girth 33 ft at 3 ft, 48 ft at ground level (Loudon 1838). 'A huge dead trunk' (Hurst 1911). Ref: Loudon (1838) Vol. III p. 1770. Hurst (1911, 192).

272. Gurney Oak. Also known as Gurneyesok. Gloucestershire. Forest of Dean. In the Bailiwick of Blakeney. Grid ref. SO 6707 (Blakeney), SO 659084 (Blakeney Woods).

A boundary oak, no longer existing. Ref: Hart (1966, 55).

273. Gurneyesok. See Gurney Oak.

274. Gutter Oak. Staffordshire. Beaudesert Park: 2½ m. SSW of Rugeley: SE of Cannock Chase. Grid ref. SK 035135 (Beaudesert Old Park).

Girth 40 ft at ground level (Loudon 1838). Ref: Loudon (1838) Vol. III p. 1770.

275. Haie House Oaks. Gloucestershire. Newnham, Forest of Dean, near the house. Grid ref. NG 673102.

A number of large oaks, about 400 years old. The largest 27 ft 2 ins girth for which the grid ref. is given (Standing 1987). Ref: Standing (1987, 26).

276. Halston Oak. Shropshire. Halston. Grid ref. SO 4107.

Girth 20 ft 6 ins (Morton 1986). Ref: Morton (1986, 104).

277. Hanged-men's Tree. Perthshire. 2 m. SE Birnam: near to Birnam Hall. Grid ref. NO 0342.

Used by the Lords of Murthly to hang thieves and other offenders. Ref: Hunter (1883, 74).

278. Hanging Tree. See Law-day Oak.

279. Hanging Tree, The. See Liberty Tree, The.

280. Hanging Trees. Cornwall. In the parish of Trebeigh, next to St Ive, near Liskeard. Grid ref. SX 302671.

Ref: Thurston (1930, 189).

281. Hangman's Oak, The. See Shilstone Oak, The.

282. Hankford's Oak, Judge. Devon. On Ley Farm Monkleigh, 200 yds E of Saltrens (on A388). Near the old house of Annery. Grid ref. SS 455219.

Girth 22 ft at 5 ft agl. Partly dead in the crown 12.8.91. Stands near group of derelict buildings (James 1991). In 1422 Judge Hankford was shot under this oak by his gamekeeper, whom he had instructed to shoot anyone found in the deer park at night. It was said that the Judge was saddened by the War of the Roses but dare not commit suicide. By this means he died by his keeper's hand. Ref: Wilks (1972, 74). Black's Guide to Devonshire (1864, 207). Visit by James 1991. **Photographs James 12/8/1991.**

283. Hannings Oak, The. Worcestershire. Kyrewood Estate ¾ m. NE of Tenbury Wells. Grid ref. SO 606680 (Kyrewood House). Ref: Elwes and Henry (1907) Vol. II p. 313.

284. Haresfield Court Oaks. Gloucestershire. Grid ref. SO 810099.

A row of oaks said to commemorate the funeral procession in c. 1327 of Edward II from Berkeley Castle, where he was murdered, to Gloucester. In 1991, six were left, one of them alive, about 12–15 ft high (James).

285. Harewood Oak. Also known as The Home Oak. Shropshire. North-west of Ross-on-Wye. Grid ref. SO 535284 (Harewood Park).

Other big oaks are in the Park but are not named. Ref: Transactions of the Woolhope Club. 1867. **Transactions of the Woolhope Club 1867 p. 12.**

286. Hart's Horn Tree. Westmorland. Whinfell Park. 2 m. NE of Penrith. Grid ref. NY 559288.

Some trunk left in 1790. Roots still in situ in 1807. In 1333 Edward Balliol visited Robert de Clifford and they put up a stag with a greyhound. The stag was chased from

FIGURE 51. a. *Above*: The Great Yeldham Oak (264) with replacement beside it. b. *Below*: Hankford's Oak (282).
a. ANTHEA SULLIVAN; b. N. D. G. JAMES

FIGURE 51. c. Jack of Kent's Oak (319). N. D. G. JAMES

Brougham Park into Scotland and back. On their return, both stag and hound died of exhaustion near the tree. The horns of the stag were nailed to the tree which gradually grew round them. They were broken off in 1658. Ref: Letter from J. M. Summerfield 25/11/1991.

287. Hatfield Broad Oak. Essex. Near Hatfield Heath. Grid ref. TL 5516.

Girth 42 ft. (Loudon 1838). Known to have existed in twelfth century. Loudon (1838). Ref: Rackham (1994). **Loudon fig. 1593.**

288. Haughley Oak. Suffolk. Haughley Park. Grid ref. TM 0262 (Haughley Park).

Ref: Rackham (1989).

289. Haunted Oak, The. See Nannau Oak.

290. Hawson Cross Oak. Also known as the Stumpy Oak. Devon. On a cross roads near Holne. Grid ref. SX 711682.

Pedunculate oak. An old oak next to a stone cross, probably marking an old route from Dartmoor. The area has been farmed since early times and has old field systems.

Estimated to be about 700 years old. A large cavity, once filled with concrete, which was removed recently. Reasonably healthy for its age in 2002. Local tradition has it as a hanging tree. Ref: Harris. **Photographed Harris Sept/Oct 2002.**

291. Haywood Forest Oak. Shropshire. Grid ref. SO 4837.

Ref: Transactions of the Woolhope Club 1867. **Transactions of the Woolhope Club (1867, 16).**

292. Hazelgrove Oak. See King's Oak, The. (II).

293. Headcorn Oak. Kent. South side of the church in Headcorn which is 9 m. SE of Maidstone on A 274 road. Grid ref. TQ 831442.

Girth 44 ft in 1967. Visited by Mr D. Drew in Aug 1991. He reported that this tree was in a poor condition with only one limb still alive. It was set on fire by vandals in May 1989 but a replacement oak has been planted in the hollow of the old tree. He was unable to get any accurate girth measurements. Local courts were held here and tradition marks it as a place where bull baiting contests were held for King John. Ref: Whitlock (1985, 105). Letter, Mr Drew (1991). **2 colour photographs by Mr Drew 1991. Picture in QJF 1967, 31.**

294. Heddon Oak. Somerset. At road junction on road from Stogumber to Crowcombe, 1 m. W of Crowcombe Church. Grid ref. ST 121371.

The tree was felled 1982 by Somerset C.C. as dangerous and has not been replaced. This oak grew on common land until the enclosure of 1780. Said to have been used as gallows for men from adjoining parishes convicted at the Bloody Assizes (1685) for supporting the Monmouth Rebellion. Judges sat at Taunton, Exeter and other places. Ref: Wilks (1972). Letter from Somerset County Council (Environment Dept) 20 Aug. 1991. **J. H. Wilks (1972, 83, 96).**

295. Hempstead Oak. Also known as Turpin's Oak. (V). Essex. 6 m. E of Saffron Walden: 5 m. SW Haverhill. Grid ref. TL 635380 (Hempstead Village).

Old stump removed in 1960. Replaced with a young tree nearby. The old tree was 53 ft in girth in 1842 (Selby). 50 ft in girth and 100 ft high in 1801. The young tree 17 ft at 4 ft *c.* 1991. Turpin was born in Hempstead. Ref: Loudon (1838) Vol. III p. 1760. Selby (1842, 254). Mee (1938, 191). Letter, D. Haylock (1992).

296. Henham Hill Oak. Also known as the Wangford Oak. Suffolk. Henham Park 4 m. E of Halesworth: 3 m. NW of Southwold. Grid ref. TM 455755 (Henham Park).

Sir John Rous hid in this oak on his estate for three days from Cromwell's men. The tree had been used as a summer house and had a door covered in oak bark so the opening was difficult to detect. His wife visited him secretly at night with food. Ref: Anon: (1853, 47). Mosley (1910, 59). Wilks (1972, 198). Whitlock (1985, 105).

297. Henry VI's Oak. Also known as the King Oak. (X). Cumberland Irton Hall, Holmrook. Grid ref. SD 0799.

Girth 13 m x 240 cm in 1998 (Holdsworth 1990). Henry VI hid in this oak after the battle of Muncaster, during the War of the Roses in 1464. The local villagers would not give him shelter. The hollow oak was filled with cement in 1976 and was alive and healthy in 1998. Ref: Wilks (1972, 64). Whitlock (1985, 104). Holdsworth (1990, 4).

298. Hensol Oak. Glamorgan. Hensol. Grid ref. ST 042790.

Girth 18 ft in 1895 Linnard (2000). Ref: Linnard (2000, 127).

299. Herne The Hunter's Oak. Also known as Herne's Oak.

(I). or Sir John Falstaff's Oak. Berkshire. Windsor Great Park. Grid ref. SU 9672 (Windsor Great Park).

Died *c.* 1796. Finally fell in a gale in 1863. 'There is an old tale that goes Herne the Hunter, sometimes a keeper here in Windsor Forest, doth all the winter time, at still midnight, walk round about this oak' (Merry Wives of Windsor). Herne is said to have hung himself on this tree. A sapling grown from an acorn off this tree was planted in Wales by Sir D. Dundas of Richmond (Loudon 1838). Queen Victoria had a cabinet made from this tree. Perry (1867) made a casket to hold a Shakespeare first folio edition. Ref: Gilpin (1791). Loudon (1838). Burt (1860, 67). Perry (1867). Mosley (1910, 63). Hurst (1911, 193). Wilks (1972, 34). Pakenham (1996, 164). **Loudon fig. 1588. Perry (1867, frontispiece, 10, 31).**

300. Herne's Oak. (I). See Herne The Hunter's Oak.

301. Herne's Oak. (II). Cornwall. Near Rezare, in the Carthamartha Woods. Grid ref. SX 371776.

Still alive but in poor state and propped up (1999). Probably a recognised place for hunts to meet in the past.

302. Heveningham Oak. See Queen Elizabeth's Oak. (IV).

303. Hoar Oak. Also known as the Kite Oak. Somerset (on boundary with Devon). On E side of Hoaroak Water, 1¼ m. W of Brendon Two Gates. Grid ref. SS 748430.

Girth 3 ft 3 ins at 4 ft (James 1991) 'Present tree planted in 1916: It is healthy and enclosed by post and rail fence' (James 1991). The site is an ancient boundary mark in Exmoor Forest. The Hoar Oak is probably synonymous with the Kite Oak. Albion (1926) states that in 1622 it was recorded that 'There were not woods in the said Forest (of Exmoor) except one oak called Kite Oak'. Ref: Albion (1926, 107). Wilks (1972, 22). Allen (1974). Visit by James 1991. **Allen (1974, 25). Photographs James 1/10/1991.**

304. Hodnet Hall Oak. Shropshire. By the lake at Hodnet Hall. Grid ref. SJ 6128 (Hodnet Hall).

Girth 21 ft 10 ins (Morton 1986). Ref: Morton (1986, 104).

305. Hollow Oak, The. (I). Also known as The Earl of Thanet's Hollow Oak; The Whinfield Forest Oak; The Wonderful Large Oak. Westmorland. Whinfell Park, near Penrith. Was near the Hart's Horn Oak. Grid ref. NY 559288 (Whinfell Park House).

Girth 31 ft 9 ins in 1765 and 42 ft in 1814. The tree was on the property of the Earl of Thanet (Loudon. 1838). Ref: Loudon (1838, 1771). Letter, J. M. Summerfield (1991). **Old prints (no refs) show a horseman inside the oak.**

306. Hollow Oak. The. (II). See Nannau Oak.

307. Holt Forest Oak. (I). See Bentley Oak.

308. Holt Forest Oak. (II). See Grindstone Oak. (I).

309. Holt Preen Oak. Shropshire. Holt Preen, near Plaish. Grid ref. SO 5396.

Girth was 28 ft 6 ins in 1983 (Morton 1986). This oak is growing over a spring. Ref: Morton (1986, 44).

310. Home Oak, The. See Harewood Oak.

311. Honour Oak. (I). Devon. Near the boundary between Whitchurch and Tavistock on the SW side of the road from Tavistock to Whitchurch and Grenofen. Grid ref. SX 483733.

This oak bears a plaque which reads as follows 'Honour Oak Tree/ Marked boundary of French prisoners on parole/ in Tavistock from Princetown/ during the Napoleonic War (1803–14). Also where money was deposited in exchange for food during a cholera outbreak in 1832'. Too difficult to girth (James 1991). Ref: Wilks (1972, 66). Brewer's Dict. (1983). Visit by James 1991. **Photographs James 1991.**

312. Honour Oak. (II). Also known as The Oake of Honour. Middlesex. One Tree Hill, Camberwell, London. Grid ref. TQ 3579 (Bermondsey).

Queen Elizabeth I is said to have dined (1602) under this oak, during the last year of her life. Ref: Wilks (1972, 157).

313. Hotel Oak, The. Co. Fermanagh. Behind Killyhelvin Hotel, on the main road east of Enniskillen.

The first tree in Northern Ireland to be protected by a Tree Preservation Order. Ref: Browne (2000).

314. Howel Sele's Oak. See Nannau Oak.

315. Hugglescote Oak. Leicestershire. Grid ref. SO 8717 (Hugglescote).

Hollow oak with doors and windows. Ref: Hewins (1945, 15).

316. Hundred Oak. Hampshire. Half a mile north of the Heckfield Stones, near Heckfield. Grid ref. SU 731613.

A meeting place for the Hundred Court which convened at Mildmas and Hocktide.

317. Hunter's Oak. Cornwall. On cross roads between St. Dominic and Bohetherick 3½ m. ESE of Callington. Grid ref. SX 413675.

The original oak has been replaced by another, planted by Lady Ernestine Edgcumbe in the 1930s. Girth 4 ft 7 ins at 5 ft in 1991. Young oak in good condition. Surrounded by a platform of earth and stones. So called because hounds met there. Adjoins N. T. Cotehele Estate. Ref: Thurston (1930). Wilks (1972, 246). Visit by James 1991. **Photographs James 25/9/1991.**

318. Huntingfield Oak. See Queen Elizabeth's Oak. (V).

319. Jack of Kent's Oak. Also known as Jacky Kemp's Oak; Pontrilas Oak, The. Herefordshire. In the Deer Park at Kentchurch Court near Pontrilas. Grid ref. SO 429256.

Pedunculate oak. Girth 37 ft 3 in (5 ft agl) over several large burrs in Oct. 1991. Stagheaded but still in leaf (James 1991). According to Linnard (2000), this tree was measured in Oct. 1997 when the girth was 11.35 m at breast height. The age was estimated at about 954 years. Ref: White (1991). Visit by James 1991. Linnard (2000, 126). **Photographs James 21/10/91.**

320. Jack of The Yat. Gloucestershire. Forest of Dean. On S side of Monmouth – Drybrook road (A4136) in Sallow Vallets near Sallow Vallets Lodge. Grid ref. SO 606143.

Blew down Sept. 1921. Girth 22 ft in 1913. Girths from 1830–1913 given in Standing (1986, 13). Percy Daniels, Crown Forester, planted a new oak in the old stump, Hart (1966). 5–600 years old. Ref: Hart (1966, 136). Standing (1986, 13). **Hart (1966) plate 7.**

321. Jack's Yack. Also known as Towd Yak. Westmorland. Lowther Park. Grid ref. NY 523236 (Lowther Castle).

Alive in 1999. A legend relates that if the branches of this oak touch the ground, the Lowther family will fall. Chocks of wood have been placed to keep the branches off the ground. Yack is the local name for oak. Ref: Letter from Mrs J. Williams (1991). Holdsworth (1999, 4). **Photograph from Mrs Williams.**

322. Jacky Kemps Oak. See Jack of Kent's Oak.

323. Jane Austen's Oak. Hampshire. Chawton. Grid ref. SU 7037.

Felled as unsafe. Ref: Letter, Hants. C.C.

324. John Bunyan's Oak. See Bunyan's Oak.

325. John Lennon and Yoko Ono's Oak. Warwickshire. Coventry Cathedral. Grid ref. SP 3379 (Coventry).

Planted in 1960 with a seat erected around it. Ref: Clarke *et al.* (1987, 38).

326. Jubilee Oak. (I). Oxfordshire. Greys Court, Rotherfield

Greys, 2 m. WNW of Henley-on-Thames. Grid ref. SU 725834 (Grey's Court).

Pedunculate oak. Girth 6.4 m or 21 ft in 1991. There is a memorial stone inscribed 'Jubilee Oak CFMS 1881'. The tree is starting to hollow and has been filled with cement. Ref: Letter, National Trust (1991).

327. Jubilee Oak. (II). Shropshire. Boscobel House. Grid ref. SJ 8308.

A tree raised from the existing Boscobel Oak was planted to celebrate Queen Victoria's Diamond Jubilee. Ref: Rodgers (1941, 124).

328. Jubilee Oak. (III). Shropshire. Admaston Spa, near Wellington. Grid ref. SJ 6313.

Planted in 1963 to commemorate Queen Victoria's Silver Jubilee. Ref: Morton (1986, 51).

329. Jubilee Oaks.

A number of oaks were planted to commemorate the Jubilee of King George V. No individual details. Ref: Rodgers (1941, 124).

330. Jubilee Tree. Surrey. Tilford. Near the Tilford Oak and King George V's Oak. Grid ref. SU 875430 (Tilford village).

Girth (1972) 8 ft 1 ins Wilks (1972). Planted 1897 to commemorate Queen Victoria's Diamond Jubilee. Ref: Wilks (1972, 186).

331. Judge Hankford's Oak. See Hankford's, Judge Oak.

332. Judge Wyndham's Oak. See Wyndham's Oak.

333. Judith Oak, The. (I). Also known as Yardley Lodge Oak. Northampton. Yardley Chase. Between Weston Lodge and Church Slade at Yardley Lodge, near Kilwick Wood. Grid ref. SP 8652 (Kilwick Wood).

Girth 28 ft 5 ins Loudon (1838). This tree was said to have been planted by Judith, a niece of William the Conqueror. She married the Earl of Northumbria and Huntingdon. After his execution for treason, she inherited his estate of Huntingdon about 1072. See also Cowper's Oak. Ref: Loudon (1838, 1764). Wilks (1972, 38).

334. Judith Oak. (II). See Cowper's Oak.

335. Kedleston Oak. Also known as the King Tree. (I). Derbyshire. Grid ref. SK 3240 (Kedleston Hall).

Girth 24 ft at 6 ft. and 60 ft without a branch (Loudon 1838). Ref: Loudon (1838, 1839).

336. Keeper's Oak. Also known as Barnes Oak. Hampshire.

Bramshill Park 2 m. NNW of Hartley Wintney. Grid ref. SU 756 595 (Bramshill Park).

Pedunculate oak. Girth 21 ft in 1963 (White 1991). Pollarded. In the early 1620s Archbishop Abbot of Canterbury aimed at a fallow buck but hit the keeper, Peter Hawkins instead, under this tree. Soon after, there were objections to him christening one of Charles I's children. The King, however, countered by saying 'he may be a bad shot but he is a very good Archbishop'. Ref: Gardner (1947, 68). Wilks (1972, 74). Bean (1976, 508). Letter, Hants. C.C. 16/11/91. White (1991). **Anon. in QJF (1963).**

337. Kempston Oak. Norfolk. Between Great Dunham and Beeston, Gt Dunham is 5 m. NE Swaffham On Woodgate Hill. Grid ref. TF 9015 (Beeston).

Ref: Grigor (1841, 337).

338. Kents Oak. Hampshire. Kents Oak. Grid ref. SU 3124.

339. Kent's Oak, Jack of. See Jack of Kent's Oak.

340. Kenya Oak. Berkshire. Windsor Great Park. Grid ref. SU 9672 (Windsor Great Park).

Alive 1991. Pedunculate oak. Ref: White (1991).

341. Kepping Tree. See Capon Tree.

342. Keston Oak, The. See Wilberforce Oak.

343. Kett's Oak. (I). Norfolk. Ryston 2 m. SE of Downham Market. Grid ref. TF 6003.

Named after Robert Kett, who led a rebellion against land enclosures and marched on Norwich, 1549. Ref: Grigor (1841, 348). Elwes and Henry (1907) Vol. II p. 324. Wilks (1972, 174). White (1991). Packenham (1996, 115).

344. Kett's Oak. (II). Also known as The Oak of Reformation; Reformation Oak. Norfolk. On side of B1172 road Wymondham – Hethersett. (Named on O.S. map). Grid ref. TG 139036.

Bears a plaque reading 'KETTS OAK 1549' Robert Kett, who led the Peasants Revolt against land enclosure, was captured and hung in Norwich in 1549. His body was hung on this tree in his home village of Wymondham. Ref: Grigor (1841, 324). Wilks (1972, 174). Packenham (1996, 115). **Wilks between pp. 96–7. Packenham p. 115.**

345. Kett's Oak. (III). Also known as the Reformation Oak. (II). Norfolk. Mousehold Heath, Norwich. Grid ref. TG 245105 (Mousehold Heath).

The men of the Peasants Revolt camped here on their way to capture Norwich in 1549, led by Robert Kett. Nine of the ringleaders were later hanged on this tree. Ref: J. Wilks (1972, 174). Brewer's Dict. (1983).

346. Kidlington Green Oak. Oxfordshire. Kidlington Green. Grid ref. SP 4913.

This hollow oak was used as a prison to keep offenders in until they could be sent to Oxford. Ref: Rodgers (1941, 18).

347. Kilgraston Oak. Perthshire. North Lodge Park, Kilgraston. Grid ref. NO 1916.

Girth 16 ft 10 ins. It was the largest oak on the estate (Hunter 1883). Ref: Hunter (1883, 142).

348. King Charles II Oak. Gloucestershire. Forest of Dean: Churchill Inclosure. On W side of ride running SW from B4431 at Shaden Tuft. Grid ref. SO 625087.

Girth 19 ft 5 ins. (Standing 1986). 20 ft at 5 ft agl. (James May 1991) This tree is thought to date from the reign of Charles II, when in 1668 the iron works which had devastated the Forest were closed down and young trees protected. It may therefore have been a young tree earlier than this date. Ref: Standing (1986, 5). White (1991). Visit by James 1991. **Photograph James 9/5/1991.**

349. King Charles Oak. (I). Northamptonshire. Salcey Forest: Salcey Little Lawn: about ¼ m. from Salcey Great Oak. Grid ref. SP 799518.

Girth: 34 ft 10 ins at 5 ft agl. Completely hollow (James 1991). King Charles is supposed to have spent a night in it. Ref: Visit by James 1991. **Photographs James 24/10/1991.**

350. King Charles' Oak. (II). See Boconnoc Oak.

351. King Dick's Clump. Leicestershire. Bosworth Park. Grid ref. SK 4201 (site of battle).

These trees mark the place where Richard III raised his banner during the battle of Bosworth field (1485) fought between him and Henry VII. Ref: Hewins (1945, 15).

352. King George V's Oak. Surrey. Tilford. Near the Tilford Oak. Grid ref. SU 875430. (Tilford Village).

Planted 1911. Ref: Wilks (1972, 186).

353. King James Oak. Perthshire. Scone Palace. Near the river in a hollow. Grid ref. NO 1126 (Scone Palace).

Girth 15 ft. Planted by James VI of Scotland (James I of England). Ref: Hunter (1883, 102).

354. King John Oak. (I). Devon. Shute Park. Grid ref. SY 2497.

A large pollard in Shute Deer Park. Other large oaks in the Park. Ref: Harding (1980, 75–6). **Harding (1980, 76).**

355. King John Oak. (II). See King's Oak, The. (II).

356. King John's Oak. Wiltshire. Clarendon Park. Grid ref. SU 195305 (Clarendon Park).

Alive in 1991. Ref: White (1991).

357. King Oak. (I). Hertfordshire. Ashridge Park in the old deer park. Grid ref. SP 9913.

Alive 1991. Girth 22 ft 5 ins at 5 ft agl (Q.J.F. 1911). Ref: Duchesne (1911, 345). White (1991). **Duchesne (1911) opp. p. 345.**

358. King Oak. (II). Gloucestershire. Razies Bottom, Ashwick Hall 1½ m. SE of Marshfield (Avon) and 3 m. N of Batheaston. Grid ref. ST 795721.

Loudon (1838) states: '28 ft 8 ins in circumference at the collar and about 18 ft as the average girth to the height of 30 ft where the trunk began to throw out branches'. Ref: Loudon (1838) Vol. III p. 1760.

359. King Oak. (III). Staffordshire. Bagots Park, Blithefield, 4 m. due S of Uttoxeter. Grid ref. SK 090273 (centre of Bagot's Park).

Alive in 1991. Ref: Elwes and Henry (1907) Vol. II p. 317. White (1991).

360. King Oak. (IV). Probably the King of the King and Queen Oaks. See Queen Oak. (IV). Hampshire. Boldrewood, New Forest. Grid ref. SU 2408.

Ref: Hurst (1911, 193): Wilks (1972, 247). Letter, Hants. C.C. 16/11/1991.

361. King Oak. (V). Lincolnshire. Burghley Park, Stamford. Grid ref. TF 0506.

Ref: Elwes and Henry (1907) Vol. II p. 211. White (1991).

362. King Oak. (VI). Wiltshire. Savernake. Grid ref. SU 225659.

Girth 24 ft (Loudon 1838). Ref: Strutt (1830, 28). Loudon (1838) Vol. III p. 1771. Hurst (1911, 193). **Strutt opp. p. 28. Loudon figs 1633, 1619.**

363. King Oak. (VII). Also known as The Tilford Oak; Novel's Oak. Surrey. Tilford 3 m. SW of Farnham railway station. Grid ref. SU 875430 (Tilford Village).

Pedunculate oak. Mentioned as a landmark in a charter of 1250 as 'Kynghoc'. Ref: Mosley (1910, 55). Hurst (1911, 193). Wilks (1972, 185).

364. King Oak. (VIII). Also known as William The Conqueror's Oak; The Conqueror's Oak. Berkshire. Windsor Great Park 'at Cranbourne' (Wilks). In the White Deer Enclosure. Grid ref. SU 9272 (Cranbourne).

Girth 26 ft at 3 ft (Loudon 1838). Hollow and '10 or 12 might sit comfortably down to dinner' in it – Professor Burnet in 1829 (Loudon). The largest and oldest oak in Windsor Forest. A favourite tree of William the Conqueror. Ref: Loudon (1838) Vol. III p. 1754. Burt (1860, 66). Grigor (1868, 267). Ablett (1880, 166). Elwes and Henry (1907) Vol. II p. 319. Hurst (1911, 190). Wilks (1972, 147). Packenham (1996). Brewer's Dict. (1983). **Picture in QJF 1967, 33. Packenham (1996, 166).**

365. King Oak. (IX). Yorkshire. Hovingham Hall. Grid ref. SE 6675 (of Hovingham).

Girth 24 ft at 1 ft, 32 ft to first branch. (Loudon 1838). Ref: Loudon (1838, 1840). Hurst (1911, 193). **Strutt opp. p. 28. Loudon figs 1633, 1619.**

366. King Oak. (X). See Henry VI's Oak.

367. King Oak. (XI). Kent. Sevenoaks. Grid ref. TQ 5355.

The only oak surviving of seven planted in 1902 for the coronation of Edward VII. Ref: Denny (1989).

368. King of The Woods. (I). Lancashire. Pott Yeats in Littledale (Wilks). Grid ref. SD 550622.

Ref: Wilks (1972, 39).

369. King of The Woods. (II). Roxburghshire. 1½ m. from Jedburgh on the Marquis of Lothian's Estate (Fernyhurst Estate). Grid ref. NT 6520 (Jedburgh).

Girth over 16 ft, 43 ft to the first branch (Selby 1842). Ref: Loudon (1838) Vol. III p. 1772. Selby (1842, 255). Grigor (1868, 270). Lauder (1883, 252). Michie (1888, 241).

370. King of Thorpe. Also known as The Great Oak. (IV); Thorpe Oak; Thorpe Market Oak. Norfolk. Thorpe Market about 1 m. from the Mansion in Gunton Park between Cromer and North Walsham. Grid ref. TG 2436 (Thorpe Market).

Girth 22 ft at 1 ft, 42 ft to first branch. Height 70 ft Grigor (1841). Ref: Grigor (1841, 133). Grigor (1868, 267). **Grigor (1841, 156–7).**

371. King Tree. (I). See Kedleston Oak.

372. King Tree. (II). See Cliff Oak.

373. King's Oak, The. (I). See Chaucer's Oak.

374. King's Oak, The. (II). Also known as Hazelgrove Oak; King John Oak; Queen Elizabeth Oak. Somerset. Hazelgrove School, Sparkford, Somerset. About 250 yds SE of Main school building. Grid ref. ST 601269.

Pedunculate oak. Girth 30 ft at 4 ft (Selby 1842). 29 ft 9 ins

at 5 ft (Elwes and Henry 1907). Girth 32 ft 3 ins, height 70 ft (Bean 1976). Girth 34 ft 5 ins above low branch (Mitchell 1991). 35 ft 5 ins at 5 ft (James 1992). Girth 34 ft 5 ins above large low branch (Mitchell 1991). Ref: Selby (1842, 256). Elwes and Henry (1907) Vol. II p. 315. Hurst (1911, 192). Bean (1976) Vol. III p. 508. Mitchell (1991, 88). Visit by James 1992. **Photographs James 6/8/1992.**

375. Kingsland Oak. Herefordshire. Kingsland. Grid ref. SO 4461.

A gateway was made in this oak. Ref: Hewins (1941). *Country Life* Dec. (1941).

376. Kirkleatham Oak. Yorkshire. Kirkleatham is 2 m. SW of Redcar and 5 m. ENE of Middlesborough. Grid ref. NZ 5921 (Kirkleatham).

Planted to commemorate the bravery of Tom Brown at the battle of Dettingen 1743 (Defeat of French). Ref: Wilks (1972, 245).

377. Kiss Oak, The. Hertfordshire. Gorhambury Park, midway between Hemel Hempstead and St Albans. Grid ref. TQ 114080 (Gorhambury Park).

Queen Elizabeth I said to have been seen kissing the Earl of Leicester under this oak. Ref: Whitlock (1985, 105). Wilks (1972, 158).

378. Kite Oak. See Hoar Oak.

379. Knightwood Oak. Hampshire. New Forest: Knightwood Inclosure: 2¼ m. SW of Lyndhurst. Grid ref. SU 265065.

Pollarded oak. Mitchell (1966) aged this tree at about 300 years. Ref: Bean (1976) Vol. III p. 508. Wilks (1972, 247). **Mitchell (1966, 275).**

380. Ladies Oak, The. Sussex. In Sheffield Park, near Uckfield. Grid ref. TQ 4721 (Uckfield).

Ref: Evelyn (1670, 158).

381. Lady Montagu's Tree. Northamptonshire. Deene Park. Grid ref. SP 9492 (Deene Park).

This tree grew from an acorn found inside a tree at Woolwich Dockyard in 1757 (Loudon 1838). Ref: Loudon (1838, 1782).

382. Lady Oak. (III). Sussex. At Rivelin, Sheffield Park. Grid ref. TQ 4721 (Uckfield).

'The tree could produce a plank, 5 ft sq at the height of 40 ft'. Loudon (1838). Ref: Loudon (1838).

383. Lady Oak, The. (I). Also known as the Cressage Oak;

Christ's Oak. Shropshire. 9 m. SE of Shrewsbury on A 458, half a mile from Cressage. Grid ref. SJ 592040 (Cressage).

Old tree damaged by fire in 1814; it finally died in 1982. A young tree is growing inside the old hollow tree. In 1814 the tree had a girth 41 ft 7 ins agl (Morton 1986). The Gospel is said to have been preached here in 598 under a tree, the site later marked with a stone cross. The Lady Oak was a remnant of Long Forest which was felled in 1616 and the tree was dedicated to the Virgin Mary. It may have been a Law Day oak where local courts met. Dean Swift is said to have married an eloping couple under the tree when sheltering from a storm. Ref: Hewins (1945, 9). Morton (1986, 50). **Morton p. 51. Clarke *et al.* p. 51. (The oak in 1789).**

384. Lady Oak, The. (II). Shropshire. Minsterley (A488) 9 m. SW of Shrewsbury at Plox Green. Grid ref. SJ 375050 (Minsterley).

Removed in the 1950s. Ref: Hewins (1945, 11).

385. Lady Powis Oak. Montgomeryshire. Powis Castle, Welshpool. Grid ref. SJ 216064.

Pedunculate oak. Girth 24 ft 5 ins and 80 ft tall (Hyde 1977). Ref: Hyde (1977, 122): White (1991).

386. Lambert's Oaks. Surrey. Oaks Estate in the Parish of Woodmanstone. Grid ref. TQ 2760 (approx.).

These oaks gave the name to the Oaks Estate owned by the Lambert family. Later owned by the Earl of Derby, who started the Oaks Race, the first of which was run in 1779 and is for fillies only. Ref: Brewers Dict. (1983).

387. Langley Oak. Hampshire. Langley 2 m. W of Calshot 3½ m. ESE of Beaulieu. Grid ref. SU 445015 (Langley).

Died and removed in 1768. The girth then was 36 ft agl and 18 ft at 20 ft (Loudon 1838). Ref: Loudon (1838) Vol. III p. 1762.

388. Larder Oak. See Shambles Oak.

389. Large Oak. Pembrokeshire. Stackpole Court.

Sessile oak. Girth 13 ft 6 ins. 100 ft high (Loudon 1838). Divided into three branches at 13 ft. Ref: Loudon (1838, 1840).

390. Large Porter. See Porters Oak, The.

391. Larmer Tree. Wiltshire/Dorset Border. Cranbourne Chase. Grid ref. ST 9617 (Cranbourne Chase).

A young tree has been planted to replace the original. A boundary tree between Wiltshire and Dorset. The traditional meeting place of King John and his huntsmen when at his hunting lodge of Tollard Royal. Ref: Rodgers (1941, 67).

392. Lassington Oak. Gloucestershire. Lassington: 1 m. W of Maisemore: ¾ m. N Highnam on B 4215. Grid ref. SO 797211 (Lassington Village).

Girth was 30 ft (Wilks 1972). Ref: A.A. Road Book of England and Wales (1965, 330). Wilks (1972, 241).

393. Laugh Lady Oak. Also known as the Law Day Oak. (II). Shropshire. Brampton Bryan Park. Grid ref. SO 3672 (Brampton Bryan).

This was a tree where Law days or Moots were held for the local Assizes. Ref: Transactions of the Woolhope Club (1871). Morton (1986, 54). **Transactions of the Woolhope Club p. 1.**

394. Law Day Oak. (I). Also known as the Bonnington Oak; The Hanging Tree. Kent. At Bonnington Corner (the village green) in Bonnington which lies on B2067 and is 6 m. SE of Ashford. Grid ref. TR 055352.

Girth 25 ft (Mr D. Drew 1991). The booklet on St Rumwold's Church, Bonnington states 'At Bonnington Corner, the village green, there is an ancient tree known as the Law Day Oak. It was under this that the Leet Court sat for the purpose of hearing and judging matters of local importance. Anything more serious would go before the Hundred Court'. Ref: J. Wilks (1972, 92). Letter, Mr Drew (1991). **Photographs Mr Drew 1991.**

395. Law Day Oak. (II). See Laugh Lady Oak.

396. Lawn Oak. Essex. Writtle Park. Grid ref. TL 6606 (Writtle).

25 ft at 5 ft (Loudon 1838). Ref: Loudon (1838, 1839).

397. Leaden Oak, The. Bedfordshire. In Ampthill Park. Grid ref. TL 0337 (Ampthill).

Sessile oak. Girth 30 ft at ground level (Loudon 1838). So called because large piece of lead fixed to it. This tree was marked in a survey of Amptill Park in Cromwell's time as being too old for naval timber. Ref: Loudon (1838) Vol. III p. 1753.

398. Leslie Troup Oak. Gloucestershire. Forest of Dean: On N side of Coleford – Cinderford Road (B4226) nearly opposite Speech House (palisaded). Grid ref. SO 618121.

Girth 8 ft 3 ins (Standing 1986). Dedicated to L. B. Troup, Deputy Survey of Dean 1973–83. Ref: Standing (1986, 7).

399. Lewis, Mrs, Oak. Hampshire. Longstock House. 2 m. N of Stockbridge. Grid ref. SU 400387 (Longstock House).

Alive in 1991. Ref: White (1991).

400. Liberty Tree, The. Also known as Hanging Tree, The. Roughfort Tree. Co. Antrim. At Roughfort, Mallusk near Newtown Abbey.

Liberty trees were planted in the 1790s to mark the liberation obtained by the American War of Independence and the French Revolution and as a symbol of freedom. This tree according to tradition was one of the assembly points before the Battle of Antrim. Ref: Browne (2000). **Browne (2000, 34).**

401. Lidiate Oak. Lancashire. Lidiate. Grid ref. SD 3604 (Lidiate).

A public house was built round this tree and named the Royal Oak. The name was changed to the Scotch Piper after one of Bonnie Prince Charlie's men hid there when wounded. He was nursed back to health by the Moorcroft family. The family held the licence for 500 years until 1945. Ref: Timpson (1987).

402. Lifton Oak. Devon. In a field on the S side of North Street, Lifton: 3½ m. E Launceston. Grid ref. SX 390852.

Pedunculate oak. A replacement for the original. Girth 16 ft 6 ins at 5 ft but this may not be strictly accurate due to ivy. Said to be an early flushing oak (James 1991). The old tree was a dancing tree and a platform was built in the branches for festivities. (Whitlock 1985). Ref: Whitlock (1985, 106).

403. Lightning Oak, The. Hertfordshire. On the Terrace Field at Haileybury College. Grid ref. TL 358106.

In 1898 was struck by lightning. A vivid flash broke pieces of wood off which were hurled far into the field. The following year it was to have been cut down but it was reprieved and has since recovered (Wright 1959). Ref: Wilks (1973, 25). Wright (1959, 75).

404. Lillington Oak. Also known as The Centre Of England Oak. Warwickshire. At the north end of Lillington Avenue, Leamington Spa. Grid ref. SP 322669.

Felled c. 1970 as it was considered dangerous. Ref: Hewins (1945, 5). Wilks (1972, 29). **Morley (19—) frontispiece.**

405. Lion Oak, The. Hertfordshire. Hatfield Park, 5 m. E of St Albans. North of the house in a shrubbery by the tennis court. Grid ref. TL 2308 (Hatfield Park).

Fell on 18 June 1992. This tree is said to have been mentioned in the Domesday Book. Ref: Letter, Col D. A. Campbell 19/4/1992.

406. Lissehall Oak. Shropshire. Lissehall by the sports pitch. Grid ref. SJ 7315 (Lissehall).

Girth 22 ft 3 ins (Morton 1985). Ref: Morton (1986, 104).

407. Little Oak. Northamptonshire. Salcey Forest. Grid ref. SP 8051.

408. Little Porter. See Porter's Oak.

409. Llanelay Oak. Glamorgan. A mile and a half from Llantrisant. Grid ref. ST 0483 (Llantrisant).

Hollow in 1838. Girth 38 ft 6 ins at ground level, 27 ft 2 ins at 3 ft (Loudon 1838). Ref: Loudon (1838).

410. Llantarnam Oak. Gwent. Llantarnam Hall. Grid ref. SO 299918.

Girth 27 ft. Ref: Linnard (2000, 126). **Picture by T.H.Thomas in National Museum of Wales.**

411. Lockwood Oak. Dumfriesshire. Lochwood, Annandale near the Castle, then the property of the Johnston family. Grid ref. NY 0896 (Lochwood).

Girth 16 ft in 1836. Still vigorous when other trees in the wood were decaying at that time (Loudon 1838). Ref: Loudon (1838) Vol. III p. 1772. Selby (1842, 254). Lauder (1883, 251).

412. Lodge Yard Oak, The. Staffordshire. Bagot's Park, 4 m. S of Uttoxeter: 2 m. N Abbots Bromley. Grid ref. SK 090275 (Bagot's Park).

Girth 33 ft 6 ins at 3 ft (Loudon 1838). Ref: Loudon (1838) Vol. III p. 1769.

413. Long Coppice Oak, The. Staffordshire. Bagot's Park, 4 m. S Uttoxeter: 2 m. N Abbots Bromley. Grid ref. SK 090275 (Bagot's Park). Ref: Loudon (1838) Vol. III p. 1769. Elwes and Henry (1907) Vol. II p. 317.

414. Long Oak. Shropshire. 2 m. S of West Felton on A5: 11 m. W of Shrewsbury. Grid ref. SJ 355233.

Ref: Hewins (1945, 11).

415. Longford Castle Oak. Wiltshire. Longford Castle. Grid ref. SU 1528 (Longford Castle).

Ref: Loudon (1838, 1839).

416. Longleat Oak, The. Wiltshire. Longleat. Grid ref. ST 8043 (Longleat).

Girth 19 ft 6 ins (Loudon 1838). Ref: Loudon (1838, 1839).

417. Lord Robinson Oak. Also known as the Forestry Commissioner's Oak. Gloucestershire. Forest of Dean. Prichards

Hill, Reddings Inclosure, Staunton: On N side of Monmouth to Staunton road A 4136. Grid ref. SO 533131.

Sessile oak. Girth 12 ft 7 ins in 1959. 14 ft 3 ins in 1986 (Standing 1986). Planted c. 1815. Dedicated to Lord Robinson, Chairman of the Forestry Commission (1932–52) who played an important part in retaining the Forest of Dean's broadleaved trees. Ref: Hart (1966, 244). Standing (1986, 7).

418. Lord's Oak, The. (I). Nottinghamshire. Worksop Park, south-west of Worksop and adjoined Welbeck Park. Grid ref. SK 570780 (Worksop Park).

Girth 38 ft 4 ins (Loudon 1838). Ref: Loudon (1838) Vol. III p. 1767.

419. Lords Oak, The. (II). Sussex. Rivelin in Sheffield Park, near Uckfield. Grid ref. TQ 4721 (Uckfield).

Felled 1653. Famous in its time. Girth 36 ft, 64 ft high (1740). Ref: Batty Langley (1740, 188). Evelyn (1670, 155, 157).

420. Loton Park Oak. See Prince's Oak.

421. Lowick Oak. Northamptonshire. Lowick Recreation Ground. Grid ref. SP 976807.

Young oak planted by Mr L. Stopford-Sackville of Drayton House 30 Nov 1975 to replace the original which was blown down in May 1968. The sapling was planted in the Recreation Ground about 35 yards north of the site of the original oak. The old tree is said to have been so big that in about 1920, 14 men could stand in the hollow trunk. Lowick was once part of Rockingham Forest. Ref: Wilks (1972, 248). Cuttings from *Kettering Evening Telegraph* (Dec 1975). Letter, J. A. Lockhart 27/11/1991.

422. Lullingstone Park Oaks. Kent. Lullingstone Castle, Nr Aynsford. Grid ref. TQ 507656.

A collection of about 90 large trees, mainly pollards. Girths from 23 ft to 33 ft. Ref: Pittman (1983), Putt (1984).

423. Lydham Manor Oak. Also known as the Big Oak. (III). Shropshire. Bishops Castle, part of Oakley Park. Grid ref. SO 3288.

Girth of 39 ft 4 ins in 1984. Another unnamed oak near had a girth of 30 ft (Morton 1986). Ref: Morton (1986, 42, 104). **Morton p. 43.**

424. Lydney Oak. Gloucestershire. Bathurst Park, Ldyney. Grid ref. SO 633029.

'Survived until … recent times' (Standing 1986). 'Girth was probably between 15 and 20 feet' (Standing 1986). Ref: Standing (1986, 14).

425. Machen Oak. Gloucestershire. Forest of Dean: Edge End. On west side of Monmouth-Micheldean road (A4136) just west of old beech avenue; palisaded. Grid ref. SO 596135.

Sessile oak. Girth 20 ft 6 ins Standing (1986) About 300 years old. Dedicated to Edward Machen, Deputy Surveyor of the Dean 1808–54. He supervised the planting of about 11000 acres in the Dean. Ref: Standing (1986, 2, 3, 9). Visit by James 1991. **Standing (1986, 2). Photograph James 9/5/1991.**

426. Magdalen Oak. Also known as The Great Oak. (VII); Alfred's Oak. Oxfordshire. Close by the gate of the water walk of Magdalen College. Grid ref. SP 5305 (of Oxford).

Fell in summer of 1788. William of Waynefleet ordered that his college should be founded near Alfred's Oak which is said to have been growing when Alfred founded a centre of learning. Ref: Gilpin (1791, 135–8). Loudon (1838, 1768). Ablett (1880, 168). Wilks (1972, 26). Whitlock (1985, 107).

427. Magii Oak. Staffordshire. Beaudesert Park. Grid ref. SK 035135 (Beaudesert Old Park).

Girth 30 ft at ground level (Loudon 1838). Ref: Loudon (1838, 1770).

428. Magog. (I). Northamptonshire. Chase Park Farm; 1 1/2 m. SSW of Yardley Hastings, close to Gog. Grid ref. SP 852550.

Girth 46 ft 6 ins a foot from the ground, 30 ft 7 ins at 6 ft. 66 ft high (Loudon (1838). Ref: Lauder (1834) Vol. I p. 259. Loudon (1838, 1765). Wilks (1972, 38). **Loudon fig. 1605.**

429. Magog. (II). Staffordshire. Mavesyn Ridware. Grid ref. SK 082169 (Mavesyn Ridware Church).

Felled in 1880s. Associated with an encounter between the Mavesyn and Handsacre families in 1403. Ref: Hewins (1945, 8).

430. Maiden Oak. Shropshire. Chepstow Castle. Grid ref. ST 5393.

This oak had unusually long leaves. Ref: Loudon (1838, 1746).

431. Majesty Oak. Kent. Fredville, Nonnington, 7 m. SE of Canterbury. Grid ref. TR 256512.

One of the Fredville Oaks; named Beauty, Majesty and Stately. Girth 39 ft 2 ins (James 1991). About 450 years old. Mitchell (1996). Ref: Strutt (1830, 52). Lauder (1834, 254). Loudon (1838, 1762). Grigor (1868, 267). Plumtree (1975, 239). Mitchell (1996). **Packenham (1996, 19).**

432. Major Oak. (I). Also known as the Queen Oak. (III); The Cockpen Tree. Nottinghamshire. Sherwood Forest. Half a mile north of Edwinstone Church on the west side of B6034. Grid ref. SK 627676.

Girth 29 ft at 9 ft in 1880. Named after Major Rooke who wrote 'Remarkable Oaks in the Park of Welbeck' (1790). The traditional meeting place of Robin Hood and his men but probably a meeting place long before (see Capon Tree). Not a very large tree although about 480 years old (Mitchell 1996). Cuttings (clones) from this tree have recently been propagated to ensure its genetic survival. Ref: Brown (1883, 19). Elwes and Henry (1907) Vol. II p. 317. Mosley (1910, 67). Hurst (1911, 193). Hewins (1945, 13). Wilks (1972, 169–70). Bean (1976, 508). Whitlock (1985, 109) Brewer's Dict. (1983, 799). White (1991).

433. Major Oak. (II). See William's Oak, Sir.

434. Malloch's Oak. Perthshire. Castle Wood, Strathallen Castle, near Auchterarder. Grid ref. NN 9315 (of Strathallen).

Girth 15 ft 3 ins at 4 ft (Hunter 1883). Malloch was a grocer who refused to sell food during a famine hoping that prices would rise. He was hung on this tree by the local inhabitants. This tree has been known as Malloch's Oak for over 200 years. Ref: Hunter (1883, 321).

435. Marton Oak. Cheshire. A farmyard in Marton. Grid ref. SJ 8468 (Marton).

Pedunculate oak. Girth 46 ft 6 ins. One of the largest pollard oaks (Mitchell 1996). Ref: Mee (1938, 116). Mitchell (1996, 316).

436. Martyr's Oak. Essex. In front of Brentwood School. Grid ref. TQ 5994.

Alive in 1972. Ref: Wilks (1972, 84).

437. Matthew Arnold Oak, The. Oxfordshire. Boars Hill, Oxford. Grid ref. SP 4910.

Planted 1910. Ref: Stewart (1981). **Photographs Stewart (1981, 150).**

438. Mawley Oak. Shropshire. At the junction of the B202 and A4117 Bewdley to Cleobury Mortimer roads. Grid ref. SO 6975.

Girth 24 ft (Morton 1986). Some limbs broke off in the 1970s. This tree marked the meeting place of the Wyre Forest tracks in the Middle Ages. The name is from Mawley Hall nearby. Ref: Hickin (1972, 6–7). Wilks (1972, 201). Morton (1986, 49, 104). **Drawing in Hickin p. 7. Tangye (1971).**

439. Meavy Oak. Devon. On the green at Meavy, opposite the Royal Oak Inn. Grid ref. SX 5411672.

Although hollow, still alive in 1999. A replacement has been planted. Girth 27 ft in 1872. A gospel oak and dancing tree. 'This tree till within this century was, on the village festival surrounded with poles, a platform was erected above the tree, the top of which was clipped flat, like a table, and a set of stairs erected … On the top a table and chairs were placed, and feasting took place' (Baring Gould 1899). King John used the oak as a 'larmer' or 'rush' halting place. In early twentieth century, the innkeeper's wife served dinner in it. Ref: Loudon (1838) Vol. III p. 1757. Murray's Handbook (1859). Baring-Gould (1899). Hurst (1911, 193). Wilks (1970, 280). Whitlock (1985, 106). Brewer's Dictonary (1983, 799). Visit by James 1991. **Loudon (1838) fig. 1591. Wilks (1970, 280–1). Photographs James 1991, Harris 1999.**

440. Meer Oak. Shropshire. Near Meeroak Farm. 4 m. NE of Knighton and 4 m. NW of Leintwardine. Near Hopton Castle. Grid ref. SO 345765 (Meeroak Farm).

Probably a boundary oak. Meer is a Saxon word meaning boundary. Ref: Hewins (1945, 11).

441. Melbury Park Oak. Dorset. Melbury Park. Grid ref. ST 570054.

Girth 33 ft (Loudon 1838). Ref: Loudon (1838, 1837).

442. Merlin's Oak. Also known as The Old Oak Tree; Priory Oak; Carmarthenshire. Priory Street, Carmarthen. Grid ref. SN 4121 (Carmarthen).

A dead stump (1972), now in the County Museum (2001). The tree was poisoned by a local tradesman in the early 19th century as he objected to people meeting beneath it at all hours. It was said to have been grown from an acorn planted on 19 May 1659 by a master called Adams from the old Queen Elizabeth's Grammer School to mark the proclamation of Charles II as King. An old poem goes: 'When Merlin's tree shall tumble down; Then shall fall Carmarthen town.' Ref: Lodwick (1972, 102–3). Wilks (1972, 135). **Lodwick (1972, 102). A photograph from National Museum of Wales.**

443. Merton Oak. Norfolk. Merton. 10 m. N of Thetford and 12 m. WNW of Attleborough. Grid ref. TF 907989 (Merton Village).

Fell in Jan. 1892. Girth 63 ft 2 ins at ground level (Loudon 1838). Other large oaks grow on the estate which at one time belonged to Lord Walsingham. Ref: Loudon (1838, 1763). Selby (1842, 254). Hurst (1911, 193). **Loudon fig. 1602.**

444. Meynell Langley Oak. Derbyshire. ¾ m. S of Kedleston; 5 m. NW of Derby. Grid ref. SK 301399 (Meynell Langley).

Wilks (1972, 38–9).

445. Michendon Oak. See Chandos Oak.

446. Mile Oak. (I). Shropshire. About 1 m. SSE of Oswestry on A483. Grid ref. SJ 301277 (approx).

Associated with Oswald, killed in the battle of Maserfield in 642. Ref: Rodgers (1941, 10). Hewins (1945, 10).

447. Mile Oak. (II). Staffordshire. Tamworth. Grid ref. SK 2004 (Tamworth). Ref: Wilks (1972, 242).

448. Milking Oak. Northamptonshire. Salcey Forest, on NW edge of Dean's Copse. Grid ref. SP 807514.

Girth 20 ft 9 ins (James 1991). It is thought to be named the Milking Oak as there was pasture here and the cows were milked under the shade of the oak. Ref: Wilks (1972, 172). Visit by James 1991. **Photograph James 24/10/1991.**

449. Millennium Derwen. Also known as The Great Welsh Oak. Gwent. Llantilio Crossenny, between Penrhos Farm and Pant Wood. Grid ref. SO 3914.

Girth 32 ft 6 ins in 1998 (Linnard). Named for the Millennium. 'The fifth largest girthed oak recorded in Wales' (Alderman 1999). Ref: Alderman (1999, 3). Linnard (2000, 126). **Alderman (1999, 3). Linnard (2000, 128).**

450. Miracle Oak. Hampshire. Burley Manor. Grid ref. SO 2103 (Burley Lawn).

An early flushing oak, leafing out at Christmas. Ref: Gilpin (1791, 227).

451. Mistletoe Oaks. See Chapter 6 for a list.

452. Mitre Oak. Worcestershire. Crossway Green, 2¼ m. SE of Stourport-on-Severn. Grid ref. SO 838685 (Crossway Green).

Pedunculate oak. 29 ft around the base. A boundary oak marking the possessions of the bishop of Worcester. Said to have been raised from an acorn collected from the tree under which St Augustine preached to the British bishops at a meeting convened by King Ethelbert. A seedling from the tree was planted in a field opposite to mark Queen Victoria's Golden Jubilee in 1888. Queen Elizabeth I on a visit met the Bishop and local gentry under the tree. Ref: Hewins (1945, 11). Wilks (1972, 113). Whitlock (1985, 107). White (1991). Stokes and Branchflower (2001). **Wilks p. 108.**

453. Moccas Park Oak. Herefordshire. On the banks of the Wye, Moccas Park. Grid ref. SO 344428 (Moccas Park).

Girth 36 ft (Loudon 1838). One of a number of large, old pollarded oaks in the Park. Ref: Loudon (1838, 1762, 1840). Hurst (1911, 193). Wilks (1973, 380). Hadfield (1970, 80). Giles (1990, 12–13). Visit by James 1991. **Loudon fig. 1595. Wilks (1969, 380). Photographs James 2/10/1991.**

454. Moccas Park Weeping Oak. Also known as the Pendulous Oak; Weeping Oak. Herefordshire. Moccas Park on the banks of the Wye. Grid ref. SO 344428 (Moccas Park).

Girth 13 ft 6 ins in 1838. This tree had pendulous branches which became less evident in old age. Ref: Loudon (1838). Hadfield (1969, 80).

455. Monarch Oak. Shropshire. Holme Lacey. Grid ref. SO 5535.

Transactions of the Woolhope Club (1867). Ref: Transactions of the Woolhope Club (1867, 56).

456. Monarch Oaks. Hampshire. New Forest. Knightwood Inclosure near Lyndhurst. Grid ref. SU 265065 (Knightwood Inclosure).

A number of oaks planted in the Inclosure to commemorate visits by various monarchs.

457. Moncrieffe's Oak. Perthshire. Halfway up the beech avenue to Moncrieffe House. Grid ref. NO 1621.

Planted in 1822 to commemorate the birth of the Lord of Moncrieffe in January of that year (Hunter 1883). Ref: Hunter. (1883, 133).

458. Monnington Oak. Herefordshire Moccas Park. Grid ref. SO 344428 (Moccas Park).

An important oak in Moccas Park. Ref: Transactions of the Woolhope Club (1867, 152). **Transactions of the Woolhope Club (1867, 152).**

459. Montague Oak. Northamptonshire. Grid ref. SP 8051 (Salcey Forest).

460. Morley Oak. Cheshire. Morley. Grid ref. SJ 8282.

Girth 42 ft (Loudon 1838). One of the largest trees in England in 1838. The trunk was hollow and used for housing cattle. The Black Prince is reputed to have dined in its shade. Ref: Loudon (1838, 1756).

461. Mottisfont Oak. See Oakley Oak. (II).

462. Moyles Court Oak. Hampshire. Moyles Court School; 2 miles N. of Ringwood. Grid ref. SU 161083.

Girth 21 ft (1947). Ref: Gardner (1947, 68). Letter, Hants. C.C. (1991).

463. Murrain Oak. Northamptonshire. Grid ref. SP 8051 (Salcey Forest).

This tree must have been associated with cattle plague in some way.

464. Mytton Oak. Shropshire. Shrewsbury. Grid ref. SJ 4912 (Shrewsbury).

Probably named after Mad Jack Mytton who lived nearby.

465. Naked Man, The. Also known as The Tree of Good and Evil; The Wilverley Oak. Hampshire. On N side of road from Sway to Burley: ¼m SW of Wilverley Post. Grid ref. SU 245018.

Dead long ago. Ref: Wilks (1972, 86). **Wilks p. 87.**

466. Nannau Oak. Also known as The Hollow Oak. (II); Derwen Cenbred Yr Ellyll; The Haunted Oak; Howel Sele's Oak. Merioneth. Nannau Park, 2 m. NNE of Dolgelly. Grid ref. SH 743209 (Nannau Park).

Struck by lightning in 1813. Girth 27 ft 6 ins in 1813 (Loudon 1838). Tradition relates that Owen Glendower murdered his cousin here and hid the body in the hollow oak. After Glendower's death, his companion, Madog, revealed the site of the murder and the body of Howel Sele was found inside the oak, standing up in its armour. Ref: Loudon (1838, 1763). Anon (1853, 53–4). Lauder (1883) Vol. I p. 251. Roberts (1890, 5). Mosley (1910). Wilks (1972, 47). **Loudon fig. 1600.**

467. Nash Oak. Shropshire. Junction of the Burford/ Correrlay and Whitmore/Wash Lane roads. Grid ref. SO 6071.

Girth 29 ft in 1983 (Morton 1986). Ref: Morton (1986, 49). **Morton (1986, 49).**

468. Neil Gow's Oak. (I). Perthshire. Dunkeld. Grid ref. NO 1242 (Dunkeld).

The oak under which Neil Gow sat and composed some of his finest pieces on the violin. Ref: Hunter (1883, 51).

469. Neil Gow's Oak. (II). See Birnam Oak.

470. Nettlecombe Oak. Somerset. Nettlecombe Court Field Centre, 2¼ m. SW Williton. Grid ref. ST 057378.

Sessile oak. Girth 'near the ground' 17 ft in 1842. Ht 85 ft (Selby 1842). Girth 21 ft 9 ins in 1959, 112 ft high (Bean 1976). Girth 21 ft 8 ins at 5 ft. 111 ft 6 ins high (Mitchell 1974). Ref: Selby (1842, 256). Elwes and Henry (1907) Vol. II pp. 314–5: Hurst (1911, 193). Mitchell (1974, 243). Bean (1976, 500). Mitchell (1982, 271).

471. Newbridge-on-Usk Oak. Gwent. Grid ref. ST 3894.

Girth 25 ft in 1870. Ref: Linnard (2000, 126). **Drawn by T. H. Thomas (1870) now in the National Museum of Wales.**

472. Newcastle Oak. Monmouthshire. In a field at the rear of the Wellington Inn at Newcastle, which is 4½ m. NW of Monmouth on road B4347. Grid ref. SO 447173.

An old tree which no-one would attempt to lop or fell because the fairies had the tree in their power. Ref: Olive Phillips 'Monmouthshire' (1951): Letter, Mrs Margery Probyn 27/4/1992, Linnard (2000, 119). **Linnard (2000, 120).**

473. Newland Oak. Also known as The Great Oak of Newland. Gloucestershire. Forest of Dean: Spout Farm, Newland (marked on 25,000 map). Grid ref. SO 551099.

The old tree fell in a storm, May 1955. A young tree planted in 1964 (grown from a cutting off the original tree). The latter was a pedunculate oak. Girth 44 ft 8 ins in 1954. This tree was held to be second largest oak in Britain and one of the oldest. Age was probably about 750 years (Mitchell 1966). Elwes and Henry (1907) Vol. II p. 320. Mosley (1910, 68). Hurst (1911, 191, 194). Mitchell (1966, 275). Wilks (1972, 247). Standing (1986, 14). **H. Townley (1910, 226): (1966). Mitchell (1966, 275).**

474. Newton St Petrock Oak. See Great Oak. (I).

475. Nigeria Oak. Berkshire. Windsor Great Park. Grid ref. SU 960710 (Windsor Great Park).

Pedunculate oak. Ref: White (1991).

476. Northern Oak. Hampshire. Possibly at Boldrewood (Wise 1863, 16). Grid ref. SU 2408 (Boldrewood).

Probably a boundary oak. Ref: Wise (1863, 16).

477. Northfield Oak. Essex. Writtle Park. Grid ref. TL 6606 (Writtle).

Girth 31 ft 6 ins Loudon (1838). Ref: Loudon (1838).

478. Northiam Oak. See Queen Elizabeth Oak, The. (VI).

479. Northwick Oak. Worcestershire. Blockley. Grid ref. SP 1634.

Girth 21 ft at 5 ft. 30 ft to first branch, about 300 years old. Loudon (1838). Ref: Loudon (1838).

480. Novel's Oak. See King Oak. (VII).

481. Nunupton Oak. Herefordshire. 3 m. WSW of Tenbury Wells. Grid ref. SO 542666.

Girth 33 ft at 5 ft. Loudon (1838). Ref: Loudon (1838). Elwes and Henry (1907) Vol. II p. 314.

482. Oak of the Reformation. See Ketts Oak. (II).

483. Oake of Honour. See Honour Oak. (II).

484. Oakleigh Oak. See Oakley Oak. (II).

485. Oakley Oak. (I). Bedfordshire. In 'the grounds of the Duke of Bedford's estate' (Burt 1860). Presumably at Woburn. SP 965325 (Woburn Park).

Girth 15 ft 9 ins at 2 ft. (Loudon 1838). Ref: Loudon (1838). Burt (1860, 73).

486. Oakley Oak. (II). Also known as The Oakleigh Oak; Mottisfont Oak; Hampshire. On the left bank of the Test, one mile north of the village near Oak Tree Farm. Grid ref. SU 331277.

Alive in 1991. Pedunculate oak. Girth 34 ft 3 ins (Gardner 1947) Hollow. Pollarded. Ref: Gardner (1947, 67). Wilks (1972, 144). Bean (1976) Vol. III p. 508. Letter, Hants. C. C. 16/11/1991. White (1991).

487. Old Churn Oak. See Churn Oak.

488. Old Crome's Oak. See Porlingland Oak.

489. Old Oak, The. See Merlin's Oak.

490. Owen Glendower's Oak. See Glendower's Oak.

491. Oxhey Oak. Also known as the Grimstone Oak. (II). Hertfordshire. In what was Oxhey Place (burned down 1954), now a building estate. Grid ref. TQ 04944 (Oxhey Hall).

Stones and other objects were placed inside oaks in the past, as gifts to the fairies. Grim is another name for fairies. Ref: Wilks (1972, 189).

492. Packington Park Oaks. Warwickshire. Grid ref. SP 2283.

Giant oaks, remains of the Forest of Arden. Ref: Hewins (1945, 6).

493. Painted Oak. Cornwall. 'In the hundred of the east' (Thurston 1930) i.e. East Cornwall. Grid ref. SX – – .

This tree had variegated leaves (see the Boconnoc Oak). Ref: Thurston (1930, 187).

494. Palmer's Farm Oak. (I). Devon. On N side of Tiverton-Tackenford road (B3221) at Palmers: 1½ m. NW Tiverton. Grid ref. SS 934141.

Branches reach to far side of road. Difficult to girth. (James 1991). Ref: Visit by James (1991).

495. Palmer's Farm Oak. (II). Devon. At Palmer's, one and half miles N. W. of Tiverton. Grid ref. SS 928141.

Girth 20 ft 6 ins at 5 ft. James (1991). Probably the largest oak in the district except for Palmer's Farm Oak. (I). Ref: Visit by James (1991).

496. Panshanger Oak. Also known as Great Oak, The. (III). Hertfordshire. Panshanger Park, between Hertford and Welwyn Garden City bounded by A414 and B1000 roads. Grid ref. TL 280120.

Girth 23 ft 4 ins at 3 ft in 1953. Gardner (1954). Selby (1842) states that it was 'upwards of 150 years old'. A maiden tree with bole of 45 feet. Mitchell (1996). Ref: Strutt (1830, 6). Loudon (1838) Vol. III p. 1762. Selby (1842, 257). Burt (1860, 60). Lauder (1883, 254). Hurst (1911, 194). Gardner (1954, 239–240). Wilks (1972, 159). Bean (1976) Vol. III p. 508. Mitchell (1996, 316). **Loudon figs 1596, 1480. Photographs Gardner (1954, 240).**

497. Parliament Oak. Also known as the Clipstone Oak. Nottinghamshire. Hewins (1945) states 'Two miles from Clipstone, on the Mansfield road is the gnarled trunk of a vast oak tree ...' Grid ref. SK 579626 (Hewin's location).

Girth 28 ft 6 ins (Loudon 1838). This oak was near the old Royal Palace of Clipstone. Both King John and King Edward I are said to have held meetings with their advisors under this oak. Here too, Edward I heard of Llewellyn's uprising in Wales. Ref: Rooke (1790, 12, 13). Hayes (1822, 126). Loudon (1838, 1767). Burt (1860, 73). Grigor (1868, 268). Ablett (1880, 169). Brown (1883, 18). Mosley (1910, 54). Hurst (1911, 194). Hewins (1945, 13). Wilks (1972, 151). Brewer's Dict. (1983, 799). **Rooke plate 8.**

498. Paschoe Oak. Also known as the Pascoe Oak. Devon. Near Paschoe House: 1¼ m. W of Coleford, nr Copplestone. Grid ref. SS 753012.

Girth: 21 ft 9 ins at 5 ft agl. James (1991). When the estate was sold, it was stipulated that this oak should not be felled. Ref: Visit by James (1991). **Photographs James 30/10/91.**

499. Pascoe Oak. See Paschoe Oak.

500. Passfield Oak. Hampshire. Grid ref. SU 8234.
Ref: Letter, Hants. C. C. (1991).

501. Pease Tree, The. Lanarkshire. The Lee 2½ m. NW of Lanark. Grid ref. NS 8843 (of Lanark).
Ref: Elwes and Henry (1907) Vol. II p. 329.

502. Pedam's Oak. Also known as Pedom's Oak. Durham. On Edmundbyers Common, 2 m. SW of Edmundbyers and 10 m. S of Corbridge. Grid ref. NY 988484.

Figure 52. *Clockwise from top left:* a. King Charles II Oak. (348); b. The Milking Oak (448);
c. Sir Phillip Sydney's Oak (650) – a burr oak. N. D. G. JAMES.

A farmer called Pedom stole sheep and hid them in this hollow oak. Ref: Wilks (1972, 78).

503. Pedom's Oak. See Pedam's Oak.

504. Pendulous Oak, The. See Moccas Park Weeping Oak.

505. Penrice Oak. Cornwall. Grid ref. SX 0351.

Planted by R. C. Graves Sawle on his coming of age. He was killed in the Great War. Ref: Thurston (1930, 193).

506. Pepperwell Oak. Perthshire. Methven Castle 5 m. W of Perth. Grid ref. NO 1225 (Methven).

Girth 17 ft in 1795, 23 ft in 1883. The tree was named after the spring by which it grows (Hunter 1883). Ref: Hunter (1883, 125). Elwes and Henry (1907). Vol. II p. 329.

507. Peter's Oak, St. Hampshire. 2½ m. SSW of Minstead. 2½ m. WSW of Lyndhurst – Holiday Hills Inclosure. Grid ref. SU 2607.

Alive in 1991. Ref: Letter Hants. C.C. (1991).

508. Petersham Oak. Dorset. Petersham Farm is ½ m. NW of Holt which is 2 m. N of Wimborne. Pig Oak (Hamlet) is ¼ m. S of Holt. Grid ref. ST 022043.

Girth 24 ft 9 ins at 5 ft (James 1992). Pedunculate: It stands on land belonging to Petersham Farm. Ref: White (1991). Visit by James 1992. **Photographs James 6/8/1992.**

509. Piddington Oak. Northamptonshire. Salcey Forest: SW corner of Atterbury Coppice or Copse. Grid ref. SP 803523.

Pedunculate oak. Girth 19 ft 3 ins at 5 ft agl. (James. Oct. 1991). The name of the tree is from the forest ride which leads to Piddington. Ref: Wilks (1972, 172). Visit by James 1992. **Photograph James 24/10/1991.**

510. Pig Oak. Dorset. Opposite Pig Oak Farm, in hamlet of Pig Oak, c. 2 m. N of Wimborne Minster. Grid ref. ST 025033 (marked on OS map).

According to Mr Jones who lives at Pig Oak Farm it was customary for the local people to turn their pigs out under this oak for the acorns (pannage). Originally the oak was free standing before the hedge was planted. The hedge was so thick, it was not possible to measure the tree. Ref: Visit by James 1992. **Photographs James 6/8/1992.**

511. Pilgrim Oak. Nottinghamshire. At the gates of Newstead Park in Ravenshead which is 4 m. SSW of Mansfield and 2 m. NNE of Papplewick. Grid ref. SK 557545 (Oak marked on OS map).

Referred to by Washington Irvine. Ref: Wilks (1972, 167–8).

512. Plaish Oak. Shropshire. Plaish. Grid ref. SO 5296.

Girth 24 ft 6 ins (Morton 1986). Ref: Morton (1986, 104).

513. Pleastor Oak. Hampshire. Selborne: 4 m. SE of Alton. Grid ref. SU 740337 (Selborne).

Blew down in the famous 1703 gale. Pleastor (or pleastow, plestor) was a playing place for games and maypole dancing. The oak was surrounded by stone steps with seats above and 'a place of much resort in summer evenings' (Gilbert White). Ref: White (1789). Hurst (1911, 88). Whitlock (1985, 107). Wilks (1972, 23).

514. Plestor Oak. Also known as Stock's Oak. Hampshire. Near Liss. Grid ref. SU 771285.

Alive in 1991. Plestor = a place for games and maypole dancing (see the Pleastor Oak). In 1922 the iron supports of the stocks, once fixed to the tree, could still be felt in the trunk. Ref: Letter, Hants. C.C. (1991).

515. Pontfadog Oak. Shropshire. West of Chirk. Grid ref. SJ 2338 (Pontfadog).

Girth 43 ft. Ref: Letter. Royal Botanical Gardens Edinburgh 1992. **Hyde (1977) plate XIX.**

516. Pontrilas Oak. See Jack of Kent's Oak.

517. Pope's Oak. (I). Berkshire. Loudon refers to 'Pope's Oak in Binfield Wood, Windsor Forest'. However the village of Binfield is 7½ m. W of the centre of the Great Park: Popeswood is 1 m. S of Binfield. Grid ref. SU 845713 (Binfield Village), SU 845696 (Pope's Wood).

'Here Pope sang' (Loudon 1838). Ref: Loudon (1838) Vol. III p. 1754.

518. Pope's Oak. (II). Sussex. West Grinstead 6 m. S of Horsham. Grid ref. TQ 1721.

Only a vestige remained in 1972 (Wilks). Beneath this oak Pope is said to have written 'The Rape of the Lock' (VCH 1907) in 1712. Stood on National Stud land. Ref: Victoria County History (1907) Sussex: Vol. II. Wilks (1972, 245).

519. Poringland Oak. Also known as Old Cromes Oak; Porlingham Oak. Norfolk. Poringland, 4½ m. S of Norwich on B 1332 road. Grid ref. TM 271016 (Poringland Church).

This tree was painted by John Crome (Artist). Ref: Wilks (1972, 41).

520. Porlingham Oak. See Poringland Oak.

521. Porter's Oak, The. Also known as The Two Porters;

The Large Porter and Little Porter. Nottinghamshire. Welbeck Park, either side of drive at the North Gate. Grid ref. SK 564742 (Welbeck Abbey).

One tree survives. The Large Porter fell in 1990s. Girth of Large Porter in 1838 was 38 ft, the Little Porter 34 ft. (Loudon). In 1894, the girth of the Large Porter was given as 36 ft 8 ins, with its top broken by a storm; the girth of the Little Porter was given as 36 ft (English Arboricultural Soc. 1893–94). The trees were named the Porters as there was at one time a gate between them. Ref: Rooke (1790, 7). Loudon (1838, 1766). Lauder (1883) Vol. I p. 259. Elwes and Henry (1907) Vol. II p. 322. Wilks (1972, 171). Packenham (1996, 124). White (1991). **Rooke (1790, 2, 7). Packenham p. 124.**

522. Powis Oak. (I). Shropshire. Bromfield Wood near Ludlow (Strutt 1830). Bromfield is 2¼ m. NW of Ludlow. Grid ref. SO 482768 (Bromfield).

Ref: Strutt (1830, 35).

523. Powis Oak. (II). Shropshire. Underhill Hall, between Picklescott and Castle Pulverbatch. Grid ref. SO 4399 (Picklescott).

Girth 34 ft. One of the largest girthed oaks in the county (Morton 1986). Named after the Powis family. Ref: Morton (1986, 46).

524. Prince Charles Oak. Gloucestershire. To the west of Speech House. Grid ref. SO 619121 (Speech House).

Planted in 1948. Ref: Hart (1966, 244).

525. Prince Consort's Oak. Gloucestershire. Forest of Dean near Speech House. Grid ref. SO 619121.

Pedunculate oak. Girth 9 ft 3 ins in 1986 (Standing 1986). Planted by Prince Albert in 1861. Grown from acorn from Panshanger Oak planted by Queen Elizabeth I. See also Queen Elizabeth II Oak. Ref: Wilks (1972, 147). Standing (1986, 6). **Hart (1966, 168).**

526. Prince of Orange's Oak. Devon. Teigngrace village about 1½ m. N of Newton Abbot on E side of road where it forms a right angle corner. Grid ref. SX 845739.

Girth at 5 ft agl: 27 ft (James 1991). Said to be where the Prince of Orange (afterwards William II) rested on the day after his landing at Brixham: 5 Nov 1688. Ref: Wilks (1972, 163). Visit by James 1991. **Wilks p. 71, 161. Photographs James 13/8/1991.**

527. Prince Philip Oak. Gloucestershire. Forest of Dean – Speech House: beside Queen Elizabeth Oak. Grid ref. SO 619121.

Sessile oak. Girth 3 ft 7 ins in 1986 (Standing 1986). Planted by Prince Philip in 1957. Ref: Standing (1986, 7).

528. Prince's Oak. Loton Park Oak. Shropshire. Near Loton Park at Allerbury. Grid ref. SJ 350146 marked on O.S. map.

Girth 22 ft 10 ins in 1985 (Morton 1986). In 1806, the Prince of Wales (George IV) rode across the border into Wales and picked leaves from this oak to prove that he had visited Wales. A plaque by the tree records this event. Ref: Morton (1986, 104). **Morton (1986, 63).**

529. Priory Oak. See Merlin's Oak.

530. Quatford Oak. Also known as the Forest Oak. Shropshire. Quatford 1½ m. SE of Bridgnorth. Grid ref. SO 742908 (Forest Oak is marked on O.S. map).

The tree was near the site chosen for Quatford Church. In 1082, Lady Adelissa was caught in a storm when crossing the Channel and she built the church in thanksgiving for a successful journey. She met her future husband under the oak tree after she landed. A stained glass window in the church depicts this legend. Ref: Hewins (1945, 10). Wilks (1972, 111). Morton (1986, 59).

531. Queen Anne's Oak. Berkshire. Windsor Great Park. Grid ref. SU 9672 (Windsor Great Park).

Pedunculate. Tradition states that Queen Anne 'often hunted in Windsor Forest' and under this tree 'generally came to mount her horse ' (Loudon 1838). Ref: Loudon (1838, 1754). Elwes and Henry (1907, 319). Wilks (1972, 147). White (1991).

532. Queen Bower Oak. Hampshire. 2 m. NW of Brockenhurst Station: 1¾ m. S of Bank. Grid ref. SU 288043 (Queen Bower marked on OS map). Ref: Letter, Hants. C.C. (1991).

533. Queen Charlotte's Oak. Berkshire. Windsor Great Park. Grid ref. SU 9672 (Windsor Great Park).

Pedunculate. A favourite tree of Queen Charlotte's. George IV 'had a brass plate with her name fixed on it' (Loudon 1838). Ref: Loudon (1838, 1754). Elwes and Henry (1907, 329). Wilks (1972, 147). White (1991).

534. Queen Elizabeth II's Oak. (I). Gloucestershire. Forest of Dean – Speech House. Grid ref. SO 619121.

Pedunculate oak. Girth 3 ft 8 ins (1987). Planted by H.M. Queen Elizabeth II in 1957. Raised from an acorn from the Prince Consort's Oak. The latter was grown from an acorn from an oak planted by Queen Elizabeth I at Panshanger, thus creating link between the two Queen Elizabeths. Ref: Standing (1986, 6).

535. Queen Elizabeth II's Oak. (II). Buckinghamshire. Dropmore. Grid ref. SU 9386.

An oak sapling from a Boscopel acorn planted by Elizabeth II.

536. Queen Elizabeth Oak. See King's Oak. (II).

537. Queen Elizabeth's Oak. (I). Also known as The Queen's Oak. (VI). Hampshire. Elvetham Park. 1 m. E of Hartley Wintney. Grid ref. SU 784564 (Elvetham Hall).

Girth 21 ft 5 ins in 1947. A plaque beside this oak states that it was planted in October 1591 by Queen Elizabeth I (Mitchell 1991). Ref: White (1991): A. F. Mitchell (1991) in *The Field* for Aug. p. 88.

538. Queen Elizabeth's Oak. (II). Also known as The Elizabeth Oak; Queen's Oak. (II). Hertfordshire. Hatfield Park 5 m. E of St Albans. Grid ref. TQ 237084 (Hatfield House).

Elizabeth was said to have been seated under this tree when the news was brought to her that Mary Tudor was dead and therefore she was now Queen. An acorn from this tree provided a sapling which was planted by Queen Victoria near this oak. Ref: Anon (1853, 47). Roberts (1890, 187). Hurst (1911, 191). Whitlock (1985, 104).

539. Queen Elizabeth's Oak. (III). London. Greenwich Park SE10. Grid ref. TQ 390773 (Greenwich Park).

The tree was blown down in 1991. Henry VIII and Anne Boleyn are said to have danced beneath this tree. As a young girl, Elizabeth played in it. Later on, the hollow tree was given a door and offenders against the park regulations were locked up in it. Ref: Wilks (1972, 158). *The Times* 1991.

540. Queen Elizabeth's Oak. (IV). Also known as The Heveningham Oak. Suffolk. In the grounds of Heveningham Hall. Grid ref. TM 350733.

Girth 35 ft in 1791 when the bole 'is a mere shell' (Gilpin 1791). Ref: Gilpin (1791). Vol. I p. 147.

541. Queen Elizabeth's Oak. (V). Also known as The Queen's Oak. (IV); Elizabeth Oak; Huntingfield Oak. Suffolk. Huntingfield: 3½ m. SW of Halesworth; orginally within 'two bow shots' of Huntingfield Hall of which nothing now remains (Wilks 1972). Grid ref. TM 344742 (Queen's Oak marked on the map).

Pedunculate oak. Girth 36 ft at 7 ft in 1911 when the bole was a shell (Hurst 1911). Part of the bole still existed in 1972. Queen Elizabeth I is said to have shot a buck from the cover of this tree. Ref: Loudon (1838, 1770). Burt (1860, 62). Hurst (1911, 191). Brewers Dictionary (1983, 799a).

Wilks (1972, 158–9). Whitlock (1985, 104). **Loudon Vol. III p. 1770 drawing**.

542. Queen Elizabeth's Oak. (VI). Also known as the Northiam Oak. East Sussex. Northiam on NW corner of village green: Northiam is 9 m. N of Hastings on A 28 and 6 m. NW of Rye. Grid ref. TQ 8324.

A replacement tree fell down in 1991 and a new tree was planted. The original tree was damaged by a storm in 1816. A plaque on the tree states 'Queen Elizabeth I, as she journeyed to Rye on the 11th August 1573 sat under this tree and ate a meal served from the house nearby. She changed her shoes of green damask silk with a heel 2½ ins high and a sharp toe, at this spot and left them behind as a memento of her visit. They are still in existence and are shown on special occasions'. They belong to the Fewin family of Brickwall. Ref: Wilks (1972, 159). Bunce (1958) Johnson, Owen (1998).

543. Queen Elizabeth's Oak. (VII). Essex. Havering Park, near Havering-at Bower. Grid ref. TQ 5193.

Girth 20 ft (Mee 1940). There was a former royal residence here, used when royalty were hunting in Hainault Forest. Under this tree, tradition relates that Queen Elizabeth learnt that the Armada had been defeated. Ref: Mee (1940, 190).

544. Queen Elizabeth's Oak. (VIII). Sussex. Cowdray Park, near Midhurst. Grid ref. SU 913226.

Girth 38 ft in 1940. 400 cms 1999. (Johnson 1999). Queen Elizabeth visited Cowdray in 1591 and is said to have visited this tree. There are a number of other large oaks in the Park but this is the largest sessile oak. Hollow and pollarded. Ref: Johnson (1999, 6–7). **Johnson (1998, 6)**.

545. Queen Elizabeth's Oak. (IX). Berkshire. Windsor Home Park. Grid ref. SU 9672.

Girth 29 ft at 4 ft in 1867. Stood 200 yards away from Herne's Oak in the Fairie's Dell. Ref: Perry (1867).

546. Queen Hive Oak. Northamptonshire. Salcey Forest: Little Straits Coppice on Queen Hive Riding which leads from the Queen Hive Rickyard on the Forest lawn in the centre, to the outside of the Forest. Grid ref. SP 809515.

Pedunculate oak. Girth 19 ft 11 ins at 5 ft agl. James (1991). The tree takes its name from the Queen Hive Rickyard. Ref: Visit by James 1991. **Photograph James 24/10/1991**.

547. Queen Oak. Yorkshire. Hovingham Hall. Grid ref. SE 6675 (Hovingham).

Girth 24 ft, 70 ft high (Loudon 1838). Ref: Loudon (1838, 1841).

548. Queen Oak, The. (I). Gloucestershire. Razies Bottom (The Razies) Ashwicke Hall, 1½ m. SE of Marshfield and 3 m. N of Batheaston. Grid ref. ST 795721.

Loudon (1838) states: 'it girted 34 ft at the base, had a clear cylindrical stem of 30 ft high and 16 ft in circumference all the way; bearing two tree like branches, each extending 40 ft beyond the bole and girting at the base 8 ft; containing in all 680 ft of measurable timber'. See also the Duke of Gloucester and King Oak. (II). Ref: Loudon (1838, 1760).

549. Queen Oak, The. (II). The 'Queen' of the King and Queen Oaks. See also King Oak. (IV). Hampshire. Boldrewood: 2 m. W of Lyndhurst. Grid ref. SU 2408. Ref: Hurst (1911, 85, 193). Wilks (1972, 247). Letter, Hants C.C. 16/ 11/ 1991.

550. Queen Oak, The. (III). See Major Oak, The. (I).

551. Queen Oak, The. (IV). Northamptonshire. Queen Oak Farm. Grid ref. SP 6865 (Althorp Park). Ref: Visit by James 1991. **Photograph James 1991.**

552. Queen of Thonock, The. Lincolnshire. Thonock Estate, ¾ m. NE of Gainsborough. Grid ref. SX 8292.

Alive in 1992. Ref: Anon. (1992, 64).

553. Queen Victoria's and Albert's Oaks. Perthshire. Taymouth Castle in the Flower Garden. Grid ref. NN 7846.

Planted in 1842. Ref: Hunter (1883, 389).

554. Queen Victoria's Favourite Oak. (I). Warwickshire. Stoneleigh, between Standing Hill and New Lodge. Grid ref. SP 3172 (the Agricultural Centre).

Girth 11 ft in 1864. Ref: Clarke *et al.* (1987, 38).

555. Queen Victoria's Favourite Oak. (II). See Queen Victoria's Oak. (I).

556. Queen Victoria's Oak. (I). Also known as Queen Victoria's Favourite Oak. (II). Berkshire. Windsor Great Park. Grid ref. SU9672 (Windsor Great Park).

Pedunculate. Ref: Burt (1860). Elwes and Henry (1907) Vol. II p. 319. Wilks (1972, 147).

557. Queen Victoria's Oak. (II). Hampshire. '150 yds from Queen's Arms Inn near the A 287 from Farnham to Odiham, Hampshire on a minor road almost opposite the Inn' (Wilks p. 164). Grid ref. SU 800503 or 813404 (two inns in the locality).

Ref: Wilks (1972, 164).

558. Queen Victoria's Oak. (III). Hertfordshire. Ashridge House Gardens. Grid ref. SP 9913.

Planted in 1823. Ref: Duchesne (1911, 345).

559. Queen Victoria's Oak. (IV). Warwickshire. Warwick Castle. Grid ref. SP 2865 (Warwick).

Planted in 1855. Ref: Clarke *et al.* (1987, 49).

560. Queen Victoria's Oak. (V). Leicestershire. Burton Overy Rectory. Grid ref. SP 6798 (Burton Overy).

A sapling was planted which had been grown from an acorn off the Boscobel Oak. This tree was planted to commemorate the Queen's Diamond Jubilee. Ref: Hewins (1945, 15).

561. Queen's Oak, The. (I) See Crouch Oak .

562. Queen's Oak, The (II). See Queen Elizabeth's Oak (II).

563. Queen's Oak, The. (III). Northampton. 'It stood directly between Crafton Castle and Whittlebury Forest' (Wilks 1972.) Note: Queen's Oak Farm lies approx midway between Grafton Regis and Whittlewood Forest. Grid ref. SP 747449 (Queen's Oak Farm).

The trysting tree for Edward IV and Elizabeth Woodville. She was the daughter of Earl Rivers and she met Edward IV under this tree and petitioned him to return to her her husband's lands after the Wars of the Roses. She later became his Queen. Ref: Burt (1860, 61). Brown (1883, 117). Mosley (1910, 53). Hurst (1911, 194). Hewins (1945, 15). Wilks (1972, 154). **Wilks (1972, 152).**

564. Queen's Oak, The (IV). See Queen Elizabeth's Oak (V).

565. Queen's Oak, The. (V). Berkshire. Donnington Park, 1¾ m. NNW of Newbury railway station. Grid ref. SU 465687 (Donnington village).

This tree was reputed to have been planted by Chaucer. When felled, it produced a beam 40 ft long. Ref: Evelyn (1670, 153). Langley (1740, 186). Gilpin (1791, 134). Loudon (1838, 1754). Ablett (1880, 167).

566. Queen's Oak, The. (VI). See Queen Elizabeth's Oak. (I).

567. Queen's Oak. (VII). See Queen Elizabeth's Oak. (V).

568. Quidenham Oak. See Winfarthing Oak.

569. Quitchell's Oak. Hertfordshire. In the grounds of Hailebury College on what was known as Quitch Hill in the Middle Ages. Grid ref. TL 358108 (Haileybury Quad).

This oak was recorded in 1634. Queach means a thicket. Wilks (1972). Ref: Wilks (1972, 25).

570. Radley Oak. Oxfordshire. Radley College Park. Grid ref. SU 5398.

Pedunculate oak. 25 ft 6 ins at 5 ft (Hamersley 1955). A pollarded Oak (Bean 1976). A maiden oak which was once forked (Mitchell 1996). There is a tradition that nine cavaliers were hung on this tree in the Civil War. Ref: Bean (1976) Vol. III p. 508. Mitchell (1996). Hamersley (1955, 143). **Hamersley (1955, 143).**

571. Rakeswood Oak. Staffordshire. Bagots Park, 4 m. S Uttoxeter: 2 m. N Abbots Bromley. Grid ref. SK 090275 (Bagots Park).

Girth 30 ft at 5 ft. (Loudon 1838). Ref: Loudon (1838) Vol. III p. 1769. Elwes and Henry (1907) Vol. II p. 317.

572. Raven Oak. Hampshire. Selborne: 4 m. SE Alton. Grid ref. SU 744344 (Selborne).

One of the famous Losel oaks on the Blackmoor Estate, famous for their length of clean timber. Ravens nested in this tree before it was felled. Ref: White (1789). Wilks (1972, 44). Whitlock (1985, 107).

573. Raven's Oak. Northamptonshire. Pilckley.

A tree with a large fork used by ravens for several generations (Loudon 1838). Ref: Loudon (1838, 1766).

574. Rawnpike Oak. Staffordshire. 'On Cannock Chase just outside Beaudesert Park' (Hewins 1945). Grid ref. SK 035135 (Beaudesert Old Park).

Destroyed by lightning and fire. 'Said to be 800 years' old (Hewins 1945). Mentioned in local records. Ref: Hewins (1945, 7).

575. Rebel Oak. Westmorland. Clifton 2 m. S of Penrith. Grid ref. NY 535266 (Clifton).

Battle of Clifton Moor was in 1745 between Prince Charles Edward and the Duke of Cumberland. This oak may have some connection with this event. Ref: Letter, J. Atkins 25/11/1991.

576. Reformation Oak. (I). See Ketts Oak. (II).

577. Reformation Oak. (II). See Ketts Oak. (III).

578. Remedy Oak. Dorset. Woodlands near Verwood. Woodlands are 3¾ m. S of Cranborne and 2½ m. W of Verwood and 6 m. NE of Wimborne. Grid ref. ST 052099.

Girth 21 ft at 5 ft (James 1992). A brass plaque reads 'According to tradition King Edward VI sat beneath this tree and touched for the King's Evil'. The King's Evil was scrofula, a swelling of the lymphatic glands and associated with consumption. The Duke of Monmouth was captured near this oak in 1685. The tree is hollow and open on east side. It is secured by two steel ropes on side furthest from the road (east side). Ref: Wilks (1972, 138). Brewers Dictionary. Visit by James 1992. **Wilks (1972) opp. p. 144. Photographs James 6/8/1992.**

579. Roan Oak. Staffordshire. In Beaudesert Park near Newee Gate. Grid ref. SK 035135 (Beaudesert Old Park).

The trunk of this tree is 26 ft 3 in in circumference. (Loudon 1838). Ref: Loudon (1838, 1770).

580. Robin Hood's Larder. See Shambles Oak.

581. Robur Britannicum. See Rycote Oak.

582. Rock Oak. Also known as the Apostle's Oak. Worcestershire. Rock 5 m. W Stourport-on-Severn (or Abberley, see below). Grid ref. SO 734712 (Rock), SO 7567 (Abberley).

The site where Augustine met the seven British Bishops to get them to conform over the date of Easter and the rite of Baptism. Finberg (1974) states the tree was at Abberley, near Rock and that the tree gave 'its name to the parish of Rock, originally R(oak), in which Abberley was included until 1289'. Ref: Wilks (1972, 111). Finberg (1974, 40). Whitlock (1985, 107).

583. Rookery Oak. Sussex. Kidbrooke Park. Grid ref. TQ 421345.

Girth 18 ft at 1 ft. in 1838. References. Loudon (1838).

584. Rosemaund Oak. Herefordshire. Felton. Grid ref. SO 5748 (Felton). Ref: Transactions of the Woolhope Club (1871). **Transactions of the Woolhope Club (1871, 34).**

585. Rossie Oaks, The. Perthshire. Rossie Hill, nr Forgandenny. Grid ref. NO 0818 (Forgandenny).

Three oaks, near the house. In 1883, one had a girth of 11 ft at 1 ft, another a clean stem of 30 ft. Tradition states that these trees were grown from acorns which George III had played with as a boy. The acorns were given to Robert Oliphant (of Rossie) by the third Earl of Bute who had been tutor to the King when he was Prince George.

586. Roughfort Oak. See Liberty Tree, The.

587. Royal Forestry Society Oak. Northumberland. Hexham Abbey. Grid ref. NY 9364 (Hexham).

Planted on 10 June 1932 by Alderman Thomas Taylor,

President 1899–1900 and the oldest past president at the time, to mark the 50th anniversary of the Royal Forestry Society's foundation. Ref: Anon (1982). **QJF 1982 Photograph opp. p. 1.**

588. Royal Oak. (I). Co. Fermanagh. Near Lisnaskea.

Named after King William and his army. Ref: Browne (2000).

589. Royal Oak. (II). See Boscobel Oak.

590. Royal Oak. Gwyneddd. Trefriw. Grid ref. SH 778628. Ref: Harris. **Harris slide 697.**

591. Rufus Oak. Also known as Tyrell's Oak; Canterton Oak. Hampshire. New Forest. 1 m. NW of Minstead: 2 m. SW of Cadnam. Grid ref. ST 270124.

The site of the tree is marked by a commemoration stone. The oak tree on which an arrow, shot by Sir Walter Tyrell at a stag, glanced, struck and killed the King (William II). 'He was placed on a cart belonging to one Purkess and drawn from thence to Winchester' (Camden 1607). Ref: Camden (1607 and 1806). Lewis (1811). Loudon (1838, 55). Ablett (1880, 169). Lauder (1883, 244). Mosley (1910, 52–3). Hurst (1911, 194). Wilks (1972, 148). Whitlock (1985, 104).

592. Ruyton Great Oak. Shropshire. Ruyton-of-the-XI-Towns which is 8 m. S of Ellesmere and 8½ m. NW of Shrewsbury. Grid ref. SJ 395221.

'A vast oak'. (Hewins 1945). Ref: Hewins (1945, 10).

593. Rycote Oak. Also known as Robur Britannicum. Oxfordshire. At Rycote, 9 miles east of Oxford. Grid ref. SU 667046 (Rycote).

A spreading oak said to 'shelter 5000 men' (Loudon 1838). Ref: Loudon (1838, 1776). Hurst (1911, 194).

594. Saint Edmunds Oak. Suffolk. Hoxne, 3¾ m. ESE of Diss; 5½ m. SW of Harleston. Grid ref. TM 183767 (St Edmund's Monument). TM225796 (Oak Farm).

Removed about 1848. Girth was 20 ft when it fell. This tree had always been associated with St Edmund (killed 870) and a Danish arrowhead was found in the tree trunk when it fell. The arrowhead still existed in 1939. Timber from this tree was used to make wooden covers for the Bible and prayer book in the wooden church at Greensted (Mee 1940). Ref: Hurst (1911, 194): Mee (1940, 177). Wilks (1972, 134).

595. Salcey Forest Oak. See Salcey Great Oak.

596. Salcey Great Oak. Also known as Salcey Oak; Salcey Forest Oak; Bull Oak; Tom Keeper's Stable. Northamptonshire. On Salcey Lawn adjoining Salcey Forest. Grid ref. SP 801515.

Girth was 43 ft in 1792 and 47 ft in 1838. (Loudon 1838). Only a heap of rotten timber remained in 1991. Elwes and Henry state that 'The Salcey Forest Oak was a mere wreck in 1822'. The tree had been used as a stable for a horse. Ref: Loudon (1838, 1766). Strutt (1830, 18.) Selby (1842, 254). Burt (1860, 73). Lauder (1883) Elwes and Henry (1907) Vol. II p. 327. Hurst (1911, 195). Visit by James 1991. **Loudon (1838) fig. 1601. Photographs James 24/10/91.**

597. Sanzen-Baker Oak. Gloucestershire. On N side of Coleford–Cinderford road (B4226): about 220 yds W of Speech House (palisaded). Grid ref. SO 618121.

Sessile oak. Planted c. 1810: girth 10 ft in 1986. Dedicated to R. G. Sanzen-Baker, Deputy Surveyor of the Dean 1954–68. The Forest of Dean was the first English National Park, created in 1938. Sanzen-Baker encouraged young people to use the Forest and developed trails, picnic places and camp sites. Ref: White (1991).

598. School Oak. Gloucestershire. Forest of Dean. N side of road opposite Parkend School. Grid ref. SO 622080.

Felled 15 Nov. 1968 as unsafe. Sessile oak. Girth (1986) over 21 feet at breast height. Planted 1657 (ring count by Forestry Commission). Comparable tree to King Charles II Oak and Forest Giant (Standing 1986). Ref: Standing (1986, 15).

599. Scone Oak. Perthshire. Scone Abbey. Grid ref. NO 1226.

Girth 10 ft ins. 40 ft of clean stem in 1883. Planted in 1809. (Hunter 1883). Ref: Hunter (1883, 103).

600. Scyre Oak. See Shire Oak. (II).

601. Sedburgh Oak. Cumbria. Sedburgh School. Grid ref. SD 6952 (Sedburgh).

Shown on maps of 1400 AD. In the school grounds. A pollarded stump. Ref: Holdsworth (1999, 4).

602. Selborne Oak. See Pleastor Oak.

603. Selly Oak, The. Warwickshire (Birmingham). Stood at the junction of the Main Street of Selly Oak and Oak Tree Lane. Grid ref. SP 039825.

Felled in 1909 and the butt placed in Selly Park. Ref: Hewins (1945, 12). Wilks (1972, 27). Whitlock (1985, 107).

604. Seven Sisters, The. Nottinghamshire. In Welbeck Park: about 3 m. S of Worksop. Grid ref. SK 564743 (Welbeck Abbey).

Despite the name this was all one tree. Ref: Rooke (1790, 7–8). Loudon (1838, 1766). Hurst (1911, 195). **Rooke plate 3.**

605. Shade Oak. Shropshire. 1¾ m. SW of Cockshutt: 6 m. W of Wern. Grid ref. SJ 412276 (marked on OS map).
Ref: Hewins (1945, 11).

606. Shaden Tuft Oak. Gloucestershire. Forest of Dean: Churchill Inclosure: S of Parkend to Blakeney road (B4431) just before it reaches W end of The Barracks. Grid ref. SO 630091.

Now a wind blown bole near King Charles II Oak. Girth 18 ft 7 in (1986). Divides into four at 15 ft agl. Possibly has been pollarded: heavily burred bole. (Standing 1986). Ref: Standing (1986, 5).

607. Shakespeare's Oak. Warwickshire. In Stoneleigh Park, Stoneleigh. Grid ref. SP 319712 (Stoneleigh Abbey).

There is a tradition that Shakespeare used to sit and write under this oak. Ref: Elwes and Henry (1907) Vol. II p. 311.

608. Shambles Oak, The. Also known as Robin Hood's Larder; Larder Oak; Birchland Oak; The Butchers Shambles. Nottinghamshire. In Birklands (Wood) 1¼ m. NW of Edwinstowe: 2¼ m. E of Warsop (Presumably the same as Birchland Wood). Grid ref. SK 606676.

The hollow oak was burnt in 1878 by schoolgirls from Sheffield who boiled their kettle in it. Deer carcases were stored in it by various people, including Robin Hood. Ref: Rooke (1790, 13). Hayes (1822, 126). Burt (1860, 68). Brown (1883, 20). Hurst (1911, 193, 195). Hewins (1945, 14). Wilks (1972, 170–1). Brewers Dictionary (1983, 799). **Rooke plate 9.**

609. Shane's Castle Giant, The. Co. Antrim. Near the ruins of the Castle on Lough Neagh.

Girth 20 ft 10 ins in 1999. Other trees nearby have been dated to 1675 and 1649. Loudon (1838) mentions two large oak trees. Ref: Loudon (1838). Browne (2000). **Browne (2000, 19).**

610. Shebbear Oak. Also known as The Devil's Stone Oak. Devon. In the main square in Shebbear village which is 7 m. NW Hatherleigh. Grid ref. SS 439093.

Girth 15 ft at 5 ft (James 1991). Said to have been planted by Bishop Grandisson (Bishop of Exeter) who lived in the 1300s. A tradition was to turn over a large stone under this oak on 5 Nov. and the church bells were rung both before and after this ceremony. Ref: Wilks (1972, 136). Visit by James 1991. **Photographs James 12/8/1991.**

611. Shell House Oak. Hertfordshire. North of the Shell House in the former Warren Coppice. Grid ref. TQ 237084 (Hatfield).

Girth 20 ft at 5 ft. (1986). About 300 years old. Ref: Rackham (1989).

612. Shelton Oak. See Glendower's Oak.

613. Shenton's Oak, Captain. Leicestershire. 4 m. ENE of Nuneaton. Grid ref. SP 428932 (Hinckley Station).

Captain John Shenton, who was in Charles I's army, hid in this tree in 1646 to escape the Parliamentary forces. Ref: Wilks (1972, 242).

614. Shilstone Oak. Also known as the Hangman's Oak. Devon. NW of A386 on N side of B3278 where public footpath crosses country road. Grid ref. SX 517878.

One of several healthy trees either side of footpath. Not a very large or old tree. Ref: Devon C.C. 21 October 1994.

615. Shire Oak. (I). Also known as the Three Shire Oak. Nottinghamshire. What is now the village of Shireoaks. 2 m. NW of Worksop railway station. Brown confirms this and states it marked junction of Notts, Derby and Yorkshire (it is now in Nottinghamshire). Grid ref. SK 554809 (Shireoaks church).

A boundary oak. Ref: Evelyn (1670, 157). Gilpin (1791, 138). Loudon (1838, 1767). Brown (1883, 24). Mosley (1910, 66).

616. Shire Oak. (II). Also known as the Scyre Oak. Staffordshire. Between Lichfield and Walsall on the boundary between parishes of Walsall and Shenstone. Grid ref. SK 0504 (Shire Oak).

Little of the tree was left by 1903 and the site is now built on. In old deeds this tree marked the boundary of Walsall and Shenstone. Ref: Hewins (1945, 7).

617. Shire Oak. (III). Also known as the Skyriak Oak; Shyre-ack. Yorkshire. A public house known as the Skyrack or Shire Oak at Headingly, Leeds. Grid ref. SE 2635 (Kirkstall).

This tree marked the site of a meeting place of the Shire Court, where every freeman had the right to vote. Ref: Mosley (1910, 65–6). Wilks (1972, 90). **Photograph Mosley (1910, 66).**

618. Shire Oak. (IV). Yorkshire. 'In Earl Fitzwilliam's Park at Wentworth' (Hayes). Grid ref. SK 3898 (Wentworth). Ref: S. Hayes (1822, 126).

619. Shordley Oak. Flintshire. Shordley Hall 5 m. N of

centre of Wrexham: ¾ m. NE of Hope. Grid ref. SJ 324586 (Shordley Hall).

Girth was 40 ft at 3 ft and 33 ft 9 ins at 5 ft. It was 51 ft high in 1838. It was hollow and had been struck by lightning (Loudon 1838). Ref: Loudon (1838) Vol. III p. 1760. **Loudon p. 1760 fig. 1594.**

620. Shyre Oak. See Shire Oak. (III).

621. Sydney Oak. See Sydney's Oak. Sir Philip.

622. Sidney Oak, The. See Sydney's Oak, Sir Philip.

623. Single Oak, The. Hampshire. Burley. Grid ref. SO 2103 (Burley Lawn).
Ref: Hardcastle letter.

624. Sir Benjamin Tichborne's Oak. See Benjamin's Oak, Sir.

625. Sir Walter Bagot's Walking Stick. See Bagot's Lord, Walking Stick.

626. Sketty Oak. Glamorgan. Lower Sketty. Grid ref. SS 6293 (Sketty, Swansea).
Girth 37 ft 9 ins at the base (Loudon 1838). Ref: Loudon (1838, 1839).

627. Skyriak Oak. See Shire Oak. (III).

628. Slang Oak. Staffordshire. Elford Park. 4 m. N of Tamworth. Grid ref. SK 1810 (Elford).
Ref: Hewins (1945, 8).

629. Sotterley Oak. Suffolk. Sotterley, on the Estate. Grid ref. TM 4584.
About 200 years old. Famous for its size and form. Ref: Barne (1998, 54).

630. Spenser's Oak. Buckinghamshire. Whaddon Hall. Grid ref. SP 8034 (Whaddon).
The tree under which Spenser is reputed to have written 'The Faerie Queen' when he was Secretary to Lord Gray de Wilton. Ref: Rodgers (1941, 17).

631. Spread Oak, The. (I). Nottinghamshire. Worksop Park, 'near the white gate' (Loudon). Grid ref. SK 5879 (Worksop).
This tree spread over half an acre (Loudon 1838). Ref: Loudon (1838).

632. Spread Oak, The. (II). Shropshire. 'About a mile and a quarter to the south of Clun' (Hewins 1945). Grid ref. SO 300805 (Clun Church).
Ref: Hewins (1945, 10).

633. Spreading Oak, The. Hampshire. N of and adjoining A31 road: 1¾ m. W of Minstead: 6 m. NE of Ringwood, New Forest. Grid ref. SU 239106 (marked on OS map).

634. Squitch Bank Oak. Also known as the Squitch Oak. Staffordshire. Bagot's Park, 4 m. S of Uttoxeter: 2 m. N of Abbots Bromley. Grid ref. SK 089265 (Squitch House).
Girth 43 ft at base, 61 ft high, solid contents about 1012 cu. ft (Selby 1842). Ref: Loudon (1838) Vol. III p. 1769. Strutt (1830, 14). Selby (1842, 256). Lauder (1883, 254). Elwes and Henry (1907, 317). Hurst (1911, 195). Hewins (1945, 7). **Loudon fig. 1613.**

635. Squitch Oak. See Squitch Bank Oak.

636. St Catherine's Oak. Worcestershire. Home End, Ledbury. Grid ref. SO 7037 (Ledbury).
Ref: Transactions of the Woolhope Club (1871).

637. St Peter's Oak. See Peter's Oak, St.

638. Staple Hill Oak. Also known as the Weare Gifford Oak. Devon. Weare Gifford, 3 m. SSE of Bideford. Grid ref. SS 468222 (Weare Gifford).
Girth 27 ft 6 ins (Loudon 1838). Ref: Loudon (1838) Vol. III p. 1758.

639. Stately Oak. Kent. Fredville, Nonnington, 7 m. SE Canterbury. Grid ref. TR 256512.
This is one of the 3 Fredville Oaks (Beauty, Majesty, Stately). Girth 18 ft 9 ins (Mr. D. Drew. August 1991). This is the smallest of the 3 oaks, which are within 100 yards of each other. Ref: Strutt (1830, 52). Lauder (1834, 254). Loudon (1838, 1762). Grigor (1868) Majesty only p. 267.

640. Stephen's Oak. Dorset. East Holme: 2 m. SW of Wareham Station. Grid ref. SY 896860 (East Holme).
Pedunculate oak. Ref: White (1991).

641. Stock's Oak. See Plestor Oak.

642. Strelly Broad Oak. Nottinghamshire. Strelly Hall. Grid ref. SK 5141.
Girth 18 ft at 3 ft. Loudon (1838). Ref: Loudon (1838, 1840).

643. Sun Oak. Sussex. St Leonards Forest 3 m. E of Horsham. Grid ref. TQ 1929.
Girth was 27 ft 4 ins at 2 ft agl. (James. August 1992). Pedunculate. The name comes from the Sun Inn, now a private house (Sun House) which is partly enveloped by the crown. Ref: Mitchell (1996, 316). Johnson O. (1998). Visit by James 1992.

644. Sunken Oak, The. Hampshire. Leigh Park (now the Sir George Staunton Country Park) nr Havant. Grid ref. SU 7106 (Havant).

Alive in 1991. Ref: White (1991).

645. Sussex Farmyard Oak. Sussex. Kidbrooke. Grid ref. TQ 421345.

Girth 21 ft (Loudon 1838). Ref: Loudon (1838).

646. Swan Mote Oak. Northamptonshire. Salcey Forest. Grid ref. SP 8051 (Salcey Forest).

647. Swilcar Lawn Oak. See Swilcar Oak.

648. Swilcar Oak, The. Also known as the Swilcar Lawn Oak; Swilcher Oak. Staffordshire. Swilcar Lawn 1½ m. S of Marchington and 4 m. SW of Uttoxeter. Needwood Forest. Grid ref. SK 130282 (Swilcar Lawn Farm).

Girth 34 ft at ground level (Loudon 1838). The tree was named after Swilcher, a Danish priest. The tree was recorded in 1802, by which time the disafforestation of Needwood Forest had begun. (Victoria County History 1967). Ref: Gilpin (1791, 121). Strutt (1830, 24). Loudon (1838, 1769). Hayes (1822, 125). Lauder (1883) Vol. I p. 253. Hurst (1911, 195). Hewins (1945, 7). V.C.H. Staffordshire (1967) Vol. II p. 350. Map on p. 358. Brewer's Dict. (1983). **Loudon fig. 1612.**

649. Swilcher Oak. See Swilcar Oak.

650. Sydney's Oak, Sir Philip. Also known as the Sydney Oak; Sidney Oak; Bear's Oak. Kent. Penshurst Place. Grid ref. TQ 530440 (Penshurst Place).

One limb remains. (1991). Girth 30 ft at 7 ft (Loudon 1838). Planted at Sydney's birth in 1554 and was his favourite tree. Commemorated by poets Ben Jonson and Haller. The name Bear's Oak is a reference to the family bearings. Ref: Strutt (1830, 48). Loudon (1838, 1762). Anon. (1853, 48). Mosley (1910, 66). Hurst (1911, 195). Wilks (1972, 37). Brewer's Dictionary (1983, 799). White (1991). Pakenham (1996). Visit by James (1991). **Loudon fig. 1599. Photographs James (1991). Packenham (1996, 108–9).**

651. Tawstock Oak. Devon. Tawstock, by St Peter's Church. Grid ref. SS 560300.

Propped up and fenced (Mee 1938). Ref: Mee (1938).

652. Tea Party Oak, The. Suffolk. Ickworth Park c. 2 m. SW of Bury St Edmunds. Grid ref. TL 820620 (centre of Ickworth Park).

Pedunculate oak. Girth 37 ft 9 ins. Thought to be 700–800 years old. Ref: Rackham (1980). National Trust (1991).

653. Thorpe Market Oak. See King of Thorpe.

654. Thorpe Oak. See King of Thorpe.

655. Thorrington Oaks, The. Essex. Thorrington, 3½ m. SE of Wivenhoe: 2 m. NNE of Brightlingsea. Grid ref. TL 095202 (Thorrington).

Four decaying stumps remained in 1911. The largest 29 ft 6 ins at 5 ft (Hurst 1911). Ref: Hurst (1911, 195).

656. Three Brethren Oak, The. Also known as The Three Brethren Tree; The Three Brothers. Westmorland. Whinfield or Whinfell Forest: 4 m. SE of Penrith and S of A66 road. Grid ref. NY 575270 (centre of Whinfell Forest).

One of these oaks was '13 yards in circumference'. Ref: Nicolson and Burn (1777) Vol. I p. 398. 'The Nic'Nac' (1925) No. 136. p. 249. **'Nic'Nac' p. 249 a print by O.Neil made in 1779.**

657. Three Brothers, The. (I). Dumfriesshire.

Blew down on 7 Jan. 1839. This oak was one tree with '3 stems or limbs' (Selby 1842). Ref: Selby (1842, 254).

658. Three Brothers, The. (II). Also known as the Charles II Oaks. Gloucestershire. Forest of Dean: Russells Inclosure: on a major intersection of forest rides [Approach E from Cannop Ponds or W from Fancy View]. Grid ref. SO 619097.

Two survive. Smallest one died between 1976–1986: Girths of two survivors 12 ft 1 in and 11 ft. Dead tree was 8 ft in girth. (Standing 1986). Ref: Standing (1986, 6). **Hart (1966) plate XIV p. 217.**

659. Three Brothers, The. (III). See Three Brethren Oak, The.

660. Three Mile Oak, The. Also known as The Tree. Staffordshire.

Near Sandwell Park Boundary, West Bromwich. Grid ref. SJ 015925 (Sandwell Valley Country Park). Ref: Hewins (1945, 8).

661. Three Shire Oak. See Shire Oak. (I).

662. Three Shires Oak. Staffordshire (West Midlands). Probably in or near Three Shire Oak Road, Smethwick – now part of Birmingham. Grid ref. SJ 020870 (centre of Smethwick).

Felled in 1908 by Smethwick Corporation (Wilks 1972). This tree was a boundary oak on the borders of Stafford, Worcestershire and Shropshire. The site is now built upon. Ref: Wilks (1972, 23).

663. Tibberton Oak. (I). Herefordshire. Tibberton Court. Grid ref. SO 9054.

108 ft high (Loudon 1838). Ref: Loudon (1838) Vol. III pp. 1745, 1756. **Loudon fig. 1587.**

664. Tibberton Oak. (II). Herefordshire. Tibberton Court. Grid ref. SO 9054.

Girth 19 ft 8 ins, 31 ft to the first fork. Destroyed by a hurricane in Dec. 1833. Ref: Loudon (1838, 1815).

665. Tichbourne Oak. (I). Hampshire. On Tichbourne Farm which is 1½ m. NE of Redlynch and 2 m. SW of Whiteparish. Grid ref. SU 218223.

Alive in 1991. Ref: Letter, Mr Jenkins (1991).

666. Tichbourne Oak. (II). See Benjamins Sir, Oak.

667. Tilford Oak, The. See King Oak. (VII).

668. Tockholes Oak. Lancashire. Tockholes Village. Grid ref. SD 6623.

Only a shell in 1958.

669. Tockwith Broad Oak. Yorkshire. Between Cowthorpe and Tockwith. Grid ref. SE 4652 (Tockwith).

Girth 15 ft 9 ins at 3 ft (Empson (1842). Said to have been grown from an acorn off the Cowthorpe Oak. In July 1644 during the battle of Marston Moor, a tent was formed beneath this oak and used as a hospital. Ref: Empson (1842).

670. Tom Keeper's Stable. See Salcey Great Oak.

671. Torwood Oak. See Wallace's Oak.

672. Tottergill Oak. Cumbria. Ten miles east of Carlisle, near Castle Corrock. Probably a remnant of the King's Forest. Grid ref. NY 5455 9 (Castle Carrock).

Girth 13 m × 240 cm (Holdsworth 1998). Pollarded and burred, with a healthy crown. In old wood pasture and recorded in the Domesday Book. Ref: Holdsworth (1999, 4).

673. Towd Yak. See Jack's Yak.

674. Treasure Tree, The. Co. Fermanagh. Crom Estate.

Alive in 1990s. The castle here was under siege in 1689 and the family buried their valuables beneath an oak tree. It is said that these were never recovered and the ground round the existing oak has been dug up by treasure seekers. However, anyone digging up the treasure who was not a member of the Crichton family lived under a death threat. Ref: Browne (2000).

675. Trebursey Oak. Also known as the Two Mile Oak. Cornwall. 1½ m. W of Launceston on old section of A30.

On small triangle of ground at junction with road to Old Tree House. Grid ref. SX 307841.

Present tree girth 5 ft 5 in at 5 ft agl. (James 1991). Badly scarred on west side. Ht of oak about 25 ft. Clearly not the original tree which was said to have been used as a gibbett. The original tree was a 'dancing tree'. The owning family held their land on condition that they dined up in the tree once a year, until a girl fell off and was killed. Her ghost had to be exorcised by the Rector of Launceston and the practice was discontinued. Ref: Thurston (1930). Whitlock (1985). Visit by James 1991. **Photographs James 25/9/1991.**

676. Tree of Good and Evil. See Naked Man, The.

677. Tree, The. See Three Mile Oak, The.

678. Tregothnan Oaks. Cornwall. Tregothnan Estate. Grid ref. SW 858416.

Four oaks planted by Queen Mary when she was Princess of Wales. Ref: Thurston (1930, 189).

679. Troup, Leslie, Oak. See Leslie Troup Oak.

680. Trysting Tree, The. See Capon Tree.

681. Turnpike Oak. Hertfordshire. Northaw 2 m. ENE of Potters Bar Station. Grid ref. TQ 289024 (Northaw Church).

Ref: Wilks (1972, 29).

682. Turpin's Oak. (I). Hertfordshire. Near Barnet (Mosley 1910). Grid ref. TQ 240960 (Barnet).

One of the trees in which Turpin hid to ambush travellers. Pistol balls were extracted from the bark. Ref: Mosley (1910, 62–3).

683. Turpin's Oak. (II). Middlesex. 'At Bedfont Green ... on Hounslow Heath' (Wilks 1972). Grid ref. TQ 1276 (Hounslow).

Associated with Dick Turpin. Ref: Wilks (1972, 85). Whitlock (1985, 108).

684. Turpin's Oak. (III). Middlesex. Opposite 'The Green Man' PH at Finchley: Finchley Common. Grid ref. TQ 2890 (Finchley).

Removed end of nineteenth century. Associated with Dick Turpin. Ref: Anon (1853, 50). Brown (1883, 35). Wilks (1972, 85).

685. Turpin's Oak. (IV). Yorkshire. Thirsk 9 m. SSE of Northallerton. Grid ref. SE 4282 (Thirsk).

Associated wirh Dick Turpin. Ref: Wilks (1972, 85). Whitlock (1985, 108).

686. Turpin's Oak. (V). See Hempstead Oak.

687. Turpin's Ring. Essex. Hempstead Village. Grid ref. TL 6338 (Hempstead).

Cock fights were held here within a ring of oak trees. Ref: Mee (1940, 191).

688. Twelve Apostles, The. Hampshire. Burley Lodge. Spelt Barley Lodge in Gilpin (1791). Grid ref. ST 238055.

Only 4 of the original 12 were in existence in 1991 (James). The largest of these had a girth of 22 ft 6 ins in 1838. Ref: Gilpin (1791) Vol. I p. 260: Strutt (1830, 54). Loudon (1838). Hurst (1911, 189): Wilks (1972, 247). Visit by James. 1991.

689. Two Mile Oak. See Treburssey Oak.

690. Two Porters. See Porters Oak.

691. Two Sisters, The. Northamptonshire. Salcey Forest. Grid ref. SP 8051 (Salcey Forest).

Only a rotten hulk exists which is thought to be one of the Two Sisters (James 1991). Ref: Wilks (1972, 172). Visit by James 1991. **Photograph James 24/10/1991.**

692. Tyrell's Oak. See Rufus Oak.

693. Umbrella Oak. Also known as the Castle Hill Oak. Devon. Eggesford Bank, Castle Hill, Filleigh, 3½ m. NW of South Molton. Grid ref. SS 663280 (Filleigh Church).

Elwes and Henry (1907) Vol. II p. 325. White (1991).

694. Venison Oak. Staffordshire. Bagot's Park, 4 m. S of Uttoxeter: 2 m. N of Abbots Bromley. Grid ref. SK 090275 (Bagot's Park).

Deer carcases may have been stored in this tree. Ref: Elwes and Henry (1907) Vol. II p. 318.

695. Verderers' Oak. Gloucestershire. Forest of Dean: 150 yards SW of Speech House beside small stream 'towards Dean Hall field boundary'. Grid ref. SO 619119.

Girth 23 ft (Standing 1987). Also 23 ft in 1991 (James). Largest oak in the Dean. Also probably the oldest. Other large oaks nearby. Ref: Standing (1987, 27). Visit by James 1991. **Photograph James 9/5/1991.**

696. Vyne Oak, The. Hampshire. The Vyne Gardens, (north of Basingstoke). Grid ref. SU 6457.

Girth 8m in 1991. Ref: Letter, National Trust (1991).

697. Wagoner's Oak. Herefordshire. Opposite Easthampton Farm house, Easthampton, 1 m. WSW of Mortimer's Cross. Grid ref. SO 409630.

Girth 33 ft 1 in at 5 ft agl. A fine tree (James 1991). Ref: Visit by James. 1991. **Photographs James 23/10/1991.**

698. Wallace Oak, The. Also known as the Elderslie Oak; Elderslee Oak; Ellerslie Oak. Renfrewshire. Elderslie: 3 m. W of Paisley. Grid ref. NS 4462.

Lauder (1834) gave girth as 13 ft 2 ins at 5 ft. Said to have sheltered Sir William Wallace and 300 men. Ellerslie was Wallace's birthplace. Wallace and others hid in branches when the tree was in full leaf. Another legend says that Wallace hid in this tree when his enemies were sacking Ellerslie. Ref: Lauder (1834, 252). Loudon (1838, 1772). Selby (1842, 254). Anon (1853, 46). Mosley (1910, 58). Brewer's Dict. (1983, 798). **Lauder Vol. I opp. p. 252. Loudon fig. 1621.**

699. Wallace's Oak. Also known as The Torwood Oak. Stirlingshire. Five miles S of Stirling: in the Tor-wood nr Falkirk. Grid ref. NS 8484 (Torwood).

Much decayed in 1771. Girth was about 22 ft (Loudon 1838). Wallace is said to have slept in this hollow oak during his campaigns against the English. 1297–1305. In 1305 he was executed in the Tower. Ref: Gilpin (1791, 143–4). Nicol and Sang (1812, 564). Loudon (1838) Vol. III p. 1773. Grigor (1868, 338). Lauder (1883, 252).

700. Waller's Oak. Buckinghamshire. Manor House, Coleshill. 2 m. SW of Amersham Station. 2½ m. N of Beaconsfield Station. Grid ref. SU 954961 (Coleshill House). SU 948952 (Coleshill).

The poet Waller (1606–1687) planted this tree in 1630. Ref: Loudon (1838, 9). Hurst (1911, 196): Wilks (1972, 38).

701. Wangford Oak. See Henham Hill Oak.

702. Warlock's Oak. Renfrewshire. In a field on the right of the bridge of Weir-St-Fillian's Church Rd, Kilmacolm, 6 m. SE of Greenock. Grid ref. NS 3569. Ref: Wilks (1972, 132).

703. Warwick Oak. Yorkshire. In Sheriff Hutton Park: 10 m. NNE of York. Grid ref. SE 6566 (Sheriff Hutton).

Ref: Alive in 1972 (Wilks 1972). **Wilks (1972, 64).**

704. Watch Oak, The. (III). Sussex. A site at Battle. Grid ref. TQ 7415.

A replacement exists. The original tree was removed to make way for a roundabout. It is said children kept a watch in the tree to see if the mail coach was coming. Ref: Johnson (1998).

705. Watch Oak, The. (I). Shropshire. ¾ m. NW of Eaton Constantine and 3 m. SE of Atcham. Grid ref. SJ 585067 (Marked on O.S. map).

Blew down about 1850. Served as a lookout in the Civil War to watch for Cromwell's troops coming from Shrewsbury. Later on it was used to look out for coaches travelling on this old high road. Ref: Hewins (1945, 9). Wilks (1972, 242).

706. Watch Oak, The. (ii). Warwickshire. Milverton, near Leamington. Grid ref. SP 2967 (Old Milverton).

Fell 'a few years ago'. Referred to in old deeds as a boundary tree. It has been suggested that this tree was an outpost and the limit of the patrol from Warwick Castle. Also, it could have been a look-out post during the Civil War in 1642 (Clarke *et al.* 1987). Ref: Clarke *et al.* (1987, 39, 51). **By R. Aspa in 1887 in the Herbert Art Gallery, Coventry.**

707. Weare Gifford Oak, The. See Staple Hill Oak.

708. Weeping Oak. (I). See Moccas Park Weeping Oak.

709. Weeping Oak. (II). Herefordshire. Whitfield Court. Grid ref. SO 4232.

Girth 14 ft 6 ins. 95 ft tall. Ref: Hadfield (1969, 80).

710. Wellbred Oak. Yorkshire. Kingston Hill nr Pontefract. Grid ref. SE 4522. (Pontefract).

Girth 33 ft in 1838 (Loudon 1838). The tree was hollow and had been used for sheltering stock. Ref: Loudon (1838) Vol. III p. 1771.

711. Welsh Oak, The. See Golynos Oak.

712. Wesley's Oak. Sussex. Winchelsea churchyard. Grid ref. TQ 9017 (Winchelsea).

Blew down in 1927. The tree under which Wesley preached his last sermon. Ref: Thurston (1930, 190).

713. Western Oak. Hampshire. 'At Boldrewood' in the New Forest (Wise 1863). Grid ref. SU 2408 (Boldrewood).

An old boundary oak. Ref: Wise (1863, 16).

714. Weston Oak. Shropshire. Between Clun and Newcastle: ½ m. S of road B4368. Grid ref. SO 279811 (Weston).

Felled in 1950s for road improvement. Housed a post box for many years. On one occasion a coffin was left in the tree overnight because of a snow storm. Ref: Hewins (1945, 10). Morton (1986, 56). **Morton p. 55.**

715. Whiligh Oak, The. Sussex. On the lawn at Whiligh, near Wadhurst. Grid ref. TQ 6531.

The oldest and largest English oak in Sussex. There is a picture of the oak on its site on the 1493 manorial map and is mentioned in a property deed of 1494. Oak from the estate was used to repair Westminster Hall in 1922. Ref: Johnson, Owen (1998). **Johnson, Owen (1998, 43).**

716. Whinfield Forest Oak. See Hollow Oak, The.

717. White Oak. Shropshire. Near Tong. Grid ref. SJ 797074 (Tong).

This oak was 'painted white, to serve as a landmark in the forest which once existed in that neighbourbood'. (Hewins. 1945). Ref: Hewins (1945, 10).

718. Whitfield Oak. Also known as the Treville Oak. Herefordshire. On the eastern edge of 'Big Wood' on the Whitfield Estate, ¾ m. N of Wormbridge on the Pontrilas-Hereford road (A465). Grid ref. SO 425323.

Fell in 1992. Sessile oak. Girth 16 ft 6 ins at 5 ft agl. (James 1991). In 1991 it was a magnificent tree but had lost a large branch in the crown and has also been damaged, probably by fire on one side. Was the tallest oak in Britain at 130 ft. 55 ft to the first branch. Ref: Elwes and Henry (1907) Vol. II p. 311. Hadfield (1970, 80). Visit by James 1991. **Elwes and Henry plate 85. Photograph James 21/10/1991.**

719. Wiggin's Oak. Shropshire. Eardington, nr Bridgnorth (Hewins). Grid ref. SO 723906 (Eardington).

Named after Edward Wiggin, a miller of Eardington who was murdered in November 1812. Ref: Hewins (1945, 10).

720. Wilberforce Oak, The. Also known as The Keston Oak; The Abolition Oak. Kent. Holwood Park, nr Keston, which is 3 m. S of Bromley and 5 m. W of Orpington. Grid ref. TQ 422636 (Holwood).

In 1911 was falling into decay. Said to be the oak beneath which William Wilberforce sought the support of the Prime Minister (William Pitt) against slavery. Wilberforce wrote 'At length, I well remember, after a conversation in the open air at the root of an old tree at Holmwood, just above the steep descent into the Vale of Keston, I resolved to give notice on a fit occasion in the House of Commons of my intention to bring the subject (of slavery) forward' (Hurst 1911). Ref: Mosley (1910, 59). Hurst (1911, 130, 189).

721. Wilkin's Oak, Billy. Dorset. Melbury Park, nr Melbury Osmond 6 m. SSE of Yeovil: 6 m. N of Maiden Newton station. In the Deer Park at Studcombe Bottom. Grid ref. ST 570054.

Pedunculate oak. Girth 39 ft 6 ins (James Oct. 1992). Pollarded. Hollow. It has a low crown making it difficult to photograph (James 1992). Billy Wilkins was a bailiff on the

Melbury estate. He was sent to warn Sir John Strangeways (the owner) at Melbury House that the Parliamentary forces were approaching. Before he could give the warning, he was overtaken and killed. About 750 years old. Ref: Loudon (1838, 1759). Elwes and Henry (1907) Vol. II p. 315. Wilks (1972, 184). Bean (1976) Vol. III p. 508. White (1991). Jones and Mabey (1993). Visit by James 1992. **Photograph in Elwes (no. 88) Vol. II. Photographs James 8/10/1992.**

722. William The Conqueror's Oak. See King Oak (VIII).

723. William's Oak, Sir. Also known as The Major Oak. (II). Herefordshire. In the Park at Croft Castle. WNW of the Castle and near the tennis court to the SW. Grid ref. SO 448655.

Girth 27 ft 2 ins at 5 ft agl. (James 1991). It was originally pollarded. Probably a hybrid oak. Ref: Visit by James 1991. **Photographs James 23/10/1991.**

724. Wilverley Oak, The. See Naked Man, The.

725. Windsor Oak. Berkshire. Grid ref. SU 9672 (Windsor Great Park).

Girth 11.2 m at 3 ft. 13 m at ground level (Alderman 1999). Probably the largest pedunculate oak in England. Ref: Alderman (1999, 3).

726. Windy Oak. Shropshire. ¾ m. NW of Ellerdine Heath and 3½ m. S of Hadnet Church. Buildings marked 'Windy Oak' on the map. Grid ref. SJ 611231.

Ref: Hewins (1945, 11).

727. Winfarthing Oak. Also known as Quidenham Oak. Norfolk. Quidenham is 5 m. SSW of Attleborough but Winfarthing is 5 m. ESE of Quidenham. The oak said to be at Quidenham Hall. Grid ref. TF 029877 (Quidenham) TF 108858 (Winfarthing).

Fell in 1956. In 1820, '70 ft in circumference; the trunk quite hollow, and the cavity large enough to hold at least 30 persons' (Loudon 1838). Hurst (1911) states '40 ft in the waist'. Said to have been called the 'Old Oak' in William the Conqueror's time. A table and chairs were put up inside the oak tree. Ref: Loudon (1838) Vol. III p. 1763. Grigor (1841, 354). Selby (1842, 254). Anon. (1853, 45). Grigor (1868, 267). Ablett (1880, 166). Mosley (1910, 67). Hurst (1911, 196). Wilks (1972, 197). Whitlock (1985, 110). **Loudon fig. 1603.**

728. Wonderful Large Oak, The. See Hollow Oak, The. (I).

729. Woolton Oak. See Wotton Oak.

730. Wotton Oak. Also known as the Woolton Oak. Buckinghamshire. 'In the park of Wotton Under Bernwood, a seat belonging to his Grace the Duke of Buckingham' (Strutt 1830). Presumably Wotton Underwood. 7 m. SE of Bicester. Grid ref. SP 688160 (Wotton Underwood).

Girth 25 ft at 1 ft (Loudon 1838). Ref: Strutt (1830, 10). Loudon (1838, 1755–6). Selby (1842, 256). Hurst (1911, 196). **Loudon fig. 1590.**

731. Wyndham's Oak. Also known as Judge Wyndhams Oak. Dorset. Parish of Silton 200 yds E of Church. Grid ref. ST 7928.

Ref: Wilks (1972, 81).

732. Yardley Chase Oaks, The. See Gog and Magog.

733. Yardley Lodge Oak. See Judith Oak.

734. Yardley Oak, The. See Cowper's Oak.

735. Yeldam Oak, Great. See Great Yeldam Oak.

736. Young's Oak. Essex. Wimbush. Grid ref. TL 5936.

Girth 8 ft 10 ins in 1803. Named after Arthur Young, agricultural writer and reformer. Ref: Loudon p. 1784.

Historic and Named Oaks, Listed by County

Note the numbers in the left hand column refer to Appendix A.

	County	Name	Other Names
1	Bedfordshire	Abbot's Oak, The (I)	
87		Bunyan's Oak	John Bunyan's Oak
397		Leaden Oak, The	
485		Oakley Oak (I)	
24	Berkshire	Barbados Oak	
66		Boundary Oak	
76		British Honduras Oak	
82		Buckleberry Oaks	
114		Chaucer's Oak	King's Oak (I)
249		Great Britain Oak	
299		Herne the Hunter's Oak	Herne's Oak (I); Sir John Falstaff's Oak
340		Kenya Oak	
361		King Oak (VIII)	William the Conqueror's Oak; The Conqueror's Oak
475		Nigeria Oak	
517		Pope's Oak (I)	
531		Queen Anne's Oak	
533		Queen Charlotte's Oak	
545		Queen Elizabeth's Oak (IX)	
556		Queen Victoria's Oak (I)	Queen Victoria's Favourite Oak (II)
565		Queen's Oak, The (V)	
725		Windsor Oak	
116	Buckinghamshire	Chenies Oak, The	
535		Queen Elizabeth II's Oak (II)	
630		Spenser's Oak	
700		Waller's Oak	
730		Wotton Oak	Woolton Oak
442	Carmarthenshire	Merlin's Oak	The Old Oak Tree; Priory Oak
14	Cheshire	Arley Oak	
64		Bostock Oak	
435		Marton Oak	
460		Morley Oak	
3	Clwyd	Abbot's Oak, The (III)	
255	Clwyd (Denbighshire)	Great Oak, The (V)	

	County	Name	Other Names
400	Co. Antrim	Liberty Tree, The	Hanging Tree, The; Roughfort Tree, The
609	Co. Antrim	Shane's Castle Giant, The	
56	Co. Armagh	Bloody Oak, The	
136	Co. Derry	Coronation Oak (II)	
37	Co. Down	Belvoir Oak	
313	Co. Fermanagh	Hotel Oak, The	
588		Royal Oak (I)	
674		Treasure Tree, The	
135	Co. Londonderry	Coronation Oak (I)	
12	Cornwall	Amy Tree	
15		Arondell's Oak	
59		Boconnoc Oak	King Charles' Oak (II)
165		Darley Oak	
280		Hanging Trees	
301		Herne's Oak (II)	
317		Hunter's Oak	
493		Painted Oak	
505		Penrice Oak	
675		Trebursey Oak	Two Mile Oak
678		Tregothnan Oaks	
297	Cumberland	Henry VI's Oak	King Oak (X)
28	Cumbria	Barras Oak	
162		Dalston Oak	
601		Sedburgh Oak	
672		Tottergill Oak	
113	Derbyshire	Chatsworth Oak	
335		Kedleston Oak	King Tree (I)
444		Meynell Langley Oak	
16	Devon	Ashton Oak	
133		Coplestone Oak	
170		Domesday Oak (III)	
210		Flittern Oak	Flitton Oak (named on OS map as this)
251		Great Oak, The (I)	Newton St Petrock Oak
282		Hankford's Oak, Judge	
290		Hawson Cross Oak	Stumpy Oak
311		Honour Oak (1)	
402		Lifton Oak	
439		Meavy Oak	
494		Palmer's (Farm) Oak (I)	
495		Palmer's Farm Oak (II)	
498		Paschoe Oak	Pascoe Oak
526		Prince of Orange's Oak	
610		Shebbear Oak	The Devil's Stone Oak
614		Shilstone Oak	Hangman's Oak
638		Staple Hill Oak	Weare Gifford Oak

	County	Name	Other Names
651	Devon *continued*	Tawstock Oak	
693		Umbrella Oak	Castle Hill Oak
130	Dorset	Compton House Oak	
163		Damory's Oak	
441		Melbury Park Oak	
508		Petersham Oak	
510		Pig Oak	
578		Remedy Oak	
640		Stephen's Oak	
721		Wilkin's Oak, Billy	
731		Wyndham's Oak	Judge Wyndham's Oak
156		Crumpler's, Samuel Oak	
26	Dumfries	Barjarg Oak	
55	Dumfriesshire	Blind Oak of Keir	
411		Lockwood Oak	
657		Three Brothers, The (I)	
502	Durham	Pedam's Oak	Pedom's Oak
32	Essex	Bedford's Oak	
132		Copford Oaks	
141		Court Oak	
164		Danbury Oaks	
172		Doodle Oak	
204		Fairlop Oak	
205		Fairmead Oak	The Chingford Oak
208		Fingringhoe Oak	
264		Great Yeldam Oak	The Great Oak (VI)
267		Grimstone Oak, The (I)	
287		Hatfield Broad Oak	
295		Hempstead Oak	Turpin's Oak (V)
396		Lawn Oak	
436		Martyr's Oak	
477		Northfield Oak	
543		Queen Elizabeth's Oak (VII)	
655		Thorrington Oaks, The	
687		Turpin's Ring	
736		Young's Oak	
619	Flintshire	Shordley Oak	
104	Glamorgan	Cefnmabli Oak	
203		Fair Oak (II)	
298		Hensol Oak	
409		Llanelay Oak	
626		Sketty Oak	
36	Gloucestershire	Bellman's Oak	
60		Boddington Oak	The Cheltenham Oak
68		Bourton Oak	

211

	County	Name	Other Names
79	Gloucestershire *continued*	Broadstones Oaks	
88		Burden Oak	
112		Charles' Oak	
146		Crad Oak	
180		Duke of Gloucester, The	
212		Forest Giant	
272		Gurney Oak	Gurneyesok
275		Haie House Oaks	
284		Haresfield Court Oaks	
320		Jack of the Yat	
348		King Charles II Oak	
358		King Oak (II)	
392		Lassington Oak	
398		Leslie Troup Oak	
417		Lord Robinson Oak	Forestry Commissioner's Oak
424		Lydney Oak	
425		Machen Oak	
473		Newland Oak	The Great Oak of Newland
524		Prince Charles Oak	
525		Prince Consort's Oak	
527		Prince Philip Oak	
534		Queen Elizabeth II's Oak (I)	
548		Queen Oak, The (I)	
597		Sanzen-Baker Oak	
598		School Oak	
606		Shaden Tuft Oak	
658		Three Brothers, The (II)	Charles II Oaks
695		Verderers' Oak	
233		Godfrey Oak	Godfraysok
410	Gwent	Llantarnam Oak	
449		Millennium Derwen	The Great Welsh Oak
471		Newbridge-on-Usk Oak	
589	Gwyneddd	Royal Oak (II)	
6	Hampshire	Adam And Eve (I)	
17		Aubrey's Oak	
35		Bell Oak	
38		Benjamin's Oak, Sir	Sir Benjamin Tichborne's Oak, Tichbourne Oak (II)
39		Bentley Oak	Holt Forest Oak
80		Brockenhurst Oak	
188		Eagle Oak	
192		Eastern Oak	
202		Fair Oak (I)	
220		Frenchman's Oak	
241		Gospel Oak (I)	Avington Oak

	County	Name	Other Names
259	Hampshire *continued*	Great Oak, The (IX)	
258		Great Oak, The (VIII)	
316		Hundred Oak	
323		Jane Austen's Oak	
336		Keeper's Oak	Barnes Oak
338		Kent's Oak	
360		King Oak (IV)	Probably the King in the King & Queen Oaks = Queen Oak (IV)
379		Knightwood Oak	
387		Langley Oak	
399		Lewis, Mrs, Oak	
450		Miracle Oak	
456		Monarch Oaks	
462		Moyles Court Oak	
465		Naked Man, The	The Tree of Good and Evil; The Wilverley Oak
476		Northern Oak	
486		Oakley Oak (II)	Oakleigh Oak; Mottisfont Oak
500		Passfield Oak	
507		Peter's Oak, St	
513		Pleastor Oak	
514		Plestor Oak	Stock's Oak
532		Queen Bower Oak	
537		Queen Elizabeth's Oak (I)	The Queen's Oak (VI)
549		Queen Oak, The (II)	The "Queen" in the King & Queen Oaks, See King Oak (IV)
557		Queen Victoria's Oak (II)	
572		Raven Oak	
591		Rufus Oak	Tyrell's Oak; Canterton Oak
623		Single Oak, The	
633		Spreading Oak, The	
644		Sunken Oak, The	
665		Tichbourne Oak (I)	
688		Twelve Apostles, The	
696		Vyne Oak, The	
713		Western Oak	
94	Hampshire - New Forest	Cadnam Oak	Cadenham Oak
174		Double Tree, The	
270		Grindstone Oak	Holt Forest Oak (II)
375	Herefordshire	Kingsland Oak	
584		Rosemaund Oak	
61	Hereford and Worcester	Bolton's Oak	
7	Herefordshire	Adam and Eve (II)	
143		Cowarne Court Oak	
150		Croft Castle Oak	

	County	Name	Other Names
155	Herefordshire *continued*	Crump Oak	
190		Eardisley Oak	The Great Oak (II); Eardisley Great Oak
248		Grafton Oak	
319		Jack of Kent's Oak	Jacky Kemp's Oak; The Pontrilas Oak
453		Moccas Park Oak	
454		Moccas Park Weeping Oak	Pendulous Oak; Weeping Oak
458		Monnington Oak	
481		Nunupton Oak	
664		Tibberton Oak (II)	
697		Wagoner's Oak	
709		Weeping Oak (II)	
718		Whitfield Oak	Treville Oak
723		William's Oak, Sir	Major Oak, The (II)
663		Tibberton Oak (I)	
201		Eve Oak	
185		Dumb-bell Oak	
234		Goff's Oak	Gough's Oak
253		Great Oak, The (III)	See Panshanger Oak
357		King Oak (I)	
377		Kiss Oak, The	
403		Lightning Oak, The	
405		Lion Oak, The	
491		Oxhey Oak	Grimstone Oak (II)
496		Panshanger Oak	Great Oak, The (III)
538		Queen Elizabeth's Oak (II)	The Elizabeth Oak; Queen's Oak (II)
558		Queen Victoria's Oak (III)	
569		Quitchell's Oak	
611		Shell House Oak	
681		Turnpike Oak	
682		Turpin's Oak (I)	
25	Invernesshire	Bard's Tree, The	
19	Kent	Augustine's Oak (II)	
31		Beauty Oak	One of the Fredville Oaks, Beauty, Majesty and Stately
54		Blenheim Oak	
67		Bounds Oak	Bounds Park Oak
170		Domesday Oak (II)	Goodcheap Oak
209		Fisher's Oak	
218		Fredville Oaks	The Great Oaks (Strutt) see under individual names, Beauty, Majesty, Stately
293		Headcorn Oak	
367		King Oak (xi)	
394		Law Day Oak (I)	Bonnington Oak; The Hanging Tree
422		Lullingstone Park Oaks	

	County	Name	Other Names
431	Kent *continued*	Majesty Oak	One of the Fredville Oaks, Beauty, Majesty and Stately
639		Stately Oak	One of the Fredville Oaks, Beauty, Majesty and Stately
650		Sydney's Oak, Sir Philip	Sydney Oak; Sidney Oak; Bear's Oak
720		Wilberforce Oak, The	The Keston Oak; The Abolition Oak
501	Lanarkshire	Pease Tree, The	
11	Lancashire	Allerton Oak	Court Tree
78		Broad Oak (II)	
368		King of the Woods (I)	
401		Lidiate Oak	
668		Tockholes Oak	
71	Leicestershire	Bradgate Oaks	
89		Burton Overy Oak	
134		Copt Oak	
351		King Dick's Clump	
560		Queen Victoria's Oak (V)	
613		Shenton's Oak, Captain	
315		Hugglescote Oak	
70	Lincolnshire	Bowthorpe Oak	Great Oak (XI)
361		King Oak (V)	
552		Queen of Thonock, The	
197	London	Elfin Oak, The	
539		Queen Elizabeth's Oak (III)	
466	Merioneth	Nannau Oak	The Hollow Oak (II); Derwen Cenbred Yr Ellyll; The Haunted Oak; Howel Sele's Oak
110	Middlesex	Chandos Oak	Michendon Oak
312		Honour Oak (II)	The Oake of Honour
683		Turpin's Oak (II)	
684		Turpin's Oak (III)	
95	Monmouthshire	Caerhyder Oak	Coronation Oak (III)
214		Foresters Oaks	
472		Newcastle Oak	
238	Monmouthshire (Gwent)	Golynos Oak	The Welsh Oak
109	Montgomeryshire	Champion, The	
226		Giant, The	
385		Lady Powis Oak	
23	Norfolk	Bale Oak	
52		Bixley Oak	
337		Kempston Oak	
343		Kett's Oak (I)	
344		Kett's Oak (II)	The Oak of Reformation, or Reformation Oak
345		Kett's Oak (III)	Reformation Oak (II)

215

	County	Name	Other Names
370	Norfolk *continued*	King of Thorpe	The Great Oak (IV); Thorpe Oak; Thorpe Market Oak
443		Merton Oak	
519		Poringland Oak	Old Cromes Oak; Porlingham Oak
727		Winfarthing Oak	Quidenham Oak
53	Northamptonshire	Blackmore Hill Oak	
69		Bowcase Oak	Bocase Tree
108		Chair Oak	
121		Church Path Oak	
144		Cowper's Oak	Judith Oak; Yardley Oak
149		Crimea Oak	
173		Double Oak	
175		Druid Oaks (I)	
178		Dryden's Oak	
235		Gog (I)	Yardley Chase Oaks; Originally 2 oaks Gog & Magog (latter gone).
333		Judith Oak, The (I)	Yardley Lodge Oak
349		King Charles Oak (I)	
381		Lady Montagu's Tree	
407		Little Oak	
421		Lowick Oak	
428		Magog (I)	
448		Milking Oak	
459		Montague Oak	
463		Murrain Oak	
509		Piddington Oak	
546		Queen Hive Oak	
563		Queen's Oak, The (III)	
573		Raven's Oak	
596		Salcey Great Oak	Salcey Oak; Salcey Forest Oak; Bull Oak; Tom Keeper's Stable
646		Swan Mote Oak	
691		Two Sisters, The	
551		Queen Oak, The (IV)	
587	Northumberland	Royal Forestry Society Oak	
83	Nottinghamshire	Budby Oak	
159		Cuckoo Oak (III)	
92		Byron's Oak	
99		Castle Hill Oak (I)	
107		Centre Tree, The	Central Oak
122		Churn Oak, The	Old Churn Oak
152		Crossed Oak, The	
181		Duke of Portland's Walking Stick	The Duke's Walking Stick
186		Dunmow Oak	
217		Foster's Oak, Simon	

	County	Name	Other Names
223	Nottinghamshire *continued*	Gamekeeper's Oak	The Gamekeeper's Tree
265		Greendale Oak	Grindal Oak
418		Lord's Oak, The (I)	
432		Major Oak	Queen Oak (III), The Cockpen Tree
497		Parliament Oak	Clipstone Oak
511		Pilgrim Oak	
521		Porter's Oak, The	The Two Porters; The Large Porter and Little Porter
604		Seven Sisters, The	
608		Shambles Oak, The	Robin Hood's Larder; Larder Oak; Birchland Oak; The Butchers Shambles
615		Shire Oak (I)	Three Shire Oak
631		Spread Oak, The (I)	
642		Strelly Broad Oak	
18	Oxfordshire	Augustine's Oak (I)	
46		Big Oak (II)	
187		Dunson's Oak	
326		Jubilee Oak (I)	
346		Kidlington Green Oak	
426		Magdalen Oak	The Great Oak (VII); Alfred's Oak
437		Matthew Arnold Oak, The	
570		Radley Oak	
593		Rycote Oak	Robur Britannicum
389	Pembrokeshire	Large Oak	
51	Perthshire	Birnam Oak	Neil Gow's Oak (II)
161		Cultoquhey Oak, The	
219		Freeland Oak, The	
225		Garter Oak	
277		Hanged-men's Tree	
347		Kilgraston Oak	
353		King James Oak	
434		Malloch's Oak	
457		Moncrieffe's Oak	
468		Neil Gow's Oak (I)	
506		Pepperwell Oak	
553		Queen Victoria's and Albert's Oaks	
585		Rossie Oaks, The	
599		Scone Oak	
698	Renfrewshire	Wallace Oak, The	Elderslie Oak; Elderslee Oak; Ellerslie Oak
702		Warlock's Oak	
98	Roxburghshire	Capon Tree, The	The Kepping Tree, The Trysting Tree
369		King of the Woods (II)	
5	Shropshire	Acton Round Oak	
9		Ale Oak	

	County	Name	Other Names
63	Shropshire *continued*	Boscobel Oak	Royal Oak or Royal Boscobel Oak
73		Brewer's Oak (I)	
77		Broad Oak (I)	
86		Bulthy Oak	
154		Crowleasowe Oak	
157		Cuckoo Oak (I)	
176		Druid Oaks (II)	
179		Dryton Oak	
221		Frodesley Oak	
222		Gallows Tree	
228		Gibbet Oak, The (I)	
230		Glendower's Oak	Owen Glendower's Oak; Shelton Oak; Great Oak (X) Grete Oak; Owen Glendower's Observatory
246		Gospel Oak (VI)	
276		Halston Oak	
285		Harewood Oak	The Home Oak
291		Haywood Forest Oak	
304		Hodnet Hall Oak	
309		Holt Preen Oak	
327		Jubilee Oak (II)	
328		Jubilee Oak (III)	
383		Lady Oak, The (I)	Cressage Oak; Christ's Oak
384		Lady Oak, The (II)	
393		Laugh Lady Oak	Law Day Oak (II)
406		Lissehall Oak	
414		Long Oak	
423		Lydham Manor Oak	Big Oak (III)
430		Maiden Oak	
438		Mawley Oak	
440		Meer Oak	
446		Mile Oak (I)	
455		Monarch Oak	
464		Mytton Oak	
467		Nash Oak	
512		Plaish Oak	
515		Pontfadog Oak	
522		Powis Oak (I)	
523		Powis Oak (II)	
528		Prince's Oak	Loton Park Oak
530		Quatford Oak	Forest Oak
592		Ruyton Great Oak	
605		Shade Oak	
632		Spread Oak, The (II)	
705		Watch Oak, The (I)	

	County	Name	Other Names
714	Shropshire *continued*	Weston Oak	
717		White Oak	
719		Wiggin's Oak	
726		Windy Oak	
81	Somerset	Brockley Hall Oak	
117		Cheriton Cross Oak	
207		Felon's Oak	
229		Gladstone Oak	
237		Gog and Magog Oaks	
294		Heddon Oak	
374		King's Oak, The (II)	Hazelgrove Oak: King John Oak: Queen Elizabeth Oak
470		Nettlecombe Oak	
169	Somerset (Avon)	Domesday Oak (I)	
303	Somerset (on boundary with Devon)	Hoar Oak	Kite Oak
22	Staffordshire	Bagot's, Lord, Walking Stick	Sir Walter Bagot's Walking Stick
34		Beggar's Oak	
42		Betts Pool Oak	
123		Cliff Oak, The	King Tree (II)
126		Codshall Oak	
236		Gog (II)	Originally two oaks, Gog and Magog, the latter gone
274		Gutter Oak	
359		King Oak (III)	
412		Lodge Yard Oak, The	
413		Long Coppice Oak, The	
427		Magii Oak	
429		Magog (II)	
447		Mile Oak (II)	
571		Rakeswood Oak	
574		Rawnpike Oak	
579		Roan Oak	
616		Shire Oak (II)	Scyre Oak
628		Slang Oak	
634		Squitch Bank Oak	Squitch Oak
648		Swilcar Oak, The	Swilcar Lawn Oak; Swilcher Oak
660		Three Mile Oak, The	The Tree
694		Venison Oak	
662	Staffordshire (west Midlands)	Three Shires Oak	
158	Staffordshire/Shropshire Border	Cuckoo Oak (II)	
699	Stirlingshire	Wallace's Oak	The Torwood Oak
75	Suffolk	Bristol's, Lord, Walking Stick	
160		Culford Oak	
244		Gospel Oak (IV)	
242		Gospel Oak (II)	

	County	Name	Other Names
243	Suffolk *continued*	Gospel Oak (III)	
288		Haughley Oak	
296		Henham Hill Oak	Wangford Oak
540		Queen Elizabeth's Oak (IV)	The Heveningham Oak
541		Queen Elizabeth's Oak (V)	The Queen's Oak (IV); Elizabeth Oak; Huntingfield Oak
594		Saint Edmunds Oak	
629		Sotterley Oak	
652		Tea Party Oak, The	
74	Surrey	Brewer's Oak(II)	
118		Chertsey Oak	
153		Crouch Oak	Addlestone Oak; Queen's Oak (I)
216		Forrard Oak, The	
271		Grindstone Oak	
330		Jubilee Tree	
352		King George V's Oak	
363		King Oak (VII)	The Tilford Oak or Novel's Oak
386		Lambert's Oaks	
544		Queen Elizabeth's Oak (VIII)	
33	Sussex	Beelzebub	
41		Betsy's Oak	Bessies Oak; Bates' Oak
101		Castle Oak	
103		Cecil Oak	
138		Coronation Wood	
380		Ladies Oak, The	
382		Lady Oak (III)	
419		Lords Oak, The (II)	
518		Pope's Oak (II)	
583		Rookery Oak	
643		Sun Oak	
645		Sussex Farmyard Oak	
704		Watch Oak, The (III)	
712		Wesley's Oak	
714		Whiligh Oak, The	
541	Sussex – East	Queen Elizabeth's Oak (VI)	Northiam Oak
177	Tyrone/Londonerry Border	Drumin Oak	
2	Warwickshire	Abbot's Oak, The (II)	
72		Brees Oak	
85		Bull Oak (II)	Wedgenock Park Oak
182		Duke of Suffolk's Oak	
245		Gospel Oak (V)	Bagington Oak
325		John Lennon & Yoko Ono's Oak	
404		Lillington Oak	The Centre of England Oak
492		Packington Park Oaks	
554		Queen Victoria's Favourite Oak (I)	

	County	Name	Other Names
559	Warwickshire *continued*	Queen Victoria's Oak (IV)	
607		Shakespeare's Oak	
706		Watch Oak, The (II)	
603	Warwickshire (Birmingham)	Selly Oak, The	
139		Coughton Court Oak	
49	West Midlands	Binley Oak	
286	Westmorland	Hart's Horn Tree	
305		Hollow Oak, The (I)	The Earl of Thanet's Hollow Oak; The Whinfield Forest Oak; The Wonderful Large Oak
321		Jack's Yack	Towd Yak
575		Rebel Oak	
656		Three Brethren Oak, The	The Three Brethren Tree; The Three Brothers
140	Wiltshire	Council Oak	
147		Creeping Oak	
151		Cromwell Oak	
166		Decanter Oak	Big Bellied Oak
183		Duke's Vaunt Oak	
356		King John's Oak	
362		King Oak (VI)	
415		Longford Castle Oak	
416		Longleat Oak, The	
391	Wiltshire/Dorset Border	Larmer Tree	
57	Worcestershire	Boar Stag Oak	
128		Colwall Oaks	Colwill Oaks
228		Gibbet Oak, The (II)	
240		Goodmoor Oak	
283		Hannings Oak, The	
452		Mitre Oak	
479		Northwick Oak	
582		Rock Oak	Apostle's Oak
636		St Catherine's Oak	
91	Worcestershire, now Shropshire	Button Oak	
145	Yorkshire	Cowthorpe Oak	Calthorpe Oak (Strutt) Cawthorpe (Ablett): Coltsthorpe (Lauder)
365		King Oak (IX)	
376		Kirkleatham Oak	
547		Queen Oak	
617		Shire Oak (III)	Skyriak Oak; Shyre-ack
618		Shire Oak (IV)	
669		Tockwith Broad Oak	
685		Turpin's Oak (IV)	
703		Warwick Oak	
710		Wellbred Oak	

Bibliography

AA 1965. *Road Book of England & Wales.*

Abell, Sir W. 1948. *The Shipwright's Trade.* Cambridge University Press.

Ablett, W. H. 1880. *English Trees and Tree Planting.*

Albion, R. G. 1926. *Forests and Sea Power.* Harvard University Press, Cambridge, Mass.

Alderman, D. 1998/9. *Registrars Report: A unique database of our tree heritage.* The Tree Register Newsletter number 8, Tree Register of the British Isles, Handcross, West Sussex, England.

Aldhous, J. 1972. *Nursery Practice.* Forestry Commission Bulletin 43. HMSO, London.

Allen, N. Y. 1974. *Exmoor Handbook.*

An Act that Timber shall not be Felled to make Coals for Burning of Iron. 1558, 1 Eliz. 1.c.15.

An Act touching Iron-Mills near unto the City of London and the River Thames. 1581, 23 Eliz. 1.c.5.

An Act for the Preservation of Timber in the Weilds of the Counties of Sussex, Surrey and Kent and for the Amendment of Highways decayed by Carriages to and from the Iron-Mills there. 1585, 27 Eliz. 1.c.19.

An Act Concerning Tanners, Curriers, Shoe-makers and other Artificers occupying the Cutting of Leather. 1604, 1 Ja. 1.c.22.

Anderson, M. L. 1967. *A History of Scottish Forestry,* edited by C. J. Taylor. Nelson.

Anon. 1998. 'Herefordshire and the Forest of Dean – 1986'. *Quarterly Journal of Forestry* LXXX, 4 The Royal Forestry Society, Tring, Hertfordshire.

Anon. 1992. 'Divisional Activity – Visit to Thonock Estate'. *Quarterly Journal of Forestry* LXXXVI, The Royal Forestry Society, Tring, Hertfordshire.

Anon. 1853. *English Forests and Forest Trees.*

Barber, J. 1983. In *Dartmoor (Early Men in Dartmoor).* Ed. C. Gill. David & Charles, Newton Abbot.

Baring Gould, S. 1899. *A Book of Devon.* Methuen & Co., London.

Barne, M. 1998. 'Have you Seen a Good Oak Lately?' *Quarterly Journal of Forestry* 92. 1 The Royal Forestry Society, Tring, England.

Bass, G. F. 1974. *A History of Seafaring based on Underwater Archaeology.* Thames & Hudson Ltd, London.

Bateman, M. 1992. *Wisdom in Wood.* A. T. Print, Tavistock, England.

Bayliss, A., Groves, C., McCormac, G., Baillie, M., Brown, F., and Brennand, M. 1999. 'Precise Dating of the Norfolk Timber Circle'. *Nature* 402, December.

Bean, W. J. 1976. *Trees and Shrubs Hardy in the British Isles.* John Murray, London.

Bennett, K. D. 1983. 'Postglacial Population Expansion of Forest Trees in Norfolk UK'. *Nature* 303.

Bevan, D. 1987. *Forest Insects: A Guide to Insects Feeding on Trees in Britain.* Forestry Commission Handbook 1. HMSO, London.

Bibliography

Billington, W. 1825. *A Series of Facts, Hints, Observations and Experiments on the Different Modes of Raising Young Plantations of Oaks.* London.

Birks, H.J.B. 1989. 'Holocene Isochrone Maps and Patterns of Tree-spreading in the British Isles'. *Journal of Biogeography* 16.

Black's Guide to Devonshire. 1864.

Blyth, J., Evans. J., Mutch, W. E. S. and Sidwell, C. 1987. *Farm Woodland Management.* Farming Press Limited, Ipswich, England.

Boutcher, W. 1778. *A Treatise on Forest-Trees.* Second edition.

Bradford, E. 1966. 'Walls of England'. *Country Life*, London.

Bradley, Richard. 1718. *New Improvements of Planting and Gardening.* Second edition.

Brewer's Dictionary. 1983.

Bridges, M. 2001. 'Tree Rings and Time: Recent Historical Studies in England'. *Archaeology International*, Institute of Archaeology, University of London.

Broad, K. 1998. *Caring for Small Woods.* Earthscan Publications Ltd, London, England.

Brough, J. C. S. 1947. *Timbers for Woodwork.* Evans Brothers Ltd, London.

Brown, J. 1851. *The Forester.* Second edition, Blackwood, Edinburgh & London.

Brown, J. 1861. *The Forester.* Third edition, Blackwood, Edinburgh & London.

Brown, J. 1882. *The Forester.* Fifth edition, Blackwood, Edinburgh & London.

Brown, J. C. 1883. *Forests of England and the Management of them in Bye-Gone Times.*

Brown, J. and Nisbet, J. 1894. *The Forester.* Sixth edition, vols 1 and 2. Blackwood, Edinburgh & London.

Brown, J. and Nisbet, J. 1904. *The Forester.* Sixth edition, enlarged. Blackwood, London.

Brown, R. J. 1997. *Timber-Framed Buildings of England.* Robert Hale, London.

Browne, D. (Compiler) 2000. *Our Remarkable Trees: A Selection of Northern Ireland's Special Trees.* The Millennium Tree Campaign, Belfast, Northern Ireland.

Browne, Sir T. 1901. *Garden of Cyrus.* Macmillan.

Buffon, M. De. 1739. *A Memorial on Preserving and Repairing Forests.* Hamilton and Balfour, Edinburgh.

Bunce, W. 1958. 'The Northiam Oak'. *Quarterly Journal of Forestry* LII, The Royal Forestry Society, Tring, England.

Bunce, W. 1959. 'A Remarkable Oak Tree', *Quarterly Journal of Forestry* LIII, The Royal Forestry Society, Tring, England.

Burt, I. 1880. *Memorials of the Oak.*

Camden, W. 1806. *Britannica or a Chorographical Description of the Flourishing Kingdomes of England, Scotland and Ireland.* Translated from the edition of 1607 by R. Gough.

Cannell, M. G. R. 1999. 'Growing trees to sequester carbon in the UK: answers to some common questions'. *Forestry* 72, 3. Institute of Chartered Foresters, Oxford University Press, England.

Carver, M. 1998. *Sutton Hoo.* British Museum Press.

Cavalli-Sforza, L. L. 2000. *Genes, People and Languages.* Allen Lane, Penguin Press.

Chambers. 1956. *Biographical Dictionary.*

Charnock, J. 1800–2. *History of Marine Architecture.* London.

Chaucer, G. 1919. 'The Parlement of Fools' in *The Works of G. Chaucer.* Ed. A. Pollard, Macmillan.

Christy, M. and Hansford Worth. R. 1922. *The Ancient Dwarfed Oak Woods of Dartmoor.* Transactions of the Devonshire Association.

Church, R. 1612. *The Manner of Planting, Preserving and Husbanding young Trees.*

Clarke, R. A. *et al.* 1987. *The Blasted Oak.* Herbert Art Gallery, Coventry, England.

Classic Boat 156, June 2001. 'Oldest is Older Still'.

Coles, J. M. and Coles, B. J. 1990. *Prehistory of the Somerset Levels.* Somerset Levels Project.

Cook, M. 1717. *The Manner of Raising, Ordering and Improving Forest-Trees.* Second edition. First edition 1617.

Cordingly, D. 1998. 'The Dutch School', *Classic Boat* 120.

Country Life, 1978. *The Country Life Book of Nautical Terms Under Sail.* Trewin Copplestone Publishing Ltd, London.

Cruickshank, T. 1830. *The Practical Planter.* Blackwood, Edinburgh.

Cunliffe, B. 1986. 'The Iron Age (800 BC–43 AD)', in *The Archaeology of the Uplands.* Ed. Darvill, Council for British Archaeology, London.

Dark, S. T. E. 1935. *Report on Trees Struck by Lightning in British Thunderstorms.* Ed. S. M. Bower, Huddersfield, England.

Darrah, G. V. and Dodds, J. W. 1967. 'Growing Broadleaved Trees in Mixture with Conifers'. *Forestry* XL 2. Journal of the Society of Foresters of Great Britain, Oxford University Press, England.

Darvill, T. 1986. *The Archaeology of the Uplands.* The Council for British Archaeology, London.

Day, S. P. and Mellars, P. A. 1994. 'Absolute Dating of Mesolithic Activity at Star Carr, Yorkshire'. *The Proceedings of the Prehistoric Society,* UCL, London.

De Bouffon, M. 1739. *A Memorial on Preserving and Repairing Forests.*

Denny, R. 1989. *King Oak.* Froglet Publications.

Dicker, G. 1969. *A Short History of Devonport Royal Dockyard.* No publisher given.

Dimbleby, G. W. 1978. *Plants and Archaeology.* Granada Publishing, St Albans, England.

Downes, W. 1848. *Report from the Select Committee on the Woods, Forests and Land Revenues of the Crown together with the Minutes of Evidence.*

Duchesne, M. C. 1911. 'The Annual Excursion of the Society'. *Quarterly Journal of Forestry* V, The Royal Forestry Society, Tring, England.

Dutton, A. and Fasham, P. J. 1994. 'Prehistoric Copper Mining on the Great Orme'. *Proceedings of the Prehistoric Society* 60. UCL, London.

Edlin, H. L. 1944. *British Woodland Trees.* B. T. Batsford Ltd, London.

Eighth Report of the Commissioners Appointed to Enquire into the State and Conditions of the Woods, Forests and Land Revenues of the Crown, 1792.

Eleventh Report of the Commissioners Appointed to Enquire into the State and Conditions of the Woods, Forests and Land Revenues of the Crown, 1792.

Ellenberg, H. 1988. *Vegetation Ecology of Central Europe.* Cambridge University Press, England.

Ellis, W. 1745. *The Timber-Tree Improved.* Fourth edition.

Elwes, H. J. and Henry, A. 1906–13. *The Trees of Great Britain and Ireland.* Printed privately in seven volumes; published in limited edition by the Royal Forestry Society 1969.

Emmerlich, A. 1789. *The Culture of Forests.* London.

Empson, C. 1842. *The Copthorne Oak.* London.

Evans, J. 1984. *Silviculture of Broadleaved Woodland.* Forestry Commission Bulletin 62, HMSO, London.

Evelyn, J. 1670 (2nd edition) and 1786 (6th edition). *Sylva or A Discourse on Forest-Trees.* (Fourth and subsequent editions spelt *Silva*). First edition 1664.

Bibliography

Fagan, B. 1995. *Time Detectives*. Simon and Schuster, New York.

Ferris, C. 'Ancient History of the Common Oak'. *Tree News*, Autumn 1996. The Tree Council, London.

Ferris, C. *et al.* 1997. 'A Strategy for Identifying Introduced Provenances and Translocations'. *Forestry* 70 3. Institute of Chartered Foresters, Edinburgh.

Fifth Report of the Commissioners Appointed to Enquire into the State and Conditions of the Woods, Forests and Land Revenues of the Crown. 1789.

First Report (1849) from the Select Committee on the Woods, Forests and Land Revenues of the Crown. 1849.

First Report of the Commissioners To Enquire into the State and Condition of the Woods, Forests and Land Revenues. 1787.

Forestry Commission. 1924. *Report on Census of Woodlands and Census of Production of Home-Grown Timber*. HMSO, London.

Forestry Commission. 1952. *Census of Woodlands 1947–1949*. HMSO, London.

Forestry Commission Guide. 1960. *The New Forest*.

Forestry Commission. 1987. *Census of Woodlands and Trees 1979–82*. Forestry Commission Bulletin 63, HMSO, London.

Forestry Commission. 1989. *Forestry Commission Broadleaved Policy: Progress 1985–88*. Forestry Commission, Edinburgh.

Forestry Commission. 1998. *Estimating the Age of Large and Veteran Trees in Britain*. Research Information Note 12, Forestry Commission, Edinburgh.

Finberg, H. P. R. 1969. *West Country Historical Studies*. David and Charles, Newton Abbot.

Finberg, H. P. R. 1974. *The Formation of England 550–1042*. Paladin, London.

Fisher, W. R. 1895. *Schlich's Manual of Forestry*, vol. iv, *Forest Protection*, adapted from R. Hess's *Der Forstschutz*.

Forest Products Research Laboratory. 1952. Princes Risborough, England.

Frazer, J. G. 1930. *Balder the Beautiful*, Volume II.

Gardner, R. C. B. 1937. 'Great Trees and Good Woodlands'. *Quarterly Journal of Forestry* XXXI. Royal Forestry Society, Tring, England.

Gardner, P. H. B. and R. C. B. 1947. 'Some Notable Trees in Hampshire'. *Quarterly Journal of Forestry* XLI, Royal Forestry Society, Tring, England.

Gardner, P. H. B. 1954. 'The Great Oak at Panshanger'. *Quarterly Journal of Forestry* XLVIII. Royal Forestry Society, Tring, England.

Gifford, E. and J. 1996. 'The Sailing Performance of Anglo-Saxon Ships'. *Mariners Mirror* 82 2.

Gibson. 1692. *Britannia or a Chorographical Description of the Flourishing Kingdomes of England, Scotland and Ireland*, edited by Gibson.

Gibson, A. 1994. *Excavations at the Sarn-y-Bryn-Caled Cursus Complex*. Proceedings of the Prehistoric Society, UCL, London.

Giles, A. September 1990. 'The Grey Old Men of Moccas'. *Tree News*, The Tree Council, London.

Gillanders, A. T. 1908. *Forest Entomology*. William Blackwood & Son, Edinburgh & London.

Gilpin, W. 1791. *Remarks on Forest Scenery and other Woodland Views*. London.

Gilpin, W. 1834. *Remarks on Forest Scenery and other Woodland Views*, Ed. Sir T. D. Lauder, Vols 1 & 2, Fraser & Co. Edinburgh; Smith, Elder & Co. London; W. Curry, Jun. & Co. Dublin.

Gilpin, W. 1879. *Gilpin's Forest Scenery*. Ed. F. G. Heath. London.

Godwin, H. 1975. *History of the Natural Forest of Britain*. The Philosophical Transactions of The Royal Society, 271, London.

Godwin, H. and Deacon, J. 1974. 'Flandrian History of Oak in the British Isles' in *The British Oak, its History and Natural History*. Ed. M. G. Morris and F. H. Perring. Published for The Botanical Society of the British Isles by E. W. Cassey Ltd, Faringdon, Berkshire.

Goodburn, D. M. 1996. *Analysis Of The Evidence For Assembly And Construction Techniques Used In The Building Of The Dover Boat*. Dover Boat Analysis Team, first draft.

Gorer, R. 1975. *The Flower Garden in England*. Batsford, England.

Graham-Campbell, J. and Kidd, D. 1980. *The Vikings*. British Museum, London.

Greenhill, B. 1982. *Garlandstone*. National Museum of Wales, Cardiff.

Greenhill, B. and Morrison, J. 1995. *The Archaeology of Boats and Ships*. Conway Maritime Press, London.

Greville, M. 1949. 'Trees of the Royal Forest'. *Country Life*.

Grigor, J. 1841. *Eastern Arboretum*.

Grigor, J. 1868. *Arboriculture*. Edinburgh.

H., A. D. 1919. 'The Oak Leaf Roller Moth in the Forest of Dean'. *Quarterly Journal of Forestry* XIII 4. The Royal Forestry Society, Tring, England.

Haddington, Earl of. 1761. *A Treatise on the Manner of Raising of Forest Trees*. Hamilton & Balfour, Edinburgh.

Hadfield, M. 1957. *British Trees*. J. M. Dent and Sons.

Hadfield, M. 1969. 'Moccas Oak'. *Quarterly Journal of Forestry* LXII, The Royal Forestry Society, Tring, England.

Hadfield, M. 1974. 'The Oak and its Legends'. *The British Oak*. Morris & Perring.

Hammersley, R. B. H. 1955. 'The Radley Oak'. *Quarterly Journal of Forestry* XLIX, The Royal Forestry Society, Tring, England.

Hammond, N. 27 March 1991. 'Tests Show Arthur's Round Table Made in 13th Century'. *The Times*.

Hanbury, W. 1770. *A Complete Body of Planting and Gardening*. Vol. I, Book I, Part I.

Handford, S. A. 1953. *Caesar The Conquest of Gaul*. Penguin Books, London.

Hando, F. J. 1944. *This Pleasant Land of Gwent*. R. H. Johns, Newport, Wales.

Hanson, C. O. 1911. *Forestry for Woodmen*. Oxford University Press.

Harding, P. T. 1980. 'Shute Deer Park, Devon'. *Journal of the Devon Trust for Nature Conservation* 1.

Harding, P. T. and Rose, F. 1986. *Pasture Woodlands in Lowland Britain*. Institute of Terrestrial Ecology, England.

Harley, R. M. 1982. 'Problems in the Silviculture of Oak in Britain', in *Broadleaves in Britain*, edited by D. C. Malcolm, J. Evans & P. N. Edwards. Proceedings of a symposium, Institute of Chartered Foresters, Edinburgh.

Harmer, R. 2001. 'Growth of Coppice Shoots Following Felling of Maiden Oaks at Different Heights Above Ground'. *Quarterly Journal of Forestry* 95 3. The Royal Forestry Society, Tring, England.

Harris, D. R. and Hillman G. C. 1989. *Foraging and Farming*. Unwin Hyman, London.

Harris, D. R. (Editor) 1996. *The Origins and Spread of Agriculture and Pastoralism in Eurasia*. University College London Press.

Harris, E. H. M. 1981. 'The National Hardwood Project'. *Quarterly Journal of Forestry* LXXV 1. The Royal Forestry Society, Tring, England.

Harris, E. H. M. 1983. 'Northern Centenary Meeting'. *Quarterly Journal of Forestry* LXXVII 2. The Royal Forestry Society, Tring. England.

Harris, E. H. M. and Harris, J. A. 1987. *A Glimpse of Forestry and the Countryside of China*. The Royal Forestry Society, Tring, Hertfordshire.

Harris, E. H. M. and Harris, J. A. 1988. 'The Society Visit to Hungary – Autumn 1987'. *Quarterly Journal of Forestry* LXXXII 2. The Royal Forestry Society, Tring, England.

Harris, E. H. M. and Harris, J. A. 1991. *Wildlife Conservation in Managed Woodlands and Forests*. Basil Blackwell, Oxford, England.

Harris, E. H. M. and Harris, J. A. 1997. *Wildlife Conservation in Managed Woodlands and Forests*. Second edition, Research Studies Press, Taunton, England.

Hart, C. E. 1966. *Royal Forest: a History of Dean's Woods as Producers of Timber*. Clarendon Press, Oxford.

Hart, C. E. 1991. *Practical Forestry for the Agent and Surveyor*. Alan Sutton Publishing Ltd, Stroud, England.

Hartig, R. 1894. *Text-Book of the Diseases of Trees*. Translated by W. Somerville and H. Marshal Ward.

Hartlib, S. 1665. *His Legacy of Husbandry*. Third edition.

Harvey, L. A. and St Leger-Gordon, D. 1977. *Dartmoor*. Third edition. The New Naturalist Series, Collins, London.

Hayes, S. 1794 and 1822. *A Practical Treatise on Planting and the Management of Woods and Coppice*.

Hedges, R. E. M. and Gowlett, J. A. J. 1984. 'Accelerating Carbon Dating'. *Nature* 308.

Henman, G. S. and Denne, M. P. 1992. *Shake in Oak*. Forestry Commission Research Information Note.

Henman, G. S. 1984. *Oak Wood Structure and the Problem of Shake*. Report of the 4th meeting of the National Hardwood Programme, Commonwealth Forestry Institute, Oxford, England.

Hennell, T. 1936. *Change in the Farm*. Second edition.

Hennell, T. 1943. *British Craftsmen*. William Collins, London.

Herron, M. H. *et al.* 1981. 'Climatic Signal of Ice Melt Features in Southern Greenland'. *Nature* 293.

Hewins, G. S. 1941. *Country Life*.

Hewins, G. S. 1945. *Famous Trees of the Midlands*. Paper read to the Birmingham Archaeological Society in 1943.

Hickin. 1972. *Natural History of an English Forest*.

Hinde, T. (Editor) 1966. *The Domesday Book*. Coombe Books.

Holdsworth, D. 1990. 'Great Oaks of Cumbria'. *The Tree Register Newsletter* 8, Tree Register of the British Isles, Handcross, West Sussex, England.

Holinshed, R. 1577. *Chronicles of England, Scotland and Ireland*. 1807 Edition, Vol. I, Book 2.

Holland, A. J. 1971. *Ships of British Oak*. David & Charles, Newton Abbot, Devon.

Houblon, A. A. 1907. *The Houblon Family: Life and Times*. Constable.

Houghton, J. 1728. *Husbandry and Trade Improved*.

Hubert, J. and Savill, P. 1999. 'Improving Oak: First Steps Towards a Breeding Programme'. *Quarterly Journal of Forestry* 93 2. The Royal Forestry Society, Tring, England.

Hunter, T. 1883. *Woods, Forests and Estates of Perthshire*. Henderson, Robertson and Hunter. Perth, Scotland.

Huntley, B. and Birks, J. B. 1983. *An Atlas of Past and Present Pollen Maps of Europe 0–13000 Years Ago*. Cambridge University Press, England.

Hurst, C. 1911. *The Book of the English Oak*. London.

Hutchins, 1800. *Forest Trees of Britain* Vol. I.

Hyde, H. A. 1977. *Welsh Timber Trees*. Fourth edition, revised by S. G. Harrison, National Museum of Wales, Cardiff.

Huyshe, W. 1907. *Beowulf*. G. Routledge and Sons, London.

Inwood, S. 1998. *A History of London*. Macmillan.

James, N. D. G. 1973. *A Book of Trees: An anthology of trees and woodlands chosen and arranged by N. D. G. James*. The Royal Forestry Society, Tring, England.

James, N. D. G. 1981. *A History of English Forestry*. Blackwell, Oxford.

Jeffries, R. 1948. *Bevis*. Jonathan Cape, London. First edition 1932.

Jenkins, J. G. 1965. *Traditional Country Craftsmen*. Routledge & Kegan Paul, London.

Johns, C. A. 1903. *The Forest Trees of Britain*. London.

Johnson, D. 1996. 'Fastening, a riveting history'. *Classic Boat* 101 November.

Johnson, O. 1998. *The Sussex Tree Book*. Pomegranate Press, Westmeston, England.

Jones, C. F. 1933. 'Description of the Golynos Oak'. *Quarterly Journal of Forestry* XXVII. The Royal Forestry Society, Tring, England.

Jones, E. W. 1959. 'Biological Flora of the British Isles. *Quercus L*'. *Journal of Ecology* 47 pp. 169–222.

Jones, E. W. 1964. 'Oak-Larch and Oak-Thuja Mixtures in Woods of Hazel, Wytham'. *Quarterly Journal of Forestry* LVIII 3. The Royal Forestry Society, London.

Jones, G. L. and Mabey, R. 1993 *The Wildwood*. Aurum Press, London.

Joyce, P. 1998. *Growing Broadleaves – Silvicultural Guidelines for Ash, Sycamore, Wild Cherry, Beech and Oak in Ireland*. COFORD, Dublin.

Kerr, G. and Evans, J. 1993. *Growing Broadleaves for Timber*. Forestry Commission Handbook 9, HMSO, London.

Kinloch, B. B. *et al.* 1987. 'Caledonian Scots Pine: Origins and Genetic Structure'. *The New Cytologist* 104.

Langley, B. 1740. *A Sure and Easy Method of Improving Estates*. Second edition. London.

Larsen, J. A. 1980. *The Boreal Ecosystem*. The Academic Press, London.

Latham, B. 1957. *Timber, A Historical Survey of its Development and Distribution*. George G. Harrap & Co., London.

Latham, P. October 1997. *The Mouse Man of Kilburn*. Forest Machine Journal.

Lauder, T. D. from Gilpin 1791. *Remarks on Forest Scenery and Other Woodland Views*. Revised 1834.

Lawson 1597. Quoted by Evelyn and Bradley.

Leather, J. 1998. 'Before the Boaters'. *Classic Boat* 121.

Leland, J. 1907. *The Itinerary of John Leyland in or about the Years 1535–1543*. Edited by L. Toulmin Smith, Vol. I.

Lewis, P. 1811. *Historical Inquiries concerning Forests and Forest Laws with topical Remarks upon the Ancient and Modern State of the New Forest in the County of Southampton*.

Lines, R. 1999. 'Seed Origins of Oak and Beech Used by the Forestry Commission from 1920 to 1990'. *Quarterly Journal of Forestry* 93 3. The Royal Forestry Society, Tring, England.

Bibliography

Linnard, W. 2000. *Welsh Woods and Forests: History and Utilization.* National Museum of Wales.

Lodwick, J. and V. 1972. *The Story of Carmarthen.* Published by the authors in Carmarthen.

Loudon, J. C. 1763, 1756 and 1838. *Arboretum et Fruticetum Britannicum.* Vol. III. L.

Loudon, J. C. 1838. *Arboretum et Fructicetum Britannicum.* London.

MacDonald, C. 2000. 'Princess of the Western Isles'. *Classic Boat* 139. Link House Publications, Croydon, England.

Main, J. First edition 1838. *The Forest Planter and Pruner's Assistant.* Second edition. James Ridgeway, London, 1847.

Main, J. 1828. 'A Review of Steuart's Planter's Guide'. *Gardener's Magazine* 4.

Mansfield, K. May 1996. 'The Shetland Sixareen'. *The Boatman Magazine* 34.

Manwood, J. 1598. *A Treatise and Discourse of the Lawes of the Forrest* (Second edition 1615, third edition 1665, fourth edition 1717, fifth edition 1741).

March, E. J. 1952. *Sailing Drifters.* Percival Marshall & Co. Ltd, London. Reprinted 1969 by David & Charles, Newton Abbot, Devon, England.

Marshall, W. 1796. *Planting and Rural Ornament.* Second edition, vol. I. London.

Marshall, W. 1815. *Report to the Board of Agriculture.*

Mason, S. L. R. 1992. *Acorns in Human Subsistence.* Unpublished Ph.D. thesis, University College, London.

Matthew, P. 1831. *On Naval Timber and Arboriculture.* Longman, London.

Matthews, J. D. 1989. *Silvicultural Systems.* Clarendon Press, Oxford, England.

Maw, P. T. 1909. *The Practice of Forestry.*

Mee, A. 1938. *Cheshire.* Hodder & Stoughton, London.

Mee, A. 1938. *Devon.* Hodder & Stoughton.

Mee, A. 1940. *Essex.* Caxton, London.

Meiggs, R. 1982. *Trees and Timber in the Ancient Mediterranean World.* Oxford University Press, England.

Mellars, P. 1986. *The Paleolithic and Mesolithic.* In Darvill 1986.

Michie, C. Y. 1888. *The Practice of Forestry.*

Miles, A. 1999. *Silva: The Tree in Britain.* Ebury Press, London.

Miles, R. 1977. *Forestry in the English Landscape.* Faber & Faber, London.

Milner, J. E. 1992. *The Tree Book.* Collins & Brown Ltd, London.

Mitchell, F. 1890. *Old and Remarkable Trees.* Transactions of the Royal Scottish Arboricultural Society Vol. XIII, Edinburgh.

Mitchell, A. F. 1966. 'Dating the Ancient Oaks'. *Quarterly Journal of Forestry* LX 4. The Royal Forestry Society, London.

Mitchell, A. F. 1974. *A Field Guide to the Trees of Britain and Northern Europe.* Collins, London.

Mitchell, A. F. 1982. *The Trees of Britain and Northern Europe.* HarperCollins, London.

Mitchell, A. F. August 1991. 'Rooted in History'. *The Field.*

Mitchell, A. F. 1996. *Alan Mitchell's Trees of Britain.* HarperCollins Publishers Ltd, London.

Mitchell, J. 1827. *Dendrologia or A Treatise of Forest Trees with Evelyn's Silva Revised, Corrected and Abridged.*

Mithen, S. J. 1994. *The Mesolithic Age. Oxford Illustrated Prehistory of Europe.*

Monteath, R. 1820. *The Forester's Guide and Profitable Planter* (Second edition 1824, third edition 1836). T. Tegg & Son, London.

Moore, P. D. 1984. 'Hampstead Heath Clues to the Historical Decline of Elms'. *Nature* 312.

Moore, P. D. 1987. 'Tree Boundaries on the Move'. *Nature* 326.

Morley, G. *Leafy Warwickshire.*

Morris, M. G. and Perring, F. H. (Editors) 1974. *The British Oak, its History and Natural History*. Published for The Botanical Society of the British Isles by E. W. Cassey Ltd, Faringdon, England.

Morton, A. 1986. *The Trees of Shropshire*. Airlife Publishing Ltd, Shrewsbury, England.

Mosley, C. 1910. *The Oak, its Natural History, Antiquity and Folk-Lore*. Elliot Stock, London.

Muir, J. R. 1938. *Messing About in Boats*. Blackie & Son Ltd, London and Glasgow.

Murray, J. 1859. *A Handbook for Travellers in Devon and Cornwall*. John Murray, London.

Newton, G. W. 1859. *A Treatise on the Growth and Future Management of Timber Trees*. L. Reeve, London.

Nic Nac Journal Number 136, 1925.

Nicol, W. 1803, *The Practical Planter*. Second edition, London.

Nicol, W. Ed. Sang, E. 1812. *The Planter's Kalendar*. Edinburgh.

Nichols, T. 1791. *Observations on the Propagation and Management of Oak Trees in General but more Immediately applying to His Majesty's New Forest in Hampshire*. Printed by T. Baker, Southampton.

Nichols, T. 1793. *Methods Proposed for Decreasing the Consumption of Timber in the Navy*. Printed by T. Baker, Southampton.

Nicolson and Burn, 1777. *History of Westmorland and Cumberland.*

Nisbet, J. 1893, *British Forest Trees*. Macmillan & Co. London.

Nisbet, J. 1894. *Studies in Forestry*. Clarendon Press, Oxford, England.

Nisbet, J. 1900. *Our Forests and Woodlands*. J. M. Dent & Co. London.

Nisbet, J. 1911. *The Elements of British Forestry*. William Blackwood & Sons, Edinburgh & London.

Oates, D. W. *The Story of Gwent*, Educational Publishing Co., Cardiff.

Ostermann, H. 1997. 'Red sails into the Sunset'. *Classic Boat* 104.

Pakenham, T. 1996. *Meetings With Remarkable Trees*. Weidenfeld & Nicolson, London.

Perlin, J. 1959. *A Forest Journey*. W. W. Norton & Co. Ltd, London.

Perry, W. 1867. *Hernes Oak*. Booth, London.

Peterken, G. F. 1981. *Woodland Conservation and Management*. Chapman and Hall, London.

Pevsner, N. 1945. *The Leaves of Southwall*. King Penguin, London.

Phillips, O. 1951. *Monmouthshire.*

Philips Price, M. 1966. 'Growing oak for future generations'. *Quarterly Journal of Forestry* LX 4. The Royal Forestry Society, Tring, England.

Pilcher, J. R. *et al.* 1984. 'A 7272 Year Tree Ring Chronology for Western Europe'. *Nature.*

Pitts, M. and Roberts, M. 1997. *Fairweather Eden*. Century, London.

Plumtree, J. H. 1999. 'Aged Oaks'. *Quarterly Journal of Forestry* LXIX. The Royal Forestry Society, Tring, England.

Pollard, A. W. 1919. *The Works of Geoffrey Chaucer*. Macmillan & Co., London.

Polwheles. 1826. *History of Cornwall.*

Pontey, W. 1809. *The Profitable Planter.* Third Edition, printed by Harding & Wright, London.

Potter, M. J. 1991. *Tree Shelters.* Forestry Commission Handbook 7. HMSO, London.

Purchas, W. H. and Ley, A. 1889. *Flora of Herefordshire.* Jackman & Calvert, Hereford, England.

Rackham, O. 1976. *Trees and Woodland in the British Landscape.* L. M. Dent & Sons Ltd, London.

Rackham, O. 1980. *Ancient Woodland; Its History, Vegetation and Uses in England.* Edward Arnold, London.

Rackham, O. 1989. *The Last Forest.* L. M. Dent & Sons Ltd, London.

Rackham, O. Autumn 1994. 'Ancient Trees'. *Tree News,* The Tree Council, London.

Raftery, B. 1992. 'Recent Developments in Irish Wetland Research'. *The Wetland Revolution in Prehistory.* Edited by B. Coles. The Prehistoric Society, UCL, London.

Richmond, I. A. 1963. *Roman Britain.* Second edition.

Robbins, S. 1992. 'Oak Apples in History and Folk-lore'. *Cecidology* 7.

Roberts, M. 1890. *Ruins and Old Trees.* London.

Rodgers, J. 1941. *The English Woodland.* Batsford, London.

Rooke, H. 1790. *Remarkable Oaks at Welbeck.* London.

Rose, W. 1943. *The Village Carpenter.* Cambridge University Press, London, England.

Rowe, J. S. and Scotter, G. W. 1973. 'Fire in the Boreal Forest. The Ecological Role of Fire in Natural Conifer Forest of Western and Northern America'. *Quarternary Research* 3, The Academic Press.

Rule, M. 1986. *The Mary Rose.* Second edition, The Conway Maritime Press, London.

Salinger, M. J. 1981. 'Palaeoclimates North and South'. *Nature* 291.

Savage, A. 1995. *The Anglo-Saxon Chronicles.* Crescent Books, New York.

Savill, P. S. and Evans J. 1986. *Plantation Silviculture in Temperate Regions.* Clarendon Press, Oxford, England.

Savill, P. S. and Mather, R. A. 1990. 'A Possible Indicator of Shake in Oak'. *Forestry* 63 4. Oxford University Press.

Savill P. S. 1991. *The Silviculture of Trees Used in British Forestry.* C.A.B. International, Wallingford, Oxford, England.

Savill P. S. 1996. 'Anatomical characteristics in wood of Oak which predisposes trees to shake'. *Commonwealth Forestry Review* 65.

Sawyer, J. 1839. *Growing Gold.* Second edition. Simpkin, Marshall & Co., London.

Scott, R. F. 1905. *The Voyage of the 'Discovery'.* John Murray, London.

Selby, P. J. 1842. *A History of British Forest Trees.* John van Voorst, London.

Seventh Report of the Commissioners Appointed to Enquire into the State and Conditions of the Woods, Forests and Land Revenues of the Crown, 1790.

Sheppard, L. 1848. *On Trees.* Jackson and Walford, London.

Sherley-Price, L. 1955. *Bede. A History of the English Church and People.* Penguin.

Shigo, A. L., Vollbrecht, K. and Hvass, N. 1987. *Tree Biology and Tree Care.* SITAS, Denmark.

Simmons, I. G. 1965. 'The Dartmoor Oak Copses; Observations and Speculations'. *Field Studies* 2.

Simmons, I. G. & Innes, J. B. 1981. 'Tree Remains in a North Yorks Moor Peat Profile'. *Nature* 274.

Sinclair, G. 1832. *Useful and Ornamental Planting.* Baldwin & Cradock, London.

Small, D. 1982. 'Reproduction of even-aged high forest oak – with special reference to the New Forest Statutory Inclosures'. *Broadleaves in Britain,* edited by D. C. Malcolm, J. Evans and P. N. Edwards. Proceedings of a symposium, Institute of Chartered Foresters.

Sobel, D. and Andrewes, W. J. H. 1998, *The Illustrated Longitude.* Fourth Estate Ltd, London.

Southern, H. N. 1964. *The Handbook of British Mammals.* Blackwell Scientific Publications, Oxford, England.

Spenser, E. 1917. *The Faerie Queen.* Everyman, Dent.

Spindler, K. 1994. *The Man in the Ice.* Weidenfeld and Nicolson, London.

Stamper, P. A. 2002. 'The tree that hid a King: The Royal Oak at Boscobel, Shropshire'. *Landscapes,* 2002 1, pp. 19–34.

Standing, I. J. 1986. 'Ancient and Notable Trees in and Around Dean'. *Journal of the Forest of Dean* 2.

Standing, I. J. 1987. 'Ancient and Notable Trees in and Around Dean'. Part 2, *Journal of the Forest of Dean* 3.

Standish, A. 1611. *The Commons Complaint.*

Standish, A. 1613. *New Directions of Experience to the Commons Complaint, for the Planting of Timber and Firewood, Invented by Arthur Standish.*

Stebbing, E. P. *Commercial Forestry in Britain.* John Murray, London.

Stebbing, E. P. 1919. *British Forestry.* John Murray, London.

Stokes, J. and Branchflower, P. 2001. 'Heritage Tree Record'. *Tree Warden News* 24, The Tree Council, London.

Stone, C. F. 1933. 'Description of the Golynos Oak'. *Quarterly Journal of Forestry* XXVII. The Royal Forestry Society, Tring, England.

Strutt, J. G. 1830. *Sylva Britannica or Strutt's Portraits of Forest Trees.* Published for the author in London.

Stuckey, P. J. 1999. *The Sailing Pilots of the Bristol Channel.* Redcliffe Press Ltd, Bristol.

Sturt, G. 1923. *The Wheelwright's Shop.* Cambridge University Press.

Sutcliffe, A. J. 1985. *On the Track of the Ice Age Mammals.* The British Museum of Natural History, London.

Switsur, R. 1986. 'New Radiocarbon Dating System', *Nature* 324.

Sykes, B. 2001. *The seven daughters of Eve.* Bantam Press, London.

Tabor, R. 1994. *Traditional Woodland Crafts.* B. T. Batsford Ltd, London.

Tangye, C. G. 1971. 'The Mawley Oak'. *Quarterly Journal of Forestry* LXV. The Royal Forestry Society, Tring, England.

Tansley, A. G. 1949. *The British Isles and Their Vegetation.* Volume I. Cambridge University Press, England, Third edition 1953.

Tegetmeier, W. B. 1904. *Pheasants, Their Natural History and Practical Management.* Fourth edition.

Temple, R. 1998. *The Genius of China.* Prion, London.

Third Report of the Commissioners Appointed to Enquire into the State and Conditions of the Woods, Forests and Land Revenues of the Crown. 1788.

Thomas, H. 1997. *The Slave Trade.* Picador, Macmillan Publishers Ltd, London.

Thomas, P. 2000. *Trees: Their Natural History.* Cambridge University Press.

Thompson, C. W. St Clair. 1928. *The Protection of Woodlands.*

Thurston, E. 1930. *British and Foreign Trees and Shrubs in Cornwall.* Cambridge University Press.

Timpson, J. 1987. *Timpson's England.* Jarrold, Norwich, England.

Bibliography

Townley, H. 1910. *English Woodlands and their Story.*

Trevelyan, G. M. 1952. *Illustrated English Social History*, Volume 2. Longmans, Green and Co. Ltd, London. First edition 1944.

Tuley, G. 1985. 'The Growth of Young Oak in Shelters'. *Forestry*, Oxford University Press.

Tusser, T. 1557. *Five Hundred Pointes of Good Husbandry.* New edition by W. Mavor 1812.

Vancouver, C. 1813. *General View of the Agriculture of the County of Devon.* Board of Agriculture, London.

Venables, C. J. 1974. 'Uses of Oak, Past and Present'. In *The British Oak, its History and Natural History*, ed. M. G. Morris and F. H. Perring. Published for The Botanical Society of the British Isles by E. W. Cassey Ltd, Faringdon, Berkshire.

Victoria County Histories, 1907. *Sussex.*

Victoria County Histories, 1907. *Staffordshire.*

Voysey, J. C. 1982. 'The Management of Lakeland Oakwoods: experiences at Grizedale'. In *Broadleaves in Britain*, ed. D. C. Malcolm, J. Evans & P. N. Edwards. Proceedings of a symposium, Institute of Chartered Foresters, Edinburgh.

Wade, A. E. 1931. *Flora of Monmouthshire.*

Walpole, H. 1796. *A History of the Modern Taste in Gardening.* Reproduced in Marshall 1796.

Wang, C. W. 1961. *The Forests of China.* Publication number 5. The Maria Moors Cabot Foundation, Harvard, USA.

Watt, A. S. 1919. 'On the causes of failure of natural regeneration in British oakwoods'. *Journal of Ecology* 7 pp. 173–203.

Webb, S. L. 1986. *Quarternary Research* 26. Quoted by Moore 1987.

Wheeler, J. 1747. *The Modern Druid.* Privately printed in London.

White, G. 1789. *The Natural History of Selborne.*

White, J. 1991. Forestry Commission list.

White, J. 1995. 'Dating the Veterans'. *Tree News*, Spring/Summer. The Tree Council, 51 Catherine Place, London.

Whitlock, R. 1985. *The Oak.* George Allen and Unwin, London.

Wilks, J. H. 1970. 'The Meavy Oak'. *Quarterly Journal of Forestry* LXIV. The Royal Forestry Society, Tring, England.

Wilks, J. H. 1972. *Trees of the British Isles in History and Legend.* Frederick Muller.

Williamson, J. A. 1959. *The English Channel.* Collins, London.

Wise, J. R. 1863. *The New Forest, its History and Scenery.* Gibbings, London.

Woillard, N. 1979. 'Abrupt End of the Last Interglacial in North-East France'. *Nature* 281.

Woolhope Naturalists Club, The Transactions of the, 1866, 1867, 1869, 1870, 1871, 1872.

Wright, C. D. 1959. 'Lightning Oak at Haileybury College'. *Quarterly Journal of Forestry* LIII. The Royal Forestry Society, Tring, England.

Young, A. C. 1790. *General View of the Agriculture of the County of Essex.*

Zvelebil, M. 1982. 'Post Glacial Foraging in the Forests of Europe'. *Scientific American.*

Zvelebil, M. 1994. 'Plant Use in the Mesolithic and its Role in the Transition to Farming'. *The Proceedings of the Prehistoric Society* 60. UCL, London.

Index

About the authors

E. H. M. Harris, B.Sc. (Forestry and Botany), Dip.For., Fic.For., M.I.Biol., is a Chartered Forester and Chartered Biologist, and has spent a lifetime working as a forester. After service in the Royal Navy during the Second World War, he worked in the Forestry Commission and in private forest management before joining the Royal Forestry Society as Director in 1975. During his time with the Society he wrote with his wife J. A. Harris the bestselling *Reader's Digest Field Guide to the Trees and Shrubs of Britain* and *Wildlife Conservation in Managed Woodlands and Forests* (1991). He retired in 1989 to run a small farm in Cornwall along conservation lines; he and his wife's renovation of woods there led to their being awarded the Duke of Cornwall's Award for Forestry and Conservation in 2002. He received the Medal 'For Distinguished Services to Forestry' in 2000, The Institute of Chartered Foresters Medal 'For Services to British Forestry' in 2003 and contributes regularly to *The Quarterly Journal of Forestry*, *Tree News* and *Country Life*.

J. A. Harris holds B.Sc. degrees in Agriculture and Zoology. Evacuation during the war to a small village in North Wales, began a lifelong interest in the countryside and its wildlife. After raising a family of four children, she worked in the pharmaceuticals industry, co-wrote two books with her husband (see above) and wrote *The Kingfisher Pocket Guide to the Wildlife of Britain and Europe*. She is particularly interested in using agricultural practices such as traditional haymaking to enhance biodiversity.

After distinguished war service, **N. D. G. James** OBE MC, TD, FRICS lectured at the Royal Agricultural College, Cirencester, where he had trained as a land agent. He later became Land Agent to Oxford University and then to the extensive Clinton estates in Devon. He wrote eight books on forestry, including *The Forester's Companion*, *The Arboriculturalist's Companion* and *A History of English Forestry*. He was President of the Royal Forestry Society and a Recipient of their Medal for Distinguished Services to Forestry. He died in 1993 having laid the foundations for this book and having done much of the initial research for it.